Social exclusion and the politics of order

MANCHESTER
1824

Manchester University Press

Social exclusion and the politics of order

Kevin Ryan

Manchester University Press

Manchester and New York

distributed exclusively in the USA by Palgrave

Published by Manchester University Press
Oxford Road, Manchester M13 9NR, UK
and Room 400, 175 Fifth Avenue, New York, NY 10010, USA
www.manchesteruniversitypress.co.uk

Distributed exclusively in the USA by
Palgrave, 175 Fifth Avenue, New York,
NY 10010, USA

Distributed exclusively in Canada by
UBC Press, University of British Columbia, 2029 West Mall,
Vancouver, BC, Canada V6T 1Z2

British Library Cataloguing-in-Publication Data
A catalogue record for this book is available from the British Library

Library of Congress Cataloging-in-Publication Data applied for

ISBN   978 0 7190 7553 7 *hardback*

First published 2007

16 15 14 13 12 11 10 09 08 07   10 9 8 7 6 5 4 3 2 1

Typeset in 10.5/12.5pt Times
by SNP Best-set Typesetter Ltd., Hong Kong
Printed in Great Britain
by The Cromwell Press Ltd, Trowbridge

To Bernie and Leah

Contents

Tables and figures

Acknowledgements

I would like to convey very special thanks to Mark Haugaard for his guidance during my doctoral research, which forms the basis for this book, and in particular for the chance to learn from the critical and creative thinking which is the hallmark of his own research. I am also indebted to Stewart Clegg for the enthusiastic observations and comments he offered as my external examiner. Siniša Malešević and the anonymous reader at Manchester University Press provided comments and advice which proved to be invaluable in preparing the final manuscript. Chris Curtin and Tony Varley deserve mention for the ongoing support they have provided during my time at the Department of Political Science and Sociology, National University of Ireland Galway. I also wish to acknowledge the faultless professionalism and relaxed efficiency of the editorial and production teams at Manchester University Press, with whom it has been a genuine pleasure to work.

Parts of chapters 8 and 9 were presented at Asia-Pacific Researchers in Organization Studies 11, hosted by the Graduate School of Business at Victoria University in Melbourne in 2005, and at the Political Science Association of Ireland annual conference in Queen's University Belfast, also in 2005. Chapter 5 was presented at the Double Vision Liminal Irish Identities conference in University College Dublin in 2005. An earlier draft of chapter 6 was presented at the Graduate Conference in Political Theory at the University of Essex in 2003. I wish to thank participants at all of these gatherings for their comments and criticisms.

I am grateful to the Salvation Army International Heritage Centre for permission to reproduce the lithograph from General William Booth's *Darkest England* in chapter 4. Oxford University Press gave me permission to reproduce Jeremy Bentham's 'Table of cases calling for relief', which also appears in chapter 4, and here I am indebted as well to Michael Quinn for assisting me in my initial inquiries. The Public Communications Bureau in Dublin provided high-quality digital images from the Citizen Traveller communications campaign as well as permission to use these images, which are discussed in chapter 5. I would also like to thank Phil Mullen from the Irish Traveller Movement for his prompt replies to my queries about the campaign. I am extremely grateful to Vincent Gribbin, head of Internal Communication at Fine Gael headquarters, for permission to reproduce images from Fine Gael's 'Ireland: A Life in the Night' campaign, which are used in chapter 7. Vincent also provided digital copies of these images. Ocean Advertising and Brand Imagination granted permission to use images from the 'Baby?' prevention and sexual health promotion campaign, which is discussed in chapter 8, and I wish to acknowledge the assistance of the Crisis Pregnancy Agency for providing copies of the 'Baby?' packs. Last but not least, Shay Hennessy from Crashed Music granted permission to use a quotation from Horslips' *Book of Invasions* at the start of chapter 9.

Introduction

One of the central problems of modernity, one which has preoccupied thinkers and actors alike, is that of understanding, explaining and contesting relations of domination. Indeed with social and political conflict driven by an enduring and pervasive desire for emancipation, modernity could be characterised as a relentless quest for an achieved end-state of freedom and/or equality. The closing decades of the twentieth century saw an important shift in the expression of social conflict, with the goal of a final emancipation giving way to a new problematic of social exclusion. As a way of understanding and addressing the problem of domination, 'exclusion' is an elastic concept which seems capable of covering all normative questions relating to difference, whether coded as economic, cultural, ethnic or otherwise. Importantly, two of the core categories of modern social thought – inseparable from the question of domination – have been recast in the course of this shift: 'poverty' and 'inequality'.

Both were central to the work of T. H. Marshall. In his classic study of *Citizenship and Social Class*, originally presented as a series of lectures in 1949, Marshall considered whether there might be natural limits to the gradual inclusion of all persons in the collective benefits of social life. Theorising the development of civil, political and social rights as a progressive and cumulative process with its origins in the eighteenth century, the object of his analysis was the relation between the formal equalities that accompany citizenship and the class inequalities generated by the market. In the wake of two world wars, the great depression, the Holocaust and the concomitant wave of fascisms, Marshall's prognosis was optimistic, and he argued that the tension between democracy and capitalism – a tension which frames the twin ideals of equality and liberty – was no cause for anxiety. As Marshall phrased it, common sense and concrete action could 'move a mountain of paradox, though logic may be unable to surmount it in the world of thought' (Marshall, 1992: 43). Marshall was not oblivious to the prevailing problems, but the point I want to emphasise is that he *could* theorise liberal democracy as a socio-political form which unfolds in stages, stages which correspond to the time-line of modernity, passing from the birth of the Enlightenment to the particular moment when Marshall himself spoke.

More than twenty years later, on the eve of events that would dislocate the basis of his optimism, Marshall retained the thrust of his earlier prognosis by asking rhetorically 'what place poverty and inequality would occupy in a democratic-welfare-capitalist society which had, so to speak, fulfilled itself'. Marshall characterised the *telos* of democratic welfare capitalism in broad brush-strokes:

> The simple answer is that in such a society poverty is a disease, but inequality is an essential structural feature. We . . . have long ago rejected the theory of the necessity of poverty, as expressed by Patrick Colquhoun when he described poverty as 'a most necessary and indispensable ingredient in society', because 'it is the source of wealth'.[1] We have abandoned belief in the evolutionary benefits of poverty, as a weeder-out of the unfit. We no longer accept poverty as the inevitable and perpetual deposit of personal failures in the competitive struggle, and we do not even rely greatly on the fear of poverty as an incentive to work, as witness unemployment benefits and redundancy payments. It has no logical place in the system, but it obstinately remains with us, so we relieve it – when we notice it. Not very long ago it became almost invisible, but now it has reappeared. (Marshall, 1972: 28)

The earlier Marshall had argued that while income inequality was likely to persist, what really mattered was equality of status in the form of citizenship, which facilitated a 'general enrichment of the concrete substance of civilised life, a general reduction of risk and insecurity, an equalisation between the more and the less fortunate at all levels' (Marshall, 1992: 33). For the later Marshall poverty had no logical place in the system, and yet it persisted. Even as Marshall cast his gaze along the egalitarian horizon of the modern welfare state, so the past was about to overtake the future as the old meanings of poverty returned: poverty as a threat to order, poverty as a sign of idleness, and poverty as a symptom of moral decline. And as the forward march of equality went into reverse, so did the general reduction of risk and insecurity which Marshall identified as a core characteristic of the welfare ideal. It is here, as Marshall's text intersects with a socio-political context marked by dislocation, that the story becomes more complex. The very notion of 'society' has been chronically problematised, recast as an agonistic field of questioning which is not simply directed at the problems of the present but also folds back onto the past.

When it was republished in 1992, Marshall's *Citizenship and Social Class* entered a very different context. In an accompanying essay Tom Bottomore delved into Marshall's benign evolutionary account, drawing attention to the role of conflict in the acquisition of equalities and rights, and arguing that 'civil and political rights have not been established once and for all, in some near perfect form, as the basis from which social rights can develop, but are also capable of further extension' (Bottomore, 1992: 85; also Walby, 1994). This insight has since been radicalised through the politics of identity and a proliferation of demands for recognition. Between the original publication of Marshall's text in 1950 and its republication forty-two years later are the social movements challenging patriarchy, imperialism, racism and environmental degradation, a growing academic interest in the construction of social identities and subjectivities, and the structural dislocations relating to the failure of Keynesianism and the demise of the Beveridgian model of 'cradle-to-grave' welfare. This complex of forces has undermined the conception of social and historical development as a process that marches relentlessly forward as a universal and universalising paradigm of progress. Furthermore, the long-standing assumption that the political, the social and the economic can be understood as discrete spheres has been all but blown away by the recognition that social space is a fluid and nebulous mixture of identities, forces and relations. In the short space of time since Marshall wrote on the topic of citizenship and social class, a new reality has emerged. The future can be planned for but it cannot be taken as given, and so the present must be continually accomplished at the level of individual biography, or at best at the level of 'community' (Beck, 1992; Bauman, 2001, 2002b; Rose, 1996a, 1996b). If we still live in 'society', then this seems to be something quite different to the one described by Marshall.

If we cast our mind back along the post-war period we are likely to recognise an enduring tension in the relation between the spheres of state, market and society. The principal ordering mechanism during this period has been, as Marshall correctly pointed out, the welfare state. This facilitated both social cohesion and, conversely, as highlighted by Bottomore, a proliferation of antagonisms, suggesting a clear case of ambivalence. On the one hand, and for the first time according to Habermas, capitalism did not subvert the 'republican promise' to include all citizens as equals before the law, but actually made it possible (Habermas, 1999b: 47). On the other hand, the growth in struggles for equality was 'the moment of deepening of the democratic revolution' (Laclau and Mouffe, 2001: 163–4). It was the dislocation of the welfare paradigm from the 1970s which opened out the possibility of realigning the relation between state, market and society. According to the dominant reading of this period, we have moved relentlessly towards one or another form of neo-liberalism. More specifically, the Thatcher and Reagan era saw the neo-liberal defence of free markets grafted onto the anti-egalitarianism of a new wave of conservatism which stood opposed to the 'nanny' welfare state. As the market replaced the state as the guarantor of liberty, so the problem of equality was recast as one of unconstrained opportunities. Meanwhile, the core objectives of social democracy, such as full employment, social housing and universal health care, were steadily abandoned as unaffordable and/or privatised through the creation of new markets (Bottomore, 1992: 86; Laclau and Mouffe, 2001: 176; Smith, 1994). The critique extends to Third Way discourse, which has continued the theme of a welfare 'crisis' through policies designed to give people 'a hand up rather than a hand out'; essentially a labour market reintegration strategy which is largely indistinguishable from economic liberalism (Levitas, 1998; Habermas, 1999b: 53; Mouffe, 2000: 121–5).

In certain important respects this movement from welfare capitalism to neo-liberalism throws the trajectory of the last two hundred years into reverse, and a brief sketch of this period will provide an outline of the terrain to be covered in the following chapters. What we have come to know as liberal government was born at the turn of the nineteenth century, and it opened out a series of problems concerning the governability of individuals, families and populations (Rose, 1996a: 39). Central to this event (the concept of 'event' is theorised in part I and examined in detail in chapter 3) was the discovery of quasi-natural economic laws, setting limits on political authority which extended to the spheres of personal freedoms and private interests. It was this formative process that instituted the oppositions we have come to take for granted: between government and market, state and civil society, the public and the private, a set of tensions rendered governable by new forms of knowledge and expertise born out of philanthropy, social economy and the human sciences, or what Michel Foucault called 'the disciplines'. From the middle of the nineteenth century one of the most pressing questions for those with a stake in social order was how to 'secure the safety of society', a problem which helped to establish a productive relay between the burgeoning fields of scientific expertise and the centres of sovereign power (Rose, 1996a: 39–41). A growing range of interventions enacted in the name of 'society' extended to questions of security, solidarity, order, prosperity and, perhaps above all, progress, with the 'social question' bringing the individual and the population into a specific type of governable relation. As the nineteenth century became the twentieth, so the frictions generated by the spheres of state, market and society were governed through various forms of welfare capitalism. No longer subjected, in accordance with *laissez faire* liberal principles, to what Nikolas Rose calls a 'kind of individualising moral normativity', the subject was recast as a subject of needs, solidarities and dependencies (Rose, 1996a: 40).

In the last third of the twentieth century the project of society withered. In its place is a management project that thinks and acts in the name of 'the social', and there are crucial differences between one and the other. The latter, which in this study is called 'inclusive governance', is a mode of ordering that governs explicitly through freedom, with a range of techniques designed to empower the socially excluded and marginalised, in particular by augmenting their employability and capacity for responsibility and choice (Rose, 1996b; Cruikshank, 1999; Dean, 1999). The excluded, dependent and incapacitated subjects to be included, enabled and empowered are located within various 'communities': of belonging, of identity, of interest, and those which are the product of targeted administrative programmes. As we will see later on, governing through communities reconfigures the terrain of government and recalibrates the status of citizenship, both of which fragment into zones, sectors and networks.

Today it seems that everyone and everything must secure its existence without depending on the solidarities and redistributive mechanisms associated with the welfare state. Whether this is normatively desirable and whether it should go by the name of neo-liberalism is something that will be bracketed for now and taken up in chapter 9. At this stage it is sufficient to note that regardless of how we position ourselves in defining an angle of critique, the figure of the 'active subject' has become ubiquitous (see Clarke, 2005). This may be the active subject desired by policy makers as an antidote to welfare dependency, or for community and voluntary sector agencies it may be the subject that emerges from empowerment programmes. In the case of radical groups it is the agent of direct action and participatory democracy. Finally, in the context of administrative reforms, the active subject is a participant in governance. The active subject is threaded through a constellation of discourses which might otherwise exist in relations of opposition. In a situation where each and all must secure their existence through responsible self-government, which requires skills and aptitudes that enable individuals and agencies to be adaptive, flexible and highly reflexive, so the active subject corresponds to a context which is structured by forces that can be harnessed at best but never fully controlled. This is the new reality that limits the role of social technicians and engineers primarily to matters of auditing, marketing and enterprise. We have in a sense redis-covered the active or self-governing subject, a figure of intense concern to social reformers during the nineteenth century, and I will be tracing out the original constitution of this mode of agency in chapters 3 and 4. For now we can note that the active subject is not reducible to an actual individual or a specifiable group but is at once a performa-tive norm and a social relation which has come to articulate the politics of order today.

Marshall was correct when he noted that we no longer speak of paupers in the same way that nineteenth-century social reformers did, which presents us with a perplexing question: how do we manage inequality in an age which has made the ideal of equality its *doxa* – the language we think with rather than about (Bauman, 2002a: 136)? If there is no natural or necessary distinction between those included or excluded from the benefits of social life then it can only be a reflection of individual failing, a symptom of structural bias, or the unfortunate product of social change. These are the three dominant discourses within which the problem of order is now suspended. The first is a discourse of 'morality' and desert, the second a discourse of power and resistance, and the third a sociological thesis of unintended effects. Filling these out in slightly more detail, we can note that the first is coded by the notion of an 'underclass', a dominant discourse in the US, and a direct descendent of the Victorian poor laws, reproducing as it does the old distinction between a deserving (self-reliant and prudent) and an undeserving (dependent, idle and criminal) poor. The second discourse of power and resistance is cast in the register of con-flict, is articulated by the political left, and is aimed at challenging rela-tions of domination. The last is an interpretative framework which can support consensus, and it plays a central role in the European context where the meaning of social exclusion is less about desert or domination than about accidental outcomes and unforeseen problems. However, this is no simple 'either/or' situation, and accepting 'inclusion' as the new sign of equality (Giddens, 1998) risks overlooking the way it can wrap the meanings invested in the 'underclass' of today and the 'pauper-ism' of the past. As we will see in due course, inclusive governance frames a constitutive tension: on one side a promise of equality which is continually reiterated and repeatedly deferred, and on the other an overriding concern to secure a manageable order. I will be arguing that this necessitates rethinking the relation between order, power and resistance.

Further to this I will suggest that a politics of inclusion and exclusion leads us into the space of a new problematic. Unlike the project of society which envisioned – sometimes implicitly, sometimes explicitly – a state of ordered perfection, inclusive governance is about managing a fluid field of social identities, objects and relations. Mindful of the entangled relationship between the will to know and that which is to be known, the strategy employed in this study is one of encircling and stalking the object in question. This is a deliberately predatory strategy, one which emphasises the importance of position and anticipates the fact that the researcher is situated within the very systems of meaning and social practices that she or he seeks to objectivise. In terms of its empirical focus, the analysis and argument presented in the following chapters take modern Ireland as the research setting. This is discussed in more detail in chapter 1; suffice it for now to note that Ireland provides a unique study of the relationship between liberal state formation, nationalism and the project of European union, and in particular of how the tension between the liberal and democratic political traditions is currently being managed. I would also like to place 'Ireland' in scare quotes, taking a certain distance from the idea of the nation-state as a natural or necessary container for analysis. While moving steadily towards an examination of the Republic of Ireland (part III), the book as a whole does not attempt to disembed the Irish case fully from its wider context. Neither will I attempt to tell the whole story as a chronologically complete time-line without omission. Instead it is intended to move around the archive of the last two hundred years, and to do so strategically with a view to elucidating the problem at hand.

Part I begins with an account of the socio-economic dislocations that characterised the 1970s. It is here that we find the discovery of a new poverty which subsequently split into relatively distinct discourses: one framed by the notion of an 'underclass' and the other by the notion of 'exclusion'. Both have since been inscribed into regimes of practices which partially reproduce and partially recode political rationalities and programmes originally consolidated during the nineteenth century. If we are to investigate the political significance of exclusion, if we are to specify the relation between past and present, and if we are to understand how order is secured today, then we must examine the present in terms of its conditions of possibility. This requires a strategic insertion into the archive to effect a 'return' to the present via the nineteenth century. A degree of caution is required in the use of terminology here. The notion of an underclass has already returned us to the nineteenth century by recollecting the notion of pauperism and reinvoking the distinction between individuals, families and communities who are deserving of public assistances, and those among the poor who are not. While the concept of exclusion is in some respects similar, it is none the less deployed in a very different way. While also drawing on notions of family, community and association as the basis of social order, this is a turn rather than a re-turn; less a neo-conservative idealisation of the past than a more explicit attempt to restructure the present. Approaching the present via the past is intended to equip us with analytical tools so that we can, if necessary, refuse both past *and* present as solutions to the problem of order today.

Part II is primarily concerned with the period 1834–90, i.e. tracing out the enactment of the Victorian poor law, the maturing of scientific philanthropy and social economy, and the institution of a normative project that I will call 'Society'. This formative period created a historically specific fracture in the social field as two distinctive ordering technologies vied for position. These will be characterised as the 'penitentiary model' and the 'social model', with both brought to bear on a range of problems associated with pauperism and vagrancy. While these often appeared to exist in a relation of antagonism, they also constituted a single ordering modality which is elucidated by examining the work of Jeremy Bentham and William Booth in chapter 4.

Part III emplaces this framework in the context of twentieth-century Ireland (the Republic), and conducts four historical case studies of nomadism, disability, youth at risk, and lone parenting, all of which bring us to the present discourse of exclusion and the new ordering modality of inclusive governance. At the end of this part we will be in a position to attempt a comprehensive and critical reading of the present.

It may already be evident to the reader that I am indebted to the work of Foucault. In terms of theoretical and methodological framework I have attempted to address a specific question by learning from Foucault, while at the same time adding to the body of work that has grown around his writings. However, it must also be emphasised that with exclusion discourse we move beyond the world that Foucault inhabited to the world he foresaw, hoped for, and in his own way tried to create. This Foucaultian projection is often referred to as the 'death of the subject' or 'the death of man', an image Foucault described in graphic terms in the closing lines of his archaeological work *The Order of Things* (1994: 387). When this projection is considered in relation to his writings on discipline and normalising power, there are good reasons to conclude that Foucault was both right and wrong. From the perspective of the social subjects examined below – from paupers and vagrants in the nineteenth century to lone parents and nomads in the twentieth century – Foucault's theory of 'the disciplinary society' would seem to be vindicated. However, the politics of order has not erased the figure of 'man' 'like a face drawn in the sand at the edge of the sea'. Instead it would seem to be more accurate to speak of the death of Society together with its perfectionist logic: the epoch within which 'man' was cast as the subject and object of knowledge.

While I will be working with and through a Foucaultian analytics, I will also be moving beyond Foucault to consider the transformation which he could do no more than anticipate and intuit, a possible discontinuity or rupture in the order of things which is still very much in train but perhaps also a little clearer at this point in time. It is important to note that Foucault never committed the error of prediction, recognising that the interventions he was attempting and the forces he was interpreting were necessarily indeterminate. Keeping this is mind, then, it should be noted that this study does not make the strong (and audacious) claim of falsifying Foucault's work. My objective is the more modest, and hopefully scholarly, one of applying Foucault's method of critique to a specific problem in our present, moving the theoretical and analytical tools he bequeathed to us into a new and localised area of inquiry.

So here is my argument in brief. While it is still correct to speak about society we no longer govern ourselves and each other through Society: a project which envisions a state of ordered perfection which is free of uncertainty and ambivalence. Instead we are engaged in the problem of governing a capricious field of relations and securing order through an apparatus I call inclusive governance. Inclusive governance takes the fact of exclusion as its starting point; it anticipates the fact that order is provisional and vulnerable to the meanings and possibilities which are foreclosed the instant any totality, any attempt at *Society*, is instituted. Inclusive governance is concerned only with *performance*: an autotelic order secured through the management of contingency and the managed inclusion of difference. The (provisional, always provisional) objectives of inclusive governance are sealed within a type of democratic decision which envelops specific possibilities while foreclosing on alternatives, securing order through an inclusive process of exclusion. Examining how this has come into being, how it works, and what the implications might be is the aim of this study.

Part I

Approaching the event

1

The new poverty, the underclass and social exclusion

Introduction

Examined as a discourse, or more accurately as a constellation of discourses, social exclusion has recoded a range of problems relating to equality, justice and rights, problems long perceived by the political left to be implicated in relations of domination, exploitation and discrimination. While international agencies and non-governmental organisations have greatly expanded the reach of the 'social exclusion approach' (Rodgers, Gore and Figueiredo, 1995), it is still most at home in Europe. This is no accident. In the bid to maintain social cohesion in an economic and political union which has recently grown to twenty-five member states, the European Commission is a driving force behind inclusion programmes. By way of contrast, in the US a set of debates has grown around the idea of an underclass, a term frequently used to frame problems of poverty and inequality as symptoms of deviancy and criminality (see Vincent, 1993). The notion of an underclass and the concept of exclusion are very different optics through which the problems of the present are perceived, yet they both emerged from the same source: the discovery of a 'new' poverty in the 1970s and 1980s, the significance of which related to a complex mix of structural dislocations and cultural transformations. Distinguished from 'simple' poverty, the new variety was seen to necessitate novel social and political innovations, with a range of anti-poverty agencies and programmes emerging to respond to the challenge. New social classes were also discovered and coded by the notion of 'risk', that is, social categories at risk of becoming mired in the new poverty (Room, 1990; Silver, 1996). In the US the notion of exclusion is used far less frequently than is the case in Europe, and when it is used it tends to be associated with affirmative action programmes which carry certain racial connotations (Silver, 1996: 117). On the other hand the idea of an underclass has for the most part failed to take hold in Europe, although it has found some purchase in the UK.

Despite this fairly neat separation, the meanings invested in 'poverty', the 'underclass' and 'exclusion' tend to slide around, and we will need to remain attentive to this slippage.

Focusing momentarily on the Irish case, John Roche conducted a poverty study for the Irish Institute of Public Administration in 1984, framing his analysis in the register of war by arguing that 'income maintenance must remain in the front line in the fight against poverty' (Roche, 1984: 193). For Roche the growing unemployment rate, particularly long-term unemployment, was 'neither economically sustainable nor socially or politically acceptable', and he went on to argue that 'the danger in the years ahead is not that there will be no economic progress but that it will be insufficient to loosen the growing tensions in Irish society'. His prognosis was grim, and he envisioned the unemployment problem threatening to 'undermine the whole edifice of the welfare state in the long run' (Roche, 1984: 193–4, 239). In fact it was becoming increasingly apparent at this time – and not just in Ireland – that the welfare state was far less an edifice than something assembled in an *ad hoc* manner over time. The 'welfare state', often discussed as a sort of intentional Leviathan, is in fact little more than a historical accretion. Made up of instruments and practices which do not always hang neatly together, and part of a living context, it is an assemblage which often generates problems from within itself.

Even as Roche published his findings, another researcher – Anne Byrne – was arguing that poverty research in Ireland was almost non-existent before the mid-1970s, and that by the early 1980s poverty had 'still not become a socially acceptable subject for debate' (Byrne, 1982: 20–1). This was definitely not the case in the wider context. Sandra Morgen notes that US federal funding for poverty-related research increased from something in the region of $3 million in 1965 to almost $200 million in 1980 (Morgen, 2002: 751). Poverty research also underwent dramatic expansion in continental Europe. Despite, or perhaps because of, the anomalous situation in Ireland, Byrne's question resonates with its wider context and merits serious attention: why did poverty become something of intense *political* significance at this time, and, adding to the intrigue, how do we get from the new poverty to the underclass on one side of the Atlantic and social exclusion on the other? We can begin to shape an answer by looking at the main categories that form my chapter title.

The new poverty

The new poverty emerged within a context framed by the register of 'crisis',[1] and it signalled general alarm amid signs of imminent social fragmentation and growing economic insecurity. Initially defined as a problem of growing long-term unemployment, its scope was enlarged as the risk of unemployment spread throughout the class spectrum, with immunity fast becoming a thing of the past (Room, 1990; Gaffikin and Morrissey, 1992; CEC, 1991). The worsening unemployment rate was also straining welfare systems capable of dealing only with cyclical and temporary fluctuations in the unemployment rate. In turn, these structural stresses were made more complex as questions of inequality and social justice were politicised (Room, 1990: 6). In ideal typical terms (i.e. bracketing case-specific differences), the model of welfare capitalism which had proven so successful in the post-war era was based on the mixed economy of Keynesian macro-economic policies and comprehensive social security systems. As noted by T. H. Marshall, poverty was largely a peripheral concern of policy making at this time, visible occasionally through social unrest but largely associated with the past, a residual phenomenon that would eventually be resolved by a mix of social engineering and economic development. It came as something of a shock to the institutional fabric of advanced democracies when poverty re-emerged as something that was generated from *within* the modernisation process itself. Even as the 'peripheral' economies of Ireland, Greece, Portugal and Spain joined the European Community expecting to catch up with their wealthier neighbours, so the critique of economic modernisation gained momentum. Originating among Marxist scholars in the non-aligned Third-World, the critique of the modernisation paradigm was appropriated by intellectuals and activists in the 'core' countries as they began to construct anti-development and post-development discourses. Political confrontation with the modernisation paradigm from *within* the modernisation paradigm seemed imminent, with the very meaning of modernity up for grabs. In short the new poverty became a key symbol of political struggle, with a whole spectrum of positions brought to bear on accounting for it, measuring it, contesting it and governing it, including non-governmental organisations and voluntary bodies, community activists, the media, academic and policy researchers, social movements, political parties, church leaders and trade unions (Room, 1990: 9–10).

Despite the diversity of these positions, there was a consensus of sorts in the idea that there was something qualitatively and quantitatively new about the emerging poverty question. Graham Room (1990) identifies five characteristics used to define it:[2]

1 There was a major increase in the number of people dependent on social assistance of one form or another. This exposed crucial

weaknesses in the established welfare mechanisms while also generating friction over the adequacy or inadequacy of minimum benefits and criteria of entitlement.

2 Unemployment rose significantly, especially long-term unemployment, with the risk of unemployment spreading to the middle classes. In turn this curtailed purchasing power and exacerbated the apparent failure of Keynesianism.

3 There was an upward trend in the number of people living on reduced incomes, many of whom were unskilled in managing limited means and were failing to meet repayments on long-term credit commitments such as home mortgages.

4 The number of single-parent families claiming social assistance increased. In part a reflection of changes in the family structure, it was also the case that one-parent families, most of which were headed by women, were overrepresented among the poor due to a mix of growing unemployment and the gendered nature of welfare systems.

5 Finally there was an increase in the number of homeless persons, making poverty more visible and raising anxiety regarding social and economic insecurity.

From these characteristics can be seen the extent to which the new poverty was implicated in the question of order. Indeed, these characteristics are also themes subject to interpretation. Assistance to lone parents, for example, was identified by some as the cause of unmarried motherhood, while long-term unemployment assistance was a possible disincentive to work. Also, the extent of poverty among ethnic minorities, many living in deprived and run-down inner-city areas, was identified as a threat to social cohesion (Room, 1990). It was the essential ambivalence of the new poverty which saw it create a gap between the past – associated not only with the failed promise of modernisation but also with pervasive conflicts over social justice, the regressive effects of public policy, and the exploitative nature of capitalism – and the present, as a space available for the institution of new practices. Poverty was re-presented as a multi-causal phenomenon requiring interdisciplinary research, new policy instruments, and new mechanisms to bring 'stakeholders' together in addressing it. Despite the diverse and often opposed positions defining the contours of the new poverty, its discursive articulation moved towards the construction of an object that was 'out there' in the real, something that could be defined, known and governed (see Hajer, 1995: 138).

While the old poverty had been coded as a zero-sum game of social rights and distributive justice, the new poverty marked out a moment of rupture in the order of things, an object around which a range of interpretations and normative interventions could coalesce. Drawing a comparison with ecological modernisation discourse – the emergence of which coincided with the new poverty – the 'multiple-stress hypothesis' was instrumental in instituting policy programmes in a context marked by conflict over the environmental question. Defined as a complex problem, the 'environment' was seen to require an integrated/multi-dimensional approach, enabling new scientific techniques and programmes to define the nature of the problem for which they were the solution (Hajer, 1995). The new poverty saw something of an equivalent to the multiple-stress hypothesis in the idea of a complex and multi-faceted phenomenon. As a new field of facticity over which no single expert could hold competency, the new poverty required novel techniques to understand the problem and innovative programmes to manage it. In Europe the meaning of the new poverty was ultimately fixed by the register of 'exclusion'. In the US, despite similarities with the social and economic dislocations experienced in Europe, a very different dynamic ensued. We will examine the latter first.

The underclass

In the US the constitution of the 'underclass' has involved the appropriation of two theses: William Julius Wilson's structural analysis of urban poverty in Chicago, and Oscar Lewis's study of poverty in Mexico.[3] Wilson's research was conducted in the tradition of the Chicago School of urban ecology, while Lewis's work was ethnographic, and both constructed their respective categories in relation to the wider socio-economic environment. More specifically, Wilson (1987) is credited with coining the term 'underclass',[4] while Lewis (1961) originally proposed the idea of a 'culture of poverty'. In the notion of an underclass as it is now used we see these ideas deformed and grafted together, producing an ideologically loaded articulation of the new poverty. Lewis used the term 'culture of poverty' to emphasise the ways in which the poor adapt to constraints and conditions imposed by social transformation, by which he meant modernisation and industrialisation, and he was clearly communicating to an audience who perceived the doctrine of market-driven modernisation to be synonymous with progress. For advocates of modernisation the culture of the poor in the so-called 'underdeveloped' societies was a product of 'traditions' which act as a fetter on progress. Lewis's use of the term operated within an anthropological frame, and he intended it to mean 'a design for living which is passed down from generation to generation' (Lewis, 1961: xxiv). He also argued that the Mexican poor were the 'true heroes . . . paying the cost of the industrial progress of the nation' (1961: xxxi), and yet like Marx he never for a moment doubted the potential of modernisation, with the political question simply one of equalising its benefits.

Nearly thirty years after Lewis published his research, Wilson studied the effects of out-migration on the part of the more successful families in black communities (see also Piven and Cloward, 1971). His research suggested that the pattern of migration was being induced by structural factors, in particular the decline in blue-collar jobs upon which the black urban communities were largely dependent, and this in turn undermined the social fabric in these areas by creating concentrations of unemployed welfare recipients. Wilson used the term 'underclass' to signify 'racial-class inequality', his argument being that the black underclass was less subjected to racial discrimination than it was constrained by the lack of economic opportunities (Wilson, 1987: 159). By the time Wilson was conducting his study the 'culture of poverty' thesis was already being used to blame the poor for their poverty, with Wilson himself using the concept in this way. And as the thesis was gathered into Wilson's text, and perhaps unintentionally reinforced within it, so too was his work discursively shaped within its context.

The underclass now tends to be presented as spatially concentrated, with much of the empirical research describing a deviant subculture that reproduces its own dysfunctional norms from within. It also anchors the wider debate on social change by providing a symbol of social danger. For example, it is used to call for tougher measures on crime while the sufficiently wealthy sequester themselves within privatised security spaces or 'gated communities', disengaging from social obligations by resisting state taxes and purchasing services directly from the private sector, including security measures to exclude the threats perceived to be emanating from the 'ghettos' (Blakeley and Snyder, 1997; Giddens, 2000). Those who subscribe to the notion of an underclass also tend to characterise the poor in terms of pathological dispositions and behavioural defects such as welfare dependency, illegal earnings on the informal economy, the eschewal of stable family relationships and commitments by males, young people dropping out of school, teen criminality and teen pregnancy (Fraser and Gordon, 1997; Morgen, 2002). This also forcefully recovers conceptions of the poor originally constituted during the nineteenth century, in particular the distinction between the 'deserving' and the 'undeserving'. Charles Murray is a leading exponent of this discourse, and he calls for a return to what he identifies explicitly as Victorian values (1994). While clearly far to the right in these debates, Murray is useful in unpacking what is often implicit in policy debates and scholarly research on the new poor more generally. For example, Robert Putnam's (2000) hugely influential work on social capital does not engage with the underclass debate directly, yet his willingness to idealise the past as a time of benevolent association and community slots into the wider intellectual project to model the present on a sociologically naïve reading of the past, a practice that invites selective amnesia, for example by omitting the fact that the so-called 'progressive era' also gave birth to the science of eugenics. More specifically, when Putnam identifies the 'stable family' as a 'vaccine' against the 'contagious [troublemaking] kids capable of infecting others' (2000: 314), his analysis connects with Murray's and also resonates with the Victorian theme of 'moral' contagion. Putnam is hardly in agreement with Murray, yet by invoking the register of contagion he helps to reinforce the neo-conservative articulation of the 'underclass' thesis.

Murray crossed the Atlantic in his analysis of the underclass, conducting research in both the US and the UK to frame the problem as one of imminent crisis. With the weight of his analysis bearing down on single mothers, Murray uses social science strategically to recover the notion of 'illegitimacy' while also targeting economic inactivity among working-aged males, a conceptual framework that assumes a natural division of labour with men providing and women nurturing. He also describes the cultural transformations of the 1960s as a form of 'irritating solipsism', drawing on the tradition of natural law to argue that 'soaring illegitimacy' among the underclass is leading to a dual society. For Murray this is a situation where the whole spectrum of social pathologies is set to increase, from crime to drug abuse, divorce, unemployment and homelessness (Murray, 1994: 17–18). While making some attempt to mask a political agenda behind the veil of science, categories such as 'the New Victorians' and 'the New Rabble' puncture any claim to value-neutrality. The loaded emblem of 'crisis' signals polarisation as the New Victorians, a class held together by self-supporting two-parent families, is set against the New Rabble of illegitimate degenerates, with Murray arguing that the increase in one-parent families, of interest to sociologists and policy makers alike for a host of reasons, is the principal source of crime and moral decline (Murray, 1994: 15, 19).

The Bell Curve (1994), which Murray co-authored with Richard Herrnstein, is similar in its agenda but more insidious in its implications. In the course of this study the thesis of a 'dull' underclass gradually becomes a 'dumb' black underclass, with the alleged intersection of rising illegitimacy and lower intelligence within ethnically homogeneous communities leading straight to 'dysgenesis', i.e. a situation whereby the dumb (black underclass) breed themselves, and possibly society as a whole, into a downward spiral where the rule of reason gives way to the law of the jungle. The normative inference and the quasi-eugenic policy recommendation is that affirmative action policies, as well as welfare programmes to lone parents, are a waste of money and a threat to society. The poverty of the underclass is a product of their own inferior genetic endowment, and the only way to reverse the slide into dysgenesis is to re-invoke the Victorian order of things: an order of immutable ranks. Meritocracy is given a genetic twist, with social order becoming the cognitive equivalent of natural order. The bottom line is that there are natural limits to social mobility, and so everyone must know their place, whatever hardships this might entail.

Francis Fukuyama, another contributor to the debate, suggests that the inclusion of ethnic minorities should be an unambiguous question of assimilation, and he also diagnoses the 'black underclass' as 'one of the most atomised societies in human history' (1995: 303). Again this exhibits a behaviourist focus and a somewhat expedient bracketing of structural factors. As with Murray, though leaning more towards the liberal end of the neo-conservative project, Fukuyama focuses on the breakdown of the traditional family which is identified in normative terms as the primary unit of socialisation. Also like Murray, Fukuyama locates the cause of decline in welfare programmes that 'subsidise' single women to have babies (1995: 353).

The account above might suggest that the notion of an underclass is articulated solely by the political right, but it is also at home in the liberal tradition, particularly if we look back to nineteenth-century liberalism, as we will in part II. In fact the underclass debate tends to dissolve the conventional ideological spectrum (see Peterson, 1991). It would be an error to assume either that it can be explained as a reflection of the conservative or liberal wings of the new right, or for that matter that it is wholly confined to the US. Similar arguments are occasionally used in the debates on social exclusion in Europe, for example in the way that 'Third Way' social democrats combine elements of liberalism and communitarianism in denouncing teen pregnancy and calling for active welfare measures to overcome the demoralising effects of 'dependency'.

It might also be alleged that the account of the underclass above is confined to its ideological dimension to the neglect of actual policy. The latter can be seen in the recent dismantling of the Federal Aid to Families with Dependent Children programme, initiated by the Democratic Clinton administration and continued unabated by the Republican Bush administration. 'Welfare reform' in the US has been codified by the Personal Responsibility and Work Opportunity Reconciliation Act, which enables competing political elites to be 'tough on work' while at the same time individualising social problems and identifying hetero-sexual marriage as the natural or necessary unit of order (Morgen, 2002).[5] The practical effect of this has been a general swing in support of compulsory workfare as the answer to alleged dependencies created by welfare (Mead, 1993; Bewick, 1997). Whether examined at the level of ideology or of policy, the framing of the underclass in the US re-invokes Victorian liberalism, with the 'undeserving poor' signifying a direct and immanent threat to the good order of society (Gans, 1996; Procacci, 1991; Byrne, 1999). This is not to suggest the simple transla-tion of ideological constructions into policy outcomes. Instead I am interested in the concrete effects which can result as a constellation of what Foucault called 'statements' come together as a formation of dis-course. These theoretical considerations will be taken up in more detail in the next chapter. For now we will consider how the underclass differs from debates on the European side of the Atlantic.

Social exclusion and the problem of cohesion

The term 'exclusion', or *les exclus*, was first used in France during the 1960s as a term of social critique, denoting such things as alienation. However, as currently used it is attributed to René Lenoir, who, as 'Secretaire d'etat a l'action sociale' in the Gaullist government in 1974, spoke of 'the excluded' as constituting some 10 per cent of the French population (Silver, 1994: 532; 1996: 63). Lenoir was referring explicitly to various classes of 'misfits' such as the intellectually and physically disabled, aged invalids, suicidal persons, substance abusers, single parents, and various other 'marginal' and 'asocial' persons unprotected by social insurance. Debates in France at this time moved to the idea of 'inserting' these 'precarious' subjects back into society, with the context defined largely by the ensuing economic problems. The scope of the concept has since greatly expanded, with the European Commu-nity/Union playing a major role in sponsoring social inclusion as an objective of policy and an area of research, consolidating it as a norma-tive concept through a series of 'combat poverty' programmes from 1975 to 1994, and subsequently embedding it in a discourse of cohesion by linking it to local partnership projects, by aligning it to the doctrine of subsidiarity, and by tying it to transfers such as the Structural Funds and Community Initiatives (CEC, 1991: 29–30; 1993; Bennington and Geddes, 2001). Tracing this formative process will provide an overview of the concept's rapid rise to prominence in Europe.

Coincident with René Lenoir's use of the phrase 'the excluded' in 1974, the European Commission published a consultation paper which formed the basis of the First European Combat Poverty Programme, which ran in two phases, from 1975 to 1977, and 1977 to 1980 (Varley, 1988: 18; Gaffikin and Morrissey, 1992: 118). The programme sponsored local pilot projects such as area-based community action projects, schemes to deal with specific types of poverty, and projects for improving social services. Half of the projects were aimed at mobilising and supporting 'communities', while others were aimed at specific problems pertaining to parenting, children, 'battered' women, the homeless, disabled persons, and the elderly (Gaffikin and Morrissey, 1992: 118–19).

The concept of exclusion itself was codified in 1984, prior to the Second Combat Poverty Programme, in a definition of the poor authored by the European Council: 'The "poor" shall be taken to mean persons, families, and groups of persons whose resources (material, cultural and social) are so limited as to *exclude* them from the minimum acceptable way of life in the member state in which they live' (cited in Room, 1990: 40; Holland, 1993: 122). Despite this shift in the language of inequality, the Second Programme, which ran from 1985 to 1989, continued to operate through the register of the new poverty and reinforced the notion of relative poverty built into the above definition, i.e. poverty measured in relation to prevailing social norms. The Second Programme was termed a 'social laboratory', on the one hand promoting the 'exchange of information, experience and models for action',[6] and on the other introducing practices of external and self-evaluation to encourage introspection and to improve project management and team motivation (CEC, 1991; Room, 1995; Gaffikin and Morrissey, 1992). The Second Programme was organised around eight themes: long-term unemployment; youth unemployment; the elderly; single-parent families; migrants and refugees; 'marginal' groups; integrated action in urban areas; and integrated action in rural areas (Varley, 1988; Gaffikin and Morrissey, 1992). The first six categories related to persons at risk, while the other two were spatial categories defining communities at risk (Williams, 1996; Scott, 1995). It was subsequently noted that other forms of inequality and deprivation were absent from the designated themes, such as low pay relating to underemployment, the feminisation of poverty related to low-wage service-sector work, and the omission of 'disability' and 'race' as categories (Gaffikin and Morrissey, 1992: 122; Varley, 1988: 22). Indeed the Commission itself acknowledged the shortcomings of the household budget data underpinning the programme, which also excluded nomadic groups and persons in institutional care from the designated inclusion measures (CEC, 1991: Appendix 1).

Towards the end of the Second Programme the European Commission, under the stewardship of Jacques Delors, published an influential document titled 'The Social Dimension of the Internal Market' (CEC, 1988).[7] This predicted imminent social and economic dislocation as a result of the impending fiscal austerity measures required to complete the single market. Anticipating a period of temporary turbulence until the market kicked in and provided jobs to a flexible and geographically mobile workforce, a third programme was sanctioned to facilitate the period of adjustment, an objective made explicit by its title: 'a medium-term programme to foster the economic and social integration of the least privileged groups' (Geddes and Bennington, 2001: 31; also CEC, 1993).

This Third Programme, or Poverty 3 as it became known, ran from 1989 to 1994 (CEC, 1995). While all three programmes were informed by principles of subsidiarity and participation, the First and Second Programmes promoted a grassroots approach through community development strategies, although in retrospect it became apparent that the concept of 'participation' was very much top-down in emphasis (Room, 1995: 109; NESC, 1994; Varley and Ruddy, 1996). Poverty 3 shifted to a smaller number of larger projects, and it sought to expand the dimension of partnership and participation beyond the community and voluntary (C&V) sector so as to include statutory and private-sector agencies. It placed greater emphasis on the transfer of successful policies, on the integration of physical, social and economic planning, on partnership and cooperation both horizontally among actors in different 'spheres' (state, market and society) and vertically among different 'tiers' (local, national and supranational), and on refining procedures for enhanced evaluation (Geddes and Bennington, 2001: 30–2). Significantly, Poverty 3 also succeeded in recoding poverty, marking a significant shift in emphasis from 'the actual conditions of poor people' to 'the forces that *generate* social and economic exclusion' (NESC, 1994: 172, original emphasis).

It is here that a political strategy for managing social antagonism becomes apparent. The discourse of inclusion eschews the normative thrust of the underclass debate, which tends to individualise social problems. It also evades the register of power and domination mobilised by the political left, moving instead to a sociological thesis of unintended effects. This marks the moment of bifurcation in the discourse of the new poverty, which is articulated in specific ways on either side of the Atlantic. In the US we find the politics of order framed by the ideas of policing, controlling and reforming a recalcitrant underclass. In Europe the problem of order is coded in Durkheimian terms as a project of cohesion, which provides a consensual hinge on which the relationship between inclusion and exclusion turns (Levitas, 1998).

In this brief discussion on the new poverty, the underclass and social exclusion, I have focused on the ideological dimension in the case of the US and the policy dimension in the case of Europe. Part III addresses the question of exclusion in much greater detail, at the level of both ideas and practices, by focusing on Ireland, which warrants a few words on this particular choice of research setting. Ireland provides an important lesson which is not self-evident if the usual markers of relative size (economic, demographic) or influence (political, military) are used. The Irish state came into existence through a mix of liberalism and nationalism, and while political and cultural nationalism often overshadowed the liberal origins of Irish state and society, it is also the case that, institutionally, Ireland exhibits a much closer resemblance to England and the US than it does to continental Europe. In the contemporary context there are good historical reasons why Ireland might have followed the US and (to a lesser extent) the UK in combining neo-liberal reforms with the notion of an underclass. However, under the tutelage of the European Union the exclusion approach has been consolidated in Ireland. As Ruth Levitas has shown (1998), the discourse of in/exclusion is something of an 'empty signifier', that is, an essentially contested concept which, precisely because it is contested, 'quilts' together various ways of thinking, speaking and acting upon the problem of order. It is the very instability and malleability of this concept that moves it to the centre of contemporary political struggles. In view of the question under consideration, Ireland provides a unique study concerning the relationship over time between liberal state formation, nationalism, the European Community/Union and neo-liberal restructuring. In short, as Europe continues to undergo significant political, social and economic reforms, a close reading of the Irish case shows how the tension between the liberal and democratic political traditions – a tension which is becoming increasingly important in Europe today – is currently being managed.

To sum up, I have indicated that in the case of the US we see the revival of themes which find their origins in classical liberalism, and this tends to preserve the order of Society by focusing on those micro-populations coded as criminal, dependent and morally degenerate. In Europe, on the other hand, there is evidence of a different kind of transformation, more a 'turn' than a 'return'. The next section considers this in more detail.

Framing the problem

In tandem with the ideological and policy-oriented debates sketched above, the problem of exclusion has of course become the subject of a growing body of academic research. The literature on this topic broadly reflects the tendency within the social sciences to favour either a macro- or micro-, structural or agency-centred explanation. In the case of the former, it is either modernity or the old bogey of capitalism which pro-vides the causal or explanatory framework (Mingione, 1996; Byrne, 1999; Room, 1995; Young, 1999; Beck, 1992; Bauman, 1998a, 1998b, 2002a, 2002b; Healy and Reynolds, 1998). What this type of analysis tends to overlook, or at least to minimise, are the ways in which the new poverty, the underclass and social exclusion are deeply implicated in contextual processes of interpretation and translation (Rodgers, 1995; Levitas, 1996, 1998; Silver, 1994, 1995, 1996; Cousins, 1996). I do not intend to rehearse the debates on the philosophy of science here; suffice it to note that I agree with Hubert Dreyfus and Paul Rabinow that we can get beyond the shortcomings of either/or approaches by subjecting the problem in question to a mode of inquiry they call an 'interpretative analytics' (1983: 202–3; also Dean, 1999). The next chapter addresses this in more detail. In the remainder of this chapter I want to consider the relation between social scientific texts and the contexts of their production, which necessitates a few provisional comments on post-structuralist thought.

In certain important respects the discursive construction of the new poverty mirrors a debate on poverty and poor relief at the turn of the nineteenth century, a debate that was instrumental in constituting the figure of the pauper. The debate itself spanned some forty years, from about 1795 to the Poor Law Amendment Act of 1834, and brought together a diverse body of texts including the well-known works of Smith, Bentham, Burke, Malthus and Ricardo as well as the lesser-known writings of Joseph Townsend and Edwin Chadwick. As we will see in chapter 3, the constitution of 'poverty' was no minor event, producing as it did a new object of knowledge, a new field of governance, and a new subject of rule (Dean, 1991, 1999). We may currently be in the midst of something no less productive as text and context form a constitutive 'event' (Foucault, 1991a: 76–8). Just as poverty and pauperism were both constituted by and constitutive of nineteenth-century liberal governance, so the new poverty seems to have played a central role in the reconfiguration of government today.

We might ask ourselves what texts are gathered into the present context. Much of the literature on social exclusion, both empirical and normative, is *about* exclusion: approaching it in terms of where it is, what its characteristics are, its impacts, and what should be done to address it. Poststructuralist thought, on the other hand, is a collection of theories *of* exclusion, which is to say that exclusion is fundamental to its social ontology (Laclau and Mouffe, 1987, 2001; Devenney, 2002, 2004; Torfing, 1999; Howarth, 2000). Poststructuralism is concerned with how a given order is constituted and instituted through the inclusion of particular meanings, identities and relations and the exclusion of others. Exclusion is thus constitutive of order, but also its limit. Ontologically there is always a 'surplus' – a symbolic residue – which harbours the radical potential to be brought into 'language' or discourse, to be articulated politically, and possibly used to realign relations of power. The next chapter looks at this in detail, using the concept of symbolic residue to conceptualise both the problem of order and the source of change. Here it is introduced for the purpose of underlining the core insight of poststructuralist thought: the impossibility of an order without exclusion.

While the modern epistemological project aimed to disclose the underlying truth hidden by ideological distortion or the capriciousness of cultural conventions, poststructuralist thought aims for something else entirely: it reaches for the possibilities which have been excluded by the truth within which we are cast as thinking and acting subjects. In other words the surplus is a potential 'solvent in which the knowable and speakable could lose its form' (Staten, 1985: 16). Moving this into the domain of politics and policy, then, the problem of exclusion cannot be resolved, it can only be anticipated and managed. There is more than a coincidental resemblance between poststructuralist thought and contemporary forms of governance. Zygmunt Bauman intuits this when he writes about the new 'hospitality to critique', arguing that we have found ways to 'accommodate critical thought and action while remaining immune to the consequences of that accommodation . . . emerging unaffected and unscathed – reinforced rather than weakened – from the tests and trials of the open-house policy' (Bauman, 2002b: 21–3). While the poststructuralist critique provides very sharp tools for the purpose of analysis and explanation, I want to consider whether its normative edge may have been blunted by a mode of ordering that transforms the core insight of poststructuralism – the argument that exclusion is both the possibility and impossibility of order – into a governing principle.

In political and policy terms the register of 'exclusion' both *anticipates* and *codes* those possibilities which are deferred as social space is ordered. The problem of order is no longer about fixing objects and relations in place once and for all through techniques of classification and control. Instead we strive for a provisional state of order, a manageable order, and we must anticipate disturbances in the form of demands for inclusion. Political struggle has been transformed, as have the perceived causes and objectives of struggle. Poverty is a case in point. As a way of explaining the tension between citizenship and social class, poverty was perceived to be *external* to the potential of modernisation: for socialists it was functional to the reproduction of capitalism but would be eradicated in the transition to communism; for egalitarian liberals it was the legacy of 'tradition', a sort of sticky substance that belonged to the past but somehow continued to cling to the present. Either way, whether because the poor had become a class for itself and realised its revolutionary potential, or through the sheer acceleration of progress, the underlying assumption was that poverty would, eventually, be consigned to history. In contrast to this the problem of exclusion is explicitly understood as something which is constituted from within the process of ordering itself. As something *internal* to the social the issue becomes one of being *at risk* of forces and relations that cannot be externalised either objectively or through modes of representation. The old poverty required us to look back along the horizon of past time for its causes; the new poverty is flanked by temporal horizons that have been chronically problematised, both past and present. Historical time, which is also the possibility of linear and continual progress, has become a foreshortened temporal horizon wherein the present cuts itself away from causal origins and predetermined destinations. We inhabit a context framed by instabilities and potential dislocations that will not and cannot be resolved once and for all, for our problems can only be managed. We have become subjects of an autotelic world, and in the course of this study I will attempt to move the reader into position to understand what it is that inclusive governance does in this context.

As a field of knowledge the 'social exclusion approach' (Rodgers, Gore and Figueiredo, 1995) incorporates a range of questions concerning what it is, where it is, how much of it there is, and how significant it is in terms of individual and collective effects. Taken as a corpus, the literature tends to affirm Hilary Silver's argument that we are dealing with something which is articulated in different ways depending on the context of its articulation (Silver, 1994, 1995, 1996). The exclusion problematic is subjected to various theoretical and methodological strategies, it is studied in a variety of contexts and examined at a number of levels, yet it must also be acknowledged that the enterprise to know exclusion also contributes to its creation, which is the problem of the 'double hermeneutic' (Giddens, 1984).[8] Indeed it is the very diversity of approaches that knits them together as a 'discourse' or 'text'. And of course my own contribution adds to this complex construction.

The literature on this topic is growing, not only in quantity but also in scope and diversity. A common thread can be traced through many individual texts, however. Though characterised in different ways, they point to some kind of discontinuity, break or seismic shift in the order of things: a phase shift (Byrne, 1999), a paradigm change (Silver, 1994), a newly reflexive (Beck, 1992; Giddens, 1994) or fluid modernity (Bauman, 2002b), or a bulimic society (Young, 1999). Whether or not this is the case, or the extent to which it is the case, it is clear that the 'how' questions must still be addressed. Defining and/or explaining what exclusion 'is' already presupposes a particular way of knowing, which is also a way of doing. We need to inquire into how this way of knowing has come into being, and to what extent it reconfigures the politics of order. The research strategy adopted here is problem-driven rather than driven by theory or methodology (Howarth and Torfing, 2005). I am not attempting to defend a specific theoretical enterprise or validate a particular research methodology; instead the task is one of tracing out a mode of ordering that thinks and governs through inclusion and exclusion, a task that requires the detail of historical investigation and a theoretical framework which can organise that detail into a coherent, problem-driven analysis. The next chapter tackles the theoretical side of this task.

2

Stalking the present:
a genealogical strategy

Introduction

> Ours is not a historical work; what we are searching for is not a convincing sequence of outstanding events, but an explanation of their trend in human institutions. We shall feel free to dwell on scenes from the past with the sole object of throwing light on matters of the present; we shall make detailed analyses of critical periods and almost completely disregard the connecting stretches of time. (Polanyi, 2001: 4)

> That punishment in general and the prison in particular belong to a political technology of the body is a lesson that I have learnt not so much from history as from the present . . . I would like to write the history of this prison, with all the political investments of the body that it gathers together in its closed architecture. Why? Simply because I am interested in the past? No, if one means by that writing a history of the past in terms of the present. Yes, if one means writing a history of the present. (Foucault, 1977: 30–1)

The quotations above are two exemplary approaches to the history of the present. Despite nominal similarities, the differences between the genealogical inquiry of Karl Polanyi and that of Michel Foucault are significant, the distance between one and the other moving towards a context we are still struggling to understand, to characterise, to theorise. Indeed at times it seems the best we can do is add the prefix 'post' to something more certain: 'modernity' or 'industrial', for example, the irony of which is that the alleged relativism of postmodernity is in fact a situation whereby we are fencing ourselves in with posts (Winterson, 1996: 6).

The purpose of this chapter is to set out a conceptual framework which will help to elucidate this context, a framework which takes the form of a specific type of genealogy. Max Weber paved the way for this type of inquiry in his study of the modern state and rational capitalism, his well-known prognosis cast in the image of an 'iron cage' (Weber, 1978a; Clegg, 1990). Weber characterised modernity as a process of rationalisation, with means–end rationality gradually becoming an end in itself: an iron cage that envelops its subject. Notwithstanding his influence on the Frankfurt School of critical theory (Clarke, 2006), Weber's pessimism was not entirely shared by those who came after him. As World War II came to an end Polanyi (2001) and Friedrich Hayek (1991) set themselves the task of tracking the causes and portending implications of the atrocities and fascisms which had unhinged the modern promise of progress, a project which Colin Gordon characterises as a 'semiology of catastrophe' (Gordon, 1986: 78; Dean, 1999: 42–3).[1] Despite their very different ideological convictions – Polanyi sympathetic to social democracy and Hayek a committed libertarian – both were in agreement that the cause of the catastrosphe could be explained by disclosing its origins, and that human error could be rectified and a better future secured. More recently Jürgen Habermas (1984, 1987, 1996, 1999a), someone who has taken much from Weber, has constructed an impressive normative theory on similar premises. While it may be frustrated at present, Habermas remains convinced that the Enlightenment promise of emancipation is immanent to our discourse, which is made transparent in his notion of an 'ideal speech situation': a communicative forum undistorted by manipulation and governed only by the force of the better argument.

There is a double movement of convergence and divergence linking the genealogies of Weber, Polanyi, Hayek and Habermas. With Polanyi and Hayek (though this says nothing about their respective normative concerns) Habermas shares the project of securing the future against forces which threaten to overwhelm the benefits of modernisation and rationalisation, and of course this is where he touches base with Weber and the Frankfurt School. At the same time, in acknowledging that human knowledge and social evolution are not determined by hidden laws or deep structures and in turning to the study of communication and discourse, Habermas shares quite a lot with Foucault. But there the similarity ends, for Habermas clearly rejects Foucault's neo-Nietzschean approach to genealogical analysis, arguing that it leads to a form of political abdication: a retreat into relativism which is incapable of transcending the specificities of context and thus unable to deliver a universal model of social and political organisation. From the Habermasian perspective the role of genealogy in critical theory is framed by the logic of 'either/or': unless there is a universal support for theoretical and ethical discourse then our particular claims to validity are groundless and we are doomed to drown in a sea of relativism (Dean, 1999: 42; Howarth, 2000: 123).

In contrast to the genealogies of Weber, Polanyi, Hayek and Habermas, Mitchell Dean characterises Foucault's genealogical method as diagnostic and anti-anachronistic. The diagnostic moment seeks to make the present strange by disclosing its contingencies and singularities. And moving in the opposite direction, the anti-anachronistic moment maintains specific links to the past while refusing to read the past through the experience of the present (Dean, 1999: 44–5). By engaging in detailed historical and empirical work the Foucaultian genealogist reconstructs and problematises the assumed continuities and discontinuities between past and present (Dean, 1999: 46; Foucault, 1984a). For Foucault, genealogy entails the 'permanent critique of ourselves': adopting a 'limit attitude' so as to interrogate our 'historical mode of being'. At the frontier of what is given to us as universal and necessary, genealogical inquiry looks for the singular and the contingent, thereby disclosing the arbitrary nature of the constraints we live under (Foucault, 1984b: 42, 45). Precisely because the world we inhabit is necessarily contaminated by a horizon of excluded possibilities, so it is possible to reach this surplus *through* the instituted order and thus to open out a space for the positing of alternatives (cf. Žižek, 1989: 215–31). Dean offers a concise definition of the approach, one which is appropriated for the purpose of this study: 'The critical ethos of genealogy can be positively described as an incitement to study the form and consequences of universals in particular historical situations and practices grounded in problems raised in the course of particular social and political struggles' (Dean, 1999: 42). Order is produced not through intention or design but through struggle. And because this may be obscured as the effects and outcomes of struggle sediment in social knowledge and social practice, so the genealogist looks for the traces of struggle and seeks to disclose the contingency of the present. It is these traces of combat that provide the key to unlocking the present.

In Foucault's own words, genealogy refuses 'the blackmail of the Enlightenment', of being forced to adopt a position either for or against the present (Foucault, 1984b: 42–3). The danger of such a choice is that the options are already coded by systems of power/knowledge. In the face of such a non-choice, Foucault's stance of refusal can be understood as a radical gesture that opens out a space for the positing of questions and possible alternatives. It is in this sense that Foucault wrote of the tactical use that could be made of 'local criticism'. By this he meant the possibility of an 'insurrection of subjugated knowledges', or those 'low-ranking knowledges' which have been 'disqualified' by the authority of 'totalitarian theories' and 'systemising thought' (1980: 80–3).

His aim was to recover 'blocs' of historical knowledge which, though excluded, continue to inhabit the discourses through which we think, speak and act. By bringing these to the fore, genealogy aims to open out a space of possibilities for the positing of alternative ways of thinking and acting. It is important at this point to note that Foucault eschewed the idea that critical thought should aim to construct a meta-narrative of emancipation, which is not to say that his style of critique is incapable of changing the world in accordance with emancipatory projects, though some of his critics seem to assume otherwise (see for example Fraser and Gordon, 1997). Taking a broadly Foucaultian approach to critique, it is crucial to be cognisant of the fact that we should not assume the possibility of emancipation in some fixed and final form. Instead it is correct to speak of a plurality of emancipatory projects which are facilitated by a 'multiplicity of genealogical researches'. The critical ethos of this 'anti-science' is not to negate the contents, concepts and methods of science itself (which would entail a sort of self-refutation on Foucault's part). Rather, it sets itself against the in-sidious 'effects', the 'centralising powers' and the institutional appara-tuses which attain the status and the concomitant authority of 'truth' (1980: 84).

Having have set out *what* it is that genealogical critique attempts to do, we now need to consider the *how* dimension, which is the conceptual framework deployed in this type of investigation.

Discourse, hegemony and epoch: the role of meaning in the politics of order

The specific objective in this study is a genealogy of a new mode of governing, one that secures social order through technologies of enclo-sure and foreclosure. Putting this less abstractly, I am interested in the constitution of a 'regime of practices' which governs – not unknowingly, but explicitly – through inclusion and exclusion. In Foucault's histories a regime of practices is part of a 'regime of truth', with the notion of 'regime' denoting systems of knowledge and practice which are assem-bled, over time, through struggle. This leaves us with the problem of scale and scope: how do we delimit a regime of truth/practice? This section begins by discussing the notion of truth regime, subsequently using the concepts 'hegemony' and 'epoch' to address the question of scope and scale.

Discourse and the formation of truth: power/knowledge/practice
As people set about governing themselves and each other, the practical

effect is the constitution of specific ways of knowing and ways of doing that circumscribe the parameters of 'the true', a term Foucault borrowed from Georges Canguilhem. On the one hand are the ways in which social knowledge constitutes a variety of object domains and subject positions, places within the social field from where true or false propositions are enunciated and inscribed into practical techniques of ordering, regulating, administering. On the other hand are the conventions employed in doing things, conventions coded by specific rationalities and principles governing classification, judgement, examination (Foucault, 1991a: 79–82). To speak and act from within the true is to make a 'statement', something that carries the force and validity of authority and is the basic element of discourse. In his *Archaeology of Knowledge* Foucault drew on structural linguistics to define the relation between statements and discourse: 'A statement belongs to a discursive formation as a sentence belongs to a text . . . But whereas the regularity of a sentence is defined by the laws of a language [*langue*] . . . the regularity of statements is defined by the discursive formation itself' (Foucault, 1972: 116). A discourse encompasses various types of statements which are ordered through specific rules of formation into programmes, apparatuses and technologies (Foucault, 1972: 31–5). Foucault defines programmes as 'sets of calculated, reasoned prescriptions in terms of which institutions are meant to be reorganised, spaces arranged, behaviours regulated' (Foucault, 1991a: 80). Programmes, then, are specific rationalities, while technologies and apparatuses are, respectively, the practical means of implementation and the modes of organisation.

While design and planning may play a role in the constitution of a programme, programmes do not originate in the minds of individual planners or bureaucratic offices. Instead they are assembled from many different sources, the practical effect of which is described by Foucault as a 'unity in dispersion'.[2] An example (given fuller treatment in the next chapter) is 'poverty', the constitution of which can be traced to the intersection of a heterogeneous universe of statements at the turn of the nineteenth century. As an object of knowledge, poverty is also a field of intervention which is invested with specific meanings, coded by forms of expertise, and articulated by social practices, some of which, like the school and the hospital, may seem to have nothing to do with poverty. It is thus meaningless to talk about the essence or limit of a discursive object such as poverty. As we will see in chapters 3–4, poverty as we have come to understand it was constituted in a specific historical context, simultaneously an object to be known and a domain to be governed (Dean, 1991). To trace out the constitution of poverty is also to disclose its contingency, which extends to its conditions of existence as an object, its meaning in specific contexts, and the way it facilitates, constrains and limits what it is possible to think and do. The meaning of poverty was not fixed by the terms of its constitution; on the contrary it remained (and remains) an object which is discursively constructed by contesting, defining and redefining its significance. In this sense poverty was and is a prize to be won in the domain of political struggle. In delimiting what can be said and what can be done in a given time and place, objects such as poverty are implicated in the production of 'truth'.

To conceptualise the social in this way is to study the conditions of existence for specific regimes of power/knowledge/practice and to reconstruct the struggles through which they are constituted, instituted and problematised. In a given society, for example, there will be a diverse, yet more or less finite and intermeshing cluster of practices such as those pertaining to punishment, medicine, public assistance and education (Dean, 1999: 21). These may be anchored in specific fields of knowledge such as justice, health and welfare, yet they are not reducible to any one of them. Punishment, for example, may find its principal institutional support in the penal system but it will also exhibit a presence in schools, families and hospitals. Practices overlap, intersect, compete, fragment, outflank and colonise (Dean, 1999: 21; Clegg, 1989). As a grid of divisions, distributions and relations, a regime is constructed, assembled, contested and transformed from multiple and heterogeneous elements (Dean, 1999: 26). The basic conceptual framework is described in figure 2.1.

There is another dimension which is not evident from this diagram but is implicit in all of its dimensions, and this concerns the subject. In Foucault's *Archaeology of Knowledge* (1972) this was conceptualised as the 'enunciative function', or the subject positions through which statements are enacted. We can fill out figure 2.1 in more detail so as to make

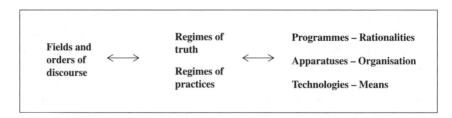

Figure 2.1 The elements of discourse

explicit this dimension of subjectivity/identity/agency by drawing on the work of Mitchell Dean, who proposes four interlocking dimensions of the subject of discourse: characteristic forms of visibility (ways of seeing and perceiving); distinctive ways of thinking and questioning (vocabularies and procedures implicated in the production of truth); specific ways of acting, intervening and directing (practical rationalities and techniques); and ways of forming the self and relations to the self (Dean, 1999: 23). The constitution of the true and its separation from the false takes place within such specifiable matrices of knowing, thinking, speaking, acting and being.

In writing specifically about the production of truth, Foucault made it quite clear that he was considering the nature of the political: 'What is history, given there is continually being produced within it a separation of true and false . . . isn't the most general of political problems the problem of truth?' (Foucault, 1991a: 82). 'A truth regime is produced, modified and transformed through a multiplicity of struggles. It is also *within* the true, as mentioned in the last chapter, that a certain surplus is found: an ineliminable residue of meaning or a horizon of excluded possibilities which exceeds the ordering force of those discourses which attain the authority of truth. Ontologically, this surplus is the constitutive possibility and impossibility of any relational system – whether a language, discourse or culture. The surplus is the spacing around written words, the void surrounding spoken sounds, and the nothingness which makes being possible; the surplus cannot be brought into discourse without extending, modifying or reconfiguring the relational whole, and is thus the source of change. At this level of abstraction the surplus is essentially a negative metaphysics. But there is also something between pure negativity and that which has the positivity of being within an ordered whole: the liminal edge between order and its other, or the margin which makes the category possible. For Bauman this is the 'stubborn and grim reminder of the flux which order wished to contain but in vain; of the limits to order; and of the necessity of ordering' (Bauman, 1991: 9). We might think of this as the empirical equivalent of spacing, void and nothingness, which is the surplus as it exists beyond representation.

In defining the boundaries of a given order this is something that *can* be represented as either external or internal to the order in question. Here we are concerned primarily with the latter, and in particular the ways in which this margin is coded by notions of the abnormal and the anomalous. The margin both bounds order from within and derives its significance from the grids of power/knowledge/practice that give form and substance to order. During the nineteenth century this liminal edge was coded in the negative as 'pauperism', 'vagabondage' and 'the residuum', and as it was discursively constituted as a threat to the safety and security of Society, so it was made into an object for the technicians of conduct and built into normalising programmes, the latter designed to cure and/or control the disorderly surplus so that order would be protected and, ultimately, perfected (Bauman, 2002b: 101; Young, 1999: 56–95). Yet the surplus is not simply the limit of an order which is complete and identical to itself – the social equivalent of an alphabet or mathematical matrix. To think of order in this way is to bracket everything that relates to change and flux, which is also to overlook the ways in which the surplus is among the possibilities of order*ing*. As a residue which is *immanent* to (an envisioned state of) order, the surplus is a constitutive 'outside' against which the will to order is constructed (Staten, 1985: 15–26). The difference between social order and social dislocation hinges on a tenuous relation between the defence of the true and the manifest scope of the surplus, a relation that makes the social intrinsically unstable or, to draw on the terminology of poststructuralism, 'undecidable' (Torfing, 1999: 97; Laclau and Mouffe, 2001: 128). In later chapters we will be tracking this constitutive tension through the archive of modern Ireland, and as we move closer to the present we will see how it has become the governing principle of the present.

Hegemony and epoch

In the chapters below we will encounter institutions such as the workhouse and the industrial school, yet rarely will we meet those who populated such institutions. The reader may well ask 'what of resistance?' and 'what of agency?' William Roseberry's reading of Gramsci will serve as a point of departure in anticipating such charges, and I will also use this to combine Foucault's theory of episteme with the poststructuralist rendering of hegemony, thereby addressing the issue of scale and scope.

Inseparable from the question of power, the concept of hegemony is generally used to understand and explain order as something that implicates subordinate or subaltern groups in their own domination. It is for this reason that hegemony is often described as a situation of 'domination through consent'. Roseberry rejects the notion that hegemony is a situation of 'ideological consensus', arguing instead that subordinate groups are not deluded and passive captives of hegemony, but neither are they autonomous agents. Hegemony is not consent in the naïve sense of that term: a situation of tacit agreement or resignation on the part of subordinate groups. Instead hegemony must be understood as an order which is characterised by struggle, or more specifically:

> [T]he ways in which the words, images, symbols, forms, organisations, institutions, and movements used by subordinate populations to talk about, understand, confront, accommodate themselves to, or resist their domination are shaped by the process of domination itself. What hegemony constructs . . . is not a shared ideology but a common material and meaningful framework for living through, talking about, and acting upon social orders characterised by domination. (Roseberry, 1994: 361)

Crucial here are the fields of force[3] through which subordinate groups act. For the purpose of this study 'field of force' can be understood as the regimes of power/knowledge/practice through which the subject is constituted and situated (but not entirely determined). When Roseberry writes of 'regionally distinct fields of force' he is concerned with the location of social powers and the way that actors are variously positioned within shared material and meaningful frameworks. The question of *position* is paramount, as are the alliances, oppositions and antagonisms which trace out the contours of a particular hegemonic formation.

This reading of Gramsci is broadly compatible with the poststructuralist rendering of hegemony, developed through an expanded conception of discourse which goes beyond the distinction Foucault made in his archaeological works between 'discursive' and 'non-discursive' practices (1972: 157). In rejecting this distinction Ernesto Laclau and Chantal Mouffe are concerned with *meaning*, which is not to deny that objects have a real existence outside of discourse but to emphasise that very little necessarily follows from this (Laclau and Mouffe, 2001: 107). The brute existence of an object might be the same from context to context but its meaning can shift radically. For example, the same rock can be a paper-weight, a tool used to drive a tent peg into the ground, or a symbol of jihad in the struggle to liberate Palestine. It is meaningful in so far as it establishes a relation with other objects: an 'element' (or statement in Foucault's terminology) in a system of relations which is socially constructed and not simply given by the materiality of the object (Laclau and Mouffe, 1987: 82; Saussure, 1983). Used in this way, the category 'discourse' is not reducible to an 'ideal' or mental realm which is distinct from a ('non-discursive') material realm. Instead discourses are, building on Roseberry's conception of hegemony, 'publicly available and essentially incomplete frameworks of meaning which enable social life to be conducted' (Howarth, 2000: 104). The emphasis on 'incompleteness' in this quotation from David Howarth points to the surplus discussed above. It is precisely because the social world is structured discursively that it remains permanently vulnerable to that which it excludes. By enlarging the scope of the category 'discourse' in this way it is possible to encompass both (incomplete) systems of meaning and meaningful practices so that discourse becomes coextensive with the social. What is often taken to be the 'non-discursive' realm is those meanings and practices which sediment in the social field, for example the practices we call 'institutions' and the codified rules and authorities we know as 'law'. In using this expanded conception of discourse I will add the prefix 'field' to indicate the conjunctural or synchronic dimension (field of discourse), and 'order' to indicate the temporal or diachronic dimension (order of discourse).

Emphasising the role of meaning in the politics of order is intended to underline the fact that social order is constructed through inclusion and exclusion as meaning is anchored in knowledge, practice and relations of power. Privileged signifiers such as 'equality', 'justice' and 'competition', for example, are interpreted in a variety of contexts and defined in different ways, creating 'obligatory points of passage' in the fields and orders of discourse through which statements must pass if they are to claim legitimacy and authority (Clegg, 1989). The struggle to anchor, direct and control meaning is precisely where we find the points of resistance which correspond to the notion of 'agency'. But resistance is not reducible solely to the intentions of human actors (Clegg, 1989). There are also certain fissures and cracks in the fields and orders of discourse that operate as points of resistance in the circuits of meaning: points of instability where the surplus of meaning can be brought into play, which is as much chance encounter as strategic intention. Struggles over meaning also bring certain normative problems to the fore: 'poverty', 'deviancy' and 'dependency', for example. By instituting hierarchies and forms of subjection, these classificatory divisions are necessarily implicated in relations of power. It is here that the category 'hegemony' is most useful and can be used to think about how a truth regime *directs* meaning through the institution of specific programmes, apparatuses and technologies (Laclau and Mouffe, 1987, 2001; Howarth, 2000; Torfing, 1999). This point can be developed by comparing the poststructuralist rendering of hegemony with Foucault's theory of the episteme, which brings us to the question of scale and scope.

Foucault tells us that discourse is not only about power/knowledge/ practice but also about history. As the basic elements of discourse, statements are ordered into formations of discourse which are suspended within and define the parameters of an 'episteme' or epoch. An episteme is an expansive envelope of time and space which is structured by what Foucault called a historical *a priori*, or 'the condition of reality for statements' (Foucault, 1972: 127). The *a priori* is the historically constituted ground upon which the struggle for truth is waged: a certain limit condition in the sense of a fundamental principle which orders statements into the discursive codes that circumscribe the sayable and the doable. Foucault's archaeological investigations disclosed three epistemes in European history, which he called the Renaissance (from the late Middle Ages to roughly the middle of the seventeenth century), the classical (from about 1650 to the end of the eighteenth century), and the modern (from the end of the eighteenth century to the present) (see Haugaard, 1997: 52–3; Dean, 1991).

During the Renaissance truth was a matter of resemblances, with all worldly things part of a cosmic order that could be known by reading the marks or 'signatures' connecting the microcosmos to the macrocosmos. In the classical period the truth of resemblances was displaced by the principle of 'mathesis', with systems of classification used to purify language so that the resulting system of signs – true knowledge reflected in language – would be the mirror of nature. It is with the birth of the modern epoch that 'Man' emerges as the subject and object of knowledge, simultaneously part of the empirical world to be known and the source of true knowledge. As both the source of knowledge and its object, the subject of the modern epoch is immersed in a horizon of obscurity – the unthought – which exceeds mind and subverts its status as the source of all intelligibility. And yet paradoxically this becomes the condition of possibility for the sovereignty of Rational Man (Dreyfus and Rabinow, 1983: 31, 90–100). Moving in the shadow of Kant, the modern subject is constructed in the image of autonomy, and as this autonomous agent strives to bring the horizon of unthought into the realm of consciousness, turning it into knowledge and making it available for technical control, so we come to believe that we are the authors of our own destiny. In doing so we overlook the fact that we are the subjects of, and subjected to, discourses which exceed the kind of design and control functions associated with Reason. Within the paradigm of problem-driven research it is precisely this 'ontological' problematic – the discursive construction of regimes of truth which conjoin subjectivity, subjectification and subjection – which is the primary concern, the overarching question one of understanding how we have come to be what we are.

In tracing out the discontinuous history of modern Europe Foucault's work demonstrated how the episteme is vulnerable to 'events' which open out conditions of possibility for a new *a priori* (taken up in detail in the next chapter). The birth of an episteme marks a point of rupture in the archive and requires us to think the contingency of our present, to trace out the conditions of existence for our programmes, apparatuses and techniques, and perhaps most importantly, to question our very mode of being. In terms of scale and scope the temporal dimension of an episteme may extend to one hundred and fifty years or more, while the spatial dimension is somewhat ill-defined. In Foucault's work the episteme is generally applicable to a rather vaguely defined referent: Western Europe, although there have been attempts to enlarge the geographical scope of his archaeological scheme, such as in the work of Edward Said (1991). The episteme, then, is an expansive envelope of time-space which circumscribes a particular way of ordering the world. Because the term 'episteme' tends to privilege knowledge over practice, and I have already emphasised the interrelation between knowing and doing, I will refer to the epochal scale as a 'mode of ordering' or 'ordering modality'.

The concept of hegemony is a more localised envelope of time and space than the epoch.[4] As with the epoch, a hegemonic formation of discourse circumscribes an order of elements and relations. And like the epoch a hegemonic formation is vulnerable to that which it excludes: the surplus of meaning which is created as hegemony is enacted and instituted. Within an epoch there may be a plurality of hegemonic formations, so that the concept of hegemony enables us to examine how order is reproduced, modified and transformed in contexts which are more localised than the epoch (figure 2.2). Importantly this also provides a conceptual tool which can go right down to the interface of epochal dislocation and transformation.

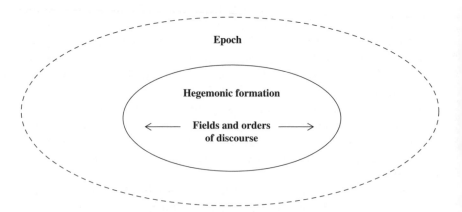

Figure 2.2 Hegemony and epoch

I will not specify these categories further at this stage as there will be ample opportunity to ground them in the analyses and case studies to follow. Suffice it for now to mention that the category 'hegemony' will be used to denote programmes, apparatuses and techniques that cut across multiple fields in a context marked by instability and antagonism. Here I want to emphasise that bringing these elements together as the conceptual nexus 'epoch–hegemony–discourse' is intended to make explicit certain aspects of Foucault's work which are otherwise implicit, the aim of which is to adapt his theoretical framework to the requirements of this particular study.

It will be clear to anyone who has read Foucault that he only rarely employs the category of hegemony, such as in his reference to 'social hegemonies' in *The History of Sexuality. Volume One* (1998: 93; see also Smart, 1986). This raises the question of commensurability: how compatible are the Foucaultian concept of episteme and the neo-Gramscian theory of hegemony? A careful reading of Foucault's theory of 'the carceral' (examined in chapter 4) together with his work on governmentality suggests that Foucault worked with a deep interest in hegemonic processes but discussed them through his own terminology. Foucault once said that he liked to use concepts, texts and phrases from Marx without adhering to the conventional rules of citation such as the footnote or the quotation mark, playing with those among his readers who waited for him to defer to the authority of Marx yet themselves incapable of recognising it when he did so (Foucault, 1980: 52–3). Foucault defended this method of writing by arguing that the physicist has no need to quote thinkers such as Newton or Einstein who constitute the horizon of thought the physicist thinks *with*, his point being that it is impossible to do history today without using the horizon of thought of which Marx is an integral part. It is possible he used Gramsci in the same way, which is not to say that he was a closet Gramscian. On the contrary, it is unlikely that Foucault would have overlooked the dangerous trace of authoritarianism in Gramsci's work. Gramsci was an innovator and a visionary but he was no ontological pluralist, and his prescriptive use of hegemony envisioned an emancipatory ethico-political unity that made little room for dissent and diversity (Martin, 1998: 87–8, 140–7). It is sometimes alleged that Foucault's style of critique was evasive, but in his assessment of the forms of knowledge which exhibit globalising pretensions he was unambiguous, describing them as 'totalitarian' and implicated in the subjugation of other knowledges (1980: 80). It is also important to note that Foucault was working within a historical context wherein the core assumptions of Marxism had been radically problematised. Foucault clearly worked with a conception of the intellectual that was almost diametrically opposed to that of Gramsci, the former working as a master of suspicion while the latter identified with the 'organic' intelligentsia charged with the role of provoking/facilitating counter-hegemony.[5] None the less there are significant points of convergence between these thinkers which can be examined in both general and specific terms, and these can be used to align the concepts of epoch and hegemony.

In general terms Gramsci's historicism and his emphasis on the conjunctural possibilities for radical change resonate strongly with Foucault's archaeological and genealogical methods, as is evident, for example, when Gramsci writes of 'historical events' and 'historical facts' by arguing that: 'It is not a question of "discovering" a metaphysical law of "determinism" or even of establishing a "general" law of causality. It is a question of bringing out how in historical evolution relatively permanent forces are constituted which operate with a certain regularity and automatism' (Gramsci, 1971: 412). Or again, when Gramsci conceptualises hegemony as the formation of a 'historic bloc', he eschews the idea that order has an essence, writing instead on the relation between state, economy and civil society as a 'complex, contradictory, and discordant ensemble' of opposites (Gramsci, 1971: 366, 137). This exhibits at least some degree of overlap with Foucault's concept of discursive formations as 'unities in dispersion' (Foucault, 1972: 31–9).

More specifically, Gramsci's use of the Italian verb *dirigere* is similar to Foucault's use of the French verb *conduire*. The meanings of *dirigere* cut through 'directing', 'leading' and 'ruling' (Hoare and Smith, 1971: xiii–xiv; Gramsci, 1971: 52–120). Foucault used the verb *conduire* in a similar way. *Conduire* or 'conduct' can be used in a double sense to mean 'to behave' (as in to conduct oneself) or 'to lead' and 'to drive' in the sense of directing (in the way an orchestra is conducted). More schematically, *dirigere* and *conduire* articulate a variety of meanings and modalities relating to power, with both Foucault and Gramsci interested in how relations of power are structured by fields of possibility which have been assembled through political struggle. The core insight here would seem to be that though the conduct of individuals and groups is facilitated and constrained (i.e. directed and conducted) by regimes of power/knowledge/practice, the outcome remains radically indeterminate. In specifying the exercise of power in this way Foucault intends to remind us of an enlarged meaning of 'government' which he thinks has been lost to the contemporary world. And by using 'conduct' in this intensely political sense, Foucault insists that to govern is to 'structure the possible field of actions of others' so that power works through and upon freedom (Foucault, 1983: 220–1). It is here that we find Foucault developing his notion of 'governmentality', which will be taken up in more detail in part II below. Moving in the groove of Gramscian analysis, Foucault asks us to rethink the question of power: to question the idea of power as something wholly negative and noxious (see Haugaard, 1997). Rather than subscribe to an understanding of power which is possessed by some and exercised over others, Foucault examines how power connects with freedom as government seeks to conduct the conduct of living individuals and populations:

> A man who is chained up and beaten is subject to force being exerted over him, not power. But if he can be induced to speak, when his ultimate recourse could have been to hold his tongue, preferring death, then he has been caused to behave in a certain way. His freedom has been subjected to power. He has been submitted to government. (Foucault, 2000: 324)

Gramsci's *dirigere* and Foucault's *conduire* meet in the concept of *government*. To govern is to act upon action, while to be governed is to think, to speak and to act within a field of possibilities and limitations: it is to articulate a regime of power/knowledge/practice.

In their own way both Gramsci and Foucault employ the register of war to rethink the political and to analyse relations of power (Gramsci, 1971: 111, 229–35; Foucault, 1980: 90; 1998: 97), and both have derived lessons from Machiavelli as they attempt to wrestle the concept of power away from its purely negative connotations associated with repression. In Foucault's work, for example, relations of power are not reducible to the apparatuses of the state, for the state stands in a 'superstructural' 'conditioning–conditioned' relation with a 'whole series of multiple and indefinite power relations' (Foucault, 2000: 123). In other words for Foucault the mode of prohibitive power exercised by the state through its monopoly over the means of coercion (i.e. Weber's classic definition of the state) is rooted in the positive power which traverses the field of social relations, or what Gramsci called 'civil society'. There is more than a casual meeting between Gramsci's conception of hegemony and Foucault's work of discourse and truth, particularly when the remaining traces of Marxist essentialism are removed from hegemony in its poststructuralist rendering. When this move is made the problem of emancipation is emptied of essence and becomes a provisional and pluralised question of 'agonism': a public 'combat' for truth. An agonistic politics in accordance with the neo-Gramscian theory of hegemony is commensurate with Foucault's refusal of Enlightenment blackmail: a strategy of 'permanent provocation' which aims to prevent the final suturing of the possible (Foucault, 1983: 222; Mouffe, 2000: 80–105; Laclau and Mouffe, 2001).

Foucault's concept of episteme works best at a generalised level of social-theoretical critique as we strive to understand the specific relations and articulations of power within which we are positioned as individuals. But it is the concept of hegemony that forces us to think about how we *collectively* embody degrees of freedom and subjection relative to the concrete 'direction' which the social exhibits at a given time and in a given place. If Foucault provides the critical tools to engage in a deconstructive enterprise of the self, then it is Gramsci who reminds us of the need for political projects to reconstruct and redirect the social (Laclau and Mouffe, 2001: 189).

An analytics of in/exclusion

As a research strategy, genealogy is interested in how regimes of power/knowledge/practice are assembled, modified and transformed through strategic forces, alliances and struggles; struggles which emerge as questions are framed, problems defined and practical solutions posited. Using the past to problematise the present, the genealogist makes a careful insertion into the 'archive' of history so that an interpretative analytics can commence; an insertion which, to a greater or lesser extent, is determined by the question asked.

This study is concerned with mapping the dislocation sketched in chapter 1, and in particular with tracing the contours of a new regime of practices which may be displacing the project of Society. Some years ago Karl Polanyi (2001) identified the period spanning. c. 1790–1834 as the 'political and economic origins of our time', a juncture when the laws of economy were discovered, when the project of Society emerged as a specific articulation of order, and when the conduct of specific social subjects thought to pose a threat to order, to security, to the very possibility of progress were moved to the centre of social and political debate. The next chapter begins the task of genealogical analysis by characterising this formative period as an 'event'.

In embarking on a critical assessment of our present I will not be opposing a 'true' reading of the facts to other 'false' representations, as in the tradition of ideology critique (Dean, 1999). An analytics of the present assumes that we are in the groove of a *particular* reading of events as the basis for our current course of action, something that inevitably involves a degree of misrecognition as a sense of necessity overrides the fundamental contingency of the present. It has become common sense to assume that welfare capitalism has either failed or is not up to the demands of the globalising economy, while social democracy is exacerbating the very problems it was intended to resolve.

Reform is aimed at establishing a break with the post-war order so as to open out possibilities for the institution of a new regime of practices. What Nikolas Rose calls 'advanced' liberalism (1996a) marks out a strategic field which, in some respects, re-collects the axioms of classical liberalism in such a way that they appear to be the one true course of action, the only game in town, which must now be rescued from the failures of 'collectivism' (Hayek, 1991). This re-invokes a number of questions of key concern to nineteenth-century commentators and reformers, in particular those concerning security, family, and the social implications of defective and deviant dispositions and conducts. Yet there are also important differences between past and present. Consequently it is important to examine this earlier period in some detail, using it as a line of approach to the present.

The theoretical framework set out in this chapter will be used to examine the politics of order in a variety of related settings, bringing the historical into a relation with the conjunctural. It is acknowledged that the theoretical framework is rudimentary as it stands, but as already noted the concerns of this study are problem-driven and not confined solely to matters of theory. It has been the intention of this chapter to set out a basic framework that can be used and adjusted as we move between different contexts of analysis, and it will be developed and adjusted as required by the specific task at hand. The analysis itself begins at the turn of the nineteenth century as the spheres of state, market and society were constituted as separate though related domains, opening out the enduring problem of how to govern this complex set of relations. It ends at a juncture where the spheres are coming together as a new type of 'enfolded' relation, establishing a new regime of truth and a new problematic of rule.

Part II

Liberal government and the problem of Society

3

The constitution of poverty and the social question: the ordering techniques

Introduction

Towards the end of World War II, Karl Polanyi published the results of his investigation into the catastrophe which had shattered what he called 'the hundred years' peace'. Sifting through the archive for its origins, Polanyi marked his spot at the end of the eighteenth century, drawing the conclusion that our 'social consciousness' was shaped by a debate which originated with thinkers such as Bentham, Burke and Malthus, and continued to spiral through the thought of Ricardo, Marx, John Stuart Mill, Darwin and Spencer. The debate in question concerned the provision of relief to the poor. It also produced a new social subject, a figure crucially important to the systems of meaning and social practices within which we are cast as thinking and acting subjects today. Polanyi was perhaps the first contemporary thinker to note that between 1795 and 1834 'the figure of the pauper, almost forgotten since, dominated a discussion the imprint of which was as powerful as that of the most spectacular events in history' (2001: 87–8; also Dean, 1991: 1). Long overshadowed by more eminent names and more notorious episodes, the idea that the figure of the pauper might be interpreted as an 'event' overlaps with Foucault's concept of 'eventalisation' (1991a: 76–7; Dean, 1991: 4; cf. Popper, 2002a: 69–70). Part of Foucault's genealogical arsenal, eventalisation traces out the strategic forces and alliances which discursively organise a field of objects and relations in such a way that it later appears to be necessarily ordered in that way. By conducting a genealogy of the event, Foucault seeks to make an intervention of a kind he describes as a 'breach of self-evidence': questioning the givenness of the present and problematising its relation to the past. As a specific type of critical intervention, this takes those things that appear to be universal and necessary and renders them contingent and precarious, always in part the product of aleatory forces and chance encounters.

And because it necessarily folds back on the present, the reconstruction of past events deconstructs our very subjectivity, recasting us as beings in possession of specific, hence contingent, ways of thinking, knowing and doing.

The pauper is in fact only one half of the event in question, the other half being the constitution of 'poverty' (Dean, 1991). From c. 1795–1834, the long debate on poor relief would see aspects of the nominally incommensurable discourses of Bentham and Malthus joined at the hip in a statement of monumental significance: the new poor law of 1834, which was implicated in the formation of a new mode of government. The name that Mitchell Dean assigns to this event is 'liberal government', the constitution of which marks out a specific problem of rule. With the birth of the modern epoch came the constitution of distinct economic, political and social spheres, which also opened out the problem of how they could or should be brought into a governable relation. Solutions to this problem were found by going to work on specific questions, with the newly con-stituted distinction between poverty and pauperism producing an ever-expanding field of interventions relating to such things as vagabondage, delinquency and illegitimacy. All of these objects provided ways to think about and act upon the problem of order. The practical problem of securing order while governing the relation between the spheres would see three distinct though related appara-tuses emerge:

1 the new poor law with its reformed workhouse, corresponding to the axioms of political economy;
2 the family relation as the object domain of a new scientific philan-thropy, organised under the banner of social economy;
3 the penitentiaries and asylums of the religious orders as they secured a role in the social question.

The relation between these apparatuses is a complex mix of opposi-tion and alliance, and in this chapter and chapter 4 we will use them to trace out the birth of liberal government. We will be tracking this to the end of the century as the discourse of Society was con-solidated, a project that was to carry the weight of post-Enlightenment modernity on its shoulders: the aspiration of human perfection governed by the rule of reason. This chapter begins by tracing out each of these apparatuses in turn, beginning with the new poor law.

From the police of the poor to governing pauperism

In Foucault's work the classical epoch encompasses a period from roughly the middle of the seventeenth century to the end of the eighteenth century, after which an epochal dislocation opens out conditions of possibility for the constitution of the modern epoch. This moment of discontinuity will be referred to here, from Dean (1991, 1992), as the 'liberal break', or the constitution of liberal government. This chapter outlines the dislocation of the classical epoch at the level of programmes, apparatuses and techniques, and is concerned specifically with how this relates to the question of 'poverty', which requires a sketch of the poor laws during this period together with an art of government known as 'police'.

The police of the poor

From the point of view of governing the poor during the classical epoch it is necessary to stretch the boundaries of Foucault's scheme, pushing it back to the end of the sixteenth century so as to encompass the Elizabethan statutes. The Tudor poor and vagrancy laws reflected a myriad of local customs and conventions, and at the turn of the seventeenth century a number of statutes were enacted to impose some degree of order on the diversity of practices, the most important of which were those of 1598 and 1601. Apart from providing for the whipping and return of vagrants to their place of origin (later codified by the Settlement Laws of 1662), it was now the duty of church wardens and overseers to raise rates so as to cover the cost of setting the able-bodied to work, relieving the impotent, and apprenticing poor children (Slack, 1990: 18–19; Marshall, 1985; Rose, 1988; Dean, 1992). It was also in this context that new rationalities of government emerged, beyond monarchs, emperors, kings, lords, princes and magistrates, to include family heads, convent superiors, classroom tutors and so on. The practical arts of government steadily spread through the territorial state as a spiralling web of ordinances and regulations, extending to households, souls, children, provinces, convents, family, and all the 'things' which had previously been part of the divine, cosmotheological order of the world (Gordon, 1991: 9; Foucault, 1991b: 90–1; Small, 1909).

In the literature on this new art of government Foucault found references to three specific domains: the art of self-government concerning morality, the art of governing a family related to economy, and the art of ruling the state, or politics. Crucially, these domains are never allowed to drift apart, with the relation between subject and sovereign anchored in a specific householding art of economy. In terms of ruling what we would now call the sphere of domestic politics, the arts of government slowly acquired a specific name: *police*. This should not be confused with the contemporary understanding of *the* police as a preventative adjunct of the state which is charged with prosecuting the law. Instead police was a condition to be achieved, with the meaning of 'good police' synonymous with the happiness and 'good order of a community' (Dean, 1992: 224; 1999; Small, 1909: 317). It should be noted too that the actual phrase 'police' was largely absent in the English (and Irish) context, with the word 'policy' serving as a better equivalent, although both find their root in the classical Greek notion of *polis* (Gordon, 1991: 9). Despite differences in terminology, the programmes, apparatuses and techniques known as police in regions of continental Europe were pervasive in the British Isles and coded by the Tudor poor and vagrancy laws, which brought the agencies and powers of the state into a coordinated relation with local officials at the level of the parish (Dean, 1992: 226; Slack, 1990; Marshall, 1985; Nicholls, 1967).

Police science marks a break with pre-Westphalian notions of rule, where worldly order was continuous with divine order, and humans were part of a fixed hierarchy that passed through princes and priests to angels and God (Small, 1909: 590). From the beginning of the seventeenth century the state became a work of reason: a 'knowing machine' with its own nature and its own laws (Gordon, 1991: 4). This also saw the rule of a given territory reconfigured by the notion of population: a complex field of objects and relations which rendered the art of government a concern with the 'due regulation of things'. The intersection between 'reason of state' and government as the due regulation of things established the conditions of existence for police science as a 'science of happiness', or alternatively the 'science of government', taking as its object the positive (rather than preventative) arts and ends of 'education, good order, security and public tranquillity' (Beccaria, 1769, cited in Pasquino, 1991: 109). Police ordinances were extensive in scope and almost illogically varied in content, from religion, foodstuffs and servants to the dimensions of saddles and horsecloths, aiming to regulate everything that went unregulated in the life of the society. Pasquale Pasquino finds a common thread in this otherwise heterogeneous field of objects: the problem of a certain formlessness or lack of order, which in practical terms translates as 'a great effort of formation of the social body' (1991: 111). Police science was to place all disorders, agitations and disobediences under total surveillance and control so that 'by means of a wise police, the sovereign accustoms the people to order and obedience' (Vattel, 1768, cited in Foucault, 1977: 213–15). Concurrent with the weakening of ecclesiastical authority and the demise of the old feudal structures, police science was about coaching citizens in how to conduct themselves in towns and regions that were becoming more populous and subject to a more centralised mode of authority (Dean, 1999: 91). Taken to its logical conclusion, police would be brought to bear over everything, linking the absolute power of the sovereign to the multiplicity of powers dispersed through the society (Foucault, 1977: 213).

Among the many things that came within the scope of police intervention were the poor. During the classical epoch the poor were governed in accordance with principles of a political economy quite different from that of thinkers such as Malthus and Ricardo. As noted above, pre-Malthusian political economy, of which Adam Smith was one of the last representatives, concerned a 'householding' conception of economy (Dean, 1992: 221; Small, 1909). The household was the basic unit of political organisation, at once the subject and object of government (Donzelot, 1979: 48). Balancing the relation between the family head and the authority that bound him was the power he exercised over his household. He could determine the employments and marriages of his children, he could punish those who failed in their obligations, and he could elicit the support of the public authorities to accomplish this latter task. An example can be seen in the *lettre de cachet* in France, which petitioned the crown to punish, exile or imprison wives who had outraged husbands, for example, or children who had offended fathers, or priests deemed insufficient by the parish congregation (Foucault, 2000: 65).

The problem of order was most acutely evident in the case of those who did not belong to a household: vagabonds, who lacked a definite place in the systems of protection and obligations. Vagabonds were either dependent on private charity and alms, a gift that honoured the giver but did nothing to integrate the receiver, or else they depended on public charity, which placed a particular type of strain on the mode of rule (Donzelot, 1979: 49). A good police of the poor required that each and all (*omnes et singulatim*) be harnessed to the wealth and strength of the state. While there were significant variations in local practices, the police of the poor meant setting the poor to work through the provision of employment, either by raising funds for a parish stock of material such as flax or hemp, or by confining the poor within a workhouse, which replicated the well-ordered household. This householding conception of economy cannot be overstated, and it is worth citing an entry in Rousseau's *Encyclopaedia* which demonstrates just how specific this is to the classical period. It was Foucault who noted the significance of this, with Rousseau defining economy as 'the wise government of the family for the common welfare of all'. The wise administration of the state required that economy be applied to the state as a whole, and this meant exercising a form of surveillance and control over the population that would be as encompassing as that which the head of the household exercised over his family and his goods (Foucault, 1991b: 92).

It is in relation to this governing principle of the orderly household that we can discern the meaning and significance of the workhouse at this time, or the house of industry, which was among the techniques to secure a police of the poor. Because it corresponds in some respects to what would later be called the labour theory of value, the workhouse of the old poor laws has at times been seen as a form of nascent capitalism; a manufactory designed to extract a surplus of labour in the form of profit. However, we are not yet in the world of 'capitalism' as it would later be theorised, even though nineteenth-century social thought would push the origins of capitalism back to this period. Instead we must examine the workhouse in its context through its relation to the secular arts of government known as 'reason of state' and 'police', and the householding conception of economy. Mitchell Dean notes that while the workhouse was indeed based on a principle of labour, the purpose it served was to augment police by combining three otherwise distinct operations, all of which were directed at the suppression of vagrancy: arresting the mobile population through the use of stocks and other techniques of public punishment; recording vagrants and making them visible through the use of branding and other forms of inscription directed at the body; and restoring order by removing the idle poor back to their 'proper' place through the application of the Settlement Laws (Dean, 1992: 226).[1] The workhouse achieved all three functions in a single operation: arresting the movement of the idle, recording and recoding their status, and inserting them into what was essentially a replica of the patriarchal household, thus increasing the number of trading households in the state and augmenting the wealth of the nation (Dean, 1992: 226–7). The house of industry placed its inmates within a 'regular course of life': instructing the young, providing for the sick, and preventing the disorderliness of idleness and beggary (Dean, 1992: 222). And while the police of the poor was predicated on harnessing their labour to the wealth of the nation, the inmates of the workhouse were not 'free labour' in the sense of nineteenth-century political economy. The house of industry was intended to ensure the moral reform of the idle poor through discipline while also recognising the utility of labour, a combination that conjoined morality and economy within a single aim (Slack, 1990: 40–1).

In summary, we can note that within the classical epoch 'the poor' were a measure of the wealth and greatness of the state. The objective of wise administration, which was also the sign of good police, was to increase the numbers of the poor. Increasing the number of households would augment the circulation of money and goods through trade, and thus swell the national treasury (Dean, 1992: 221). The governing statement in the discourse of the poor in the classical epoch concerned the 'numbers of the nation's poor', and despite local variations in methods of administration, a uniform logic can be detected in the way that 'populousness' functions as both the sign and index of the military strength, prosperity and relative greatness of the state (Dean, 1992: 220–3). While it is possible to talk about the poverty *of* specific objects such as a nation, city or even the poor themselves, the meaning of 'the poor' is articulated within an epoch that cannot think the discourse of nineteenth-century political economy. Prior to the debate on the abolition of poor relief at the turn of the nineteenth century, that thing we have come to know as 'poverty' in our present has no meaning.

As the eighteenth century drew to a close a three-way problematisation of the existing system of poor relief emerged, and this would see 'poverty' constituted as a new object of knowledge and a new terrain of government (Dean, 1992: 229–33; 1991: 143). First, the workhouse came under sustained critique as costly and ineffective and, as a mode of provision, was charged with generating contagions relating to both disease and morality. Gilbert's Act of 1782 empowered parishes to combine as unions for the purpose of poor relief, to dispense outdoor assistance and to provide relief through employment, effectively abandoning the workhouse as the principal mode of provision for the able-bodied poor (Marshall, 1985; Slack, 1990). Secondly, the development of friendly societies among labourers, together with insurance annuity schemes, established alternatives to the poor laws and instituted the practice of saving today in order to secure an uncertain tomorrow. Lastly, and perhaps most importantly in view of its scope, a new type of philanthropy developed. Nineteenth-century philanthropy positioned itself against the failings of the poor laws and set about questioning the axioms of political economy. Opposing a range of specific 'moral' deficiencies, the philanthropic and statistical societies gathered under the banner of 'social economy', which is examined below. First I want to consider a number of concurrent theoretical challenges to the extant order of things with a view to tracing the practical effects generated by the realm of ideas.

In some respects Adam Smith's *Wealth of Nations* (1976a) departed from his earlier *Theory of Moral Sentiments* (1976b), particularly in his reading of Mandeville's 'fable of the bees', yet Smith none the less remains within the realm of what is generally referred to as 'moral economy' (Dean, 1992: 233–4). From the point of view of nineteenth-century political economy, the import of Smith's work lies in the way it helped to dislodge the sphere of market exchange from the political and legislative framework of sovereignty. Yet in Smith's work the field of exchange remains a moral sphere, with the invisible hand coordinating the self-interested activities of sympathetic individuals. Smith's 'system of natural liberty and perfect justice' was one in which the unconstrained pursuit of individual self-interest under competitive conditions would, and ought to be allowed to, create a harmonious order. Among the self-interested individuals who were capable of rational calculation were the labouring poor, who could and should augment their happiness by exchanging their labour for goods (the 'division of labour' thesis). Smith's political economy was one in which rational individuals faced each other as equals: the poor as owners of their own labour facing those who possessed land and property (Dean, 1992: 233). The poor did not have a *right* to subsistence apropos of that thing we today call 'welfare', but they were entitled to a 'liberal reward' for their labour, which should be consistent with 'common humanity' (Smith, 1976a: 22–30, 91–6). Smith tied the economic and moral value of labour to his vision of opulence and progress, wherein the lower ranks could improve their circumstances in accordance with principles of 'equity', while his conception of opulence was framed by the idea of the 'progressive state'. However, Smith did not develop a fully fledged labour theory of value, which was not possible before thinkers such as Malthus and Ricardo had appropriated the newly annexed sphere of exchange relations and grafted it to different mechanisms. It is only after this move was made that the new science of political economy transformed labour into a commodity which regulates the value of all other commodities (Dean, 1992: 234).

While Smith had considered the implications of stagnation and decline, he was clearly an optimistic child of the Enlightenment, with his vision of the future cast along a horizon defined by the notion of the 'progressive state'. Malthus would puncture this optimism. And while Smith theorised free labourers as rational subjects who could increase their happiness by exchanging their labour on the market, it was Bentham who noted the existence of conditions – conditions relating to public assistance – wherein it would be irrational for the labourer to do so. Perhaps more than any other statement constituting this field of discourse, it was Malthus's thesis on population which presented a fundamental challenge to the French and Scottish Enlightenment. Malthus discovered that population increases at a geometric rate, while the means of subsistence increases at an arithmetic rate (Malthus, 1992: 17–19). This law of essential scarcity had a direct bearing on the poor laws, because public assistance countered the 'checks' on the growth of population, and would, if it continued to go unchecked, outstrip the means to feed it. If 'positive' checks such as disease and famine, or 'preventative' checks such as moral restraint, were absent, then the numbers of the poor would, in accordance with the laws of nature, increase to such an extent that wages would be depressed and the poor would lack the means of subsistence. The inevitable result would be an increase in misery, vice and disorderliness, ultimately creating the conditions for revolution (Malthus, 1992: 21–9, 100–9). Malthus's solution lay in the normative doctrine of moral restraint: the poor had to be taught, by harsh measures if necessary, to delay marriage and limit the numbers of children they bore, the latter to be determined by the means they could secure by their own labour.

In the face of this natural law of scarcity the sign of 'populousness' was recast. No longer the index of the prosperity, strength and greatness of the state, the numbers of the poor were now a sign of immanent disorder, and a new discourse was born that would articulate the movement pressing for the abolition of the poor laws. The break with the householding conception of economy turned on this Malthusian thesis of an ineradicable gap between population and subsistence, a disequilibrium that was thought to motivate labour although the gap itself could never be closed. This law of scarcity, or 'ontological lack' as Mitchell Dean terms it, was both the engine of wealth creation and the limit of state intervention (Dean, 1992: 237–8, 242). The name given to this natural scarcity was 'poverty'. The pre-Malthusian world is one in which population is the sign of the wealth of the nation, not a problem defined by natural laws of scarcity; where 'police' is an ideal to be sought by government, not a force in defence of order; where 'economy' is the art of household management, not a quasi-autonomous reality; and where the family is contiguous with political authority, not external to it (Dean, 1999: 95). By the time the debate on the poor laws was stabilised by the reforms of 1834, each of these relations can be turned on its head and we have crossed the threshold to the modern epoch.

The poor law of 1834
The work of Adam Smith may well be among the conditions of possibility for the emergence of liberal government, but in terms of

the statements gathered into this mode of rule, it is the texts of Malthus and Bentham that we must examine. We must trace how each of these very different texts, these originally distinct statements, came to articulate the other as an *other* statement, one linked to, but also departing from, the intentions of its authors. This process of discursive formation is a specific mode of power which Foucault described rather cryptically as 'non-subjective intentionality', by which he meant a strategic field of force relations produced through the intersection of a number of different elements, but not reducible to any single source (Foucault, 1998: 94–5; 1980: 97). Examining the texts of Malthus and Bentham will help to sketch out precisely why the Poor Law Amendment Act of 1834 is such an important marker in the birth of the modern epoch.

The Act of 1834 was the culmination of a debate some forty years long, a discursive struggle that was brought to a (provisional) halt by a Royal Commission (Checkland and Checkland, 1974). While the debate had been driven by the Malthusian position calling for abolition, the Act of 1834 did not abolish the practices of public relief so much as reform them. The main objective of the reform was to do away with outdoor relief to all able-bodied paupers, a task to be accomplished by the 'workhouse test' of 'less eligibility'. As the brainchild of Jeremy Bentham, the 'less eligibility' principle was conceived in accordance with the doctrines of utilitarianism, and was to render conditions inside the workhouse 'less eligible' than any form of paid employment outside. Its rationale was that the poor would govern themselves in accordance with the utilitarian calculus of pleasure and pain. In other words, the able-bodied poor would volunteer to enter the punitive conditions of the workhouse only if this increased their happiness and reduced their suffering. It was also the case that public assistance to the wives and children of able-bodied men was conditional on their entering the workhouse along with their husband/father. Upon entering the workhouse all would surrender whatever civil or political rights applied to their rank, with the family divided and housed in separate wards according to sex, age and ability to work. It is here that we can locate the trace of Malthus's principle of moral restraint, which was predicated on the idea that public relief to the poor encouraged improvident marriages and bastardy (discussed below).

In terms of institutional supports, the Act made provision for a national system of administration under the authority of a central Board of Poor Law Commissioners. As Secretary to the Board, Edwin Chadwick was head of an office supported by an inspectorate of assistant commissioners who were charged with enforcing uniformity of standards and practices throughout the system. Regarding implementation, the new regime was to reorganise the old system based on the civil parish so that clusters of local units would be grouped into Poor Law Unions, each with its own workhouse governed by an elected Board of Guardians and managed by a permanent salaried staff. It was also the case that after 1834 the reformed workhouse was brought into a specific relation with the old settlement laws, now operating in accordance with the new political economy. Before 1834 the settlement laws had reflected the science of police with its concern for 'the due regulation' and 'right disposition of things': arresting vagrancy and restoring order by removing the poor back to their 'proper' place. After 1834 it was placed in the service of a national labour market. With its test of less eligibility, the reformed workhouse would ensure that the poor travelled to avail themselves of work rather than surrender their liberty and their dignity. But in cases where the movement of the rural poor in search of work placed an unacceptable burden on urban ratepayers, the powers of removal would ensure that the cost of relief would be suppressed and order maintained (Englander, 1998: 14).

If in the past the settlement laws had been a technique to arrest mobility, they were now employed to direct and regulate the movements of the labouring population. And while the old poor laws were articulated by a rationality of rule that governed in the interests of morality and order, the aim of which was to make a territory and its population completely transparent to knowledge, that of the new poor law concerned the discovery of natural laws which required that government be restricted in the interests of liberty and economy (Rose, 1996a: 39, 43). The governing principle of the old poor laws concerned the numbers of the poor and the wealth of the nation, while that of the new poor laws was predicated on the invention of the pauper and the distinction between pauperism and poverty. It is in Bentham's *Essays on the Poor Laws* of 1796 that we find this distinction formulated with customary precision:

> Poverty is the state of everyone who, in order to obtain subsistence, is forced to have recourse to labour. Indigence is the state of him who, being destitute of property . . . is at the same time either unable to labour, or unable, even for labour, to procure the supply of that which he happens thus to be in want. (Bentham, 2001: 3)

Later, in his *Principles of the Civil Code*, Bentham noted that civil law could do nothing relative to subsistence other than to create 'motives' in the form of rewards and punishments, and so the law should not remove the pressure to labour by assisting poverty independent of labour (Bentham, 1843a: 303, 314). Two years after Bentham's death the Royal Commission on the Poor Laws published its report, with the Benthamite distinction between indigence and poverty used to codify what was clearly a labour theory of value:

> The most pressing of the evils which we have described are those con-nected with the relief of the able-bodied . . . in no part of Europe except England has it been thought fit that the provision, whether compulsory or voluntary, should be applied to more than the relief of *indigence*, the state of a person unable to labour, or unable to obtain, in return for his labour, the means of subsistence. It has never been deemed expedient that the provision should extend to the relief of *poverty*; that is, the state of one, who, in order to obtain a mere subsistence, is forced to have recourse to labour. (Checkland and Checkland, 1974: 334)

For Bentham the problem of indigence had to be understood in relation to the larger question of security. Security took lexical prece-dence over equality in Bentham's scheme of things, which is structured as a great pyramid with the principle of utility at the top. Security, especially of property, was the condition of existence for industry, abundance and equality, which are the four elements of Bentham's civil law (Poynter, 1969: 117–18; Dean, 1991: 187). Strictly speaking the problem of subsistence was not the proper object of government, and could only be promoted indirectly by offering security to the fruits of labour, meaning property. Yet security was also an end which justified the relief of indigence, because the indigent would be pressed by starvation to commit offences in obtaining the necessities of life. Bentham was a thinker in search of principles of administrative cer-tainty, and against the grain of the abolition movement he identified necessity as the correct criterion of poor relief. The question of desert, good or bad, made no difference to the quantity of indigence. To assume otherwise was a sign of confusion, which in this case saw the rules of punishment applied to the domain of public assistance (Bentham, 2001: 6–7). In discarding the moral distinction of deserving and unde-serving poor as the basis of provision, Bentham argued that govern-ment must provide subsistence to those who could not provide for themselves, not because it was desirable to increase equality but because the greater good of security required it (Dean, 1991: 187). Likewise the creed of private charity sponsored by the abolitionists was unacceptable to Bentham, because it was infused with obscurity and uncertainty, because it was prone to error in the form of excessive leniency and excessive severity, and because (*contra* Smith) it would be unevenly regulated by emotions such as sympathy (Dean, 1991: 188).

It is also in Bentham's writings that we find the principle of less eligibility formulated.[2] Two years before Malthus published the first edition of his *Essay* (1798), Bentham wrote his *Fundamental Positions in Regard to the Making Provision for the Indigent Poor*, reasoning that:

> If the condition of individuals, maintained without property of their own, by the labour of others, were rendered more eligible than that of persons maintained by their own labour, then . . . individuals destitute of property would be continually withdrawing themselves from the class of persons maintained by their own labour, to the class of persons maintained by the labour of others . . . The destruction of society would therefore be the inevitable consequence, if the condition of persons maintained at the public charge were *in general* rendered more eligible, upon the whole, than that of persons maintained at their own charge, those of the latter not excepted, whose condition is least eligible. (Bentham, 2001: 39)

Here Bentham's poverty–indigence distinction defines his standard of public assistance, to be set below the comfort afforded by the lowest wage in the labour market. In accordance with liberal principles of government, this would ensure that the poor entered the less eligible conditions of the workhouse *voluntarily*, and would do so only in circumstances that would reduce their suffering. Indeed it would be irrational to do otherwise. While providing an objective distinction for administrative purposes, the technique would also prevent free labourers from being lured into a state of pauperism.

The translation of this principle from text to context was facilitated by Edwin Chadwick, who first met Bentham in 1829 and, as secretary of the Poor Law Commission from 1834 to 1846, was one of the chief architects of the reformed poor law.[3] In the section of the *1834 Poor Law Report* which deals with the 'principle of administering relief to the indigent', the imprint of Bentham is unmistakable:

> The first and most essential of all conditions . . . is that his situation on the whole shall not be made really or apparently so eligible as the situation of the independent labourer of the lowest class . . . in proportion as the condition of any pauper class is elevated above the condition of independent labourers, the condition of the independent class is depressed; their industry is impaired, their employment becomes unsteady, and its remuneration in wages is diminished. Such persons, therefore, are under the strongest inducements to quit the less eligible class of labourers and enter the more eligible class of paupers. The converse is the effect when the pauper class is placed in its proper position, below the condition of the independent labourer. Every penny bestowed that tends to render the condition of the pauper more eligible than that of the independent

labourer, is a bounty on indolence and vice. (Checkland and Checkland, 1974: 335)

Framed by the recently discovered laws of economy, the indigence–poverty distinction was to be inscribed into practices of administration given practical expression in the 'workhouse test'. The standard of comfort afforded by public relief was never to be more eligible than the situation of the independent labourer of the lowest class, because if it was more eligible then it would transform the labouring poor into paupers (Checkland and Checkland, 1974: 335).

If poverty was the natural and unchangeable lot of man, then indigence would mark out the terrain of government and the limits of state intervention. In this mentality of rule we see the outline of a specific relation between the spheres of economy, society and state appearing which would articulate an enduring problem: how to bring them into a governable relation. However, the pauper–poverty distinction and the less eligibility principle were not simply translated into the new poor law in the form envisaged by individual authors such as Bentham. Instead they would be grafted to other elements which were strictly Malthusian.

In tracing out this relation between the texts of Bentham and Malthus, it is important not to confuse the historical figures with the discursive effects of 'Benthamism' and 'Malthusianism'. This is Dean's argument, who proposes that the constitution of poverty is 'an invention without an inventor'. Ultimately it does not matter whether Bentham is the origin of the less eligibility principle, or indeed whether he merely enunciated an innovation which originated elsewhere. Similarly, as an individual Malthus certainly campaigned for the abolition of the poor laws, an abolition which clearly did not happen. But does this mean that there is no 'Malthusian effect' (again, Dean's term)? If we note the way in which the idea of rolling back expenditure on poor relief and enforcing the independence of the patriarchal family became a hegemonic doctrine – an unquestionable axiom – then the answer must be that there was an important Malthusian effect (Dean, 1991: 87; 1992: 232–5). After 1834 poor relief outside of the workhouse was to be strictly prohibited, with the question no longer one of *whether* or not the independence of the poor should be enforced. Rather the lines of battle were drawn around the poverty–indigence distinction, with all commentary bearing down on the problem of *how* pauperism should be repressed. The Act of 1834 did not signal the triumph of the abolitionists, but it did introduce a number of innovations that were clearly Malthusian. In particular it was in the principles of moral restraint and checks on improvident marriages built into the new regime that we see the imprint of Malthus most clearly.

The laws of nature, Malthus explains, dictated that a child was 'confided directly and exclusively to the protection of its parents', and by the same laws the mother of a child was confided 'almost as strongly and exclusively to the man who is the father of it'. The laws of nature were inviolable and the administration of the poor could do no more than reflect this; indeed it would be foolish to do otherwise:

> It may appear to be hard that a mother and her children, who have been guilty of no particular crime themselves should suffer for the ill conduct of the father; but this is one of the invariable laws of nature, and knowing this, we should think twice upon the subject, and be very sure of the ground on which we go, before we presume *systematically* to counteract it. (Malthus, 1992: 266)

Improvident marriages and bastardy would be encouraged by violating natural laws, and so to maintain order and property, and to limit the 'degree of power given to the civil government', it would be necessary to exclude relief to all children. For the man who married and bore children without the means to support them through his labour, then it should be made clear through 'punishment' that he had committed an 'immoral act' and so 'all parish assistance should be denied him, and he should be left to the uncertain support of private charity'. The married man who went on the rates was to be 'taught to know [that] the laws of nature, which are the laws of God, had doomed him and his family to suffer for disobeying their repeated admonitions' (Malthus, 1872: 430–1). If moral restraint was the preferred option in preventing the growth of the 'redundant population' of paupers, then the required checks would best be accomplished not by dispensing public assistance but by establishing parochial schools to instruct the poor in the doctrine that their happiness or suffering depended on themselves, and that if they multiplied beyond their means then they should not expect government to provide (Malthus, 1872: 433, 437).

The Malthusian trace gathered into the new poor law is not to be found by looking for evidence of abolition, but by looking closely at the line of exclusion erected against relief to able-bodied men and all those defined as their natural dependents. In the classical epoch the political significance of the patriarchal household was derived from the feudal order of estates, with wealth and rank underpinning the obligations linking masters and subjects. After 1834 the significance of the house-hold was transformed by the laws of economy. All able-bodied men –

those whose only property was their labour – were now economically responsible for themselves, their wives and their children, and they would have to secure their subsistence by selling their labour. This governing principle would be enforced by excluding all able-bodied males from assistance outside of the deterrent institution of the workhouse, bearing in mind that the decision to enter the workhouse was not an imposition decreed by the coercive powers of the state but a voluntary decision on the part of the family head (Dean, 1991: 96-7; also Spensky, 1992: 104). The line of exclusion would stop only with the infirmity or death of the male family head, after which certain classes of women and children, such as widows with dependent children, could go to the Union for relief. However, in strict accordance with the Malthusian position on bastardy, those who *should* be supported by their husband or father, such as unmarried mothers, would be subjected to the same principles governing pauperism, and would be obliged to enter the workhouse as the condition of eligibility for relief (see chapter 8).

In the reform of 1834 we find Benthamism come into an unlikely relation with Malthusianism. This is no superficial innovation but rather a hegemonic bloc within the newly emerging epoch. In the writings of Bentham we find an elaborate scheme for a massive administrative system directed at the management of pauperism (see chapter 4), while in the work of Malthus we find a thesis on natural laws which necessitate the total abolition of all public assistance to the poor, certain types of charity notwithstanding. Yet the constitution of poverty brought these apparently incommensurable statements into a productive relation. Among the conditions of possibility for liberal government, this is the basis of practices to regulate and order the various sub-populations associated with deviant and defective conduct. The Benthamite principles and the Malthusian position on bastardy converged as a mode of administration that would coach and discipline the poor so that they would learn to govern themselves in accordance with the axioms of liberal rule. The fact that liberal government harbours an illiberal impulse might alert us to the critical value of Foucault's notion of 'intentionality', as heterogeneous elements intersect and form a strategic field of force relations, the effects of which exceed the intention of individual thinkers and reformers.

The liberal break

What Dean calls the 'liberal break' marks an epochal moment of dislocation and transition, or to draw on Foucault's archaeological scheme, the end of the classical era and the birth of the modern episteme. By calling it the 'liberal mode of government' Dean does not equate 'government' with a political executive, or 'liberal' with the ideological and philosophical corpus known as liberalism. Instead, drawing on Foucault's writings on governmentality, this use of the term 'government' covers all calculated practices as they are brought to bear on the conduct of individuals and groups, and is thus more encompassing than *the* government, or political governance narrowly defined. On the other hand, the term 'liberal' denotes rationalities and practices which are opposed to older forms of rule and aim to limit the scope of sovereign power as it had developed during the classical epoch. Extending to fields as diverse as economy, education, medicine, hygiene and philanthropy, and concerned with bringing conducts and habits into line with specific conceptions of responsibility, independence and health, liberal government is less a doctrine than an ethos: a practical way of reflecting on the problem of rule through the recognition that to govern too much is to undermine the very ends of government (Dean, 1992: 218; 1999). If the sword is the symbol of sovereign power, then the power of liberal government entails a much lighter touch – more the carrot than the stick (Barry, Osborne and Rose, 1996).

With the birth of liberal government, 'poverty' – now framed by the principles and axioms of a new political economy – came to articulate the discourse of wealth and exchange in a historically novel way. No longer synonymous with the numbers of the poor, the question of poverty was distinguished from an internally heterogeneous object called 'pauperism', or in Bentham's vocabulary 'indigence'. Pauperism denoted various forms of voluntary or involuntary transgression in relation to natural laws and social norms. Ontologically, poverty was straightforwardly factual: the natural condition of man and the impulse to labour. Pauperism, however, was intensely normative. As a state of dependency, the significance of pauperism was derived not simply from the principle of labour, but from the state of independence made possible by free labour (Dean, 1992). In essence the problem of pauperism was one of securing particular habits among the poor, meaning a mode of conduct conducive to a state of responsible self-dependence. And this is the specific concern that would shape the relation between competing disciplinary technologies. The manifold problems associated with pauperism would see the illiberal workhouse of liberal government continually problematised by philanthropists operating under the banner of 'social economy'. Just as liberal government was made possible by the discovery of economic laws and regularities, so social economy would carve out its own distinct field of objects and relations. If the 'social question' corresponded to the category 'pauperism', then its cause could be traced back to the administrative shortcomings of political economy, in large part symbolised by the reformed workhouse.

Social economy

Economie sociale emerged in France and Italy during the first half of the nineteenth century, while in Germany a similar set of concerns came under the name of *sozialpolitik*. In England and Ireland, as was the case with police science, the objects and techniques of social economy took a slightly different form: a question concerning the 'condition of the labouring classes'. In the English and Irish contexts the actual term 'social economy' was used only infrequently, and when it was used it often deferred to the question of *condition*. Here the discussion is confined to the task of tracing the general contours of this field of discourse rather than examining regional differences. Focusing on the French case, we will thus be working with the premise that in terms of programmes, apparatuses and techniques, the registers of *economie sociale*, *sozialpolitik* and 'the condition of the working classes' are coterminous (see Dean, 1992: 243).

As an ensemble of statements, social economy emerged alongside political economy through the discovery of Society, but it also directed itself against political economy by championing the social and staking a claim in the complex problem of pauperism (Proccaci, 1991). Writing on the misery of the labouring classes in France and England in 1840, for example, Antoine Buret was cognisant of the fact that the political economy of Adam Smith had been political precisely because it sought a science of wise administration which could not be removed from moral considerations. Buret explained that economy 'neither can nor should constitute an independent science because the facts on which it rests are connected indissolubly to facts of moral and political order, which determine its meaning and its value' (cited in Procacci, 1991: 157). The new political economy had opened out a 'moral' void in the order of things which social economy would attempt to fill.

Moving in the shadow of the liberal break, social economy connects with but also disengages from the old charitable practices of eighteenth-century philanthropy, and Giovanna Procacci defines its 'strategic location' as occupying a space halfway between the public and the private (also Donzelot, 1979). Social economy marks the transformation of philanthropy as it engrafted the techniques of statistics and social inquiry onto the tradition of good works and oriented itself to the problem of order. The primary object brought within the scope of the new scientific philanthropy was the figure of the pauper. Social economy took as its object a specific relation between 'moral facts' and 'industrial facts', but it is important to be sensitive to what exactly is signified by these terms (Procacci, 1991: 157–8). The term 'moral' in particular codes a concern which is directed at the problem of conduct, the meaning of which was succinctly captured by Louis Villerme in 1840: 'The behaviours of a people are its morality; the task therefore is to give them nothing but good ones' (cited in Procacci, 1991: 158). 'Morality' signified the problem of order, and order was confronted by a range of adversaries gathered into the discourse of pauperism. If the pauper was a complex of deviations which derived its meaning from the project of Society, then 'morality' was the name for a range of techniques brought to bear on the practical task of re-forming deviant habits and defective conducts.

During the middle decades of the nineteenth century the social economists used the symbol of pauperism to point to the ever-present dangers threatening the security of Society. If the problem of pauperism was not resolved then civilisation itself would be threatened and it would be necessary to 'prepare for the convulsion of the world'. Pauperism was 'the class of men omitted by society so that they rebel against it'; or again, pauperism was the intensification of indigence such that it became a 'scourge' and a 'permanent nuisance to society'. Pauperism was the spectre of the mob, it was dangerous associations and mixtures, and, most ominously, it encircled society from within (Procacci, 1991: 158). Echoing the logic of police science, the problem of pauperism was all disorderly and unruly habits, conducts and associations: the dispositions and contagious relations that might escape the grip of rational control. If pauperism was to be conquered and order secured, then the conduct of each and all had to be monitored and, where necessary, modified.

While poverty and pauperism articulated each other within the same formation of discourse, the abolition of the latter would not obliterate the former. On the contrary, as Antoine Cherbuliez reasoned in 1853: 'when pauperism has been successfully overcome, only the poor will remain' (cited in Procacci, 1991: 159). The eradication of pauperism would not touch poverty; in fact it would preserve poverty in its proper state, free from the taint of indigence. On this point there is a direct link to Bentham. In his survey of the various 'positions' determining the 'necessity of relief', Bentham notes a fundamental tension between the positions that take humanity as their motive and security as their object, and those that take justice as their motive and frugality as their object. For Bentham the principle of provision should take its cue not from motives but from the ends of security and frugality; only in this way would the desired end of 'perfection' be achieved (Bentham, 2001: 10). Despite their points of opposition, political economy and social economy were in agreement that the problem of pauperism required a solution in the form of a well-governed state of good order where poverty did not degenerate into indigence. By comparison with Bentham's scheme, social economy took 'morality' as its motive, but its object was clearly a combination of security and frugality. Order had to be secured against the tendency in human nature to desire freedom and equality, because equality was a state of things that could exist only in 'primitive' society. In civilised society it was necessary to bring human nature under forms of tutelage so that people would pursue their satisfaction only through 'the means permitted them by the social regime' (Procacci, 1991; Donzelot, 1979). Social economy would constitute what Jacques Donzelot calls a 'tutelary complex', and it would govern through a form of regulated freedom. Using a mix of guidance and restraint to conduct the conduct of the lower orders, the family would be the principle site of intervention (Donzelot, 1979; Gordon, 1991: 48; Foucault, 1983: 220–1).

In her analysis of this discourse Procacci poses a rhetorical question: if the discourse of pauperism does not seek the elimination of poverty, then what was its strategic purpose? The answer is not to be found by seeking evidence of efforts to reduce inequality. What is required is an inquiry into the techniques directed at the control and eradication of *difference* (Procacci, 1991: 160–2). It is the dangers associated with difference that define the 'moral' dimension of social economy, and difference can be represented as an indefinite variety of defective, deviant or otherwise abnormal habits and conducts. Pauperism always corresponds to specific problems even though there is no limit to the number and type of problem to be addressed. Pauperism is *mobility* in the sense of fluid forms of sociality: the problem of vagabondage. Pauperism is *promiscuity*, or the depraved and dangerous couplings among the slum-dwellers which threaten to spill out into the wider society: the problem of improvident marriage and bastardy. It is habits of *independence* that refuse to take up their correct place in the social order of ranks; habits such as living with the present and refusing to be blackmailed by an uncertain tomorrow: the problem of intemperance and improvidence. Pauperism is *ignorance*, precociousness, and a willingness to engage in insubordination: the problem of truancy and delinquency. If it was nature that made man *as such* then it was education that would make the citizen, and so the teacher should replace the policeman, and the school should replace the prison. Ignorance was not only the lack of skills conducive to self-supporting labour, it was also the absence of dispositions that would serve as a bulwark against idleness, immorality, uncleanliness and improvidence. The politics of pauperism marks out an antagonistic field of relations where a veritable arsenal of techniques is brought to bear on the problem of securing Society, from the application of statistics to the practice of home visiting, to the regulation of hygiene, to the expansion of mass education.

Although the discourse of pauperism envelops a universe of objects as diverse as those of police science – the insane, imbeciles, beggars, criminals, drunks, prostitutes, vagrant children – it none the less resists decomposition into its constituent micro-populations (Procacci, 1991). Pauperism exhibits a stubborn cohesiveness despite the fact that it wraps an ever-expanding range of problems. As a discourse it betrays a certain fictitious character – an 'empty signifier' with the capacity to absorb an ever-expanding horizon of meanings (Žižek, 1989: 97; Torfing, 1999: 98). Within the orders of discourse 'pauperism' operates as a signifying vessel: it is filled and refilled with meanings, deployed in a variety of contexts, and invested in a range of programmes: a discursive surface for inscription and an unlimited capacity to symbolise the problem of order. Perhaps the most ominous and enduring effect of this order of discourse is the way it formulated the fiction of the 'normal family relation', at once a normative standard and an expansive field of normalising interventions, in particular the technique of child rescue. It was in relation to the fictitious normal family that the themes of child neglect and neglectful parents emerged in the second half of the nineteenth century, producing a range of disciplinary and eugenic interventions which we will encounter in part III.

Social economy both emerged from and organised itself in opposition to political economy, with the reformed workhouse one of its principal objects of critique. The workhouse of the liberal state and the idealised family relation of the social economists faced each other as rival answers to the problem of order, and yet they also formed a constitutive relation, each indispensable to the other even as they competed to define the definitive path of progress. It was within the cracks and fissures of this conflicted relation that the closed asylum of the religious orders endured and adapted to new conditions of possibility. In both architectonic form and practical effects the enclosed asylum continued to develop through a mix of established conventions and innovations. With one foot in the classical period and the other in the emerging modern epoch, the large establishments under the control of the religious orders would be coupled to the workhouse and social economy in a variety of ways. As a disciplinary technique directed at the administration of specific populations, the enclosed asylum also constitutes a crucial third dimension in a three-way relay articulating the problem of order during the nineteenth century.

The convent asylum

Opposition to the workhouse existed well before the reforms of 1834, but in the wake of the amended poor law it became increasingly organised through the mission of 'rescuing' certain classes of women and children from the demoralising environment of the workhouse. For the social economists the dangers that brought women and children to ruin were compounded in the workhouse, populated as it was by those hardened in the ways of idleness, insobriety and licentiousness. The technique of rescue saw many types of small-scale institutions established – homes, refuges and day schools – all of which were intended to provide an alternative to the workhouse. Another strategy was based on the old practice of boarding out foundling children by placing them with nurses. It was thought that the scope of the practice could be enlarged through private subscriptions and voluntary effort. In the case of girls who had 'fallen', or showed signs of falling, into moral depravity (prostitution), for example, it was thought that the boarding-out model could be used to place them with 'respectable' families. This would train them in habits of moral self-restraint, and ultimately mould them into responsible and self-supporting individuals. However, as the rescue movement became more systematic it also began to experience financial constraints due to its dependency on private subscriptions. The result, and here we are looking at the case of England and Ireland, was the gradual transfer of the rescue enterprise to the religious orders, where the model of small-scale homes was transformed into the large penitentiary.

The practical effect of this process was that the old logic of enclosure and exclusion, which originates with the medieval lazar house, became part of the modern administrative system (see Foucault, 1977: 198–9; 1988). The paradoxical effect was that what began as a movement to resolve the problems associated with the workhouse had the effect of creating new versions of the old problem, with the rescue movement gradually producing a complex of large penitentiaries and asylums. By the end of the nineteenth century the religious orders had a monopoly over a vast network of Magdalen penitentiaries, reformatories and industrial schools, all large-scale institutions which housed specific colonies of women and children. A brief examination of one of these institutions – the Magdalen penitentiary – will complete this overview of the ordering technologies assembled during the nineteenth century.

In England and Ireland the first Magdalen refuges and asylums were established during the second half of the eighteenth century (Finnegan, 2001: 8; Luddy, 1995: 110–12). Initially admittance required a letter of recommendation, with some homes operating a policy of discrimination by favouring young and unskilled women who were 'not hardened in the ways of vice'. Inmates, or 'penitents' as they were coded, were expected to stay for between eighteen months and two years, and were to leave only if their future could be guaranteed, either by securing a position as a domestic servant or by returning home (Luddy, 1995: 111). Close examination of these practices in the context of London reveals a significant degree of variation in the type of home and its treatment of inmates, at least in the sphere of private philanthropy (Higginbotham, 1985). However, of primary interest here are the institutions managed by the religious orders, which exhibit a more enduring and standardised practice.

The technique of rescue spread rapidly in the early decades of the nineteenth century, with a proliferation of Magdalen-type homes, refuges and asylums established under lay management. It was also the case that the initially fastidious procedures of vetting and selecting inmates gave way to the imperative of filling the institutions in order to staff the commercial laundries at the heart of the venture. A classic example of Weberian rational bureaucracy, the institution became its own end as 'over-zealous' rescue workers began to scour workhouses, hospitals and courts for potential penitents (Finnegan, 2001: 11–12, 84). By mid-century it was felt that a central organisation was required to consolidate efforts and prevent duplication among rescue agencies. The Reformatory and Refuge Union was established in 1856, and two years later its Social Evil Sub-Committee formed an association called the Female Mission to the Fallen. Men involved in rescue work faced an additional problem in that they needed to enter brothels in order to prosecute their mission, and their intentions could be misconstrued if they were spotted going into the brothels by members of respectable society. It thus became imperative to recruit women, and the Home Missionary Society (later the Women's Mission to Women) was formed to fulfil this function (Finnegan, 2001: 12–15).[4] By the end of the nineteenth century the rescue enterprise had become a veritable industry, with more than 300 Magdalen institutions in England housing some 6,000 inmates, and with at least 1,200 full-time rescue staff, not to mention vast numbers of part-time workers, district visitors, street and city missionaries, members of refuge committees and chaplains (Finnegan, 2001: 7). In England most towns had at least one Magdalen asylum by the 1890s; many had several competing refuges and homes, and the inmate population was no longer confined to prostitutes. Rescue had been extended to unmarried mothers, some of whom were victims of 'seduction' (including incest and rape), while others were classed as 'feeble-minded', 'deaf and dumb', 'idiotic', 'half mad' or simply 'in need of restraint' (Finnegan, 2001: 37, 143, 149; Luddy, 1995: 112).

From the 1840s the reliance on private subscriptions saw many of the private establishments experiencing financial problems, one reason why orders such as the Sisters of Mercy and the nuns of Our Lady of Charity of the Good Shepherd were able to take over the management of the homes (Luddy, 1995: 122–3). Once under the control of the religious orders the homes achieved economies of scale: huge penitentiaries running commercial laundries without the burden of wages. The average asylum housed 140–230 inmates, with the larger ones accommodating over 300 (Finnegan, 2001: 20–1). These were tightly regulated regimes, and they succeeded in maintaining strict disciplinary rule despite being run by relatively small numbers of nuns. The Good Shepherd Order provides a good example. In 1898, thirty years after her death, a book of detailed regulations on the government of the penitents was published in the name of the Order's foundress, Mother St Euphrasia Pelletier.[5] Titled *Practical Rules for the Use of the Religious of the Good Shepherd for the Direction of the Classes*, the *Rules* reflected the nature of the task at hand, with the perceived disposition of the inmates, the scale of the institutions, and the nature of the Order's work seen to require strict discipline and unquestionable obedience (Finnegan, 2001: 22). Discipline was to reflect the pastoral relationship between shepherd and flock, with the penitents reduced to the status of children and enveloped by an austere environment of care, compassion and charity. In practice this translated into absolute subordination to the authority of the Mistress (Finnegan, 2001: 23, 42).[6]

Once inside the penitentiary the women, like the nuns, were stripped of their individuality and inserted into the corporate body of the order, albeit at the bottom of a rigid hierarchy. The semiology of the institution was coded by the distinctiveness of dress and a uniformity of rule imposed on bodies, space and time (Luddy, 1995: 113–21). Upon entering the enclosed environment the penitent would be assigned a new name, with all links to the past severed. Visiting was discouraged as this risked 'awakening memories' which might disturb the state of mind required for penitence. Topics of conversation were to be selected and approved so as to prevent 'improper mental associations', while the content of all written correspondence was to be vetted. To ensure the 'good order of a class', a strict rule of silence also applied to specific parts of the day. For true penitents adherence to the rule of silence was a sign of 'virtue and true happiness', while for the rest it was a prophylactic 'against dissipation and dangerous conversations'. The rule of silence was enacted by the Mistress in the form of a specific look, a gaze that marked the precise moment when all penitents were to come to attention at their post (Finnegan, 2001: 23–4).

The rule of silence was part of a continuous regime, the elements of which were segregation, labour, surveillance and hierarchy.[7] In terms of labour, every minute in the life of the penitent was to have its appointed task so that there would be no time for uncontrolled mental reflections, and industry was at once a barrier against the dangers of idleness and a means to 'tranquilise' the inmates so that they would be 'more amenable to religious instruction'. Daily life was a relentless routine of religious instruction, vocational training and imposed silence. Washing and working for the public were both punishment and penitence, with the inmates deliberately detached from their maternal role as mothers, their babies usually sent out for adoption (Luddy, 1995: 113–21). The *Rules* instructed Mistresses to 'let your surveillance extend to everything', so that penitents were never to be left alone or allowed to retreat into some corner from where they might evade the gaze of the Mistress (Finnegan, 2001: 30). A lamp was to burn continuously throughout the night in the dormitories while the Mistress would lock herself into a cell, carefully fitted with a slide opening or grill so that the whole of the dormitory could be observed at a single glance (Finnegan, 2001: 234).[8]

Stepping back from specifics so as to examine the practice within its context, then, it can be noted that the technique of rescue brought philanthropic agencies and religious orders into a relation of enrolment. Social economy helped to establish what Foucault called the 'disciplines', with 'discipline' used in the dual sense to encompass both the human sciences as a domain of knowledge and a constellation of practical techniques directed at the moulding of conduct (Foucault, 1977: 305). The (re-)formation of conduct could take place within the social field, in particular through the family, or it could be accomplished through the technique of enclosing an inmate population within the walls of an institution that closes itself off from the wider society. Reconfiguring the monastic technology of the lazar house, and paralleling the development of reformatory punishment as an alternative to capital punishment or transportation to the penal colonies, the Magdalen penitentiary was but one in a series of such institutions, with further innovations taking the form of the reformatory school and the industrial school (Foucault, 1977; Hughes, 1986; Ignatieff, 1978). What these institutions shared was the combination of classification, segregation and exclusion as the means of securing and defending order. The various homes and schools were intended to provide answers to the problems associated with the mixed workhouse, and they were to replicate, as far as possible, the ideal family with the father providing and punishing and the mother cherishing (see Hancock, 1855). Yet the main accomplishment of the rescue movement, against the stated intentions of its practitioners, was the creation of an extensive system of 'monster schools', all cast in the mould of the workhouse (see Tod, 1878; O'Shaughnessy, 1862a, 1862b). The penitentiaries managed by the religious orders, the disciplines of social economy, and the workhouse instituted by the new poor law together formed a complex administrative system which brought together a variety of authorities: convention, science and law. In the final part of this chapter I will conceptualise this order of authorities in terms of specific ordering technologies.

The ordering techniques

We have seen how liberal government bears the imprint of Smith, Bentham and Malthus. From Smith the economy is annexed from the political and legal framework of sovereignty; from Bentham comes the indigence–poverty distinction together with the less eligibility principle; and from Malthus is a law of scarcity which drives the economic mechanisms and determines the need for checks on population, either positive checks in the form of famine and disease, or preventative checks in the form of sexual abstinence and moral restraint. These statements were assembled into an internally complex formation of discourse which continues to influence the politics of order today. The constitution of poverty established a sort of discursive hub through which passed (and continue to pass) debates on economy, labour, the family and individual conduct. As a related object, pauperism delimited the realm of public administration, with the pauper a class of subject who had voluntarily rescinded his liberty, and that of his family, in exchange for public assistance. Vagabondage should also be mentioned, for while the vagabond was at times indistinguishable from the pauper this was not always the case, with the relation between the pauper and the vagabond of crucial importance to liberal government. As a recipient of public assistance, the pauper was too dependent. The vagabond, on the other hand, moved in exactly the opposite direction. Associated with mendicity, idleness and a lack of respect for property, the vagabond exhibited an excess of liberty. Gathered into the discourses of pauperism and vagabondage was everything that threatened to subvert Society, but this also made

Society possible, because a project like Society requires a measure of itself. Between the pauper and the vagabond was the central problem of liberal government: the need to combine freedom and discipline. While delimiting the normative boundaries of Society, the pauper–vagabond complex also inscribed an enduring yet productive fracture into the heart of this project, for between conducts which are excessive and those that are deficient was scope for administrative expansion.

The possible movements within this grid – between the private sphere of the self-governing family and the punitive regime of the workhouse; between the undisciplined freedom of the vagabond, the state of dependency associated with pauperism, and the free labourer as a self-governing subject – opened out a division and a relay between specific and at times opposed technologies of government. On one side were the enclosed institutions of the poor law and the religious orders, while on the other was a normative and normalising fiction of the family home. Both connect liberty to discipline, and both are concerned with creating a specific type of subject. And yet there is a difference in how the subject of rule is to be formed. The workhouse and the penitentiary subject the inmate to a punitive mode of control, while scientific philanthropy, which is properly called a 'social' model, is concerned with inducing specific dispositions on the part of its subjects as they are positioned within the social field.

Liberal government confronted a number of pressing questions; questions such as how the problem of pauperism was to be addressed without allowing the state to encroach upon the laws of economy, or how the labouring classes were to be disciplined in a situation where the old ties of association and obligation no longer applied (Donzelot, 1979). Two answers, or more specifically two technologies, would slowly come into view, one based on exclusion, the other on strategic inclusion, with both a specific mode of discipline. In both cases it was agreed that, for the sake of liberty and economy, the reach of the state must be limited. The strategy derived from political economy tapped into utilitarianism with its psychological calculus of pleasure and pain, and it sought to compel individuals and families to conduct themselves in accordance with the laws of economy. Social economy sought to mould and shape the conduct of individuals and families through various forms of close inspection and direct intervention. Linking these technologies was the objective of governing the conduct of the individual and the population by reforming deficient, defective and deviant dispositions and desires.

In very general terms the dominant strategy from the side of philanthropy was simply to empty the disorderly population out of the mixed workhouse so that its contents could be carefully separated, classified, and subjected to specific interventions. However, the practical effect of this was the development of a whole range of social disciplines as the workhouse was split into a nexus of specialised institutions. Before looking at the detail of this I want to retrace the ground we have covered thus far, taking Bentham's scheme of public provision as a point of departure and moving towards a schematic presentation of what I am calling the 'ordering techniques'.

In his *Pauper Systems Compared* Bentham analysed what he considered to be all possible modes of public assistance, and it is for this reason that I will use Bentham's scheme as a point of departure. In other words he provides us with an empirically informed conceptual model. Bentham begins at point zero by considering the argument by the abolitionists, and the name he gives to this scenario is the 'no-provision system'. The most convincing argument in defence of the no-provision system is, according to Bentham, the argument that if public relief was abandoned then it would not only be replaced by private charity but would also actively encourage benevolence. Bentham reveals the absurdity of this argument by suggesting that if it held for indigence then it would also be reasonable to apply it to gin drinking, sedition, war, plague, famine and 'every species and cause of misery', which should also be left untouched or even encouraged 'for the better promotion of sobriety, patriotism, courage, medicine and benevolence' (Bentham, 2001: 150). He also critiqued the no-provision system by drawing on the distinction between motive and object discussed above. In terms of providing for the 'impotent part of the necessitous poor' the motive of humanity was sufficient, as one could have regard for their suffering, but when it came to relieving the able-bodied poor then the object of security was paramount. When confronted by a troublesome beggar one could say 'go to your parish', but without some form of public assistance the outcome of such a confrontation was entirely contingent. The English were not used to facing starvation and would not be willing to bear it, and so the primary reason for considering some kind of positive relief to the poor was 'regard for the safety of the other classes' (Bentham, 2001: 150). Having discarded the no-provision system, Bentham worked his way carefully through the 'limited or inadequate-provision system', the 'home and community provision' system, the 'small establishment systems', and finally the 'large establishment system'. His overall objective was a defence of the last of these, to be run on a commercial basis, and, as we shall see in the next chapter, this would provide the platform for his great plan for the management of pauperism, a scheme which would be built around his panopticon principle of inspection. For now we can use his three positive modes of provision as an initial sketch of the ordering techniques that would vie for position right up to the present: the home-provision system, the small-establishment system, and the large-establishment system.

Taken together these cover the techniques corresponding to social economy, the workhouse of the new poor law, and the convent asylum. Social economy encompasses the first two, while the poor law workhouse and the convent asylum converge on the large and centrally administered institution. During the classical period the model of home provision would have corresponded to out-relief. And while outdoor relief would gradually return after the reforms of 1834 (in England, much less so in Ireland), it remained a marginal practice and was formally discouraged by statute. I will thus use the category of home provision here to describe the practices of rescue which took the family relation as their normative standard, including the techniques of boarding out and home visiting. The small-establishment system corresponds to the various refuges, asylums, homes and schools intended to reform deviant and deficient individuals before returning them to society. Despite the significant differences between the workhouse and the convent asylum, both correspond in their own way to the large-establishment system. This is populated by a corporate inmate-body which is subjected to a disciplinary regime under central management. For the purpose of analysis the three-way model can be organised into a diagram of two models: a 'penitentiary model' based on the governing principles of separation and exclusion, and a 'social model' based on the governing principle of correcting defective habits and conducts within the social field itself. These are filled out in more detail below.

1 *The penitentiary model:* based on an enclosed order under central authority. The institution is governed by principles of hierarchical classification, segregation, and exclusion from the wider society, with the inmate population ordered as a corporate body which is stripped of individual characteristics and subjected to a disciplinary regime of unquestionable obedience. The model can be subdivided according to the governing authority:

1a *The workhouse of the new poor law:* the inmate body is organised into a master–subject relation. Stripped of whatever civil and political rights may apply, the citizen becomes a ward of the state. Men must bring their wives and children into the workhouse whereupon they are separated into distinct wards. As the chattel of men who have become a burden on the rates, women and children (including unmarried mothers and illegitimate

children) pay the price of dependency. All who enter the workhouse relinquish their status as subjects and become objects of
administration.

1b *The convent asylum:* the inmate body is organised in a parent–
child relation corresponding to the pastoral logic of the shepherd
and flock. The individual is stripped of the ability to reason and
is positioned as an obedient and subordinate lamb in the fold of
the shepherd. Just as for the child under the authority of natural
parents or legal guardians, authority is unquestionable and the
child is the object of pity or punishment as circumstances demand.
The inmate is not a subject endowed with autonomy or reason but
is an object governed by the principle of absolute obedience.

2 *The social model:* based on directing individual dispositions in order
to fit the flawed individual with the habits required for responsible
self-governance. The philanthropic register of 'association' signifies a
type of order to be secured through pervasive surveillance and socially
induced compliance. The technique of rescue is aimed at policing
deficiencies and defects, which are identified through home visiting
and corrected by boarding out individuals with 'respectable' families,
and/or by training them within small-scale replicas of the family home.
Again, the model can be subdivided:

2a *Boarding out:* aims to place those who exhibit abnormal dispositions in the charge of and under the influence of normal families.
Families are selected on the basis of their suitability in regard to
social rank and religion.

2b *The small-scale establishment:* attempts to replicate the normal
family and thus overcome the deficiencies of the mixed workhouse, and in this way it resembles the practice of boarding out.

In both approaches under this second heading the home is not a
mechanism of exclusion but a technique of strategic inclusion. While
it shares the parent–child relation with the convent asylum it is not
necessarily based on the logic of absolute obedience. At stake is the
task of inducing the formation of habits and desired dispositions
through a careful mix of the carrot and the stick. The home of the
philanthropic enterprise is derived from an idealised conception of
normality invested in the family relation. While coded as a child
the delinquent or defective is, as with the convent asylum, stripped
of a capacity to reason. But in contrast to the convent asylum
the individual is not merely an object to be disciplined; she or he
is also to be examined, trained, and re-formed by the technicians
of conduct, and ultimately returned to society as a self-governing
subject.

This conceptualisation is intended as a rough guide rather than an ideal type, and it is important to emphasise that the outline describes the techniques as they came into existence, and there is no necessary correspondence between authority and ordering technique. For example, in the context of Ireland the state-run workhouse and the convent asylum would steadily shade into each other as the workhouse was transformed in a 'county home' for the aged and infirm, while the religious orders took over the day-to-day running of most large institutions from hospitals and asylums to schools. For its part the state extended the use of home provision through contributory benefits, old-age pensions, the extension of outdoor assistance, and the introduction of unemployment assistance. And of course, as was the case elsewhere, professional social work gradually became a recognised discipline, blurring the boundaries between philanthropy and public administration (Skehill, 1999). The precise ways in which the ordering techniques are articulated is an empirical question which will be taken up in detail below.

In concluding this chapter we can note that the relation between the ordering techniques opened out a fracture in the fields and orders of discourse. As the penitentiary model became more complex so it preserved the logic of exclusion, linking the old lazar house of the classical epoch to the workhouse of the reformed poor law and the various schools, asylums and refuges established during the nineteenth century. The social model, on the other hand, operated through the development of novel knowledges and techniques, which is to say the social disciplines linking philanthropy to the human sciences. This fracture is less a relation of opposition than a productive relay, a mildly antagonistic relation to be sure, but also one that continually opens out spaces for administrative expansion. Between the ordering techniques which operate on the basis of enclosure and exclusion, and those that govern through strategic inclusion in the social field and the family relation, it is possible to detect a single ordering modality.

The next chapter examines the modality itself, focusing on two programmatic statements directed at the problem of order. By programmatic statements is meant specific rationalities of government which are coded in the form of comprehensive and idealised schemes for representing, knowing and acting upon the world. These statements are blueprints for the construction of actual political apparatuses to conduct the conduct of individuals and populations in accordance with specific ends (see Rose, 1996a). The first is derived from the work of Jeremy Bentham at the end of the eighteenth century, while the second concerns a social scheme constructed by 'General' William Booth at the end of the nineteenth century. As we move from one to the other we will see a transformation in the subject of government, from the subject of what Nikolas Rose calls an 'individualising moral normativity' at the turn of the nineteenth century, to the social 'subject of needs' at the beginning of the twentieth century (Rose, 1996a: 40). At the end of the chapter we will be in a position to place this analytical framework within the context of the Irish Free State so that we can move towards the constitution of inclusive governance in the present.

4

Two programmatic statements in the politics of order: the ordering modality

Question: Does your Grace consider that that discipline operates benefi-cially upon the character of the child that is the subject of it?

Response: The system of discipline I speak of is one which fits a man for the purposes of society, and which in truth cannot be had, unless coupled with large numbers on which it is to act. This, if well wrought, and upon a sound principle, converts the subject into a moral and religious machine, and ensures the regularity and tranquillity of the social system. (arch-bishop of Dublin before the Commissioners of Irish Education Inquiry, 1826)

Introduction

As the nineteenth century drew to a close, one E. D. Daly delivered a paper to the Statistical and Social Inquiry Society of Ireland on the topic of child neglect, calling attention to an ambitious reform scheme in England associated with the name of 'Booth' (Daly, 1891: 538). Daly himself opposed the leviathan-type programme; in fact he was against all such programmes whether organised by the state or by private enterprise, and he stood in defence of 'individual efforts widely distributed'. The precise meaning of 'Booth' may have been self-evident to Daly and his audience, but from where we stand today there is something more interesting in the imprecision of the reference, which envelops both techniques vying for position in the politics of order at this time: the penitentiary model and the social model. There were in fact two reformers called Booth, and either one could have been the target of Daly's invective. Today the better known of the two is Charles Booth, the entrepreneur and social reformer who produced the first major empirical survey on poverty in his *Life and Labour of the People of London* (1969). His lesser-known contempo-rary was 'General' William Booth, who co-founded the Salvation Army with his wife Catherine. This moment of ambiguity in the archive will be used to commence an inquiry into the intrinsic logic of Society itself.

Both of the Booths agreed that indiscriminate alms-giving and unregulated public relief demoralised the poor, yet they had quite different views on what should be done about it. The work of Charles Booth fell into two halves, one descriptive and based on his survey, the other normative and taking the form of recommendations of a governmental type. It is in the latter that we find his vision for an encompassing system of administration in the spirit of the 1834 reforms. In order to control the 'springs of pauperism' paupers were to be brought under a system of 'state tutelage', the objective being to prevent the pauperisation of the self-supporting classes (Booth, 1969: 296–7). Beggars and idlers were 'the ready materials for disorder', and they were to be subjected to a great 'experiment' of disciplinary training, the cost of which would be shared between private and public sources (Booth, 1969: 11, 298). Charles Booth maintained that the shiftless poor were motivated by the pleasure of idleness rather than the pain of industry, and so the abolition of the poor laws and the disciplinary influence of the workhouse was unthinkable (Englander, 1998: 67–72). The utilitarian logic of his reasoning was impeccable: society was to be 'purged of those who cannot stand alone', with state interference in the lives of a small fraction of the population acceptable because it would augment the liberties of the rest. Charles Booth referred to his scheme as limited socialism or 'socialism in the arms of individualism', with his use of 'socialism' denoting the institutions of the poor law (Booth, 1969: 297). Both in the technique of the survey and in the thrust of his recommendations, his thinking was clearly influenced by Bentham. In contrast to this, General William Booth's vision was rooted in the tradition of philanthropy, although he was also critical of the piecemeal nature of the existing philanthropic practices. William Booth remained intensely suspicious of all those who thought the answer to pauperism lay in any single sphere, whether state provision, the free market or social economy, and he sought to bring all of these realms together as a centrally governed whole.

The relation between the texts of Bentham and the two Booths is complex rather than linear, and a few words are required to explain the choice of material used in this chapter, and why we will not be examining Charles Booth further. First, we have a relation of influence linking Bentham to Charles Booth. Both thought it necessary to sequester certain classes of subject within an enclosed space cut out of the wider society. The space of reform was one of controlled isolation where the deviant, the defective and the recalcitrant could be subjected to specific techniques of training. For Bentham this space would be the panopticon (discussed below), a machine to engineer a particular type of subject. For Charles Booth the sphere of strategic exclusion would be the work-house and the labour colony, and like Bentham's model these were to 'influence' and 'enable' (i.e. compel) the individual 'to act more freely and intelligently for himself' (Booth, 1969: 303). Second is a develop-mental relation connecting Bentham to William Booth. During the nineteenth century the panoptic principles and techniques moved beyond the physical limitations of Bentham's original architectural model to become coextensive with the social itself (also discussed below). Finally there is a relation of contiguity between the Booth schemes, which reflects the unresolved tension between the ordering techniques, or the struggle characterised by one contemporary reformer as a battle between 'the institutionalists and the boarders out' (O'Connell, 1880). For the purpose of clarity this complex relation will be simplified by focusing on the programmatic statements of Jeremy Bentham and William Booth. It is not intended to propose a cause–effect relation between one and the other. Instead I would argue that the relation between past and present is neither linear, circular nor recursive, and if a form is required to visualise this relation then it might be possible to speak of a long and fragile arc which bends and warps, folds back on itself here and there, makes connections and relays between seemingly random points, entangles itself in elegant knots, and occasionally snaps and creates a synapse or junction. Bentham and Booth provide a way to trace this arc, and while these works might not be the only way to conduct a genealogy of the present mode of governance, each in its own way is exemplary in systemising the modern problem of order.

In examining these two schemes I am not suggesting that either was simply translated into the 'real' world in its entirety. Nor is it intended to propose that they are ideal types in the tradition of Weberian analy-sis. Instead the schemes are being used to trace specific *programmes*, and while they certainly have their moment of idealisation, each is a comprehensive scheme for representing, knowing and shaping the world: for thinking the world in such a way that it is made available for political programming (Rose, 1996a: 42). In distinguishing his concept of the 'programme' from the 'ideal type', Foucault pointed out that the latter involves the historian engaging in an exercise of 'retrospective interpretation'. Given the historical context of Weber's work, it may also be the case that Foucault was suspicious of the ideal type because he saw a trace of the 'normal' in it, something against which abnormal types could be constructed and acted upon. Speculation aside, Foucault was clearly closer to Weber than he was willing to admit, his genealogies of power/knowledge, for example, anchored in the study of rationalities and modes of organisation – classic Weberian concerns. However, Foucault was also correct to point out the specificity of the programme, with its concern to regulate conduct and to order the spaces within which things are thought, said and done (Foucault, 1991a: 80). This is what Foucault means when he writes about governing as a way of structuring 'the possible field of action of others' (1983: 221). It is certainly the case that governmental programmes are transformed as they are interpreted and translated in specific contexts. In this sense to describe the programme in its 'pure' form does share something with the analytical device of the ideal type. Yet it also remains the case that the programme is intended to shape the world in its historical context, while the ideal type is distilled from the world as it has come to be.

As the classical epoch drew to a close it was Jeremy Bentham who remained cognisant of the fact that even the most diligent and virtuous could be thrown 'headlong' into the abyss of indigence by one false step, and it was necessary to maintain vigilance in the interest of security. Bentham's scheme for a comprehensive and centrally administered system of large workhouse establishments foresaw the possibility of, and attempted to prevent, the 'abyss' of growing indigence. A century later William Booth spoke from within the heart of darkness itself. Separated by a century, both envisioned a solution to the social question in the form of a comprehensive system of administration, with Booth echoing Bentham's maxim that 'wisdom, true wisdom, consists not in the scantiness of measures, but in the amplitude of means' (Bentham, 1843b: 397). However, while they might have agreed on the need for a comprehensive system of administration, they nonetheless framed their object in quite different ways. Bentham designed a machine within which a specific type of individual would be formed: the subject of liberal rule. A century later Booth's project was of a different magnitude and density. If Bentham is characterised as the rational planner who seeks to transform the jungle into a well-ordered garden, Booth was concerned with equipping the individual to make her or his way in the jungle itself. Booth was certainly a gardener of sorts, but his vision of order was predicated on a Spencerian/Darwinian struggle for existence, and he accepted that the logic of the jungle would endure in the pauperised depths of the industrial city. Despite their differences, between Bentham and Booth lies the constitution of a project which supports the meanings invested in questions of mendicancy, delinquency, illegitimacy, vagrancy, lunacy and idiocy, a constellation of problems which are among the condition of possibility for the vision of ordered perfection which goes by the name of Society.

Bentham's pauper kingdom[1]

Bentham's plan for the management of pauperism was built on scientific principles of administration, with his utilitarian principle of less eligibility providing both an objective distinction between paupers and the labouring poor and a mechanism to prevent the latter from becoming pauperised. The movement from the world of liberty to the disciplinary environment of the poor-house would be governed (more or less; there were also more sinister aspects to the plan) by the individual's ability to discern between pleasure and pain. If all wage labour outside of the workhouse was more eligible than conditions within, then it would be rational to claim relief only in cases of genuine necessity.

For Bentham the objectives of public relief should combine principles of economy, moral influence and justice, and should be universal in application. Relief outside of the workhouse – or 'home provision' as Bentham called it – failed to meet these criteria. It could not be universal since there were classes among the infirm and the vagrant who either could not be relieved at home or lacked a home altogether; it was not an efficient way to organise the employment of paupers; it could not be tied to educative influences; and it was bound to be less economical than a system of large establishments (Poynter, 1969: 127–8). It was also prone to abuse since, while out-relief might serve the needs of the 'strictly virtuous', it escaped the public eye and could be squandered on alcohol and other luxuries. The existing houses of industry were prone to the same irregularities and were too small to be efficient, and Bentham rejected the idea of partial reform such as the incorporation of parochial administrative units.[2] Against these disorders and irregularities stood the merits of a comprehensive public system, and what Bentham envisioned was an 'analytic division of the whole country' with a view to administrative perfection (Poynter, 1969: 128; Bentham, 1843b: 392).

Bentham wrote to Arthur Young, the editor of the *Annals of Agriculture*, in 1797 outlining his plan to collect and collate information that would form the basis of two related volumes: *Pauper Systems Compared* and *Pauper Management Improved*. He also enclosed two tables with his letter, one a blank 'pauper population table' which would serve to gather statistical information on the pauper population from as many parishes as possible, and the other a 'table of cases calling for relief', also described by Bentham as the 'general map of pauper-land, with all roads to it' (Bentham, 1843b: 361–2). Mitchell Dean argues that the table of cases could be interpreted, incorrectly, as belonging to the classical period. Bentham's project was in fact concerned with counting the numbers not of the poor, but only of that segment of the general population which constituted the 'cases calling for relief'. The table systemises the distinction Bentham had made the previous year between poverty and indigence, and is consistent with his view that poverty is an 'unalterable and general state of humankind' and 'indivisible by any system of classification' (Bentham, 2001: 3). Poverty was the source of productive labour, the motor of civilisation, and the condition of possibility for progress, unlike indigence, which was a fetter on all of these (Dean, 1991: 178). It was thus only the 'burthensome part of the poor' which was the object of Bentham's plan, and he set about 'extirpating mendicancy' with a view to securing 'good order' (Bentham, 1843b: 401, 420).

The pauper population table was intended to document the numbers claiming both indoor and outdoor relief, and would enumerate all classes of pauper whether orphan, bastard, lunatic, idiot, cripple or bedridden. Differences within the pauper population had a direct bearing on the cost of relief and the value of return by way of actual or potential labour, and the table was designed to gather the information required to calculate profits and losses in relation to the various classes of pauper (Bentham, 1843b: 362). The main questions informing the statistical branch of Bentham's project concerned the amount of food a class of pauper consumed and the value of labour that could be extracted in return for relief. Bentham wanted to reclassify the 'stock of pauper hands' according to the logic set down in his table of cases, a taxonomy that would reach beyond the permanent stock of paupers in the workhouses to the 'degraded classes' of thieves, deserters, beggars and prostitutes who were currently at large in society (Bentham, 1843b: 365).

Perceiving the existing 'order of things' as an administrative mess, Bentham set out to impose order on the classification of paupers through a universal labour theory of value. His table of cases was based on three considerations: the nature and degree of indigence in terms of efficient cause; the cause, degree and duration of the inability in respect to work; and finally the mode and degree of relief or prevention, as practised or practicable, adequate or inadequate, eligible or ineligible. With rhetorical flourish Bentham asked his reader: 'What say you to this idea of forming a valuation on that part of the national livestock which has no feathers to it, and walks upon two legs?' (Bentham, 1843b: 366–7).

Bentham's rational approach to 'general economy' would facilitate precise calculation as to the type and quantity of labour that could be extracted through weighing up 'mouths to be fed' and 'hands to work with' (Bentham, 1843b: 363–4). And through the 'art of management and book-keeping' he would render the net cost of maintenance perfectly transparent and visible at a glance. To this end his table was organised as a taxonomic system of 'hands' (figure 4.1), with each of the

EXTERNAL CAUSES ;

Which are all temporary, and of uncertain duration ; viz.

VI. LOSS of WORK	**VII. INABILITY to obtain WORK ;**
(Original Property being also wanting).	(Property being also wanting) through
as in the case of	*I. Badness of Character ;* *as in the case of*

VI. LOSS of WORK

(Original Property being also wanting).

as in the case of

[IX.]¹ OUT-OF-PLACE-HANDS (*d*) (*e*) ;
ex.gr.

1. Labourers, *on completion of the job—*
2. ———— *on disagreement with the Employer, through the Labourer's fault—*
3. ———— *through the Employer's fault—*
4. Journeymen—Manufacturers—Handicraftsmen and—Artists—Shop-keepers and—Warehouse-keepers, *on the shutting-up of the Manufactory, Shop or Warehouse, by reason of death, failure, or leaving off business—*
5. Journeymen—Manufacturers—Handicraftsmen and—Artists—Shop-keepers and—Warehouse-keepers, *on disagreement with the Master, through the Servant's fault—*
6. ———— *through the Master's fault—*
7. Seamen, *on completion of the Voyage—destruction, capture, or breaking-up of the Ship—or on disagreement with the Commander, through the Seaman's fault—*
8. ———— *through the Master's fault—*
9. Domestic Servants, *on the death, or going abroad, of the Master—the breaking-up or reduction of his establishment—or on disagreement with him, through his fault—*
10. ———— *through the Servant's fault—*
11. Domestic Servants, discharged without Characters, *through the Servant's fault—*
12. ———— *through the Master's fault.*

X. CASUAL-STAGNATION HANDS,
ex.gr.

13. Husbandmen, *on the conversion of Arable into Pasture—*
14. Canal-Diggers, *on completion of the Canal.*
15. Miners, *on the failure or working out of the Mine—*
16. Quarrymen, *on the working out of the Quarry, or failure of the demand—*
17. Manufacturers, *in the event of a general stagnation of the Manufacture—*
18. Handicrafts and Artists, exercising occupations dependent on Fashion—*on failure of the Fashion.*

VII. INABILITY to obtain WORK ;

(Property being also wanting) through

I. Badness of Character ;
as in the case of

XIV. STIGMATIZED HANDS (*f*) ; *ex. gr.*

1. Thieves, including Pickpockets—
2. Highway Robbers, including Footpads—
3. Housebreakers—
4. Incendiaries—
5. Coiners—
6. Cheats, including Gaming-Cheats, or Sharpers, Swindlers, and other Obtains by false Pretences—
7. Smugglers—
8. Forgers—
9. Perjurers—
10. Soldiers, Militia-men, Marines and Seamen, drummed out, or otherwise discharged with infamy.

Pardoned, or at large after expiration of their sentence.

XV. SUSPECTED HANDS.

11. Classes from 1 to 9 as above, acquitted or (after trial or examination) discharged without punishment, *through uncertainty of guilt, or technical defect in procedure or evidence—*
12. Children, under age, *living with parents, &c. belonging to Classes* 1 to 7.

XVI. UNAVOWED-EMPLOYMENT HANDS.

13. Classes 1 to 7—
14. Gypsies, *viz.* occasionally Fortune-tellers, *i.e.* Cheats ; occasionally Thieves—
15. Deserters.

XVII. LAZY HANDS.

16. Beggars (*Habitual.*)

XVIII. UNCHASTE HANDS.

17. Prostitutes—
18. Mothers of Bastards—
19. Loose Women—
20. Brothel-keepers (female)—
21. Procuresses.

Figure 4.1 Detail from Jeremy Bentham's 'Table of cases calling for relief'

categories and subdivisions based on (in)ability or (un)willingness to labour.

The table divides the pauper population into internal causes and external causes, the former including insane hands, feeble hands, unripe hands (children), sick hands, child-burthened hands and lazy hands; the latter encompassing out-of-place-hands, casual-stagnation hands, periodical-stagnation hands, superseded hands, stigmatised hands (thieves, forgers, smugglers), suspected hands (uncertainty of guilt), unavowed-employment hands (gypsies and deserters), strange hands (travellers, foreigners) and decayed-gentility hands. Among the latter classes (to the right of the table) are all the 'dangerous and disreputable classes'. Bentham attempts to exhaust all causes of indigence and to arrange them in relation to a single governing principle: self-supporting labour. As things stood, every 'man' had the right to be maintained in the character of a pauper at the public charge, the problem being that this tended to maintain the indigent in a condition of idleness. And coupled to this was the problem of the common beggar whose means were more eligible than those of the pauper maintained in the state of idleness, because if this was not the case then the beggar would quit his or her occupation and become a pauper. It was clear to Bentham that an element of compulsion – meaning coercion – was required if the problem of pauperism was to be governed. Beggars set a bad example to the industrious poor and, because they caused pain in the form of sympathy and disgust among the charitable, they also depressed the quantity of happiness. The solution was to apprehend beggars and subject them to the discipline of labour, and to this class would be added 'insolvent fathers, chargeable bastards, and disreputable mothers' (Bentham, 1843b: 404).

Once sequestered within the poor-house, the various classes of pauper would come under the rule of the 'all-employing principle' and the 'labour-division principle'. For reasons of health, morality and economy Bentham explained that:

> Not one in a hundred is absolutely incapable of all employment. Not the motion of a finger – not a step – not a wink – not a whisper – but might be turned to account in the way of profit in a system of such magnitude. A bed-ridden person if he can see and converse, may be fit for inspection; or though blind, if he can still sit up in bed, may knit, spin, etc. etc. Real inability is *relative* only – i.e. with reference to this or that species of employment, or this or that situation. In the situation in question employment may be afforded to every *fragment* of ability, however minute . . . In a limited local establishment on the present footing, the stock of ability lies oftentimes unemployed, for want of those appropriate means and

opportunities of employment which could not be afforded to any profit in any other than an establishment of the largest scale. (Bentham, 1843b: 382, original emphasis)

Echoing Adam Smith's account of the pin factory (1976a: 14–15), Bentham argued that the division of complex tasks into several simple operations would create new forms of employment and bring more classes of pauper within the compass of useful labour. This would require large houses of industry so that inability and infirmity could be greatly reduced (or even eradicated) through an expansive division of labour. Males should not be given work that could be done by females until the female stock of hands was fully provided; adults should not be given work that could be done by children of a workable age until the stock of non-adult hands was provided; and so with the able against the unable, the willing against the lazy, and the skilled against the unskilled. The principle of compulsion was to be flexible, fitted to the exact circumstances of the class in question and governed by two principles: the 'self-liberation principle', meaning no liberty until the cost of relief was covered by the value of labour, and the 'earn-first principle', meaning no sustenance until the daily requirement of labour was met (Bentham, 1843b: 383).

The plan also provided for the systematic application of Bentham's panopticon principle of inspection. Designed by Bentham's brother Samuel, the inspection principle was to be the perfect instrument of order. It worked by placing the manager of the poor-house (or prison, school, manufactory, asylum or hospital – this was to be a versatile technique) in a central tower surrounded by a circular arrangement of cells. In this way the inspector would occupy a 'centrical spot' from which 'without any change of situation, a man may survey, in the same perfection, the whole number [of inmates] without so much as a change of posture' (Bentham, 1995: 39, 43). Whether the object of inspection was to punish the incorrigible, guard the insane, reform the vicious, employ the idle, maintain the helpless, cure the sick or train the young mattered not, for in all cases 'the more constantly the persons to be inspected are under the eyes of the persons who should inspect them, the more perfectly will the purpose of the establishment have been attained' (Bentham, 1995: 34). Unless one were willing to concede the need for as many guards as there were inmates, it was clear that total surveillance was impossible. However, the panoptic technique was one of 'apparent omnipresence' which took the form of an 'invisible eye' and an 'inspective force'. By placing the inspector within the central inspection tower, and concealing his precise whereabouts through the use of special contraptions, the agent of surveillance would be able to see without being seen. And this was the genius of the machine: the inmates would never know precisely when they were being watched, and so they would conduct themselves as if constantly under the gaze of inspection (Bentham, 1995: 42–5, 74, 100). In other words they would internalise the panopticon's disciplinary gaze.

Augmenting the centrical spot of the inspection tower were spatial principles of separation, aggregation and vicinity, together forming an apparatus that would control all disorderly and contagious relations among the inmate population. The principles of aggregation and separation related to matters of preservation and prevention. Once the pauper population was divided into the classes of hands, the classes would be kept apart. Not only would this preserve moral order by separating the sexes, it was also the case that the 'indigenous and quasi-indigenous stock' could be separated from the 'coming and going stock who might excite hankerings after emancipation'; adults could be separated from children, petty criminals from hardened criminals, the morally depraved from the innocent, and so on (Bentham, 1843b: 372). The principle of vicinity cut through the principles of aggregation and separation, transposing the logic of the table of hands onto the three-dimensional fabric of the pauper panopticon. Married couples would occupy a special ward of double cells with high partitions, with small children 'of the innocent and unobserving age' placed between each couple. Raving lunatics would be positioned next to the deaf and dumb; prostitutes next to elderly women; the blind beside silent lunatics and the 'shockingly deformed'; and between the dangerous classes and the susceptible classes would be a 'barrier ward' (Bentham, 1843b: 373). The administrative logic would preserve health from infection and morals from corruption, with the central inspection lodge ensuring that the 'censorial eye' of the governing class was cast over 'the evil disposed among the governed'. The internal organisation of the house would be extended to the surrounding grounds, with roads used to create isolation wards which would never be occupied by more than one class at a time. And as a barrier against strangers the pauper panopticon would be surrounded by a double fence and a 'sequestration belt' of trees (Bentham, 1843b: 372–73, 385).

Through careful positioning and uniform visibility, the panopticon would transform the complexity of human populations into an order of efficient simplicity: 'no false musters, no running to and fro, no mislayings and huntings, no crossings and jostlings . . . every person and every thing is within view and within reach at the same instant'. Delinquent acts would be known the instant the offence was committed, with defendant, witness and judge co-present; while the transgression, the trial, the sentence and its execution would all exist within the compass of the same moment (Bentham, 1843b: 392–4).

In terms of its immediate goals the plan sought to replace the 'mixed multitude of independent authorities' with a unified authority. This would be organised as a joint stock company called the National Charity Company, which for Bentham was 'the best, or rather the only tolerable form of government for such an empire' (Bentham, 1843b: 369; 1995: 113). At a minimum the Company would protect property-owners against future increases in the poor rates, and if possible it would include ratepayers in a share of the profits (Bentham, 1843b: 371). The Company was to be given coercive powers to 'execute with unremitting vigilance . . . the suppression of mendicity and habitual depredation', apprehending and detaining all persons, able-bodied or otherwise, with no visible property or evident means of livelihood (Bentham, 1843b: 404).

Bentham's pauper empire was to be a national network of panopticon poor-houses, each one surrounded by enough land (waste if possible) to provide for the subsistence of its own population (Bentham, 1843b: 369). Originally planning for 500 houses to cover the entire country (Poynter, 1969: 128), Bentham settled for an initial goal of 250 to be spaced no further apart than a man or a woman could cover in a day on foot (Bentham, 1843b: 374). Each house was to hold 2,000 paupers, giving a total of 500,000 for the system as a whole (Bentham, 1843b: 369–70). Bentham was also determined to abolish 'disinterestedness' in the running of his system through a mix of punishments and rewards. The 'moral' motive of humanity towards inmates would be regulated by the positive and negative sanctions of publicity, while duty to the Company would be secured by a salary tied to profit or loss. The principle of interestedness would place the governors themselves under a second level of panoptic inspection, this time effected by a public with a vested interest in the management of the houses, with periodic public inspections helping to keep the system in check.

While the model was built on standardised principles it would also be sensitive to local exigencies, something that would enable the system as a whole to learn from itself. Because every aspect of the system was available for comparison, it would be 'advanced to the highest possible pitch of perfection' (Bentham, 1843b: 392). Useful knowledge would be augmented and disseminated while the fruits of observation and experiment would be accumulated and stored, no longer scanty, accidental, irregular or incomplete:

[The] proposed Company would afford the first opportunity ever presented to mankind, of enriching the treasury of useful knowledge by contributions furnished on a national scale, and on a regular and all-embracing
plan; and would thus form an epoch – not only in political economy, but
in many and many another branch of science. The sciences which now
await this epoch, for a degree of improvement altogether unattainable
by any other means, would thus be raised to a new pitch of certainty.
(Bentham, 1843b: 425)

Bentham's immediate objective was to carve an enclosed space out of
the social fabric, with the panopticon poor-house transforming the idle,
the deviant and the defective into useful subjects. The larger objective,
however, was, on the one hand, to create a system of administration
capable of permanent improvement, and, on the other, to engineer the
self-governing subject of a liberal order.

Panopticism[3]

The inspection principle at the heart of Bentham's plan combined a
degree of actual surveillance, which could never be more than partial,
with an omnipresent and inescapable fictional mode of surveillance. It
is this latter dimension that Foucault seized on in his *Discipline and
Punish*, a study in which he developed his theory of 'the carceral': a
mode of discipline which takes the form of hierarchical observation and
normalising judgement (Foucault, 1977). Foucault greatly enlarged our
understanding of the relation between power, order and exclusion by
theorising two related modes of power which connect up with the
sovereign state and form a triangular relation between discipline, government and sovereignty (Foucault, 1991b: 102). The intimate relation
between these modes of power – disciplinary power and biopower – is
clearly in evidence in the quotation at the start of this chapter.

The exemplary form of disciplinary power is training, which is exercised over the body by external authorities and over the self through
self-discipline. Foucault described this as a 'humble modality' of power,
one that operates through 'minor procedures', so that from a useless
multitude of bodies training creates a multiplicity of forces that can be
combined in a variety of ways and used for a variety of tasks (Foucault,
1977: 170). Training is a 'modest, suspicious power which functions as
a calculated, but permanent economy' of normative regulations and
procedures, with its objects also the instruments of its exercise
(Foucault, 1977: 170, 184–5). With training working primarily through
techniques of inducement and reward, the negative logic of coercion is
reserved for those unwilling or unable to conform to a standard which

is applied to individual bodies and derived from living populations: a mode of authority and a normative standard known by such names as 'average social man' (Lawson, 1847).

'Average social man' is an object constituted within the domain of what Foucault called biopower, a concept derived from the argument that a society's 'threshold of modernity' has been reached 'when the life of the species is wagered on its own political strategies' (Foucault, 1998: 143; 1997: 73–9). Life entered history in conjunction with the science of police and the discovery of population in the classical epoch, and during the nineteenth century it was carried into the 'great technologies of power' engendered by philanthropy, scientific social inquiry and the human sciences. In contrast to sovereign power, which is deductive and exercised over its subjects through the juridical power to take life or let live, biopower is productive and takes charge of life by subjecting it to the rule of the normal, which is to say the 'true state of facts' (Foucault, 1998: 139–44; 1977: 305). Objectively the normal is simply a statistical average, derived simultaneously from living individuals and a living population. But as its dimension of facticity is abstracted into standards and measurements such as normal health and normal intelligence, it no longer corresponds to any particular individual and becomes the basis of hierarchical observation and normalising judgement. And of course there are consequences attached to being coded as a person with above-average or below-average intelligence, or defined as a risk to the community following psychological evaluation.

Taken together, the standard of 'average social man' intersects with the disciplining of bodies and the biopolitical regulation of populations to institute the 'constraint of a conformity that must be achieved': a mode of authority which makes possible a whole spectrum of distributions which divide the normal from the abnormal and the desirable from the deviant (Foucault, 1977: 182–3). Foucault drew on two forms of division to tease out the significance of this, the first based on exclusion within the lazar house, and the second based on control of the plague through quarantine. Both are concerned with the problem of contagious relations, with Foucault arguing that they slowly came together during the nineteenth century (Foucault, 1977: 198). The 'disciplinary partitioning' and 'constant division between the normal and the abnormal' begins with the leper and the plague but is consolidated in the disciplinary and biopolitical techniques of nineteenth-century government, with the panopticon giving architectonic form to a new mode of power. With its radial distribution of cells around a central inspection tower, the inmate is positioned within a spatial grid marked out by axial visibility linking the prisoner to the inspector, and lateral invisibility with the cell walls separating each prisoner from all others. The inmate is positioned as an object of information but prevented from becoming a subject in communication, visible at all times but never knowing precisely when under the gaze of the inspector (Foucault, 1977: 200). As the guarantee of order, the panopticon would ensure that 'the crowd, a compact mass, a locus of multiple exchanges, individualities merging together, a collective effect, is abolished and replaced by a collection of separated individualities' (Foucault, 1977: 201).

For Marx the 'collective effect' of the crowd was the condition of possibility for the proletariat as a class 'in itself' to become a class 'for itself'. For Bentham the ungoverned crowd was the opposite of order, and he positioned his reader right at the centre of the central inspection tower as he described the inspector's gaze: 'to the keeper, a *multitude*, though not a *crowd*; to themselves, they are *solitary* and *sequestered* individuals' (Bentham, 1995: 50, emphasis in the original). The panopticon positions its objects in such a way that those subjected to its disciplinary force are also recruited into the labour of its operation and its reproduction (Foucault, 1977: 201). This is a paradigmatically *social* power.

When Foucault wrote *Discipline and Punish* he was actually researching three figures and not just the delinquent, the other two being the human monster and the onanist (masturbator). Taken together, these figures gradually come to constitute the abnormal (Foucault, 2003). With the birth of the abnormal comes the problem of danger, a living realm of disorder which goes beyond the actual criminal act (as the object of sovereign power) to the things that certain types of individual are capable of doing (Foucault, 1977: 291; 1998: 89). Foucault's account of the panopticon operates within this wider investigation into the constitution of the abnormal and normalising power, which gradually colonises the social and establishes a disciplinary grid linking each to all, simultaneously individualising and totalising as the disciplines are brought to bear on the problem of governing bodies, behaviours, conducts, habits and dispositions (Foucault, 1977: 184, 249). In the specific context of liberal government, normalising power establishes a relation of equivalence between the subjects that make up its domain (i.e. the subject of liberalism is the individual, and all individuals are essentially the same and equal before the law), but once the apparatus is operational it distinguishes and ranks individual differences, so that the initial homogeneity results in hierarchies which split the normal from the abnormal. Furthermore, while the disciplinary techniques promise to isolate and cure or reform abnormal habits, conducts and dispositions – thus restoring the state of formal equality – their practical effect is a proliferation of the very things in need of normalisation (Dreyfus and Rabinow, 1983: 193–8; also Bauman, 1991: 14). This is the disavowed political dimension of scientific expertise. When the abnormal is cast as an object of scientific investigation and technical intervention, the disciplines are simultaneously depoliticised and extended through processes of continual technical refinement and adjustment (Dreyfus and Rabinow, 1983: 195–8). It is the panopticon – a machine designed to normalise the abnormal – that systemises this mode of power.

Panopticism establishes (or rather envisages – it was never actually built to Bentham's specifications) a relation between the repressive power of the state and the positive power of the human sciences, between the disciplinary penitentiary and the social disciplines, and between 'two modes of production of truth': confession and examination (Foucault, 1998: 64–5). In the course of this transformation the citizen-subject of sovereign rule is enveloped by a 'region of juridical indiscernability': a constellation of behaviours, drives and dispositions which define the domain of the human sciences (Foucault, 2003: 21). The relation between law and science, or what Foucault calls the twin protectors of normalising power, can already be detected in the way that Bentham connects legal punishments (the apprehension of beggars) to a disciplinary mechanism which is outside of the law (the decision to enter the workhouse is voluntary). The global functioning of normalising power is one of colonising the juridical realm, creating an uneasy alliance – at times giving rise to antagonisms – between the realms of law and scientific expertise, and between the spheres of state administration and social economy. A good example of this is a figure discovered during the nineteenth century and known as the 'moral lunatic', with the subject of this discourse neither entirely a prison inmate nor a hospital patient (McDonnell, 1863; Kitching, 1857). Foucault argues that medicine provides a means to govern this type of unstable relation, with the generalised medicalisation of behaviours, conducts, discourses and desires placing medicine in a strategic position as an 'arbitrating discourse' (we will return to this theme in part III) (Foucault, 1980: 107; 1977: 296). This complex relation of extension, colonisation and arbitration suggests the gradual formation of an internally heterogeneous but otherwise unified social logic.

The panopticon, then, is but one moment or statement in the institution of the disciplines. If the penitentiary can be described as the 'discipline-blockade', or the enclosed institution on the edge of society which is turned inwards on itself through the negative function of exclusion, then the panopticon is what Foucault calls a 'discipline-mechanism' which improves the exercise of power by making it lighter and more mobile. And if the former is a mode of 'exceptional discipline', then the latter is a mode of 'generalised surveillance' which goes beyond the reductive logic of sovereign power to a mode of power which strengthens social forces by increasing production, developing economy, spreading education, raising the level of public morality, and more generally increasing and multiplying social forces and capacities (Foucault, 1977: 207–11). While the penitentiary model expands throughout the nineteenth century (spiralling through the hospital, the Magdalen penitentiary, the industrial school, the reformatory), so the disciplinary technologies are dispersed as they emerge from the penitentiary environment with its massive and compact disciplines, establishing a mobile and flexible mode of control (Foucault, 1977: 294–8). While operating with various purposes, some religious (pastoral care), some economic (the workhouse test) and some political (public assistance), the disciplines gradually become coextensive with the social (Foucault, 1977: 211–12). The panoptic principles of 'observing hierarchy' and 'normalising judgement' come together as a regime of practices which 'manifests the subjection of those who are perceived as objects and the objectification of those who are subjected' (Foucault, 1977: 184–5). Normalising power envelops the individual and the population alike; nothing is wasted, there is no outside, and everything is saved by the technicians and engineers of conduct: judges, teachers, supervisors, officers and parents (Foucault, 1977: 294–302).

Foucault suggests that the boundary between disciplinary power and biopower, or what I have been calling the penitentiary model and the social model, was gradually effaced as normalising power was diffused, 'placing over the slightest illegality, irregularity, deviation or anomaly, the threat of delinquency' (1977: 297). A carefully balanced technical relation was established through a proliferation of institutional supports and methods, from the growth of auxiliary services (dispensaries, hospitals and schools) to the fields of expertise dedicated to educating, treating, training and correcting. Foucault's carceral archipelago stretches from the prison to the family via the hospital, the school and the factory, on one side dealing with transgressions which violate the law and warrant incarceration, and on the other side correcting petty departures from the norm. Domains of crime, sin and bad conduct, which had previously existed as separate orders, are gradually brought together as a single governable relation, and Foucault concludes that it is possible to speak meaningfully about 'the universality of the carceral' (1977: 303). In this sense the figures of the pauper and the vagabond can be conceptualised as a discursive surface for the inscription of the abnormal and the articulation of normalising techniques: nodal points in the constitution of Society.

In the remainder of this chapter I want to look at a programmatic statement which organises this machinery into a systematic whole: the great social scheme of General William Booth. What links Bentham's vision to Booth's is the dream of the perfectly ordered Society. The relation between them, which spans an entire century, is not one of law-bound determination but rather a heaving, swaying, swirling field of forces and relations which is never wholly random but also never the product of design. Among the conditions of possibility for the Booth scheme (and the project of Society itself) is Bentham's plan for the management of pauperism. By no means does this assume that Bentham is the author of Society. The claim being made is both more modest and more ambitious: it is to suggest that Bentham*ism*, which includes such things as the poverty–indigence distinction, aspects of the amended poor law, and the interventions of people such as Edwin Chadwick, Nassau Senior and George Nicholls, helps to assemble a truth regime called Society. What holds the texts of Bentham and Booth together, what brings them into a relation and makes the exercise of comparison meaningful, is the manifold articulations of the pauper–vagabond complex: the many struggles between 'the institutionalists and the boarders out' (O'Connell, 1880), and the various marginal subject positions implicated in the constitution of Society.

General Booth's scheme to rescue Society

Just shy of a century after Bentham formulated his great plan, General William Booth proposed a comprehensive programme of social 'crusades'. Like Bentham, Booth defines the social question as the problem of idle hands,[4] with the growing population of unemployed paupers marking out the 'field of battle' which would bring the school, the home, the street, the tavern, and all places where people associate into the compass of his scheme (Booth, 1890: Appendix: xxxi). Bentham sought to control dangerous mixtures and associations by removing paupers *from* the field of social relations. Booth, however, would take the project of Society itself as his object.

Publishing his scheme in 1890 under the title *In Darkest England and the Way Out*, Booth drew on a range of discourses to formulate his programme, from Darwinism to nationalism to the colonial scramble for Africa. The European conquest of Africa at that time was framed by the notion of discovery and described as a Darwinian struggle for existence, and if the former was a sign of advancing civilisation, the latter was a rationale of ruthless competition among the great powers (see Hochschild, 1999; Kahn, 2001: 35–43; Jacques, 1997). Booth was enchanted by the publications of Henry Morton Stanley, which provided him with the imagery and the logic he would use to construct his scheme. In particular it was Stanley's account of pathological human development in the African forest that caught Booth's eye, and he used it to create a dramatic story of doom and salvation anchored in the authority of science. Like the African 'pygmies', the pauper 'residuum' of England was the product of both an inferior hereditary endowment and a degraded environment:

> This summer the attention of the civilised world has been arrested by the story which Mr. Stanley has told of 'Darkest Africa' and his journeyings across the heart of the Lost Continent. In all that spirited narrative of heroic endeavour, nothing has so much impressed the imagination, as his description of the immense forest . . . The intrepid explorer, in his own phrase, 'marched, tore, ploughed, and cut his way for one hundred and sixty days through this inner womb of the tropical forest'. The mind of man with difficulty endeavours to realise this immensity of wooded wilderness . . . where the rays never penetrate, where in the dark, dank air, filled with the steam of the heated morass, human beings dwarfed into pygmies and brutalised into cannibals lurk and live and die . . . As there is a darkest Africa is there not also a Darkest England? Civilisation, which can breed its own barbarians, does it not also breed its own pygmies? May we not find . . . within a stones throw of our Cathedrals and palaces similar horrors to those which Stanley has found existing in the great Equatorial forest? (Booth, 1890: 9–12)

Stanley's pygmies were organised into two classes: the first a 'very degraded specimen . . . more nearly approaching the baboon than was supposed to be possible', and the second a 'very handsome' type with open, innocent features. Aligning these to the pauper residuum, the human baboon and the handsome dwarf became two modes of arrested development, respectively the animal and the infantile, with their correlates in Victorian England the 'vicious lazy lout' and the 'toiling slave' (Booth, 1890: 11–12). On one level this is simply a reconstruction of the long-established distinction between the deserving and undeserving poor. Yet the interventions envisioned by Booth moved to a new degree of density and intensity, going well beyond those provided for under the poor laws.

By the end of the nineteenth century the Darwinian struggle for existence (which should actually be attributed to Spencer) had become an axiom of the human sciences (see Huxley, 1898). However, this reached its limit in the project of Society, for if the negative effects of competition broke the bounds of the slums and infected the wider society then all might find themselves in a Hobbesian state of nature. For vicious, lazy louts and toiling slaves alike, the 'world is all slum'; a desperate existence where 'the savages of civilisation lurk and breed' and where the workhouse was an intermediate purgatory before the grave (Booth, 1890: 12, 156). The poor law was emblematic of the failure to secure good order through minimal government intervention and an over-reliance on market forces, with the state accepting responsibility for the maintenance of the destitute by imposing conditions on relief that Booth considered impossible to meet. Nowhere was this more evident than in the application of the workhouse labour test in the casual ward.[5] The stipulation that casuals be subjected to a demanding quantity of oakum picking or stone breaking before being allowed to leave the workhouse prevented them for seeking work and escaping their condition of indigence (Booth, 1890: 67–72). Not only did the workhouse preserve the pauperism it was intended to deter, it also increased it. To counter these regressive trends it was necessary to organise rescue expeditions such as the Salvation Army slum brigades, with 'slum sisters' working at the front line at close quarters with the 'enemy', living in the same kind of hovels as the poor and sharing 'an equal plane of poverty' (Booth, 1890: 158–9). Booth's Army was to be as 'indomitable as Stanley' himself.

The nature of the social problem continued to be defined by the poverty–pauper distinction, and Booth paid homage to the 'decent working people who are poor indeed, but who keep their feet, who have not yet fallen, and who help themselves and help each other' (Booth, 1890: 207). This group was the bedrock above the 'submerged tenth',[6] and was not to be lost sight of in dealing with the residuum. For Booth the instruments of state and those of philanthropy were equally inadequate, with the existing schemes reaching only the thrifty, the industrious, the sober and the thoughtful, or 'the aristocracy of the miserable', and missing the improvident, the lazy, the vicious and the criminal. To counter this required 'a social lifeboat institution' so as to 'snatch from the abyss those who, if left to themselves, will perish as miserably as the crew of a ship that founders in mid-ocean' (Booth, 1890: 43). All existing modes of assistance and relief caused, exacerbated or failed to address the problem of the residuum. Trade unions came closest to meeting with Booth's approval, yet while they succeeded in banding people together in voluntary organisations, 'created and administered by themselves for the protection of their own interests', they also failed to accomplish the kind of unity envisioned by Booth (Booth, 1890: 77–8). The social question demanded an answer in the form of a truly encompassing scheme, and it was with this object in mind that Booth proposed his 'new message of temporal salvation'. His scheme would encompass each and all, and there would be no disorderly residue.

Booth's objective was simultaneously to modify defective individuals and improve ineffective social structures. In this sense his critique of political economy was not a refutation of market principles; on the contrary, these were accepted as invariable laws. Instead Booth's scheme set about harnessing the economy to social ends,[7] which would require the 'reformation of human nature in every form which its depravity can assume' (Booth, 1890: 73, 78). The problem then was not the capitalist mode of production itself but the way it impacted on the poor, and one of the crucial tasks facing the social reformer was to facilitate every labourer in becoming his own capitalist (Booth, 1890: 229). In the game of temporal salvation no assistance would be given without a return by way of labour, and there was to be no place for idlers in Booth's scheme (Booth, 1890: 271–2). A solution to the social question required that all 'out of works' submit unquestioningly to the discipline of organised labour schemes (Booth, 1890: 38–9).

Order was to be secured by creating prudent and self-governing individuals. Here the subject of liberal government is transformed, or perhaps it is more accurate to suggest that a shift in emphasis occurs. The individual and the family were now to be *subjected to Society* as a unified order with a definite purpose. This type of order could not be built on consent alone. What was needed was authority, and the lesson from the French Republic was that the ideals of liberty, equality and fraternity could not be attained without iron discipline in the ranks, stretching from the highest to the lowest. The 'motive power' which had fuelled the French Revolution would have ended in disaster if 'the instinct of the nation' had not tempered the doctrine of the rights of man (Booth, 1890: 230–1). As a functionally integrated division of labour, the social body was to be governed not by democracy but by a central 'directing brain' (Booth, 1890: 232). Booth's little cooperative commonwealth would be built on principles of obedience, discipline and rank, so that within the associational logic of his scheme lurks the shadow of sovereign power, its governing principle one of (voluntary) subjection to an absolute authority (Booth, 1890: 242). While communistic experiments were doomed to fail because of their utopian commitment to equality, Booth's commonwealth would succeed because it would reflect the assertion that:

[T]he fittest ought to rule, and it will provide for the fittest being selected, and having got them at the top, will insist on universal and unquestioning obedience from those at the bottom. If anyone does not like to work for his rations and submit to the orders of his superior Officers he can leave. There is no compulsion on him to stay. The world is wide, and outside the confines of our Colony and the operations of our Corps my authority does not extend ... There cannot be a greater mistake in this world than to imagine that men object to being governed. They like to be governed, provided that the governor ... is prompt to hear and ready to see and recognise all that is vital to the interests of the commonwealth. (Booth, 1890: 232)

Membership in Booth's commonwealth would be voluntary and dissenters could leave if they so wished, but for those who stayed there would be no room to question or challenge authority. Booth's commonwealth was beginning to look like an 'organic' authoritarian state, and as we shall see shortly, its boundaries would become increasingly solid.

The scheme hinged on the reformation of the residuum into 'self-helping and self-sustaining communities, each a cooperative society, or patriarchal family' (Booth, 1890: 91).[8] The Boothean state would be an integrated system, beginning with city colonies where the travelling hospital, slum sisters, prison-gate brigades, inebriate homes, rescue homes and refuges, preventative homes, industrial schools, asylums and labour bureaus would gather up criminals, drunkards, fallen women and street children. This residuum would be moved to the city factories and on to the farm colonies via model suburban villages. In the farm colonies they would be set to work in industrial and agricultural villages and cooperative farms. In turn the city and farm colonies would be transit points to the overseas colonies, where the scheme would continue to colonise space and time as it extended toward the future:

The Scheme, in its entirety, may aptly be compared to a Great Machine, foundational in the lowest slums ... drawing into its embrace the depraved and destitute of all classes; receiving thieves, harlots, paupers, drunkards, prodigals, all alike, on the simple conditions of their being willing to work and to conform to discipline. Drawing up these poor outcasts, reforming them, and creating in them habits of industry, honesty, and truth ... Forwarding them from the City to the Country, and there continuing the process of regeneration, and then pouring them forth onto the virgin soils that await their coming in other lands, keeping hold of them with a strong government, and yet making them free men and women. (Booth, 1890: 93)

The visual depiction of Booth's scheme (figure 4.2) exhibits an unmistakable imprint of the panopticon, with Bentham's scientific table of

Figure 4.2 General William Booth's *Darkest England*

hands now translated into a visual narrative: a canvas designed to win hearts and minds. It is worth noting that Bentham also looked beyond the relief of indigence to the possibility of general social progress:

> This plan is not a plan for a day – it looks onwards to the very end of earthly time . . . sooner or later the yet vacant lands in the country will have been filled with culture and population. At that remote but surely not ideal period the Company will have turned its thoughts to colonisation: and the rising strength of these its hives, will by art, as in other hives by nature, have been educated for swarming. (cited in Poynter, 1969: 123)

As with Bentham's plan for the management of pauperism, Booth's scheme was as boundless as empire. Expansion should be planned for, even hoped for rather than simply emerge as an *ad hoc* response to population pressure. In Booth's lithograph we find the heterogeneous elements of the social question gathered into a unified ensemble with a *single purpose*: progress and perfection.[9] At the bottom of the image we see a depiction of chaos and darkness, with the many categories of evil and misery described as an amorphous and unordered mass of swirling elements. As we read from bottom to top we also move from the present to the future, with the panoptic inspection tower now a lighthouse that brings everything under its gaze while lighting the way into the future. The panoptic eye transforms chaos into order, social regression into evolutionary progress, and pain and privation into opulence and plenitude. The beacon is not simply a mode of surveillance but an apparatus of Enlightenment, and as it embraces the chaotic residuum it lifts it up, its left and right arms transforming the quagmire of human misery into an orderly table of problems to be addressed, statistics to be analysed, and curative measures to be implemented. As each element is moved from the abyss into the realm of Society, so it is given its place in the system of knowledge and practice.

As we read this visual narrative we move from the darkness of the present, through a transitional stage of ordering, and onto an ordered utopia marked out by well-defined roadways and passageways into the future. Bounding the whole are the symbols of mathematical precision and scientific control: column and archway. Combining solid foundations, permanent structure, straight lines and right angles, the structure banishes ambivalence, while statistics – the sign of facticity and impartiality – are inscribed on the pillars, immortalising the social problems which are to become nothing but a memory in this perfectly ordered world (see Bauman, 1991; Harvey, 1990). And here we find the normativity of the scheme, with the symbol of the directing brain enunciating the simple and universalising message: 'work for all'. *Darkest England* amplifies the disciplinary focus of the panopticon, transforming it from a technology of individual bodies into a social technology of populations. While the inspection tower of Bentham's poor-house still remains at the centre of everything, the walls of the pauper panopticon now bound the project of Society itself.

In Booth's vision the panoptic techniques become coextensive with the social. Paupers are to be re-formed at large in the social body, while the Benthamite principles of aggregation, separation and vicinity have become a generalised system of administration. Following the route marked out by Bentham, Booth shows us how Society can be engineered by correcting its defective parts. It was imperative to 'get hold' of the 'denizens of Darkest England':

> You may clothe the drunkard, fill his purse with gold, establish him in a well-furnished home, and in three, or six, or twelve months he will once more be on the Embankment,[10] haunted by delirium tremens, dirty, squalid, and ragged. Hence, in all cases when a man's own character and defects constitute the reasons for his fall, then character must be changed and that conduct altered if any permanent beneficial results are to be attained. (Booth, 1890: 85, 96–7)

The fallen individual must be 'made': made sober if a drunkard, made industrious if idle, made honest if a criminal, made clean if impure, and given the ambition to rise if 'deep down in vice' (Booth, 1890: 85–6).

The salvation of the morally depraved – 'the lost, the outcast, and the disinherited of the world' – was based on achieving the standard of the Cab Horse Charter.[11] Booth explained that every horse drawing a taxicab in London was given three things: shelter for the night, food for its stomach, and work by which it could earn its corn (1890: 19–20). Animal and infantile beings, even if they were deformed and degraded representatives of the human species, could with a little planning and foresight be elevated to the standards that had been attained for the working horse of urban England. Animal standards for human animals marked out by two criteria of entitlement: 'when he is down he is helped up, and 'while he lives he has food, shelter and work'. Booth insisted that the cab horse standard could be attained on 'cab horse terms . . . If you get your fallen fellow on his feet again, docility and discipline will enable you to reach the cab horse ideal.' Docility and discipline could be induced in the grateful individual who is helped from the gutter into Society. This was an enterprise requiring the directing brain to adopt the technique of the horticulturalist: 'You must in some way or other graft upon the man's nature a new nature, which has in it the element of the divine' (Booth, 1890: 45).[12] Even withered supports could be made to bear fruits in the jungle of industrial society. While Booth is not using the term 'welfare' here, we have nonetheless passed from the logic of the poor law with its principle of compulsion to the pastoral logic of the welfare state, a discourse of national unity that would recode the governability of the state–economy–society relation (see Rose, 1996a: 48).

This encompassing scheme, which seeks a useful place for all things, finds its internal limit in a residuum among the residuum, which is the outer limit and the internal margin of Booth's little commonwealth. Importantly this is the moment when the exclusionary logic of the penitentiary re-enters the scheme. The relevant category here is the strange figure of the moral lunatic mentioned earlier. In Booth's scheme the moral lunatic is deemed to be 'incapable of self-government'; a 'residuum of men and women who have, whether from heredity or custom, or hopeless demoralisation, become reprobates':

> men so incorrigibly lazy that no inducement that you can offer will tempt them to work; so eaten up by vice that virtue is abhorrent to them, and so inveterately dishonest that theft to them is a master passion. When a human being has reached that stage, there is only one course that can be rationally pursued. Sorrowfully, but remorselessly, it must be recognised that he has become lunatic, morally demented, incapable of self-government, and that upon him, therefore, must be passed the sentence of permanent seclusion from a world in which he is not fit to be at large. (Booth, 1890: 204)

It would be a 'crime against the race' to allow this class to wander abroad so that they might 'infect their fellows, prey upon society, and multiply their kind' (Booth, 1890: 204–5). While extending compassion to these lesser beings Booth nonetheless insisted that there be an impassable barrier between them and Society which, once crossed, should be re-crossed no more for ever. The reprobate carried 'the contagion of moral leprosy' and if given the chance would produce offspring doomed even before birth 'to inherit the vices and diseased cravings of their unhappy parents' (Booth, 1890: 205). The principle of exclusion is here conjoined with the science of eugenics, with social pathologies cast in the double register of environmental and biological determinants. Moral lunacy was a problem that could only be governed by removing the class from the circuits of association and procreation.[13] As a class among humans they were more than mere weeds, and yet like a weed they must be cut away from the fruits and vegetables and left to die in a state of exclusion (cf. Bauman, 1989, 1991). While Booth agreed that liberty was a universal birthright, he did not shrink from the possibility of extending the principle of permanent exclusion to habitual criminals, drunkards and vagrants (Booth, 1890: 206).

The moral lunatic closes off the possibility of exit from Booth's little cooperative commonwealth. Membership has become permanent and compliance with authority is to be enforced. For those stripped of the ability to reason and classed among the morally insane, there is no possibility of autonomous action or decision, and for the rest there is a regime of absolute obedience. Moral lunacy is an ambivalent category, and can be extended to all who raise their voice and question the unquestionable doctrine of obedience. Excluded from the domain of freedom, this leprous class would not be external to Society; on the contrary, it would be permanently excluded from within and subjected to the prevailing norms. The excluded would not escape the regime of industry, sobriety and religious instruction, and once within the penal settlements they would resign themselves to the disciplinary regime because it had become 'their fate'. We have returned to Foucault's insight that there is no outside to the carceral: 'the delinquent is not outside the law, he is, from the outset, in the law ... in the midst of those mechanisms that transfer the individual imperceptibly from discipline to law, detention to offence' (Foucault, 1977: 301). The constitution of Society does not follow the logic of inclusion and exclusion in the literal sense of unrelated domains. Instead we have a hierarchy which is constructed by defining an 'outside' from *within*, and in this way the horizon of perfectibility called Society bounds itself through its internally constituted margins.

Between Bentham and Booth is more than the expansion of the disciplines. There are also certain ethico-political ideals which invest the project of order with particular meanings. Bentham would have governed *through* a specific type of individual, a subject created within his panoptic machine who would think, talk and act the truth of utilitarianism. In Booth's commonwealth the individual is to be subjected to Society as a corporate subject with a single purpose. At the general level both are examples of the grand narratives associated with modernity: progress and perfection. However, at the level of the particular there are important differences. It is worth noting that Booth – leader of a Christian organisation which takes all of humanity as its flock – argued that it was 'absurd to speak of the colonies as if they were a foreign land'; they were simply pieces of Britain (1890: 144). Booth's commonwealth is built on dangerous principles, principles that were at home in the nationalisms and fascisms of the late nineteenth and early twentieth centuries. Indeed Thomas Huxley, a contemporary of Booth, waged a campaign against the scheme in a series of letters to *The Times* precisely because of its totalitarian impulse (Huxley, 1898). Booth assigned a place to everything and everything would remain in its place, with the only permissible movement of things being the temporal and geographical expansion of the system itself. This was never about social reform as we tend to idealise it today, i.e. social justice and the extension of rights and entitlements to all individuals as beings of equal moral worth. For Booth the social ranks had to be maintained because they could not be transcended without violating natural order. This was imperative not only to preserve God's will, but also to ensure *national* progress. Booth's scheme sets out to correct the balance of social inequity only to the degree that it ensures the security and order of the *nation* (see Malešević, 2002).

The birth and consolidation of Society

In his genealogical works Foucault liked to mark the birth of a regime by identifying the precise moment of its gestation. For example, in his study of the prison he proposed 22 January 1840 – the day the Mettray agricultural reformatory in France opened – as the moment when the disciplinary society was instituted (Foucault, 1977: 293; see also Carpenter, 1968; Garwood, 1853). Polanyi's turn of phrase, 'the origins of our time', which is a looser claim, is perhaps more suitable to this particular study, bearing in mind that we should use it with caution. What we identify as the 'origins of our time' depends very much on the questions we pose. Yet whatever question we ask of our present, it is likely that its conditions of existence were instituted between the texts and contexts of Bentham and Booth, a period that spans the constitution of liberal government and the consolidation of that normative regime we have come to know as (the National) Society.

In Booth's little commonwealth the pastoral expert was to live among the poor, listening, observing, guiding and directing: an agent who induces, coerces or excludes as the individual case requires. Each of his shepherds would be an individual node in a totalising system, each carefully positioned to identify and extricate the wolves among the flock. 'Power belongs to the best informed', Booth tells us, and he goes on to explain that 'at the present there is no central institution, either governmental or otherwise, in this country or any other, which charges itself with the duty of collecting and collating the ideas and conclusions of Social Economy' (Booth, 1890: 227). The social question required that the technicians of order 'compare notes and store information', which in turn necessitated a mode of administration built in the image of the university so that even 'the humblest toiler in the great work of social reform' could avail himself or herself of 'the accumulated experiences of the human race'. Such a system would condense 'the essence of all the best books that have been written' and would utilise all eyes, ears and brains; it would be a 'great index of sociological experiments' (Booth, 1890: 227–8). Booth's scheme builds on the genius of Bentham by stretching the panopticon over the entire field of social relations. Social interventions were to cover all classes of subject, all stages of the life-cycle, and all possible contingencies. Society would be secured through comprehensive planning and expert guidance, the whole steered by an uneasy combination of market forces and a central executive. We see here a biopolitical blueprint for the modern welfare state.

Examined as programmatic statements, the visions of Bentham and Booth set about explaining the causes of disorder as each proposes a comprehensive scheme to address it. Bentham identifies the specific causes of indigence so that it could be subjected to rational principles of administration, while Booth looks to a future where the social question has been resolved. The two schemes lie at either end of the nineteenth century, both in their own way concerned with resolving the problem of order. Indeed when viewed chronologically Bentham's table of hands and Booth's rescue scheme read as a narrative, with Bentham's tabular system described as a general map of pauper-land and all roads leading to it, while Booth provides a detailed pictorial map describing the way out of pauperism (figures 4.1 and 4.2). Bentham seeks the original cause of present problems while Booth foresees a future wherein these problems have been resolved: a future where order would no longer pose a problem. In the intervening period we find a series of frictions, negotiations and adjustments within the space of a problematic that would pass beyond the time of Booth to the optimistic stance of T. H. Marshall – the moment used to commence this study. Between Bentham and Booth we have the constitution and institution of an enduring technical-administrative system.

Both programmes exhibit a willingness to sequester conducts and dispositions that pose a threat to the vision of order, and this is the precise moment of *the political*. In both cases this exclusionary moment is wrapped in an authority or combination of authorities – reason, natural law, scientific objectivity – that itself requires no justification. Authority is rendered impartial, it works in the service of order, and it derives its normative force from the notion of progress. The ordering programme moves into the space of the universal and attempts to transcend its contingent conditions of existence, its disavowed political dimension found in the way its rationality, its objects and its techniques – its truth claims – could be otherwise. The programme evades the fact that it is contaminated by possibilities and alternatives which it excludes, and it is for this reason that the programme can be conceptualised as an ethico-political 'decision': the moment when certain ways of thinking and acting are enclosed within a regime of truth, which by default forecloses on alternatives. Yet the authority of the decision always remains vulnerable to its immanent horizon of exclusion (Torfing, 1999: 67–9).

As mentioned above, there is a certain banality to this argument given the centrality of this insight to contemporary discourse. But this is precisely why it is important to be clear on this point, because certain aspects of the nineteenth century are being recollected today even as the claim to the universal is (partially) abandoned. We are currently witnessing the consolidation of a hegemonic discourse that recovers aspects of the nineteenth century, in particular the search for disciplinary techniques to mould the conduct of the incompetent and the recalcitrant so that all are capable of responsible self-government (see chapters 5–8). If we are moving away from the old disciplinary logic of the penitentiary model we are also retrieving the rationalities that originally enabled that model to adapt, endure and expand.

To understand this relation between past and present requires careful attention to detail. While the problem of order links the nineteenth century debates on pauperism to twenty-first-century debates on exclusion and the underclass, the very meaning of 'order' has changed. The politics of order today breaks with the past but also returns to past practices and rationalities, reassembling them in new contexts. Over the last two hundred years we have come to think of power as coercive and concentrated somewhere between capitalism and the state, while the possibility for resistance, for emancipation, for equality is in the hands of a universal subject: the citizen and/or the worker. Even as the universal subject began to fragment into a plurality of struggles waged in the name of feminism, civil rights, environmentalism and anti-imperialism, it also remained the case that repressive and coercive power was perceived to have a place which could be opposed through organised political action (see Newman, 2004). But what happens when the old boundaries delineating the spaces of power and resistance are effaced, when state, market and society are folded one into the other, when the public and the private are indistinguishable, when political subjects are dissolved into a generic consumer?

Today the walls of the penitentiary have been all but demolished (the growth of the prison notwithstanding), yet the logic endures as a mobile region of the social. Like the enclosures which Booth set aside for his reprobates, it is those states of exclusion which are by definition outside of the social order even though they are within. The penitentiary has become a marginalised position or a disadvantaged place – individuals and communities marked out by a certain lack or risk – the absence of employable skills and entrepreneurial dispositions in the case of excluded persons, of inward investment and the requisite quanta of 'social capital' in the case of disadvantaged places. More generally it is an administrative category and an embodied condition: a least eligible situation which excludes certain individuals and micro-populations from the benefits of social life, thus warranting interventions to stimulate, enhance or activate the abilities and dispositions which define the fluid contours and shifting meanings invested in the generic goal of 'inclusion'.

We have recently abandoned the project of Society, shifting instead to the task of stabilising and ordering a fundamentally unstable field of objects, identities and relations. In the remaining chapters of this study I will be attempting to move the reader into position to see how the quest for ordered perfection has been displaced by a mode of ordering which is in essence a management programme. To understand this shift – from governing through Society to inclusive governance – it is necessary to approach the event we are currently living carefully and in detail. The technologies of government born during the nineteenth century were gathered into the discursive fabric of the twentieth century, and it is to this period that we now turn, focusing in detail on the case of Ireland. We will approach the present cautiously and patiently by working across a number of case studies, combing back and forth between past and present several times before proposing a critical reading of the new governmentality.

Part III

From governing through Society to inclusive governance

In this final part, the analytical framework developed above is placed in the context of twentieth-century Ireland and used to examine four specific fields of discourse: nomadism, disability, youth and lone parenting. This is not an attempt at a fully comprehensive analysis of social exclusion. Instead these fields have been selected with a view to mapping a new governmentality, and before commencing I would like to make a few general comments on the historical period covered in this section. Born from a struggle which combined a primordial conception of 'the nation' with a global theme of subjection, the Irish Free State was both a political project and a symbolic space which opposed nationhood to a monolithic power that stood in the way of sovereignty. An example of this mode of representation, and one of central importance for this study, is the Democratic Programme of the first Dáil in 1919:

> The Irish Republic fully realises the necessity of abolishing the odious, degrading and foreign Poor Law system, substituting therefore a sympathetic native scheme for the care of the Nation's aged and infirm who shall not be regarded as a burden but rather entitled to the Nation's gratitude and consideration. (Dáil Éireann, 21 January 1919)

The poor law would help to transform a population into a polity, and an inquiry into the poor laws commissioned by the Free State in 1925 translated the pledge into a programme. I will be using the report of this commission, published in 1927, as a point of insertion into the archive of twentieth-century Ireland, as well as the point of departure in the case studies that follow.

The report of the 1927 commission – one of many such documents examined in the following chapters – is treated as a technology of government, similar to but not quite the same as the programmatic statements of Bentham and Booth. When a specific region of the social is problematised, the technique of the public inquiry secures order by bringing authorities and expertise to bear on the problem, defining its nature, delimiting its boundaries, and fixing its meaning in the fields and orders of discourse. What distinguishes the public inquiry from the enterprises of Bentham and Booth is that in the case of the inquiry we are looking at a type of discursive mechanism intended to secure the governability of an already-existing order. The public inquiry brings the authorities of state and scientific expertise into alignment, simultaneously depoliticising the issue in question and 'scientising' politics (Ashenden, 1996: 81; Bourdieu, 1989). As a technique of government the public inquiry is brought to bear on questions that mark a departure from the state of normality, providing a forum of public accountability, a symbol of openness and objectivity, and a discursive site of 'government in the making': a space where facts and norms are grafted together and codified (Ashenden, 1996).

The First Democratic Programme has not been the only articulation of the theme of domination and emancipation in recent history. Others have been cast in the vein of subaltern studies, attempting to recover the voice of those who have been written out of official histories (Burke, 1987; Prunty, 1998; Kearns, 1997; Finnegan, 2001; Luddy, 1995; Powell, 1992). It is worth recalling Foucault's thoughts on genealogy at this point. Foucault noted that the subjugated knowledges he was using to problematise the present could never be insulated from the possibility of their appropriation:

> After all, is it not perhaps the case that these fragments of genealogies are no sooner brought to light, that the particular elements of the knowledge that one seeks to disinter are no sooner accredited and put into circulation, than they run the risk of re-codification, re-colonisation? In fact, those unitary discourses, which first disqualified and then ignored them when they made their appearance, are, it seems, quite ready now to annex them, to take them back within the fold of their own discourse and to invest them with everything this implies in terms of their effects of knowledge and power. (Foucault, 1980: 86)

To think the relation between domination and emancipation as a passage engendered by political will or scholarly integrity risks overlooking the complexity of 'empowerment', which has its own peculiar politics in linking freedom to discipline and subjectivity to subjection (Cruikshank, 1994, 1999). In this part of the book I will be practising a form of critique derived from Foucault which is neither for nor against the present. At times it may seem that I am opposed to normative programmes designed to empower the marginalised, and to avoid misunderstanding I want to make it clear that I am not opposed to these interventions. But neither am I necessarily for them.

In each of the next four chapters we will see a gradual shift, or rather a series of shifts, from punitive practices of incarceration, assimilation and normalisation to participation within an inclusive mode of governance. Chapter 9 is dedicated to the analysis of this new governmentality.

5

Vagabondage and nomadism

I would put large windows into every cottage as a first step. Light is a severe questioner . . . a thorough system of friendly visiting at unexpected times . . . would gradually exercise a most salutary influence on the homes and habits of the people. (Miss Menella Smedley, 1880)

Introduction: the question of origins

Among the larger Traveller organisations in Ireland are Pavee Point and the Irish Traveller movement, both of which define Travellers as the nomads of Ireland, an indigenous minority, ethnically distinct from the Roma and Sinti of continental Europe, and distinguished from the sedentary ('settled') majority population of Ireland by a shared history, value system and language.[1] Referring back to the theoretical framework set out in part I, I will be analysing the marginality of this social subject (and those discussed in the chapters to follow) as a liminal state: a residue or surplus which is squeezed out from regimes of power/knowledge/practice and a margin that bounds order from within.

One of the popular myths concerning Travellers is that there was no 'problem' prior to the 1960s and 1970s, with Travellers and the settled community living in harmony prior to this. Jane Helleiner has gone some way towards falsifying this sociological framing of Travellers – which assumes a relation of incommensurability between a traditional form of life and a rapidly modernising society – by sourcing documentary evidence of anti-Traveller bias in Galway going back at least as far as the foundation of the Irish Free State (2000: 51–61). However, until Helleiner's research is replicated in other parts of the country it would be erroneous to assume that her findings can be generalised. Also, there is at least some available evidence to suggest that neither the sociological thesis nor the political thesis of early systematic discrimination is entirely correct. For example, a census of 'homeless persons, casuals, and tramps' commissioned by the Irish Free State in 1925 (discussed below) makes no mention of 'tinkers' or 'itinerants' (as the travelling people were then called) as a specific group. Similarly, the records of parliamentary debate make only occasional reference to tinkers or itinerants before the mid-1940s.

In contrast to these two distinctive theses, the point of departure for this chapter will not be to push back an anti-Traveller bias in time so that the scope of culpability is enlarged, or to contrast the traditional with the modern. Instead I will suggest that the relation we need to understand is less that between 'Travellers' and the 'settled community' as historically stable subjects, or between the traditional and the modern as distinct stages of social development, than that between Society and its Others. If 'vagrancy' denotes persons, relations and forces that lack a fixed place in the order of things, Society is a will to order that thrives on the very things it constitutes as a threat. As more people were incorporated into the project of Society through slum-clearance and social housing programmes, through mass education, and through the gradual development of a welfare state, so many of the questions long circumscribed by the pauper–vagabond complex were recast as the 'itinerant problem'. This is not to say that 'tinkers' and 'itinerants' (or indeed 'Travellers') did not exist, and it will help to sketch the representation of 'Gypsies', tinkers and vagabonds during the nineteenth century before moving to the detail of more recent developments in this field.

Prior to the nineteenth century Gypsies were not entirely distinguished from the general itinerant population associated with vagrancy and mendicancy (Helleiner, 2000: 33; Rose, 1988: 3–16). This can be seen from a statute during the reign of Charles I, enacted in 1634/5 and adopted by the Irish Parliament, declaring that:

> All persons delivered out of gaols that beg for their fees, or otherwise travaile begging . . . all such as wandering pretend themselves to be Egyptians, or wander in the habit, form or attire of counterfeit Egyptians – shall be taken adjudged and deemed rogues vagabonds and sturdy beggars, and shall sustain such punishment as [is] appointed by [law]. (cited in Nicholls, 1967: 30)

The law accords with the arts of government and the science of police of the classical epoch. By the nineteenth century there was a clear distinction drawn between those for whom travelling was a way of life and those who tramped in search of employment, and the closing decades of the century saw a number of moveable-dwellings statutes enacted which, together with the enforcement of compulsory school attendance, were part of a systematic effort to settle the mobile populations (Helleiner, 2000: 35; Rose, 1988).

With the emergence of a British Gypsiology movement the figure of the Gypsy became the object of a specific field of expertise. In part a reaction to industrialisation, the Gypsiologists set about documenting and preserving Gypsy folklore, language and custom before it disappeared (Delaney, 2001). By the end of the nineteenth century the Gypsies of England had been Orientalised, their origins tracked to India by an expert gaze that romanticised them as proud and independent persons driven by wanderlust, while at the same time casting them as criminal, treacherous, idle, parasitical and sexually deviant. In the hierarchy established by the Gypsiologists, the Irish 'tinker' was located midway between the pure Oriental Gypsy and the 'half-blood' of the Gypsy/Anglo-Saxon hybrid, while at the very bottom was the common vagrant. The interest in racial purity rendered the lifestyle of the small cohort of 'true Gypsies' acceptable because it was racially determined, while the itinerancy of the other classes was considered to be socially deviant and morally degenerate (Helleiner, 2000: 35–9).

The figure of the tinker also played a role in the Irish literary revival movement. Spearheaded by writers such as Lady Gregory, J. M. Synge and William Butler Yeats, the past became a resource in defining the essence of the Irish nation, with folk tales and epic narratives forming the basis of a cultural nationalism. Representations of tinkers in poetry, plays and prose posited them as the original and authentic forebears of the Irish nation, and yet they were also portrayed as outside of and inferior to the moral community, figures unconstrained by the norms of respectable society and thus a type to be feared (Delaney, 2001; Helleiner, 2000).

This interpretative framework was reproduced in the 1950s when the Irish Folklore Commission set about documenting the tinkers 'before it was too late'. Tinkers were cast as 'one of the oldest classes of Irish society', a living legacy of the original Irish and a repository of authentic Irish traditions. The symbolic function of the genuine tinker retained its other in the form of the vagrant, who, in the mould of the counterfeit Egyptian, was an impostor charged with duping the public into giving alms. In 1955 the folklorist Sean McGrath argued that the vagrant tinker was a 'shame and a disgrace to the genuine tinkers of the country', a viewpoint affirmed by members of Parliament (Helleiner, 2000: 48–9, 63). Gradually the debate moved to a consensus that tinkers had a recent and humble origin, as either the descendants of dispossessed peasants or simply an outcast group. But we have already moved too far and too fast. The point to be taken from this brief survey is that somewhere between the Gypsiologists and the folklorists is an inversion: from the tinker/itinerant as a subset among the mobile classes to the tinker/itinerant as the sign of vagabondage *as such*.

The missing thing: the Poor Law Commission on vagrancy

The first Commission of Inquiry into the Poor Laws in Ireland made no reference to tinkers or itinerants. It was clear, however, that matters concerning vagrancy and mendicancy were of central importance to the proceedings. The principal concern of the Commission was to devise permanent legislation 'for the effective and economical relief of the sick and destitute poor' (including the insane poor), something that required mechanisms to distinguish the deserving from the undeserving. Among the Commission's priorities was the demand for economic efficiency, reflecting the interests of ratepayers in general and the Dublin Board of Guardians in particular. The latter body was concerned with the burden of maintaining 'foreign' paupers, and demanded the introduction of settlement laws in Ireland so that either the mobile poor could be returned to where they had come from or the cost of their relief could be recovered from the ratepayers in the paupers' place of origin.

Given this concern with the wandering poor, the Commission's research into the populations inhabiting the workhouses revealed an unexpected absence. Missing from the disorderly contents of the mixed workhouse was a figure long known to use it as a port of call or shelter of last resort, a figure traditionally subjected to the workhouse labour test: the tramp, casual or night lodger, or as coded in legislation, the vagrant (Ireland, 1927: 17). Research carried out by the Commission found that casuals were occasionally being received in some county homes (the new name for the workhouse), but the number seeking admission was so low that it raised a question as to what might be happening to this class. Stating clearly that 'although this class are not recognised we know they exist', the Garda Siochana (police force) was requested to conduct a census of 'homeless persons observed wandering on the highways in a single night in November 1925'. The results of the census are reproduced in table 5.1.

It is not possible to discern from this information the extent to which, if at all, tinkers/itinerants are enumerated among the general population of 'homeless persons', although it seems reasonable to assume that they

Table 5.1 Number of homeless persons and their dependent women and children, November 1925

Category	Outside Metropolitan area			Metropolitan area		
	Men	**Women**	**Children**	**Men**	**Women**	**Children**
1 **Travelling in search of work**	248	33	44	116	18	–
2 **Willing to undertake casual labour but unfit or unwilling to work continuously**	238	48	58	120	18	–
3 **Habitual tramps**	652	416	614	34	7	–
4 **Old and infirm persons**	150	63	14	13	5	–
5 **Bona-fide pedlars, hawkers, etc.**	141	77	122	7	1	–
Total	*1,429*	*637*	*852*	*290*	*49*	–

Source: **Ireland (1927)**

are likely to have been counted among classes 3 and 5, which together account for 64 per cent of the total. The fact that most people in these sub-categories are from rural society is commensurate with knowledge of the travelling people at this time, and the large numbers of women and children, especially in category 3, would suggest that we are looking at travelling families here rather than individuals. Interesting too is the way in which the question ('homeless persons and their dependent women and children') assumes the adult male as its subject, thus continuing the patriarchal principles of the 1834 poor law. While it would be some time yet before a national 'itinerant problem' was identified, we can none the less keep this table in mind while considering how the wandering poor were classified at this time. In the context of the new Free State, the 'reform' of the poor laws would run counter to the promise of the First Democratic Programme cited in the introduction to this part of the book. Far from replacing the 'odious, degrading and foreign Poor Law system' with a 'sympathetic native scheme', the old model was to be translated into a new context, reinstating the enduring tension between the discipline of the penitentiary and the social disciplines. The promise to expel the dividing practice of the 'foreign and degrading poor law' became an exercise in translation as the poor law unions became the basis of a new county system of administration, outdoor assistance was renamed home assistance, and the workhouse was turned into the county home. The will to order was now in the service of the national interest, yet the same residual categories which had characterised nineteenth-century administration were set to endure. This is clearly visible in the census above, which distinguishes between the impotent poor, the involuntarily idle and the habitual wanderer. It is the last class that poses a threat to order, and we will see this become a distinction that separates the 'itinerant' from the mythical 'real' tinker. In general terms there has never been a call for sanctions against the 'real' tinker/itinerant/Traveller. It is the dangerous vagabond posing as the real thing who is to be punished, 'absorbed' or otherwise normalised.

Unity and distinction: the discourse of contagion

The French semiologist Roland Barthes once explained that he did not wish to '*arrange* the uncertainties or contradictions of the past' in order to give retrospective unity to his writings (Barthes, 1985: 26, original emphasis). In an explicitly postmodern gesture, Barthes refused the modern impulse to order the orderable and to interpret the present as the unfolding of some metaphysical force of necessity. The discursive construction of 'Ireland', however, has entailed precisely the sort of retroactive ordering that Barthes is suspicious of, with the labour invested in tracing out the origins of itinerants part of the search to uncover the essence of the Irish nation. Tinkers and itinerants became a living link to the past, with the relation between the 'settled' community and the nomadic minority framed as a paternal relation between moderns and their primitive kin. Itinerants were fixed in past time, were studied as an artefact and, having served their archaeological purpose, were to be subjected to modernising influences. Tinkers and itinerants are the 'true' Irish while at the same time posing a threat to the nation: a symbol of national origins while at the same time denied a history of their own (MacLaughlin, 1995; Mac Gréil, 1996; Helleiner, 2000; Delaney, 2003; Acton, 1994). In the account that follows there will be no attempt to interpret or represent actually existing Traveller life, culture or history. Instead the objective is to trace out a process of formation as Society is constituted against a constellation of counter-norms which are symbolically framed by the signifying complex 'tinker–itinerant–Traveller'.

The theme of contagion has been central to this process, a pervasive theme during the nineteenth century and generally split into a biological dimension (infectious diseases) and a 'moral' dimension (undesirable habits and dangerous relations). Rogues, vagabonds and 'sturdy beggars' have long played the role of social bacterium in the narratives of contagion. During the nineteenth century typhus was among the most feared of infectious diseases, and an epidemic in England around the time of the Irish famine saw the emigrant Irish identified as the cause of the disease, while in the context of race theory the Irish gained the reputation of being an infectious race (Rose, 1988).[2] Among the domestic population, moral and biological contagion was associated with the tenement slums, and from the perspective of 'respectable society' vagrants and pauperised slum-dwellers were largely indistinct, the difference a matter of whether their presence was confined to the slums or not. As the labouring classes were ordered into the nation-building project through slum clearance, social housing, public health, compulsory education and new forms of social assistance and benefits, so vagrancy was gradually emptied of its internal complexity. Over time it was the 'roving wrong-doer' – a term used to describe itinerants in Northern Ireland in the 1960s – that came to signify contagion. We can trace out the contours of this displacement by looking at the discourse of public health.

Tuberculosis was one of the main illnesses targeted for eradication by the public health authorities of the Irish Free State, and as the war on TB gained momentum during the 1940s there was a concerted effort to medicalise the disease by demolishing its 'moral' meanings associated with inferior disposition and questionable character on the part of slum-dwelling families. An editorial in the *Irish Press* in 1949, for example, pointed to the practical difficulty of dealing with TB as long as people refused to attend sanatoriums because of the stigma attached to the disease (*Irish Press*, 1949). The *Press* argued that susceptibility to TB was not a reflection of character or class, so that all people must learn to trust in medicine and curative treatment. In the context of nation-building, TB was recast as a disease that anyone could contract, and it would be conquered by a science that would benefit all irrespective of status.

By the 1950s the National BCG Committee, responsible for anti-TB inoculation, was waging a propaganda campaign on two fronts. On the one hand it set about educating the public to avail themselves of state medicine, and on the other it aimed to falsify the representation of the Irish as an infectious race. In 1953 the Committee explained that young emigrants from the rural West of Ireland were 'the most vulnerable section of our population' and, due to their lack of resistance to infection, were prone to 'invasion by the tubercle bacillus' (NBCGC, 1953:

4–5). By 1954 the Committee was able to 'take pride' in the fact that it was in a position once and for all:

[T]o refute the theory so often expressed abroad that the Irish as a race are tuberculous and are frequently responsible for spreading the disease when they emigrate ... there has been a complete reversal of medical opinion, particularly in England, concerning the hazards of the young Irish emigrant. (NBCGC, 1954: 4–5)

The problem was no longer one of shunning the Irish emigrant 'for fear of contracting TB from him', but of ensuring that the emigrant did not contract the disease 'in the urbanised surroundings to which he has come, uninfected and unprotected' (NBCGC, 1954: 4–5). By the following year the Committee had coded the Irish 'innocent abroad' as a 'tuberculin-negative subject' and a 'negative reactor', a diagnosis confirmed by Dr Barnett Stross, an English MP for Stoke-on-Trent, who apologised in the Commons for having 'misunderstood the problem' of the Irish immigrant (NBCGC, 1955: 4). By 1956 this was all more or less given, and the Committee's annual report referred simply to 'our peculiar "Celtic" predisposition for the disease' (NBCGC, 1956: 3).[3]

Shifting to a separate though related region of this discourse, a Public Health Bill published in 1945 incorporated venereal disease (VD) into the code of infectious diseases and proposed to make it a criminal offence if an infectious person or the guardian of an infectious person failed to make provisions to quarantine the disease (Barrington, 1987: 168–72).[4] Ireland was the last country in Western Europe where louse-borne typhus was still endemic, and the powers of arrest being sought were primarily aimed at prostitutes and itinerants. Each represented one half of the contagion problematic, the moral and the biological respectively, and while VD necessitated the control of prostitution it was the 'mobile tinkers' who were suspected of spreading typhus, a concern which saw the 'itinerant class' identified explicitly as a 'menace to the community'.[5] Even as the National Society was consolidated through the discourse of public medicine, so there was a process of internal separation as prostitutes and itinerants were defined as social bacteria posing an internal threat to the moral and physical health of 'the' people. While in this instance itinerants were coded as a biological threat, the problem of itinerancy never drifted too far from the 'moral' meanings associated with contagion. In England it was the Irish emigrant *as such* that was associated with the problem of vagabondage, but the Irish emigrant could be redeemed by slicing off a segment of 'the people' and sacrificing itinerants to the national interest. The first

Commission on Itinerancy established in 1960 played a part in doing just this.

A. D. McDonald, secretary of the Commission, wrote to the town clerk in Birmingham during December of 1961, inquiring about a report in *The Times* which apparently held 'the Irish tinker class' responsible for rendering 'whole neighbourhoods uninhabitable'. In his reply the town clerk apologised for the paucity of information he had at his disposal, explaining that he was aware that immigrants from the West Indies, India, Pakistan and Ireland had settled in certain areas of the city, and because they were apparently willing to live in overcrowded conditions they tended to depreciate those areas. However, he did not refer to an 'Irish tinker class'. Instead his referent was a generic Irish immigrant, and he wrote that 'I have never heard it suggested . . . that there are large numbers of Irish "tinker" families although I think it is common knowledge that a considerable number of Irish immigrants have come to this country' (Ireland, 1963a: 161). The Commission wrote back nineteen months later, drawing attention to new reports from *The Times* and the *Guardian* concerning 'Irish tinkers' in Birmingham. On this occasion the town clerk consulted with the local medical officer and confirmed that there had indeed been a 'considerable influx of Irish "tinkers" into the Sparkbrook area of Birmingham'. Further to this he noted that 'many of the landlords of the houses in which the Irish tinkers are residing are Pakistanis and some of them have complained that their lodgers are destructive and unsatisfactory in regard to the payment of rent' (Ireland, 1963a: 162). By the second half of this second letter the scare quotes were removed and a distinction had been made between a generic (i.e. normal) Irish emigrant and those of the tinker class. Indeed the clerk began to use the tautological label of 'itinerant tinkers', while also placing tinkers at the bottom of a hierarchy among immigrant groups associated with depreciating property.

The second article cited by the Commission did in fact report specifically on Irish tinkers in Birmingham (*The Times*, 1963), but the first one, which initially caught the Commission's attention, was concerned with 'the Irish immigrant population' as a whole (*The Times*, 1961). In this report the Irish were divided into three strata: the 'top group who settle down and are well liked'; the 'second group' who 'settle down but take little interest in the cleanliness of their homes or keeping their children under control'; and the 'third group of the gypsy or tinker class who tend to make whole neighbourhoods uninhabitable'.[6] Notwithstanding this mention of tinkers, the piece had more to say about the 'deserted mothers' and the 'motley assembly of youths and men' who were arriving from Ireland to the UK with 'no job, little or no prospect of a job

and with no real desire to do any work when they get here'. If Irish
tinkers were cause for concern, then so too were all Irish men and
women travelling to England to avail themselves of the 'better national
assistance benefits', and in particular those who were destined to fall
into prostitution and crime. In the UK the problem of the Irish was
framed as a question of public order and social security, but the way
the problem was actually phrased was of crucial importance: a minority
of Irish immigrants were (to paraphrase) 'blackening the reputation of
the larger numbers of decent Irish people'.

During this correspondence the concerns of the Commission appear
to be impartial as they seek information regarding their object of inquiry:
means of livelihood, migration patterns and such. Yet something
more takes place as their interlocutor in Birmingham is *persuaded* of
the distinction *within* the category of Irish immigrant. Of course this
is but a segment of a more complex issue. The Irish Commissioners
are responding to news reports, which in turn are representations of
local social relations. But we can none the less see how a distinction
is created in defending the reputation of the Irish abroad. Even as a
programme to absorb itinerants into Society was inaugurated within
the space of the Irish state (see below), so they were segregated and
sacrificed to redeem the reputation of the Irish abroad. And this helps
to constitute the very distinction which defines the problem in need of
a solution.

As parliamentary secretary to the minister for justice at this time,
Charles Haughey spoke before the Commission on Itinerancy at its
inaugural meeting. When Haughey defined the object of inquiry as the
'presence of itinerants', he also provided the Commission with a predetermined conclusion to its work when he stated that 'there can be no
final solution of the problems created by itinerants until they are
absorbed into the general community'. The end defined the means and
was justified by the alleged need to 'reduce to a minimum the disadvantages to themselves and to the community resulting from their itinerant
habits' (Ireland, 1963a: 110–11). This was no dialogic process; judgement had already been passed, and the inquiry was simply charged with
the task of initiating a programme of assimilation. While it would be an
'onerous task', the project of absorption would be guided by the enlightened ideal of humane treatment. In the background to all this lurks a
larger strategy, however, one that awards itinerants a semio-political
function in the orders of discourse:

> You will bear in mind that our itinerants have no respect for the Border
> and pass back and forward as they see fit . . . It will be of interest to

establish why the itinerant population here has been steadily going up while the itinerant population in the Six Counties has been steadily going down. Can it be that, on the whole, life is more pleasant in this part of the country? (Ireland, 1963a: 111)

Tracing the movements of the itinerant population would provide a comparison between the twenty-six counties and its recalcitrant off-spring in the North. The nation-building project was in fact a race, and there was everything to gain if those who resided in the North could be convinced that they were lagging behind: prosperity would act as a powerful persuader. The register of 'absorption' was more than a programme of assimilation; the southward movement of itinerants (a wishful fallacy as it transpired) might also be a vote of confidence on the part of a minority who (apparently) had no political affiliation – an auspicious sign of impending national unity.

The Commission thus constructed the 'itinerant problem' in terms of three interrelated dimensions, with all three articulating the project of national unity. The first was the project of constructing the National Society as a homogenous entity with no disorderly residue of vagabond-age, pauperism and immorality. This was the problem of an anomalous 'presence' within the body of the nation, a threat to good order which had to be 'absorbed'. The second concerned the dominant symbol of national division – the border separating North and South. The mobility of 'our itinerants' who 'have no respect for the border' was a sign of preference among a people who were by their nature geographically mobile, and thus perfectly suited to pass judgement on the best form of life. Finally, the third and more tacit dimension was implicated in the ongoing project to redeem the reputation of the Irish abroad. This stain was to be removed by displacing the negative meanings of the emigrant onto itinerants. While there is no evidence of intention on the Commission's part, it is precisely the way such unobtrusive gestures define and defend Society by delimiting a margin which is of interest here.

Manifold relationships between insides and outsides, inclusions and exclusions, came into play in constituting Society. Like the vagabond of the nineteenth century, the itinerant in the twentieth century exhibited an excess of freedom and a deficiency of self-discipline. To become a subject of the National Society, the indigenous primitive would have to be 'absorbed' into the present, but there were already limitations imposed on this programme. The 'itinerant problem' denoted an unde-sirable 'presence' within the social body: a contagious threat to national health, welfare and prosperity, but also something which gave discursive form to the project of national unity. Whatever it was that actually existing 'itinerants' were doing, saying or thinking, *itinerancy* had become a resource in the service of nation-building.

The techniques of assimilation: child rescue and rehabilitation

In May of 1931 an anonymous letter was published in the *Irish Times* on the subject of the 'tinker menace'. The letter, signed 'Pro Bono Publico', was titled 'Tinkers' Children':

> It is true that these little children are dirty to the last degree, ignorant of the humblest amenities of civilised life, of all the things that are taught to little children in their national schools, and above all ignorant of God. Their present condition is bad, but what of their future if our only consideration is to rid ourselves of the nuisance of their presence? This is a matter for the State. Surely no Christian government should allow a heathen community to continue unchecked in its country. The only means I see to rid the whole country of the nuisance is to take the children, from two years and upwards, from all vagrant tinker camps, and to place them in nursery homes, where they will be taught and trained in all those social and moral principles which go to the making of decent citizens . . . After school age the girls should get a course of domestic training to equip them for domestic work, and the boys at fourteen years of age should be passed on to an Industrial School . . . In this way a generation or two should see the last of the 'tinker menace' and in its stead our farmers and householders would have at their command a supply of well trained and efficient workers. (Pro Bono Publico, 1931)

The letter presents Society as a hierarchical order of essences, its author envisioning a regime where the authorities of state, church and philanthropy work in concert to eradicate the primitive tinker population. The proposed technique – essentially eugenic in orientation – aims for a total separation between adults and children, with the latter perceived as empty vessels to be filled with the values and habits of 'decent citizens' and 'efficient workers'. Nazi Germany provides the most extreme example here, with the Roma one of two groups soon to be targeted for extermination on racial grounds. Less well known perhaps is the case of Sweden, where, even as Pro Bono Publico penned his or her letter, a group known as Tattare (Travellers) came under the gaze of an emerging eugenics regime organised around the practice of sterilisation (Broberg and Tydén, 1996). And the type of intervention proposed by Pro Bono Publico was already being implemented in Australia with the complicity of the religious orders, with Aboriginal children removed from their natural parents under the White Australia programme through a mixture of persuasion and coercion (Bird, 1998).[7] While there would be further calls for interventions of this kind in Ireland (Helleiner, 2000: 71), the dominant techniques of normalisation would combine the themes of 'rehabilitation' and 'settlement', both articulated by the logic of child rescue. We need to be careful in approaching the meaning of 'child' in this field of discourse, however, for it is entangled in theories of primitivism.

During the 1950s the terms 'tinker', 'itinerant', 'travelling' and 'vagrancy' were used interchangeably,[8] with the theme of child rescue threading them together. During July of 1951, the minister for justice was asked if he was aware 'of the loss and inconvenience caused to farmers and rural dwellers by travelling tinkers and other itinerant dealers'. The minister replied that he was aware 'that vagrants are a source of annoyance and loss to farmers', but explained that he held out no prospect of 'a satisfactory system of control'. James Dillon intervened by proposing that Garda authorities be instructed not to allow itinerants to camp on trunk roads 'lest their children be knocked down by passing motorists'. The justice minister agreed, stating that 'I think the protection of children is necessary', with the exchange concluded by deferring the matter to the Gardai.[9] The regulation of itinerancy was not a question of a punitive state or a repressive law singling out a particular group. Saving children was non-partisan – normatively desirable and politically neutral – it operated on the plane of the universal moral good.

A later report in the *Connacht Tribune* shows how the theme of child rescue came to articulate the assimilatory logics of 'absorption' and 'rehabilitation':

> There should be no delay in undertaking the work of rehabilitating the itinerant class. It will, no doubt, be heart-breaking and at times, exasperating work. They will not be willing pupils when it comes to introducing them to the age of the 60s. Nevertheless, work spent saving the life of a child is well spent. (*Connacht Tribune*, 1964)

At stake was not simply the reform of an outmoded form of life, but the saving of innocent lives, a moral action of the first order. But note the movements within this debate: from 'their' children in the case of Dillon to a relation of equivalence between 'a' child and the 'itinerant class' in the *Connacht Tribune* piece. When two itinerant children died in a campfire on the outskirts of Dublin later that year, an editorial in the *Irish Times* explained that 'it is not sound to argue that they know best what is good for them' (*Irish Times*, 1964b). Itinerants were a leftover from history, dependent on the obsolescent trade of tinsmithing, so that if the problem was to be resolved the 'former tinker' had to 'mend his ways instead of his pots and pans'. But this could not be done without external guidance. It was noted that 'the difference between itinerants and the rest of us is the difference between our upbringings', the point being that they could be resocialised, or more specifically, trained, so that it was 'our' responsibility to 'try to the largest extent to which we are capable to see that their children get every chance to become normal citizens' (*Irish Times*, 1964b). This was the positive-panoptic version of Pro Bono Publico's plan: not removing itinerant children but reconstructing the form of life itself.

A certain repetition becomes evident here, something which resonates with the established practices for policing the abnormal. The basis of a liberal order, the rule of law, of liberty itself, is reason. Good order requires that those not in possession of reason or incapable of rational conduct – the hysterical woman, the delinquent child, the criminally insane, the imbecile – be either sequestered in the penitentiary or controlled within the family relation. This is the generic meaning of 'rehabilitation', which seeks to discipline disorderly dispositions, habits and conducts. In the case of itinerants the disciplinary technology employed would not be the workhouse, the penitentiary or the asylum, but the camp, with the theme of child rescue establishing a nodal point in the orders of discourse – a point of convergence – which brought a variety of agents into agreement. As the itinerant population as a whole was infantilised so the possibility for dialogue and dissent was closed off and we again catch a glimpse of the pastoral power of religious authority and the modern state: the obedience demanded by the shepherd, and the discipline exercised over those among the flock who are reprobate. Referring back to General Booth's little cooperative commonwealth, exclusion is effected through the internal colony, with the constitution of Society allowing nothing to escape the grip of the ordering technologies.

Rehabilitation and settlement

In the field of Traveller discourse, what is unsaid is just as important as what is, and just as a Great Silence enveloped the figure of the unmarried mother (see chapter 8), so a Great White Lie surrounded the figure of the itinerant. Those who set about 'rehabilitating' itinerants participated in the myth that, in the long run, assimilation was for their own good. The problem, however, was that while everyone wanted to see itinerants 'settled' nobody wanted to be close enough to see it happen. Itinerants were being pauperised by a modernising Society that knew only one form of life, and yet the reason they were dying young and living in poverty was not because they were being forced to survive within the shrinking margin of an expanding order, but because they either refused to become, or were prevented from becoming, modern subjects. All signs pointed in the same direction. There was unanimity on what to do; the problem was how to do it.

After the 1925 census on homeless persons for the Poor Law Commission, a number of other censuses were undertaken, such as the censuses of 'vagrants camping out' in 1944, 1952 and 1956 (Helleiner, 2000: 59, 61). Notwithstanding these earlier counts, it was the 1960 census by the Commission on Itinerancy that was heralded as 'the first census of itinerants ever taken in the country' (*Irish Times*, 1961a). This might be taken as a sign of heightened interest in the context of the Commission's work. Following comparative international research, the Commission concluded that Holland had made the greatest progress, and a delegation dutifully travelled to Holland to see for themselves how the Dutch were handling 'their itinerant problem', apparently missing the irony of their excursion (Ireland, 1963a: 21–8). News reports on the trip described the 'regional camps' for the 'concentration' of itinerants as a suitable intermediary step on the way to the eventual 'assimilation' of 'the tinker population'. The camps were described as entirely modern and progressive, with electric lights, piped water, chapels and schools all exerting an educative effect so that 'the petty crime and vandalism which we associate with tinkers can be largely eradicated, and a decent and worthwhile life for them can be made' (*Irish Times*, 1961c; *Irish Press*, 1961c; *Irish Times*, 1961d).

The data derived from the 1960 census also provided an answer to Haughey's interest in the southward migration of the Ulster itinerants. Although the 'age of material progress' had made life on the road more difficult:

> It is astonishing to note that the tinker population of the Republic is growing ... The high birth rate, allied to the traditional disinclination of itinerants to work outside of their own world, has enabled this small class to do what the population as a whole cannot achieve – increase itself. (*Irish Times*, 1961d)

While dashing Haughey's hopes, the statistics were also politically loaded in so far as they problematised the very logic of the settlement programme. Even bracketing the fact that not all Travellers want to be housed, that many who do move into houses refuse to relinquish life on the road fully, that is, assuming that the travelling population could be herded into a given number of houses and 'settled', the new data punctured the very rationale of a programme which assumes it is dealing with a dying culture. However, it would be some time yet before the full implications of this were confronted.

In the meantime the settlement programme was taken up by concerned citizens, such as the County Dublin reformer who wrote to the *Irish Times* in 1964 to explain 'how splendid it would be if the problem of the unfortunate tinkers (their true name) was taken up by a group of active Christian people' (Thomas, 1964). The envisioned scheme would see active Christians 'borrow a few acres from young farmers' so that 'willing' tinkers could 'make a start on growing potatoes and cabbage for their own use'. The land itself would remain in the hands of the settlement committee, however, so that 'no squatters rights would arise and evil-doers could be expelled'. Three years later another letter to the *Irish Press* expressed the same impulse but in less sympathetic terms, describing itinerants as being 'without property and trade', 'primitive', 'unable to help themselves' and mired in 'illiteracy, disease, and desperation' (Clarke, 1967). Again it was proposed to establish camps – under conditions acceptable to the settled community – wherein begging and littering would be prohibited, and camping beyond the compound strictly forbidden. The 'nuisance of these people' was to be controlled within the camps by subjecting the inmates to round-the-clock surveillance, to be conducted by volunteers with the assistance of the Gardai. Like criminals on probation, itinerants were to be given the chance to prove their worth under the watchful gaze of their masters, occupying a tenuous position in the social order that was fully revocable. To apply the panoptic principles to itinerants required that they be spatially concentrated, and in the camp we see how the penitentiary can be built without walls. It was clear that the itinerant was not perceived at this time to be capable of responsible self-government, something to which we will return a little later.

A national network of voluntary settlement committees and itinerant welfare organisations subsequently emerged, an organisational structure of spatially dispersed but functionally interrelated nodes resembling Bentham's plan for the management of pauperism. The first was established in Dublin in 1965, and four years later the Irish Council for Itinerant Settlement was formed to coordinate the project and to lobby the government for support (Gmelch and Gmelch, 1974: 2; Gmelch, 1987: 305).[10] The declared goals of the settlement movement were to establish camp sites, to organise education for itinerant children, to encourage regular employment, and to 'educate the public' so that they would accept the presence of the camps (*Irish Times*, 1967d; Helleiner, 2000: 82). The programme of settlement and the technique of the camp combined as a strategy to envelop and sequester conducts and relations that exceeded the instituted regime of power/knowledge/practice: a master plan to secure Society. In the shadow of the strategy was its disavowed political dimension, with order built on the foundation of an internal margin it was constructing, policing and reproducing.

We can see this in the way that the campsites provided a justification for forced eviction: itinerants could be moved on to the camps even when the camps were nowhere to be found. It was argued that because makeshift camps posed the danger of fire and disease, so it was 'for their own good' and for 'the health of their children' that they be moved on (Healy, 1964; Cowan, 1964). The phrase 'moving them on' sounds quite congenial, a bit like the shepherd moving the flock to greener fields, and it masks the violence of the actual act, such as the case in Limerick in 1964 when a force of twenty local authority workers, equipped with two tractors and under the orders of the city engineer, evicted ten itinerant families from waste ground owned by the City Corporation. After two caravans had been towed onto the road the families apparently 'agreed to go peacefully' (*Irish Press*, 1964a).

Between settlement and eviction emerged a new strategy to control the presence of itinerants. A letter published in the *Irish Press* and the *Irish Times* in 1970 captured this succinctly, the author reasoning that 'if we wish to keep our parish clear of the travelling people, we should do so . . . We should first, however, ensure that we do our share of solving the national problem.' Calling for support among residents of his locality, the author explained that 'if we accept [three families] as our contribution to the problem . . . we can gladly evict all other travellers' (Clarke, 1970a, 1970b). This was the 'we have our quota' strategy, discussed in more detail below.

A conflict was brewing: on the one hand an increasingly politicised Traveller identity contesting discrimination and demanding recognition, on the other growing antipathy among residents of housing estates who began to organise against the presence of Travellers beyond what was considered to be the 'normal quota'. But there was also something else. The project of Society was about to be massively problematised.

Conflict and mediation

The theme of 'housing the people' has played a crucially important role in Irish nationalism, particularly after Fianna Fáil entered the parliamentary sphere in 1927 and quickly politicised the continued existence of tenement slums (see Kearns, 1997; Prunty, 1998). By the mid-1980s 'housing' had become a symptom of deep-seated failure, however.

Against the backdrop of the new poverty, with inner-city residential areas being demolished to make way for grant-assisted office development, with the state withdrawing its commitment to social housing, with unemployment and crime burgeoning in inner-city areas, with homelessness on the increase, and with the emergence of a militant tenants' rights movement in the private rented sector, it seemed that the great promise of modernisation was coming apart at the seams. Against this backdrop, Traveller discourse shifted away from the idea that 'itinerants' were simply a remnant of the past to be fast-forwarded into the present. Not only had the number of Travellers grown since Haughey announced his 'final solution'; many Traveller families who had been housed had also gone back on the road (Gmelch, 1987: 307; Helleiner, 2000: 115). There was also growing friction as the tenants and residents of public and private housing estates organised to prevent Travellers from settling in their area. It was in this context of growing instability that Oscar Lewis's (1961) 'culture of poverty' thesis was brought to bear on the Traveller question (see Gmelch, 1987: 306; Helleiner, 2000: 92).[11] Recasting the distinction between Travellers and non-Travellers in cultural terms, the old coercive techniques of assimilation started to give way to facilitative methods of inclusion, with settlement committees calling for 'interim' measures under the guidance of professionals (Helleiner, 2000: 94). We can examine this shift by working outwards from the anti-Traveller strategies of tenant and resident associations.

Sharon Gmelch suggests that for the working classes, many of whom lived on local authority estates at the edge of the cities, the presence of Traveller camps served as a reminder of their hopes for upwards mobility being thwarted (Gmelch, 1987: 307). Given the trend in long-term unemployment at that time, and particularly in view of its impact on unskilled blue-collar workers, this seems plausible. It was also the case that Travellers were moving to urban areas in larger numbers, with a subsequent increase in the number and size of Traveller camps and a rise in the frequency of anti-Traveller protest marches, rent strikes and vigilante attacks (Gmelch, 1987; Helleiner, 2000; MacLaughlin, 1995). One example was the case of Annie Furey in the Shantalla area of Galway city in 1970, a 50-year-old mother of two who had qualified for a local authority house having lived in a condemned property for ten years. When it was announced that the Furey family was to be given tenancy, the Shantalla Residents Association organised a protest and took the local authority to task for 'putting the Shantalla people in this situation'. Six weeks later the number of police assigned to protect the family was doubled as locals rampaged, smashing street lights, lighting fires and stoning the windows of the Furey home. The Shantalla Residents Association finally stood down after the bishop of Galway threw his support behind city officials (*Irish Times*, 1970f; *Irish Press*, 1970d; also Helleiner, 2000: 87–8).

A more protracted confrontation ensued when Galway City Corporation announced a plan to build a Traveller 'village' in Castlegar for twenty families in 1976. The Castlegar Development Association (CDA) quickly mobilised to block the plan. Entering into negotiations with the local authority, the CDA agreed that settling Travellers was a responsibility of the community and each area should do its bit. However, there were already eight Traveller families housed in the area, which was 'four more than normal', and so it was unreasonable to expect the local community to do more (Helleiner, 2000: 93).[12] Resident associations subsequently called on the local council to resign over its handling of the 'itinerant problem', a judgement endorsed by the minister for industry and commerce, who referred to a nearby Traveller camp as an 'industrial embarrassment' when he visited the city in October (Helleiner, 200: 93).[13] The plan was abandoned (although it returned in 1979), with the assistant city manager announcing that he would resume housing Travellers in local authority estates. However, this merely relocated the ensuing conflict, with the Galway branch of the National Association of Tenants Organisations (NATO) losing no time in mounting opposition, arguing that they were being unfairly victimised because they were poor, while residents in private estates were relieved of their share of the burden (Helleiner, 200: 90, 93).

Attempting to mediate in this conflict, the settlement committees concentrated on changing public attitudes towards Travellers. In 1976 Victor Bewley, head of the National Council for Travelling People (formerly the Council for Itinerant Settlement), took local authorities to task for their duplicity, on the one hand officially endorsing the settlement policy, and on the other participating in the 'we have our quota' strategy through an unofficial policy of limiting the numbers of Travellers housed in any single locality (Bewley, 1976a, 1976b).[14] Conflict was particularly acute in Dublin, in no small part owing to the fact that some 25 per cent of Travellers were living in the greater Dublin area by 1981. But this proximity also facilitated political organisation (Gmelch, 1987: 309), and in 1980 a Traveller obtained a court injunction to prevent Dublin County Council from evicting her family from a roadside campsite on the outskirts of the city. When the Supreme Court ruled against the Council's appeal, a precedent was established requiring local authorities to provide suitable accommodation before Travellers could be evicted (Gmelch, 1987: 310).

The number of documented Traveller families increased by over 50 per cent between 1973 and 1979, with nearly half of these families living on the side of the road. More Travellers were dependent on state assistance, the size of the average Traveller family had increased, and less than 50 per cent of Traveller children were attending school regularly (Ireland, 1983a: 3). Even from a strictly administrative perspective (i.e. setting aside the political question) it was becoming clear that the nature of the 'problem' needed to be rethought, and the Travelling People Review Body, established in 1981 by the Department of Environment and Local Government and the Department of Health, was charged with precisely this task. The review body codified an official shift in terminology from 'Itinerant' to 'Traveller' and included three Travellers on its board (the first indication of a shift to inclusive governance in this field of discourse). This also introduced a number of categories, rendering the relation between Travellers and the 'settled' community more complex.

The first of these was the distinction between 'transients', denoting 'traveller families who neither have nor desire a fixed place of abode', and 'non-transients', or 'families who desire a fixed place of abode in a house or on a serviced site, and who in the meantime must, through no fault of their own, move from place to place' (Ireland, 1983a: 4). While intended to recognise differences within the category 'Traveller', the new classification risked reproducing the old distinction between 'real' tinkers and their vagrant counterpart (Ireland, 1983a: 20, 23–32; see also Helleiner, 2000: 123–5). Individual Travellers could *in principle* be given a place in the project of Society, but the 'transient' symbolised trespass, nuisance, drunkenness and criminality, and provided a discursive resource for the continued exclusion of Travellers as a group.

A second distinction was drawn between 'authorised' and 'unauthorised' camping sites. The review body presented this in graphic terms by contrasting pictures of the orderly 'group housing scheme' and the 'authorised service site' with the filth and chaos of 'the unauthorised site' (Ireland, 1983a: 39, 48, 50). On the one hand the Review Body marked a shift towards the recognition of Travellers as a group with the right to preserve and enjoy their own identity and culture. On the other hand a new statement had emerged within this field of discourse. Bearing a strong imprint of Bentham's plan for a system of panopticon poorhouses, the logic of absorption was replaced by a technique to enclose the Traveller population within a system of 'authorised sites'. The authorised site was a panoptic technique built for the electronic age: a system of fixed nodes connected by fluid pathways. It recoded the techniques of rehabilitation and settlement so that Travellers would be fixed in place without preventing them from moving. That they moved and would continue to move was now accepted, and so order would be maintained not by preventing that movement but by directing and channelling it. Travellers would be governed within a space of flows positioned within yet distinct from the National Society.

Travellers were still to be rehabilitated, albeit in such a way that the skills and knowledge imparted to them should be 'appropriate' to their preferred way of life, yet this would also entail re-engineering the Traveller disposition. This is evident from the report of the review body, which noted that 'they have little notion of time and are unaccustomed to following a rigid timetable', and while recommending a degree of flexibility in the training regime, there was an alleged need 'to instil an awareness of the need for time-keeping and discipline' (Ireland, 1983a: 76). In an approach like the rehabilitation of the 'handicapped' at this time (see chapter 6), Travellers were to be incorporated into training programmes – managed by expert 'teams' – with a focus on communication skills, self-esteem and personal development (Gmelch, 1987: 312).

Ruth Barrington, who represented the Department of Health on the Review Body, was one of three members who expressed reservations about the final report. Barrington was specifically concerned with 'the risks to the lives and health of traveller children arising from poor living conditions' (Ireland, 1983a: 115). Maintaining that Traveller children experienced physical disadvantages as a result of life on the road, she called for detailed research in order to 'pinpoint the reasons for any deviation from the standards of health enjoyed by the population as a whole'. Barrington was drawing on research published in the *Journal of the Irish Medical Association*, with titles such as 'retarded brain growth in Irish itinerants' (1974), and 'growth and development in travelling families' (1975), her argument being that 'the shorter the period on the road, the greater is the success with housing', and this in turn would increase the likelihood of Traveller children benefiting from uninterrupted attendance at school (Ireland, 1983a: 115–16). The normative emphasis on health resonated with a lecture given by Joyce Sholdice, from the National Council for Itinerant Settlement, a decade earlier. Sholdice had spoken of 'two separate groups' among the population, and explained that since the Report of the Commission in 1963 'more and more people have become aware of the urgent need to bridge the gap'. It was not simply a question of securing 'a better way of life for the Travellers', but of reducing 'the disadvantages to themselves and to the community resulting from their itinerant habits':

> We have looked for too long at the sins of the fathers and have ignored the distress of the children, forgetting that these parents were once themselves little children, and that they have become what they are, not because they are wicked, but because they have never had the opportunity or the education to be any different. (*Connacht Tribune*, 1973; also cited in Helleiner, 2000: 202–3)

There were intimations of something old and something new here. Sholdice and Barrington were looking out from the normative ideal of Society and offering an invitation. Somewhere between Sholdice's lecture in 1973 and Barrington's comments a decade later, a space had opened out for the inclusion of Travellers, recognising them as equals even as it was made known that they embodied a redundant form of life, an attachment that marginalised and excluded them. To be the opposite of this, i.e. to be included, they must be given the opportunity to be, in Sholdice's words, 'different'. But when Sholdice enunciated 'different' what she meant was 'the same'. To be included in Society, itinerants must be different from themselves: they were to learn to govern themselves in accordance with the norms of the prevailing order.

Managing nomadism

In 1960 a Traveller by the name of Joe Donohoe led a deputation to meet with the Commission on itinerancy in order to express grievances regarding evictions and harassment – the one and only dialogic encounter between the Commission and its object. From then on the Commission decided this type of arrangement made itinerants 'ill at ease' and the exercise was not repeated. Instead the Commission decided to conduct its work through covert surveillance and surprise inspections (Ireland, 1963a: 30–1). Joe Donohoe quickly vanished from the pages of the Commission's report but he was not so easily deleted from social space, and he formed the Itinerant Action Committee with the help of a young English journalist named Grattan Puxon (Gmelch, 1987: 311–13). Supported by a group of university students, the Action Committee picketed the offices of Dublin Corporation and demanded an end to evictions. And following the publication of the Commission's report they organised the first Traveller protest march on the streets of Dublin and presented a petition to the Dáil (lower house of Parliament) demanding the provision of legal camping sites in accordance with the Commission's recommendations. Puxon also established contact with the World Romany Community, and in October 1964 the leader of the organisation together with the head of the Romany Evangelical Church announced their intention to visit Ireland, where they would petition the government on behalf of Irish Travellers (*Irish Times*, 1964a). However, the campaign lost momentum after Puxon was arrested under the Offences against the State Act on a charge of possessing explosives.[15] Although denying the charges, Puxon was forced to return to England and the campaign withered.

It is difficult to find a fitting way to describe the nature of this campaign. The idea of 'resistance' comes to mind, but this is not entirely suitable. I say this because it seems that in the wake of the Commission's work the demands of the settlement movement and Travellers were moving into alignment. The 'problem' of itinerancy had long been articulated in temporal terms: a relation between moderns and primitives. In this interpretative framework there is only one space: Society, so that when the primitives are absorbed into the present there will be only one subject: Society. Modern subject and living space are identical, and that which exceeds it, its surplus, is simply a disorderly residue, an anomaly left over from the past to be mopped up through the disciplinary technologies of the camp and training. Because space is negotiated in temporal terms there is no need to negotiate space in *spatial* terms. Momentarily in the 1960s – much more so by the 1980s – the question characterising this field of discourse was how to manage space *in spatial terms*. The technique of the 'authorised site' was one practical expression of this, albeit one still entangled in the modern apparatus of enclosure and assimilation. However, a change was being instituted as the politics of order was reconfigured.

The struggle for recognition

As noted in the last chapter, the concept of 'decision' can be used to denote the (provisional) outcome of political struggle, with the decision fixing those meanings that have become unstable and stabilising the undecidability of the social field. To be within the realm of the decision is a form of effective agency, capable of directing power relations and creating power resources. If we understand 'consultation' in this way we can understand why Travellers began to demand that they be consulted on programmes relating to settlement and housing (Kilfeather, 1982). If the demand to be included in the realm of decision is to be taken seriously, then what is required is a Foucaultian statement – a candidate in the politics of truth – and in the case of Travellers such a statement was constructed in the form of a Committee for the Rights of Travellers, later becoming Mincéir Misli (Travellers Movement). The organisation lobbied for rights, organised demonstrations and protest marches, informed the media of evictions, hired media consultants to train Travellers on how to handle interviews and present Traveller issues, and sent representatives to local authority and community meetings (Gmelch, 1987: 310f).

A protest march in 1985 saw the organisation tap into the international anti-apartheid movement in calling on the government to 'end the evil of inaction', with the marchers demanding accommodation, health care, and an education that would ensure future prospects and the right to be treated with dignity and respect (*Irish Times*, 1985b). A draft Charter of Travellers' Rights had been presented to government the previous year,[16] which sought to secure the 'recognition of a distinct identity' and 'the right to maintain this identity through following their traditional way of life'. The Charter was based on twelve articles covering general rights as a minority as well as more specific rights to travel and to accommodation compatible with Traveller culture (Gmelch, 1987: 315–16). The trade unions also lent their support, with twenty-one representatives from eight unions publishing a letter in the *Irish Times* denouncing the privations endured by four hundred Traveller families around Dublin, described as 'a state of siege comparable with the black townships of South Africa'. The unions endorsed 'the concept of the Travellers being a distinct cultural group [who] deserve to be treated as such', arguing that 'in the European courts the lifestyle of ethnic groups is protected by law' (McGrath et al., 1985). With the far right gaining ground in Europe, and with immigration fast becoming a volatile issue, questions of 'race', ethnicity and identity moved to the centre of political debate. But the strategy of using identity and ethnicity to lobby for recognition and rights exposed a new fault-line in Traveller discourse.

The Irish State moved to ratify the United Nations Covenant on Civil and Political Rights in 1989, completing a process begun in 1973. To accomplish this it was first necessary to introduce legislation prohibiting incitement to hatred on grounds of 'race', religion, nationality or sexual orientation (eventually carried into Irish law as the Prohibition of Incitement to Hatred Act 1989), and as the Bill made its way through the legislature, the ensuing debate saw questions of ethnicity and identity move to the centre of Traveller discourse (Helleiner, 2000: 228–33; Yeates, 1994). The scope of the Bill extended to 'any group of persons on account of their colour and ethnic or national origins, as well as on grounds of their nationality, race or religion'. Despite its comprehensiveness, it appeared that the Bill failed to encompass Travellers, who became something of an anomaly in the ensuing debate (Helleiner, 2000: 229). The process was initially seen as 'fulfilling international obligations', with the legislation thought to be of little relevance to Ireland. After all, although there was the old problem of 'religious' sectarianism, there was apparently no problem of racial or ethnic prejudice. Some commentators anticipated immigration in the future, and as this might create racial/ethnic tensions it was best to be prepared. It was only when parliamentary deputies in opposition began to press for an amendment to the Bill in the form of a specific reference to Travellers that things became complicated (Helleiner, 2000: 230–4).

The complication arose in relation to the contentious issue of 'ethnicity' (Yeates, 1988; *Irish Times*, 1988b). Some commentators argued that Travellers were an ethnic group because they *had* a separate culture, way of life and language; others spoke of common origins which had *resulted* in these characteristics. The minister of justice evaded and parried on the matter and ultimately refused to clarify whether or not the state considered Travellers to be ethnically distinct, deferring the matter as something for the courts to decide (Helleiner, 2000: 230). Entangled in this question was a whole bundle of essentially contested concepts: ethnicity, race, identity and culture (see Malešević, forthcoming). Niall Crowley from the Dublin Travellers Education and Development Group attempted to clarify the issue by explaining that Travellers should be recognised as an ethnic minority with their own separate culture, history and identity, while ra*cism* was prejudice combined with the power to act on that prejudice (Yeates, 1988). The debate settled on the idea that Travellers had a distinct culture, but the question of ethnicity remained unresolved. At stake was an unsettling encounter with the contingency of collective identities. Long represented as the original and authentic Irish, if Travellers were both different from and the same as the 'settled' Irish, then maybe there was no essential Irishness to speak of. A consensus of sorts was reached by equating 'ethnicity' with minority, or rather a disempowered minority, which derived its meaning from the national identity. The debate demonstrated just how deeply ingrained was the assumption that Travellers were not a people but a supplement to the Nation – a community within the larger National Society. It was this that saw the pragmatic amendment 'membership of the Travelling community' grafted onto the legislation as the basis of legal protection (Helleiner, 2000: 233).

The National Council for Travelling People subsequently split into two organisations over the question of ethnicity, a parting said to have brought 'a long simmering private dispute into the open' (*Irish Times*, 1991a; Cummins, 1991; Yeates, 1994). Traveller organisations have since reached agreement on the question of ethnicity, which is now crucial to their strategy of combating racism through the United Nations

CERD framework (International Convention on the Elimination of All Forms of Racial Discrimination) (Ireland, 2004). The Irish government, however, while conceding the 'cultural identity' of Travellers, maintains that 'Travellers do not constitute a distinct group from the population as a whole in terms of race, colour, descent or national or ethnic origin' (Ireland, 2004: 90). Interesting here is the fact that these frictions and realignments seem to pose little problem for the newly emerging mode of governance.

Inclusion?

Earlier I suggested that under the settlement programme, Travellers were not deemed capable of responsible self-government, and thus were to be subjected to the authority of external controls and disciplines. This has since changed, with Travellers incorporated into social partnership negotiations since 1996,[17] which was the moment when corporatism in Ireland was extended beyond the traditional partners to include a com- munity- and voluntary-sector 'platform' comprised of more than twenty organisations. This followed the *Report of the Task Force on the Travel- ling Community* published the previous year (Ireland, 1995), which played a key role in agreeing a National Traveller Accommodation Strategy codified by the Housing (Traveller Accommodation) Act 1998. Local authorities were now required to prepare a five-year plan for the provi- sion of 'Traveller-specific' accommodation in their area, with the strategy managed by the Department of the Environment and monitored by a National Traveller Accommodation Consultative Group (GTSG, 1999: 13; CWC, 2002a). Further to this, a Traveller Communication Committee was established with financial support from the Department of Justice, Equality and Law Reform. The objective of the Committee, managed jointly by the Irish Traveller Movement, the Parish of the Travelling People, Pavee Point and the National Traveller Women's Forum, was to develop a 'Traveller communication programme', a project that would combine a Citizen Traveller theme and an anti-discrimination theme (figure 5.1; Murphy and McDonagh, 2000: 115–19, 179–204; Ireland, 2002: 12). By the end of the 1990s there were tangible signs that the new inclusive mode of governance was delivering not only greater prosperity (the 'Celtic Tiger' economy) but also greater equality.

Or maybe not. While I will be looking at this in greater detail in chapter 9, here it can be noted that the Citizen Traveller strategy is one example of new contractual technologies of control which have emerged in the context of concerns over 'anti-social' behaviour. The technology of contract aims to draw individuals and groups into the voluntary

Figure 5.1 Citizen Traveller

acceptance of imposed obligations (Crawford, 2003), and in the case of groups – such as Travellers – this requires compliance on the part of the group as a whole. With respect to the Traveller Communications Committee, there seem to have been reservations from the outset on the part of government as to whether a public awareness campaign specifically for Travellers was warranted. With a National Anti-Racism Awareness Programme planned for 2001, it was suggested that 'the Citizen Traveller campaign might get lost within the Anti-Racism campaign' (Ireland, 2002: 11; 2005c). Further to this, when representatives of the Communications Committee met the Taoiseach (prime minister) in November of 2001 to discuss funding, they were asked to consider the issue of anti-social behaviour on the part of Travellers, a concern raised again in a subsequent meeting with officials from the Department of Justice, who informed the Committee that the campaign should be 'two way' (Ireland, 2002: 15–18).

The reference to anti-social behaviour was almost certainly a comment on Traveller encampments along the banks of the Dodder River in the Rathfarnham area of Dublin the previous summer. Media reports on the encampments turned the Citizen Traveller project on its head, with Travellers accused of abusing their rights and reneging on responsibilities:

> The number of jobs that travellers are capable of doing has decreased dramatically over the years . . . A job they have perfected is turning an unspoilt scenic spot into a teeming mass of filth and rubbish overnight. The fact that there's not a demand for this unique service doesn't worry our traveller friends. They do it anyway, out of the goodness of their hearts . . . In a strange twist on normal holiday procedure, they don't settle up the bill or check out at the end of each of these holidays. The opposite is the case with many travellers getting (and demanding) financial remuneration from residents for ending their sojourns . . . Let's get a couple of simple things straight. It's not racist to question the rights of travellers to roam freely and set up camp all over the country . . . and it is not, despite what the wets in the *Irish Times* and RTE[18] say, 'incitement to hatred' to argue they should not be allowed to do what they do. (*Sunday World*, 2001)

The *Sunday World* is a tabloid, and perhaps easily dismissed as a result, yet this type of account was by no means out of step with events then in train, or indeed reports in the broadsheets (see Farragher, 2001; Hennessy, 2001; Ireland, 2002: 13). In fact the subsequent Housing (Miscellaneous Provisions) Act 2002 gave legal force to the sentiments expressed in the *Sunday World* report. Prior to the enactment of this law landowners were obliged to obtain a court order before removing people from their land, but under the terms of the new Act Gardai are empowered to arrest trespassers without a warrant and to confiscate property, including caravans, which in the case of Travellers means their home (Haughey, 2002). Those charged under the Act face a €3,000 fine or three months' imprisonment.

From the point of view of the 1,200 Traveller families on 'unofficial' campsites, the Act effectively overturned the Supreme Court ruling of 1980 which required local authorities to provide alternative sites before evictions could be served. Traveller organisations responded by using the resource of the Citizen Traveller campaign, representing the new legislation as racist and presenting the argument – endorsed by Amnesty International – that it criminalises their way of life (figure 5.2; Love, 2002). Furthermore, as the 2004 deadline for the provision of Traveller-

Suddenly, in caring Ireland, to be a Traveller is a terrible crime.

The racist and unworkable law on trespass criminalises 1200 unaccommodated Traveller families.

Figure 5.2 Resisting the Housing Act

appropriate accommodation approached, there was little indication of any real change materializing; that is, beyond the production of a fiction within the inclusive theatre of Social Partnership. By July 2002 the target of 2,200 serviced halting sites set by the task force had seen only 129 provided by local authorities (CWC, 2002b; Delaney, 2003).

The Housing Act is a statement within the emerging discourse of 'anti-social behaviour', and more specifically a sanction enacted in the name of order. The current minister for justice is drawing up legislation to introduce British-style Anti-Social Behaviour Orders (ASBOs) to Ireland, but this is by no means a party-specific agenda. Chapter 7 considers this issue in more detail. Here I simply want to draw a parallel with developments in Britain, where the Anti-Social Behaviour Act of 2003 extends the offence of aggravated trespass so that it can, in practice, be applied to anyone occupying private property, whether a building or in the open air. In fact the trespass dimension of the legislation seems to be directed specifically at Travellers, ravers and political activists (Padfield, 2004: 723–4).

The minister for justice responded to the final Citizen Traveller poster by commissioning a consultancy firm – Talbot Associates – to conduct a 'value for money' audit of the Traveller public relations project in 2002, after which financial support was withdrawn (Ireland, 2002). Again, as with the contractual mode of discipline used in the Citizen Traveller strategy, the audit is another pervasive technology deployed by inclusive governance, and we will return to both in due course. In announcing the termination of the project, the minister cited the Talbot report in explaining that the campaign 'represented the Traveller perspective exclusively and did not address the concerns of the settled community', concluding that 'Government objectives for Citizen Traveller were unlikely to be met in the future.' In short, irrespective of how Travellers conduct themselves as individuals, the Citizen Traveller campaign failed to modify their conduct as a *group* sufficiently, and we see here the failure of a strategy based on a fixed ethnic identity, a strategy which tends to reify the categories and boundaries of inclusion and exclusion. Travellers are to be empowered, but not as the authors of the message described in figure 5.2. Instead they are to be empowered as the responsibilised subject described in figure 5.1.

It seems that inclusive governance is itself a disciplinary technology. When parents boycotted a rural school in County Galway in 2001 after a number of Traveller children enrolled, a TD (elected representative) for East Galway used the consensual register of inclusion to explain that the situation was difficult for the Department of Education, for the parents, for the school management and for the Traveller families involved in the dispute. While agreeing that every child was entitled to an education, in this *particular* case things 'had not been properly thought out and prepared'. Locals were not saying 'no' to Travellers *per se*, the problem was that the school 'does not have the usual back-up services for the disadvantaged such as remedial teachers' (McDonagh, 2001). Here is the exception which allows for the exercise of 'reasonable prejudice' (Billig et al., 1988: 100–23). It is the special needs of Travellers that provide the means to exclude them, which is not a matter of excluding them but a question of how best to include them. Enveloped by the ordering apparatus of inclusive governance, Travellers appear to have little alternative available other than to use the discourse of exclusion to contest the limitations of inclusive governance.

In the technologies of contract and audit, in the example of reasonable prejudice, and in the discourse of anti-social behaviour we can begin to see an outline of the new governmentality as well as the subject of inclusive governance. Neither has been specified with any degree of precision at this stage of the analysis, as I am deliberately leaving this task until the final chapter. In the meantime I aim to continue tracking the constitution of inclusive governance and mapping some of the constituent features of its subject.

6

Defectiveness and disability

To show his extraordinary knowledge of the subject, he gave me a sheet
of paper, as big as that, with a list of the forms of insanity. I counted them
up, and they were forty in number. 'My dear Sir', I said, 'this will never
do; if you reduce your principles to practice, you will shut up nine-tenths
of the people of England', and so they would. You may depend upon this;
if you ever have special doctors they will shut up people by the score.
(Lord Shaftsbury, cited by Sigerson, 1886)

Introduction: governing disordered minds

It was noted in the last chapter that the Irish Free State partially
reformed the poor laws, changing the name and the function of the
workhouse so that it became a county home for the infirm and the
elderly. The lunatic asylum was similarly recoded by the Local Government Act of 1925, becoming the mental hospital (Ireland, 1927: 99). In
fact the insane poor were housed in both institutions. Patients in the
district mental hospitals were medically certified as dangerous lunatics,
idiots or persons of unsound mind, while the inmates of the county
homes were received 'not by reason of their mental condition but as
persons being eligible for relief' (Ireland, 1927: 101). In this way the
question of disordered and defective minds can be seen to traverse
the fields of law and medicine, establishing a strategic relation between
the authority of state and the authority of science, and yet there is a
certain lack of precision regarding the domain of this complex authority.
In 1965, for example, a Commission on Mental Handicap (discussed
below) traced the categories 'idiot' and 'lunatic' back to the middle ages,
noting that during the nineteenth century 'the term "lunacy" was used
in a variety of ways, sometimes in contradistinction to "idiocy", some-
time including it and frequently in conjunction with the terms "insane"
or "of unsound mind" . . . The fact that the deaf and blind and deaf
mutes were in law presumed to be idiots made for greater confusion'

(Ireland, 1965a: 4). From the point of view of medical expertise and public administration this lack of precision was unacceptable. But it also circumscribed an arena within which a struggle was waged over the meaning of 'mental disorder', a phrase used by the Poor Law Commission in 1927 and still in use during the 1960s (Ireland, 1927: 93; 1965a: 6). From Foucault we can define this arena as a struggle for truth; a struggle articulated by a constellation of actors as they set about governing lunacy and imbecility.

Within the realm of mind the great division concerns the relation between the 'normal', the disordered and the deficient. Entangled in this is the question of difference, which can also be physical, the latter sometimes treated separately, and at other times interpreted as a sign of abnormal mind (see Robins, 1986: 157–9). Difference pertaining to the mind–body complex has long been the sign of the monster: that which threatens but also makes possible the domain of the normal (see Foucault, 2003). In the present we have come to think the distinctions and divisions between disordered and deficient minds and bodies through the language of psychiatric illness and specific (physical, intellectual and sensory) disabilities, though in this chapter I will be moving quite freely between the divisions separating illness and disability, mind and body, rejecting the idea that they have ever been entirely distinct, with the present proving no exception, an example being attention deficit and hyperactivity disorder (ADHD). As a relatively new domain of medical expertise, although by no means a new 'problem', ADHD belies the possibility of any easy distinction between normal and abnormal, illness and impairment, mind and body (see chapter 7). My intention here, as with the case of Travellers, is not to tell the story of the disabled but to examine how this field of discourse is implicated in innovations in both the arts of government and the subject of government.

The Poor Law Commission on mental defectiveness

As the Irish Free State came into existence there were some 36,000 inmates within the penitentiary complex: 700 in nine local prisons, four convict prisons and one borstal; 6,000 in four reformatory schools and fifty-two industrial schools; 11,000 in the county homes; 17,298 in district and auxiliary mental hospitals, private mental hospitals and the criminal lunatic asylum; and 1,000 in the Magdalen asylums (Kilcommins, O'Donnell, O'Sullivan and Vaughan, 2004: 38–9). Close to 50 per cent of this inmate population was interned in some form of mental institution. It is perhaps no surprise, then, that a survey of these institutions by the Poor Law Commission revealed a problem of overcrowding. The Commission also made explicit the strategic function of the mental hospitals by describing them as places of detention. In fact, as noted above, the subject of this discourse is undecidable, simultaneously an 'inmate' and a 'patient'. Those coded as mentally defective were positioned within a regime spanning the prison (criminal lunatic asylum), the workhouse (the county home) and the hospital (public and private), subjected to practices both custodial and curative.

Expressing its concern over the year-by-year increase in the numbers of mentally defective inmates, the Commission identified three possible causes: an increase in life expectancy due to 'medical advances', a related increase in age-related 'mental decay' because people were living longer, and an increase in the rate of detection due to the vigilance of medical professionals. Taken as a whole, it seemed apparent that the inmate population was set to rise; a trend that would exert greater pressure on a system already overstretched. The Commission thus recommended that lunatics, idiots and imbeciles be removed from the county homes altogether so that the institution would be reserved for the aged, the infirm and chronic invalids (Ireland, 1927: 82, 124). However, this would not in itself resolve the problem. A mechanism was also required to distinguish within the population of mental defectives by separating the curable from the incurable. With a proportion of juvenile defectives in the county homes deemed to be educable to some degree, it was recommended that they be trained so as to become independent or to work under supervision (Ireland, 1927: 106). Coupled to this was the idea of extending the practice of boarding out, placing at least some defectives in the care of families (Ireland, 1927: 109).

The pressure to reform the hospitals and homes was also driven by medical professionals as they organised to monopolise this field of discourse. Even as the Poor Law Commission commenced its inquiry in 1925, Lord Birkenhead addressed a meeting of the National Council of Mental Hygiene in London, arguing that the conception of the asylum as an adjunct to the prison was barbarous, out of date, and should be superseded by the 'timely curative treatment' which 'medical men' were striving towards. Dr Donnellan of the Grangegorman Mental Hospital in Dublin made a similar argument before the Poor Law Commission, explaining that there were large numbers of 'feeble-minded' and 'mentally deficient' children who were being left to degenerate and to fill the asylums, citing the example of one 'idiot boy, who was deformed, being taught to use a sewing machine and thereby making himself very useful' (*Irish Times*, 1925a; *Irish Independent*, 1925d).

As the Free State embarked on the great adventure of nation-build-ing, so the ordering technologies continued to vie for position. But they could also work together, with confinement, 'timely curative treatment', and the idea that defectives should be trained to 'make themselves useful' – and here we are close to the Benthamite logic of hands – com-bined within a single apparatus.

Constituting the nation: the defective as 'subject to be dealt with'

The Poor Law Commission was part of a context where a new state was tinkering with an administrative system established during the nine-teenth century. Tinkering is a form of maintenance or repair, and in this case helped to reinstate the old regime of power/knowledge/practice. As part of this process of translation, a public inquiry into the industrial and reformatory school system (also known as the 'certified' schools) was commissioned in 1934.[1] Among its terms of reference was the ques-tion of 'the treatment and/or disposal of children committed to indus-trial schools who are found to be suffering from physical or mental defects' (Ireland, 1936: 4). In its report the Commission confirmed that it had indeed found children in the schools who were 'unsuitable for training' due to 'physical or mental defects', as well as 'children suffer-ing from contagious and infectious diseases'. It was deemed 'undesir-able that mentally defective children, and certainly children in whose cases the degree of mental deficiency is at all marked, should be sent to a certified school' (Ireland, 1936: 35). The Commission wanted a new procedure of compulsory medical examination so that 'physically or mentally abnormal' children would be identified prior to committal and sent to an 'institution specially certified for such cases' (Ireland, 1936: 18). Medical examination and legal judgement were to work together so that if 'a low grade mental defective' came before a court the child could be detained in a 'mental colony'. The same applied to 'the higher type of mental defective', with the Commission noting that 'it is in every way undesirable that [they] be placed with normal children'. The reason, based on a mixture of efficiency and sympathy, was that it was in the interests of all: mental defectives were a burden to their teachers and a handicap to the other children, and because they could not keep up, their own condition tended to worsen (Ireland, 1936: 35). The envi-sioned reforms would cater for both mental and physical defectives and 'would be of such a type that strict classification of cases could be easily accomplished', thus sorting those susceptible to training from the rest. Because the permanent and complete cure of mental defectives was not possible, the task of governing defective minds and bodies required continuous supervision (Ireland, 1936: 36). The Benthamite techniques of examination, aggregation and separation are all in evidence, as is their purpose: to control contagion while transforming the incompetent and recalcitrant into self-governing subjects in the service of the National Society.

Two years after the Commission published its report, Dr Louis Clifford presented a paper to the Statistical and Social Inquiry Society of Ireland on mental defect amongst Dublin children (Clifford, 1939). The findings, based on a survey of 2,000 Dublin children from the north side of the Liffy, suggested a pandemic problem with 21 per cent found to be mentally defective. Clifford's research sought precision within the master category of 'defect', using intelligence scales to distinguish the idiot and the imbecile child from the feeble-minded. Of crucial importance was this last category, with 75 per cent of defectives belonging to this 'grade', some of whom 'presented no stigmata' and might 'pass as ordinary children' (Clifford, 1939: 30). The mark of distinction was 'educability' and a capacity to 'adapt to social conditions' characterised by competition and struggle. Mental defect was interpreted through a Darwinian register of unfitness: endowed with a 'subnormal' capacity for adaptation, defectives were prone to idleness and disposed to 'anti-social' or 'rebellious' behaviour and inattentiveness. In short they were likely to become a burden to themselves and to the wider community (Clifford, 1939: 39).

Inquiries into the 'home circumstances' of defectives had found many of the parents to be of 'poor mentality', with Clifford suggesting that in other countries they would certainly be classed as 'subjects to be dealt with' (1939: 36). This phrase was lifted straight out of the infamous Mental Deficiency Act of 1913 in the UK, a piece of legislation implicated in eugenic practices (Walmsley, 2000). Clifford's incorporation of this phrase into his own normative programme is an example of how the logic of practice can enter a social context even when unsupported by the instruments of state. Clifford wanted a special school in Dublin for 7–16-year-olds where the number of mental defectives was largest. At the end of this term the child would be reassessed and either returned home, boarded out with foster parents, or classed as 'still a subject to be dealt with'. In the last of these cases the defective would be transferred to one of a number of special 'colonies' organised on the basis of age and sex, with juniors separated from seniors, and males from females. In the colonies girls would be trained in housecraft and needlework, while boys would be instructed in shoe-making and simple furniture-making. Clifford's scheme could have been taken directly from the pages of General Booth's *Darkest England*.

Four years later Clifford's scheme was placed in the realm of public debate and condensed into questions of educability and compliance. Drawing on Clifford's study, a report in the *Irish Times* reasoned that:

> [T]hese defectives can be educated to a considerable degree in mental and manual processes, but do not make much progress in the ordinary schools because of the difficulty of giving them special attention . . . Instead, these children are a source of worry to the teachers because of the fear that inspectors may judge the school on answering made by defectives, and that they may leave school almost illiterate and possibly with anti-social tendencies. (*Irish Times*, 1943b; see Clifford, 1939: 37)

A range of concerns came together in the problem of mental defectiveness, from teachers concerned with how their competency would be perceived by their superiors to the possible sources of anti-social conduct.[2] According to the *Irish Times* report the Department of Local Government was keen to place responsibility for reform in the hands of local authorities, but it was also made clear that 'if an effort was made along voluntary lines then a subsidy would probably be given' (*Irish Times*, 1943b). As with the certified schools in the nineteenth century, so the task of training defectives was delegated to the social economists and the religious orders.

Less than two weeks later the *Irish Press* carried a story on what was described as 'the first colony for adult mental defectives in the country', run by the Brothers of the Hospitaller Order of St John of God, on a 170-acre estate near Gormanstown in County Meath.[3] Preceding but also resonating with the infantilisation of itinerants, the report described how 'seventy men of mental ages ranging from three to six years are living to the full their child-like lives . . . Free from fear and want they live the dreamy lives of children.' Rev. Brother Norbert McMahon was quoted on his views that while the 'patients' had been graded by simple intelligence tests, they also graded themselves due to the fact that their 'limited intelligence, out of its depth in the company of normal minds, quickly finds its own level in such a colony and achieves companionship and friendship with its equals' (cf. Rose, 1985: 112–45). There were also echoes of Clifford's research, with the *Irish Press* disseminating the statement that feeble-mindedness accounted for 75 per cent of mental defect, a cohort that could be 'trained and fitted for ordinary life in a suitable environment'. Below this grade were the 'imbeciles', a class deemed 'unsuitable' for life outside of the total institution. It was this class that populated the Gormanstown colony. The unnamed journalist went on to explain that:

By experience, the Brothers have found that the easy agricultural work is best suited to them. Yesterday I saw them bronzed and supremely happy helping to harvest a 12-acre field of wheat. A healthy young man, who in his native village might have moped in tuberculosis, proudly and skilfully drove a horse from a high-piled load of grain . . . Though they appear to understand each other, much of what they say cannot be understood even by the Brother in charge. (*Irish Press*, 1943b)

As with the discourse of itinerancy, the representation of defectiveness exhibits traces of primitivism, with both fields bearing the stamp of General William Booth's human baboon and handsome dwarf. In contrast to Brother McMahon's reference to 'patients', the journalist noted that the Brothers hoped to extend the capacity of the colony to about 200 'inmates', and here it becomes evident that the discourse of mental defectiveness had been only partially medicalised. The reference to tuberculosis is also instructive in this respect, for it still carries a 'moral' as well as a medical meaning: the sign of character defect and the mark of stigma going back to the old discourse of pauperism.

The reassessment of the certified schools loosened the grip of the penitentiary model of discipline, but only with respect to those classed as curable/educable/trainable. From Foucault we can note that the practices directed at the subject to be dealt with simultaneously individualise and totalise, bringing each and all under a mode of surveillance that classifies, separates and disciplines in the name of cure and care. Augmenting the techniques being developed in the field of itinerancy at this time, here the productive organs of the National Society are divided from its defective parts. Like General Booth's reprobate, the subject to be dealt with would be excluded from the realm of Society and consigned to the margins of order.

The Mental Treatment Act of 1945 gave legal expression to the medical mode of classification and treatment, introducing a new office in the form of an inspector of mental hospitals. Among other duties, the inspector was charged with maintaining surveillance over the hospitals so that the forms of discipline, restraint and sedation would be known and recorded. It was not so much that mental patients were no longer *to be* restrained or disciplined; rather the job of the inspector was to know whether this was being conducted by 'medical treatment or otherwise'. The law now determined that the 'mechanical means of bodily restraint' would be recorded in a special log, and would be permitted only so as to expedite medical treatment or to prevent persons of 'unsound mind' from injuring themselves or someone else (Ireland, 1945a: §237, 263, 266). Beyond this the meaning of mental defect continued to oscillate between patient and inmate, care and control, with §251 of the Act making it a criminal offence to assist the escape of a person maintained by, or undergoing treatment in, a mental institution. Looming on the horizon of this field of innovation was the technique of 'rehabilitation', which would recalibrate the discourse of defectiveness and produce a new 'handicapped' subject, moving the trainable defective further away from the asylum and towards the 'community'.

Rehabilitating the handicapped

The Rehabilitation Institute, established in 1949 as an independent voluntary body, was originally concerned with training former TB patients (Browne, 1986; Curry, 1993: 161). However, as the rehabilitation movement gained momentum it began to cater for all types of 'handicap' (Ireland, 1975: 18). A decade after its establishment, and the same year that the number of patients in the mental hospitals peaked at 21,000 (Ireland, 1984a: 1), Captain P. O'Toole spoke at a Dublin Rotary Club luncheon and explained that the Rehabilitation Institute was saving the Irish state £60,000 each year by returning disabled persons to full employment. Furthermore this was primarily a voluntary effort, beyond which little else was being done to 'restore our 30,000 disabled people to full working capacity' (*Irish Press*, 1958c). By 1961, the year after the National Association for the Mentally Handicapped of Ireland was formed, and the same year as two separate inquiries into Mental Handicap and Mental Illness commenced, the National Rehabilitation Committee (NRC)[4] was managing fifteen institutions and announced that it was 'unable to cope' with the growing demand for its services. The Committee's president, Mr James Mooney, declared that rehabilitation was going to be 'a tremendous task' (*Irish Press*, 1961b).

Later that year the NRC organised a seminar on *Trends in Rehabilitation* at the Lourdes Hospital in Dun Laoghaire (*Irish Press*, 1961d; *Irish Times*, 1961e). The Rev. Dr J. R. M. Nolan from the Department of Psychology at University College Dublin spoke on the techniques of 'vocational testing' and 'vocational rehabilitation', an approach deriving its significance from the post-war economic boom. While the economic recovery bypassed Ireland during the 1950s, the 1960s brought a brief period of optimism, with much talk of economic and social progress driven by the government's first Programme for Economic Expansion (Ireland, 1958a, 1958b; Kennedy, Giblin and McHugh, 1988; Lee, 1989). Dr J. P. Ryan, medical director at St John of God Services for the Mentally Handicapped, explained that employers in Ireland should be able to give a percentage of jobs to mentally handicapped people, especially in the 'more humble occupations for which such persons were most suitable'. Echoing Bentham's notion of relative ability, Ryan proposed that the 'severely handicapped' could be taught repetitive movements commensurate with mass production techniques, 'moderates' could be 'fitted' for simple factory labouring through 'the best possible training', while the 'mildly handicapped' had a much brighter outlook. Given special education and training, this last class could be fully rehabilitated as 'normal citizens'.

From these beginnings the discourse of rehabilitation developed through an interesting slippage of meaning. In the context of TB or some other debilitating illness or accident, rehabilitation is a therapeutic counter-measure concerned with restoring the independence of someone who has lost it. However, when applied to 'the handicapped', that is, beyond those disabilities that result from illness and accident, it entails something more strategic. No longer a counter-measure to restore something lost, it becomes instead a normative programme concerned with creating habits and abilities which are perceived to be lacking. Rehabilitation was a new name for the disciplinary technologies born during the nineteenth century, and in combining the training of individual bodies with the regulation of micro-populations, it connects up with the logic of 'absorption' emerging in the field of itinerancy at this time (see Foucault, 1977: 302). Common to both fields is the governing standard of the 'normal'.

The normal child

When the Commission on Mental Handicap reported in 1965 it defined mental handicap as 'one of our gravest problems in the fields of health and education'.[5] Positioning itself as the agent of a new 'liberal and enlightened attitude', the Commission set about rethinking the mode of treatment in the context of a 'greatly increased interest in the problems presented by mental handicap' (Ireland, 1965a: xiii, 49; *Irish Press*, 1964b). The nature of the problem was defined as the 'great loss to the nation through lack of productivity, through underproductivity of the mentally handicapped and through the dependency of the mentally handicapped on others' (Ireland, 1965a: xiii). Added to this was the fact that the rehabilitation model faced limits in the form of technological developments. Anticipating a reduction in unskilled occupations due to mechanisation and automation, the Commission noted that the loss of such jobs would make the 'absorption' of the mentally handicapped into the general community more difficult (1965a: 117). Again, as with the programmes to govern itinerancy, the underlying premise here concerns the problem of establishing a relation of equivalence between a unified order and a singular subject.

Consistent with Dr Louis Clifford's definition of feeble-mindedness in 1939, the Commission defined the mentally handicapped as 'those who, by reason of arrested or incomplete development of mind, have a marked lack of intelligence and, either temporarily or permanently, inadequate adaptation to their environment' (Ireland, 1965a: 18). And rejecting the idea of handicap as a 'disease entity', the Commission characterised it instead as 'varying degrees of impairment' relative to maturation, learning and social adjustment (Ireland, 1965a: 19–20). While the mentally handicapped were not suited for mental work, and notwithstanding the limits confronting the rehabilitation enterprise, it remained the case that the bodies of the mentally handicapped could be trained for manual work. It was thus noted that the 'inability of the mentally handicapped to take up or retain employment is more often due to emotional instability, or lack of concentration, motivation, or social competence, than to insufficiency of particular work skills'. We will encounter this notion of 'emotional instability' – developed by the eugenicist and educational psychologist Cyril Burt – again in the next chapter. Here we should note the intimate relation which has been established at this time between the techniques of training and the authority of the 'psy' sciences. Training the handicapped was to be geared towards remedying 'personality defects' and forming the correct 'work habits' of punctuality and concentration (Ireland, 1965a: 97–8). In other words, the handicapped were to be trained 'to observe the procedures and the social attitudes which would be expected of them in the normal work situation':

> [T]here are still several forms of work suitable for the mentally handi-
> capped, for which normal workers are not in sufficient supply . . . In the
> production of a wide variety of industrial goods the work can be broken
> down into a number of simple processes. Where it is so broken down and
> the mentally handicapped are confined to a limited number of processes,
> they have been found to make excellent workers. Repetitive work does
> not bore them as it does many persons with higher intellects and their rate
> of production and standard of work compares very favourably with those
> of normal workers. (Ireland, 1965a: 100)

Again in a way resonating with Bentham's ingenious plan to extract labour from even the most 'insane', 'imperfect' and 'unripe' hands, the handicapped individual was to be grafted to the machine, or more specifically, positioned as a human interface between the machines of mass production and the makers of the machines: those with 'higher intellects'. The important difference between this model and Bentham's plan is that we are no longer within the panopticon poor-house. Instead we are within the realm of Booth's little commonwealth, with the walls of the panopticon extended to envelop the National Society.

The Commission noted a certain 'difficulty', however, in 'locating and assessing all persons who may be mentally handicapped and of applying accurately and uniformly the criteria upon which a diagnosis . . . depends' (Ireland, 1965a: 23). The problem was that 'mild cases, which may merge almost imperceptibly into the general population, constitute the majority of the mentally handicapped and conflict of opinion occurs most frequently, therefore, in relation to the group of cases whose quantitative effect on statistics is the greatest' (Ireland, 1965a: 23). In terms of both knowing and acting upon it, handicap was difficult to define: there was always a trace of doubt as to where the normal ended and the abnormal began. Conquering ambiguity was the task of the 'test battery', a technique intended to fortify the diagnosis by spreading the niggling presence of doubt over a wider body of evidence. Using personality tests, vocational testing, social attainment tests, and tests on specific aptitudes, the battery was supplemented by the expert gaze as the trained eye looked for signs of alertness, initiative, stability, maturity, concentration, motivation, autism, emotional disturbance, neurosis, psychosis and physical fitness (Ireland, 1965a: 167). Ultimately the overall assessment hinged on the individual's 'performance' relative to 'others in his group':

> [T]he person being tested is given standard tests to perform (problems to solve, relations to determine, symbols to allocate properly, words to understand, etc). His performance is compared with the performance of a known group who have been given the same tasks in exactly the same way and he is given a score to indicate his level of intelligence within his group. (Ireland, 1965a: 166)

In the test battery we see a maturing of the biopolitical technologies going back to 'average social man'. To be sure the methods have been refined and the authority of science consolidated, yet the domain of facticity continues to mesh with the realm of normativity. The Commission noted that 'the decision that a person is mentally handicapped is a grave one' (Ireland, 1965a: 168). And yet a *decision* it remained, with the standard of normalcy a statistical artefact and an empirical fiction contaminated by the contingency of its cultural circumstances. Yet this is precisely where the productive potential of the apparatus lies. Operating through an integrated system of detection, diagnosis, assessment and advisory services, the decision would secure authority and legitimacy through an organisational innovation known as 'community care'.

The notion of community care was attracting much attention at this time, with experiments in other countries finding it 'therapeutically better'. Interestingly the Commission traced the practice to the Brehon Laws (Ireland, 1965a: 164), so that community care was defined as a natural, hence essential part of the national heritage: always-already there and thus 'posed as presupposed' (Žižek, 1989). The 'expert team' was to be a central component of the new model, and would encircle the problem of handicap by coming at it from two directions: a school team and a general team, each combining medical professionals and social workers. This would anticipate and respond to 'cases of doubt', with data gathered on the child's parents and home conditions, as well as on the child's general behaviour at home and in school. Instances of cruelty, neglect, lack of stimulation and lack of security should be recorded. High priority would be awarded to schemes of preventative research, monitoring the 'birth records' of children exhibiting mental handicap and gathering data on specific categories of child, such as orphaned, unwanted and illegitimate. The scientific-administrative complex was to detect and document all forms of mental handicap, including its various sources and contexts (Ireland, 1965a: 53–5; cf. Rose, 1985).

The model was a practical response to the insight that 'no assessment or treatment programme could be effective unless all facets of the individual' were taken into account, with the 'whole person' to be traversed by the expert team (*Irish Times*, 1970c). With new legislation paving the way for a system of regional Health Boards, the combination of expert teams and community care marked what would turn out to be a crucially important shift in organisational thinking, codified with the help of McKinsey and Company Inc., a company that had built its reputation as a 'management engineering service'. Commissioned to report on the health services, McKinsey's advice to the Irish state was that 'the structure does not tell you how effective the services are', and so health-sector reforms were to be effected by identifying measurable targets, by defining the steps necessary to achieve those targets, and by assigning responsibility to individuals charged with completing the necessary steps by a specified date (Ireland, 1970b: §1.7). The innovation was born out of the managerial insight that 'local knowledge ... is of great assistance' in achieving 'efficient administration', so that 'constant communication and contact with the local population is essential' (Ireland, 1970b: §2.9). In the McKinsey Report can be found the basic ingredients of a major innovation in the arts of governance, with administrative reforms preparing to bring service provider and service user closer together through the organisational practice of 'integrated community care'. The strategic logic of the model was succinctly captured in a letter from McKinsey and Company to the Irish government: the new Health Boards were but 'one link in a chain that stretches from the individual patient, through the clinician, back to national determination of needs, priorities and available resources'. In other words the managers, providers and consumers of health and welfare services were to be 'forged into a single, powerful force at the local level' (Ireland, 1970b: iii, §1.4). There were signs of a new regime of practices being instituted.

As applied to the 'grave problem' of handicap, the new approach also had a symbolic dimension. Indeed the official definition of handicap – arrested and incomplete development – carried a larger meaning in the Irish context. In the past it had been possible to assume that national development had been retarded by foreign rule: the external cause scenario. The idea of an innate lack, on the other hand, would suggest an inability to develop: the mark of inferiority. There were signs of a growing impatience, a push to accelerate the project of modernisation, with a discursive shift away from the register of destiny and towards the idea of an engineering project: *to develop* through a coordinated mix of determination, planning, expert knowledge and, again crucially important, *partnership* between a variety of authorities and those long subjected to the authorities of state and science. This was the larger significance of the expert team and the community care model. An innate lack would be a problem of monumental proportions, but defective and inefficient machines could be improved through retooling, redesign and re-engineering.

The normal family

A second inquiry into the industrial and reformatory school system was commissioned in 1967. The subsequent report, published in 1970, is generally known as the Kennedy Report after the Committee's chairperson Justice Eileen Kennedy, and it essentially continued the nineteenth-century critique of the workhouse by moving to abolish the large institutions once and for all. The basic argument was that the system of certified schools was failing because it was 'haphazard and amateurish', no longer suited to 'the requirements of our modern and more scientific age and our greater realisation of our duty to the less fortunate members of society' (Ireland, 1970a: 13). The schools created 'inadequate persons' and were to be replaced by an integrated child-care system organised along two axes: the first to

prevent family breakdown by keeping the child within the family relation; the second to institute a new model of residential care based on
the 'normal family'. Deferring to the definition of handicap provided
by the 1965 Commission, the Kennedy inquiry located the individual
mind along a continuum from normal to abnormal, with deficiencies due
to either an innate lack or inadequate adaptation (see Ireland, 1970a:
109–13).

The Department of Psychology at University College Dublin conducted research for the Committee and found that a very high proportion of children in residential care could be classified as 'generally
backward'. It was also noted that a number of the children examined
exhibited 'linguistic deficiency' and an inability to 'read or express . . .
thoughts adequately', and thus could be classed as 'mentally handicapped'. Backwardness and handicap were associated with the 'cultur-
ally deprived person', meaning a type of individual who 'cannot meet
and deal adequately with the demands which his culture makes on him'.
The list of things that could give rise to inadequacy included lack of
personal contacts, lack of emotional, social and intellectual stability and
development, lack of emotional support at home, lack of both parents
at home, and a lack of financial stability in the family (Ireland, 1970a:
110). The register of lack formed a complex of forces that should nor-
mally converge on the child, many of which were associated with particular socio-economic circumstances. Importantly, the problem of
disordered and deficient minds and bodies was (once again) becoming
a poverty-related problem.

Defined in the negative, the 'inadequate family' corresponded to
problems such as 'illegitimacy, orphans, young offenders, the children
of large families, [and] the children of inadequate parents', all of which
helped to define the normative standard of the 'normal family'. The
standard was to be inscribed in new, small-scale residential homes or
'units' intended to replace the industrial schools and reformatories.
Coded as a 'normal home', the units were to have a housemother
looking after their day-to-day running, while the housefather would 'go
out to work in the usual way', thus simulating the 'good family environment' (Ireland, 1970a: 16). The fictions of the normal family and the
normal child converged as the ideal subject of Society:

> [T]o function adequately at a basic level, an individual must have attained
> a normal standard in terms of general intellectual development, language
> development with which intellectual development is closely related,
> reading attainment, attainment in numbers, and emotional and social
> development. If it is seen, from a study of our institutions of care, that our
> children have not a competence in these areas of development which is

up to the standards attained by the majority of the population then we can speak of cultural deprivation in such institutions as a fact. (Ireland, 1970a: 111)

There was also an evident shift in the way that children in residential care were to be taught to value individual choice and private property. The Kennedy Report explained that teaching children to respect private property necessitated that they had the right to personal property themselves: 'only in this way can a respect for property and a realisation of its purpose develop in children' (Ireland, 1970a: 19). The disciplined uniformity and drill of the penitentiary inmate was giving way to a standardised subject of choice.

Beyond the asylum

As with the Commission on Mental Handicap, the concurrent Commission of Inquiry on Mental Illness interpreted change as progressive and cumulative, stating in its report that 'there has been no similar period of time in the past which has seen such a marked improvement in therapeutic practice'. 'Profound advances' in 'psychiatric knowledge and methods' – more specifically, new drugs – had made it possible to move patients out of the asylum and into the community (Ireland, 1966: xiv; *Irish Times*, 1967b). Forming the background to this new awakening was a problem of 'gross overcrowding' in the mental hospitals, confirming the prognosis of the 1927 Poor Law Commission. This was compounded by the discovery that Ireland had the highest rate of psychiatric beds per capita in the world, at 7.3 per 1,000 of the population.[6] By way of comparison, the rate for Northern Ireland was 4.5, for England and Wales 4.6, for France 2.1, and for the USA 4.3. The Commission noted that 'at any given time, about one in every 70 of our people above the age of 24 years is in a mental hospital. When it is remembered that every mentally ill person brings stress into the lives of people around him, it will be clear that in Ireland mental illness poses a health problem of the first magnitude' (Ireland, 1966: xiii). The anomaly was something the Commission could not answer but could only ponder by deferring it as a question for further and future research.[7]

As a question of 'incipient mental illness' the problem was potentially a pandemic, and thus had to be dealt with through meticulous detective work among experts and lay actors alike, a form of labour that could not be contained within the walls of the asylum. Instead surveillance was to extend to the home, the 'community' and all other 'normal surroundings'. What was needed was to 'close the gap between psychiatry and general medicine', and to 'inculcate throughout the community . . . the basic principles of mental hygiene' (Ireland, 1966: xiv–xv,

16). This would require an effort of societal proportions, bringing together local and national health authorities, universities, medical schools, hospital management, medical practitioners, nursing authorities, trade unions, rehabilitation and welfare organisations, print and broadcast media, and the public at large. The answer to the problem was to be found not merely in the realm of knowledge but in concerted action. A strategy was required to manage the incipient nature of the problem and to anticipate its society-effect: this was to be a hegemonic programme.

Dr R. A. McCarthy, resident surgeon at Our Lady's Mental Hospital in Cork, commented on the overcrowding problem by announcing that at least 400 of the 2,000 patients in the hospital could be discharged if they had somewhere to go.[8] McCarthy argued that 'we are a dumping ground for all types of patients, geriatrics, epileptics, and those suffering from social problems' (*Irish Times*, 1970a; *Irish Press*, 1970a). The long process of sequestering lunatics and imbeciles into hospitals and colonies was going into reverse, with the defective subject to be dealt with now reconstructed as a handicapped subject to be inserted into the 'community'.

The new poverty and psychiatry

A number of prominent thinkers began to question the authority of the 'psy' sciences during the 1960s, foremost among them R. D. Laing (1990), Erving Goffman (1961), Michel Foucault (1988) and Thomas Szasz (1960). In 1967 the *Irish Times* published an interview on 'modern psychiatry' with Dr Joshua Bierer, and it seemed that the so-called anti-psychiatry movement had arrived in Ireland. Founder of the Marlborough Day Hospital in London and director of the British Institute of Social Psychiatry, Bierer outlined his plan to establish a 'therapeutic community', intended to give patients an active role in their treatment (see Bierer and Evans, 1969). He had originally proposed this in the 1930s while working in Essex, when his superintendent had responded to Bierer's idea by telling him that he was 'off his head'. Thirty years later Bierer interpreted the trend towards community care as the vindication of his vision. He explained that he had been 'preaching for about forty years that mental illness does not exist' and that 'we create mental illness by locking people up . . . you need only go to the zoo . . . if you lock up an animal he will either sit in a corner like a depressed patient or walk up and down like a manic patient'. As Ireland had twice as many mental patients as other countries, Bierer cautioned that there was 'twice the potential for creating mental illness – the hospitals were factories for mental illness' (*Irish Times*, 1967e). Dr James J. Wilson of St Brigid's Psychiatric Hospital wrote to the *Irish Times* in reply to Bierer, explaining that the interview 'could be regarded as a highly diverting piece of light entertainment (even if in slightly bad taste) if it were not for the fact that this is a very serious subject in which exaggeration, distortion and specious logic has no place' (Wilson, 1967). Wilson countered Bierer's constructivist argument by drawing on the authority of clinical science, stating that 'the psychiatric hospital exists because of the fact of mental illness and not the reverse'. Like Bierer's superintendent in Essex, Wilson also diagnosed him as a madman, stating that 'it is sad to see [Beirer] rant and kick against a door that is no longer closed'.

On one level this was simply a disagreement between clinicians over how to govern the problem of disordered minds. But on another level a struggle over truth was in train, and even as the authority of psychiatry was extended to new problems – in particular the role it acquired in diagnosing the new poverty (see below) – so the field of discourse itself became increasingly unstable.[9]

A few years later Professor Ivor Browne of the Eastern Health Board expressed his concern over the 'enormous' increase in the numbers of people seeking help from the psychiatric services. He also tapped into the 'hospital dumping' debate when he argued that a psychiatric hospital is:

[A] large collection of human beings who are not like each other, who do not fit in society, but who do not fit together ... old people who have nothing to do with psychiatry, mentally handicapped people who have nothing to do with psychiatry, people with social problems who may have something to do with psychiatry or people who are not able to manage their lives ... a whole lot of human beings who could not live in society or whom society did not want. (*Irish Times*, 1973)

When Browne identified the asylum population as a collective anomaly he also pointed to an administrative problem which was becoming apparent as the penitentiary model of discipline went out of favour: how to manage 'a whole lot of human beings' who do not fit in society, who could not live in society, and whom society does not want. It was less the issue of disordered minds that was in question than the disordering of Society, symbolised by all those who could not or would not conform to the fiction of the normal. Here we should note that the field of itinerancy was also becoming chronically unstable at this time, as Travellers organised to demand recognition and rights.

In 1982 the Adam and Eve Counselling Centre in Dublin defined its role as dealing with the psychological mal-effects of modern urban life, cataloguing an impressive list of problems which, when taken together, bridge the medicine–morality divide: obsessive-compulsiveness, stress and hypertension, unmarried motherhood, dropping out, loneliness, sexual infidelity, alcohol and drug abuse, poor self-concept, mental fatigue, anorexia, hysteria, schizophrenia, transvestism, voyeurism, masochism, neurosis, gambling, agoraphobia, hypochondria and impotency. The Centre was on the site of a former Simon shelter for the homeless and was adjacent to a former penny dinner parlour, a symbolically appropriate location given the intimate relation then being forged between the new poverty and psychiatric discourse. The Counselling Centre had over two thousand patients on its books, a collection of men and women described as being 'utterly distraught with the pressures of modern life' (O'Cuanaigh, 1982). As the project of Society was confronted by questions that it had not anticipated and was not equipped to answer, so the category of the normal unravelled, its contents mixing with the realm of the abnormal. The inside and outside of Society were becoming indistinguishable.

One of the key signs of the new poverty, and an object that *could* apparently be acted upon, was long-term unemployment, increasingly linked to questions of mental and physical health. In 1985 the World Conference on Health Education met in Dublin and discussed the implications of youth unemployment. Notable was the causal link established between unemployment, psychiatric illness and behaviours associated with negative health effects, including smoking, lack of exercise, poor diet and alcohol consumption (O'Byrne, 1987; *Irish Times*, 1985c). Six years later the Irish Economic and Social Research Institute (ESRI) published a report confirming the link between unemployment and 'psychological distress', with one-sixth of the national sample classified as 'non-psychotic psychiatric case[s]' (Whelan, Hannan and Creighton, 1991; Clarke, 1991). In the context of the new poverty the 'psy' sciences came to play a central role in making sense of new pressures and insecurities (see also Fraser and Gordon, 1997: 136–9). But what exactly did this mean for those classed as 'handicapped' and 'disabled'?

Resisting rehabilitation

Disability was still widely perceived to be an apolitical issue; that is, a matter for medical treatment supplemented by the vocational technique of rehabilitation. However, disabled persons were becoming increasingly vocal and visible in resisting this representation. An example is the case of Martin O'Donoghue, who was actively politicising disability from at least 1968 when he challenged the Gaelic Athletic Association – a sacred symbol of Irish nationalism – on the lack of accessibility of its sports stadiums (O'Donoghue, 1970). He also challenged the Irish Wheelchair Association for its lack of assertiveness in campaigning for the rights of the disabled. In 1976, as general secretary of the Irish Association of Physically Handicapped People, O'Donoghue took both the state and the National Rehabilitation Board (NRB) to task, alleging that 'physically and mentally handicapped people were being exploited in a state-backed factory operated by the National Rehabilitation Board'. He went on to explain that the NRB employed some thirty people at its factory at Ballybane in Galway, which had been built with government grants two years previously. As workers these people were earning less than those who stayed at home on the Disabled Persons Maintenance Allowance,[10] and O'Donoghue petitioned the NRB (unsuccessfully) to pay the workers union rates (McHale, 1976). The technique of rehabilitation was turning out to be less a form of emancipation than a mode of control even more disabling than the old public assistance code (see Gill, 2005).

As the disabled became politically organised, so it became increasingly clear that they were no longer willing to be acted upon or spoken for by carers and custodians. Questions of recognition and rights would come to the fore during the 1980s, with growing emphasis on the exclusion of the disabled from the spheres of opportunity and decision-making. Interventions such as O'Donoghue's, however, also overlapped with and reinforced a larger process of change. No longer confined to the realm of 'handicap', the rehabilitation enterprise was being extended as a strategic response to social dislocation.

Rehabilitating Society

The various meanings articulated by the category 'handicap' – inmate, patient, trainee and worker – became the basis of a special working party on 'Training and Employing the Handicapped'. Appointed in 1973 by the minister of health, the working party reported that 'persons *employed* in the *training* centres and sheltered workshops' were in receipt of a payment generally less than half the average Disabled Persons Maintenance Allowance (Ireland, 1975: 21, emphasis added; also Ireland, 1983b). There is a clear slippage – and tension – between 'employee' and 'trainee' here, with the category of handicap having no fixed identity in relation to labour law or the welfare code. It is also right here, in the space of this slippage, that this field of discourse begins to articulate the problem of 'dependency' in the larger sense of the term.

The working party employed the imagery of systems theory, a rhetorical style which framed the handicapped as a latent resource to be 'activated':

> Motivating the handicapped person involves bringing him to a state where (a) he accepts that he is capable of working and (b) he is prepared seriously to undergo whatever preliminary activation and training may be necessary. Unfortunately far too many handicapped persons think of themselves as permanently incapacitated for work. Furthermore, the payment of weekly allowances to persons unable to provide for themselves because of physical or mental disability creates in some, at least, an absolute dependence on financial assistance of this sort and to [*sic*] discourage them from making an effort to fit themselves for employment. An effective policy for the integration of the handicapped person into the working community must counteract these attitudes by removing or reducing the psychological barriers and financial disincentives that have developed. The establishment of training services of high standard will . . . rapidly demonstrate to many handicapped persons that they need no longer think of themselves as incapable of work. But it will also be necessary to encourage the development of an appreciation that the quality of life and the dignity of the individual is enhanced by work and reduced by unnecessary dependence on State benefits. (Ireland, 1975: 27–8)

This is some years before the assault on welfare peaked, yet we can already glimpse the logic of workfare in the quotation above. The report went on to explain that the existing practices made the error of treating handicapped persons as patients, while the correct criterion should be the 'ability to do the job'. Thus the old 'diagnostic labels' were to be of 'secondary importance to the question of the individual's abilities or potential, *vis-à-vis the task required of him*' (Ireland, 1975: 25–7, emphasis added). Disabled persons were already challenging the medical model at this time, yet the report *Training and Employing the Handicapped* was one indication of how the grip of the medical model was being loosened, or at least supplemented, for other reasons. Whether or not 'the dignity of the individual' was 'enhanced by work and reduced by unnecessary dependence on State benefits' was moot, because the disabled qualified only for residual entitlements left over from the poor laws. As a statement in the orders of discourse, *Training and Employing the Handicapped* was part of an emerging programme directed at *all* forms of dependency, and it redefined the significance of unemployment by constructing a new type of worker: the permanent trainee.

According to the report of the working party, the 'paramount reason for helping the handicapped person' was 'social and humanitarian', yet behind this was the 'secondary but important reason' of economy. With the humanitarian rationale providing an alibi (Barthes, 1993: 128), the submerged rationale was neatly summed up by Dr Garrett Fitzgerald in his views on rehabilitation:

> It would be difficult to think of a more productive form of social invest-
> ment, yielding such a high return in social and human terms, as well as
> providing an economic return through the reduction of unemployment
> benefit assistance payments and through the enhancement of the produc-
> tive potential of the community, which is badly in need of the skills created
> by the rehabilitation service. (cited in Ireland, 1975: 28)

Though appearing to meet in an antagonistic relation, administrative reforms and the disabled were struggling to accomplish the same thing: autonomy. The 'ability to do the job' might begin with the handicapped – a social subject actively seeking reconstruction and hence a suitable site to anchor the new practices – but the potential of permanent train-ing was far greater. This was a mode of subjectivation that could dis-pense with punitive techniques such as the old workhouse test (although the rate of remuneration for trainees still bore the stamp of the less eligibility principle). Instead this was a right which should not be denied. As minister for health, Charles Haughey spoke on this 'right to work' in 1979 when he opened a new workshop for the Rehabilitation Insti-tute. Haughey declared that 'the freedom to exercise his right to work is one of the most powerful reassurances that any citizen can have that he is fully accepted as an equal member of the society in which he is living' (*Irish Press*, 1979b). What is left unsaid here is that the dependent poor were to avail themselves of the right to work whether they volun-teered or not. This was a right not to be refused.

The rehabilitation enterprise and the community care model merged as a single strategy in 1984, published under the title *The Psychiatric Services – Planning for the Future* (Ireland, 1984a). The cover of this little booklet was decorated with a pencil sketch of a provincial town, replete with two churches (possibly bridging the sectarian divide), a school, a chemist, a supermarket, and a pub (figure 6.1; see also Bierer and Evans, 1969: 50–7). In the middle of the drawing is a large single-storey building, the exterior of which has been cut away so that we can see its interior. Mapped onto the freehand lines describing the town are a number of thick dark lines, all running perfectly parallel and perpen-dicular to each other with bulbous heads at their end, very much like solder tracks on an electronic circuit board. The solder tracks join spe-cific areas of the town to a column of words which describe the functions of this fictional community: sector HQ, workshop, reception, day centre, out patients, crisis intervention and hostels. This is a statement in a

Figure 6.1 Planning for the future

newly emerging order of discourse: a plan for the future which is super-imposed on and re-describes 'traditional' Ireland. If the old Ireland was a project in search of unity, the new Ireland would be a network of zones, or more specifically 'sectors' and 'community units'. Here the problem of order is re-imagined and reassembled.

Just as the Kennedy Report on the industrial and reformatory schools deferred to the 1965 Commission on Mental Handicap, *Planning for the Future* deferred to the 1966 Commission on Mental Illness, with the conclusions of the study group who authored the plan 'in the same spirit' as those of the Commission – essentially an endorsement of the community care model (Ireland, 1984a: viii). Community care was presented as the culmination of a process set in motion by the 1945 Mental Treatment Act, and so the past was gathered into the present as if the relation between them was one of predestination (Ireland, 1984a: 2–3). Explaining that the asylums of the Victorian era were 'designed to isolate the mentally ill from society', it was noted that the numbers of inmates had peaked in 1958, after which there had been a steady decline, part of a 'pattern of expansion and contraction common to most European countries'. The historical trend took the form of a bell curve, moving logically towards reforms which are posed as presupposed (Žižek, 1989).

To accelerate the process it was recommended that psychiatric hospitals and psychiatric units in general hospitals establish 'screening procedures to prevent inappropriate admissions'. The new administrative apparatus was to be organised as a 'sectorised service' and a collection of 'catchment areas', each resembling the circuit-board village sketched on the cover of *Planning for the Future*. Within these administrative zones the hospital would be folded into the community, blurring the precise location of the rehabilitation regime. Patients would be moved around a comprehensive therapeutic space and monitored at all times by the 'expert team', who would ensure 'continuity of care' by 'encouraging patient movement from one component to the other as needs change'. Rehabilitation was no longer confined to techniques of vocational training; instead it was to become a regime of 'active treatment' to deliver 'social skills', 'communication skills' and 'daily living skills', enabling all classes of patient to 'cope in domestic, occupational, industrial, social, and recreational settings'. The new regime would create 'an air of activity and optimism', essential not only for 'realising the potential of patients' but also for 'improving the morale and job satisfaction of nursing, medical and other staff'. Monitored by senior hospital management as the agents of 'foresight, drive, commitment, and leadership', the new therapeutic regime would adopt new techniques in managing the dynamic nature of the system. Picking up where the McKinsey Report left off, each Regional Health Board was to draw up targets and objectives to be reached over a ten-to-fifteen-year period, with time itself sectorised as a succession of five-year phases. Clear priorities were to be identified, energies directed, information regularly appraised and evaluated, with goals flexible and broad enough to allow for 'modification as circumstances or attitudes change' (Ireland, 1984a: xi–xv, 1–10, 71–8; see also Ireland, 1985b). Context, structure and objectives were no longer stable entities, with the new ordering modality designed to adapt to a shifting field of possibilities.[11]

In his foreword to *Planning for the Future*, the minister for health deferred to the authority of the new national development plan, bearing the pragmatic title *Building on Reality* (Ireland, 1984b). The new reality was one of structural change and financial constraints, with little room for the old ideals, so that the health services were to be 'slimmed down' by 'shifting resources into the community'. Moving away from the policy of direct provision, health policy was to reflect a paradigmatically biopolitical strategy of regulation, constructing strategies to prevent disease and promote health by removing the causes of unhealthy lifestyles. Air quality, alcohol consumption, dietary patterns, exercise levels and care-lessness were all to be monitored by adopting 'modern management information systems in administration', and removing the 'insulation' which protected 'healthcare providers' and 'healthcare consumers' from 'the full economic consequences of their actions' (Ireland, 1984b: 95–100). Ireland was to be governed by acting upon the action of autono-mous individuals and agents, governing through the related though otherwise discrete zones of a sectorised society, with 'tripartite sectoral development committee' coordinating a range of 'sectoral consultative committees',[12] each of which would conduct performance-oriented 'sec-toral analysis' (Ireland, 1984b: 32–9, 70–5, 157).[13]

It seemed that the long struggle to govern lunacy and imbecility through technologies of enclosure was about to come full circle. In July of 1991 a 28-year-old homeless man was jailed for six months for causing malicious damage to a bus and handling stolen goods. Recently released from the Central Mental Hospital, the young man explained that he had no place to go and no money for food. The judge criticised the 'appalling circumstances that many mentally ill around the city survive in . . . People like this need to be cared for by the community, but that just does not happen . . . The only people who care for them are the Gardai, the courts and the probation services . . . The public policy is quite simply not working' (*Irish Times*, 1991c). In passing sentence the judge described the prison time facing this man as 'psychiatric care by proxy'. Given the strategic objectives of the community care model, it seems difficult to discern whether this case should be construed as its failure or success. Either way, the old discourse of pauperism seemed to have returned. For those who fail to embody the norms of responsible autonomy there is the prison. Bierer's ambition for the 'therapeutic community' has been realised, but not in the way he envisioned it. Even as the disabled organised to contest their exclusion, so the project of Society itself dissolved.

Managing disability

The Forum of People with Disabilities published a new recruiting leaflet in July of 1991, stating that people with disabilities would continue to experience discrimination as long as they were represented as passive victims and objects of charity. The Forum advocated 'positive political action' so that the 'voices and experience' of people with disabilities would 'inform government, planners, service deliverers, voluntary and statutory organisations, and other people with and without disability of our views and demands' (*Irish Times*, 1991b). Three years later Mary

Duffy of the Disability Equality Trainers Network used the discourse of exclusion to argue that:

> People with disabilities have begun to realise that they do not need to be changed, fixed or made more 'whole' and their problems are not caused by impairments or medical conditions. It is clear to us that it is society that needs to change, to be fixed and made more inclusive. (Gallagher, 1994)

The disabled in Ireland were poised for militant action, with the discourse of exclusion providing a means to articulate their demands.

Recognition and rights

By 1996 the field of disability discourse in Ireland was anchored in the emerging apparatus of inclusive governance in three places. First, as noted in the last chapter, was the *Partnership 2000* National Agreement – the first to incorporate fully the community and voluntary (C&V) sector. Among the organisations represented in the community platform was the Forum of People with Disabilities. The second nodal point was a review group, commissioned by the Department of Health in 1992 to make recommendations on services for people with physical and sensory disabilities. The review group published its report in 1996 under the title *Towards an Independent Future* (Ireland, 1996a). The third element was a Commission on the Status of People with Disabilities, established in 1993, and again publishing its report in 1996 as *A Strategy for Equality* (Ireland, 1996b). Even as these statements began to stabilise the field, so the Irish Wheelchair Association and the Disability Federation of Ireland destabilised it again by protesting against the lack of resources being made available to implement the recommendations made by these bodies (*Irish Times*, 1997a, 1997b; *Irish Independent*, 1997a).

Partly in response to this, in 1997 the new Fianna Fáil/Progressive Democrat government announced that it was establishing a National Disability Authority (NDA) to oversee policy and services to disabled people.[14] The new body was to subsume the National Rehabilitation Board, and the Chair of the outgoing Board, Dr Arthur O'Reilly, described the change as 'a new dawn for people with disabilities in Ireland'; a move away from the 'patronising attitudes' of the past to an 'inclusive rights agenda'. The minister for justice, equality and law reform endorsed this assessment by noting that the new Authority would 'enable people with disabilities to achieve and exercise their economic, social, cultural, political, and civil rights' (Pollack, 1997; *Irish Independent*, 1997b). This shift to a rights-based approach was reinforced by the report of the Commission on Disability, with the NDA set up to monitor compliance with the Commission's recommendations and to coordinate national disability policies (Pollack, 1997; *Irish Independent*, 1997b). The Commission's report explained that 'people with disabilities do not want to be pitied nor do they want their disabilities to be dismissed as of little importance' (Ireland, 1996b).[15] What they did want was clearly articulated by the tone and content of the document:

> People with disabilities are the neglected citizens of Ireland. On the eve of the 21st century, many of them suffer intolerable conditions because of outdated social and economic policies and unthinking public attitudes. Changes have come about, influenced by international recognition that disability is a social rather than a medical issue, but many of those changes have been piecemeal. Public attitudes towards disability are still based on charity rather than on rights . . . Whether their status is looked at in terms of economics, information, education, mobility or housing they are seen to be treated as second-class citizens . . . People with disabilities are angry . . . The picture that emerged [during the process of inquiry] was one of a society which excluded people with disabilities from almost every aspect of economic, social, political and cultural life. People with disabilities and their families made it clear that they want equality, that they want to move from reliance on charity towards establishing basic rights . . . One of the most striking features of the submissions was the sense of absolute frustration which emerged . . . Another theme to emerge clearly . . . was that of marginalisation . . . Many people with disabilities felt that they were being either kept out, or pushed to, the margins of society. (Ireland, 1996b: 1.1–1.4)

Drawing on developments in the international arena at this time, the Commission adopted three guiding principles in setting out its recommendations: equality, maximising participation, and enabling independence and choice, all of which were intended to reverse the 'existing exclusions' so that 'people with disabilities [are] recognised as having equal status with all other citizens' (Ireland, 1996b: 1.34–40).

The question of rights – an approach which posits 'persons with disabilities as subjects of law' (NDA, 2003: 5) – has come to play a central role in stabilising this field of discourse. During February of 2002 the minister for justice, equality and law reform moved to pass a new Disability Bill through the Dáil, a piece of legislation intended to bring the process of public inquiry and legislative reform to a close. However, because it legislated only for 'duties of care' on the part of the state, the Bill was opposed by the National Disability Authority, the Irish Equality Authority and the UN Committee on Economic, Social and Cultural

Rights (Humphreys, 2002; Long, 2002).[16] Finally enacted in 2005, the new framework provides for the legal right to an 'assessment of dis-ability-related health, personal social service and education needs' (Ireland, 2005a). However, under the terms of the Act, meeting those needs is dependent on 'available resources', so that the rights-based approach to disability in Ireland is coupled to, and dependent on, eco-nomic performance. Furthermore, the Act has been written specifically to enable 'provision to be made for the assessment of health and educa-tion needs occasioned to persons *with* disabilities *by their* disabilities' (Ireland, 2005a, emphasis added). Moving against the grain the 1996 Commission, the substance of the Act assumes individual impairment rather than social disablement (see also NDA, 2003: 5; Gannon and Nolan, 2005).

Inclusion?

Disabled persons have been sequestered within the walls of the asylum, treated as objects of charity, and trained in the arts of self-government. Whether governed as an object or a subject, disability has long been implicated in defining the boundaries and internal contours of Society. Within the context of inclusive governance this remains largely unchanged, although the mode of ordering is being reconfigured. As enunciated by the minister for justice and codified in the new legislation, inclusive governance *enables* people *with* disabilities to *achieve* and exercise *their* rights. It is for the individual and/or the 'sector' to achieve and exercise rights, rights already inscribed in the social fabric. In other words, inclusive governance invites the disabled to comply with the 'rules of inclusion' (Crawford, 2003), which means managing their employability and conforming to norms of responsible autonomy. The agency of the excluded is to be enabled or facilitated ('activated' in the jargon of the 1975 report) so that they take their place in the social order. There is nothing really wrong with the existing order; it simply needs to be made more inclusive. Dr Arthur O'Reilly's metaphor of a 'new dawn', something the print media latched onto, makes a cut in disability discourse so that the past drifts away from the present: the new context is something we can all participate in together. The dis-abled are now recognised as having rights, but these are largely the right to recognition, the right to participate in the forums of inclusive gover-nance, and the right to be included in a variety of market settings. To go further than this, that is, to meet the redistributive demands of the disabled, would require the kind of solidarity that belongs to the dis-placed discourse of Society (see Bauman, 2001: 74–88).

The disability rights movement in Ireland has tended to confront what are sometimes called traditional disabilities, and perhaps one reason why the rights-based approach is deliberately constrained by 'available resources' is the challenge posed by emerging disabilities, those relating to poverty, age, stress, chronic fatigue, toxic exposure, multiple chemical sensitivity, HIV, ADHD and child abuse (Fox and Kim, 2004: 327; Gannon and Nolan, 2005). It is also worth mentioning that research commissioned by the National Disability Authority in 2002 found that of 25,448 persons with intellectual disability known to service providers, some 8,000 also have a psychiatric condition, 4,500 may require some sort of specialist psychiatric assessment and treatment, and between 900 and 2,400 exhibit 'severe challenging behaviours' (NDA, 2003: 6–19). This is what the NDA calls the 'dual diagnosis population in Ireland', a category spanning psychiatric illness and intellectual disability, and one that reaffirms the 'multi-disciplinary team' as the most suitable mode of treatment. There are good reasons to consider the possibility that the new universe of disabilities is directly related to the performative norm of the active subject, a new fiction to replace the old fictions of the normal child and the normal family: the flexibilised, reflexive, adaptable, prudent, responsible, self-governing, self-supporting consumer-worker and active member of various 'communities' who performs at optimal efficiency and never breaks down. This is the subject of inclusive governance, and maintaining this subject can be expensive. Far more efficient are the strategies to enable and activate the subject so that she or he is encouraged, induced and, if necessary, gently coerced into acquiring the skills, aptitudes, attitudes and credentials to exercise a responsible form of autonomy. We have already encountered this in the Citizen Traveller campaign, and we will see it again in the fields of youth and lone parenting. While I will return to this in greater detail in the final chapter, here we can note that governing through the inclusion of historically marginalised subjects in the decision-making process is about the management of power relations. As with the case of Travellers, the disabled are unlikely to be awarded any special place within the space of this problematic. Their role is to *inscribe* themselves within the social order, and the new politics of order awaits the act of inscription.

7

Juvenile delinquency and youth at risk

The statement that 'the hygiene of the growing child is scientifically of more importance to the nation than is that of the adult' is irrefutable . . . Not alone the obviously ailing but also the apparently normal child must be inspected. And not alone must the child himself be examined but his physical condition must be studied in relation to the hygienic conditions of his home and his school. (Dr M. O'Leary, school medical officer for Dublin City, 1930)

Introduction: the object of training

In 1925, an inspector from the National Society for the Prevention of Cruelty to Children (NSPCC, later ISPCC) sought a court order to commit five children from a Connemara family to the industrial school system; the reason: the family was starving, the roof of the house had collapsed injuring one of the children, they could not afford to light a fire, and the only bedding in the house was straw (*Irish Independent*, 1925b). In the vernacular of the times the NSPCC inspector – from an authority with its origins in social economy and scientific philanthropy – was referred to as 'the cruelty inspector'. If the family home exhibited signs of neglect then it could be broken up by the professional home visitor, who was invested with the power to place children in the care of state and clergy.

Only rarely was it suggested that poor families should be provided with the means to maintain their own children (see, for example, *Irish Press*, 1934b). More common was the Malthusian view that this would demoralise the poor, and might even encourage them to have children they were unable to support. Awarding a grant to foster-parents was more acceptable as they would be selected on the basis of their respectability. However, this too was subject to abuse on the part of mercenary nurses who profited from 'baby farming' (*Irish Times*, 1928; Ireland, 1927: 71–4; also Higginbotham, 1985).[1]

Aside from the difficulty of administering the problem without demoralising the poor was a more technical matter: whether or not those sent to the certified schools should be criminalised through the existing procedure of committal. Commenting on a Bill to remove 'the degrading and unnecessary' practice of committal in 1928, an editorial in the *Irish Independent* noted that:

> The industrial schools serve a very useful purpose . . . The poor children sent to them are well fed and well treated. They receive a good education and are taught at least the rudiments of a trade [but] it is regrettable that, to secure admission to one of these valuable institutions, a child must be first convicted of some offence, and thus branded a criminal. (*Irish Independent*, 1928)

The committal question articulated the larger problem of vagabondage, which in the case of juveniles related primarily to issues of truancy and beggary. Because children had to be committed before being placed in institutional care, it was not uncommon for poor families to stage an act of begging in the presence of a civil guard so as to have the child charged under the 1908 Children's Act. There were also cases where children were entrapped by cruelty inspectors who offered them a coin in the presence of a police officer (Barnes, 1989: 64–5, 81; *Irish Independent*, 1931b). Between committal and vagabondage was yet another problem: idleness, with the Free State Prisons Board warning that:

> We have within the last few years to deal with an entirely new class of criminal, composed of half-educated youths who would appear to have escaped early from parental control. They have grown up in lawless habits, and the streets and the cinema have been the main sources of their moral education. Full of new and unsatisfied desires, these youths have been dazzled by sensational reports in newspapers of large sums of money obtained by organised robbery, and they are seduced by the prospect of getting money easily without having to work for it honestly. (cited in Molony, 1925: 183)

Since the middle of the nineteenth century, the search for the hereditary and/or environmental origins of 'misbehaviour', 'misconduct' and 'anti-social propensities' (Burt, 1923a) had gradually brought legal, medical and educational authorities into alignment (see Rose, 1985). Medical professionals framed the problem of delinquency through competing discourses of 'moral imbecility' and 'emotional instability'. For Cyril Burt, a prominent educational psychologist and eugenicist, emotional instability was the primary source of just about all social problems, and in 1925 a report in the *Irish Independent* drew on his theory of the 'unstable child' to explain that 'if the purpose of the ordinary school were the training of character as well as the instruction of the intellect', then the 'disorders' pertaining to crime, unemployment and insanity 'would be largely obviated, and the numbers of future criminals and lunatics largely reduced' (*Irish Independent*, 1925c; Burt, 1917, 1923a, 1923b, 1931). The condition of 'emotional instability' bridges questions of mental defect and delinquency, and the key word here is 'future'.

To secure the future required that principles of good order be inscribed into its subject: the youth of today; and so – echoing General Booth – the treatment of young offenders was to be 'animated by a desire to do good to the rising generation', enabling 'those who have fallen to regain their character and start afresh on the path of honesty and hard work' (Molony, 1927: 453). Building the character of the nation's children required the school – as the realm of organised training – to merge seamlessly with the discipline of labour (*Irish Independent*, 1925a). As things stood there was a gap between one and the other which allowed youths to deviate from the path marked out by the project of the National Society, a gap called unemployment. The problem was not entirely subject to the laws of economy, however, and there were things that could be done by filling this gap. But first the existing stock of untrained youth had to be inspected and inventoried.

The Poor Law Commission on dependent children

Following its investigations into the inmate populations of the mixed workhouse, the Poor Law Commission found four classes of child maintained under the public assistance code (Ireland, 1927: 69–70): orphaned and deserted children; legitimate and illegitimate children of workhouse inmates, including the children of widows with one child (a class not entitled to outdoor relief); children other than orphaned children who had been taken from their parents; and finally children whose parent or parents were in prison, hospital or an asylum. The only alternative to the workhouse was the practice of boarding out, and in considering it the Commission presented what was essentially a balance sheet. On the positive side it approximated the normal family, thus providing a suitable environment in preparing the child for independent adult life. On the downside was the old problem of baby farming. Not all foster homes were good homes, children could be taken in for monetary gain and used as drudges, and if illegitimate the stigma of their birth would be known and they would most probably be shunned. With respect to illegitimate children the Commission proposed a new institution specifically for unmarried mothers and their children (see chapter 8), which would also house other classes of child unsuitable for boarding out. However, this would still leave a 'residue' of youths, an anomalous class which ensured the continuance of the certified schools, and the Commission drew on the evidence it had compiled to offset fears regarding their efficacy (Ireland, 1927: 69–74). Impressed by the results of its field work, the Commission reported that the managers were excellent and made 'every effort . . . to fit the pupils for a life of self-dependence'. And so the established practices spanning the penitentiary and the family relation would continue, albeit in slightly modified form (see below).

As there will be reason to return to this later, it is worth mentioning a novel administrative scheme put before the Commission: a government department dealing exclusively with all matters relating to infant life protection and child welfare, from illegitimacy, adoption and boarding out to delinquency and defectiveness. The Poor Law Commission saw no benefit arising from the establishment of a 'single "mixed" authority', however, which would only create confusion by combining unrelated duties. In 1927 the idea of a single mixed authority failed to resonate with the existing regime of truth, a truth which still bore the trace of police science and sought a distinct place for all things, but it would later reappear. In the meantime there was a steady process of formation which maps onto the fields of nomadism and disability.

Recalibrating the regime of training

Readjusting the penitentiary model
In the last chapter we briefly encountered the work of the first Commission on the reformatory and industrial schools, which was charged with reporting on the care, education and training of all children and young persons in the certified schools and 'other places of detention' (Ireland, 1936: 4). Pressed by notables such as Sir Joseph Glynn, president of the St Vincent de Paul Society and a prominent member of the Catholic Protection and Rescue Society, to abolish the practice of criminal committal, the Commission recommended that committal be replaced by a procedure called the 'admission order' (Ireland, 1936: 17–20; *Irish Times*, 1934b, 1934c). Keen to dispel the 'misconception' equating the certified schools with juvenile prisons, the Commission explained that:

> Shortly after the reformatory school system came into operation, the necessity for dealing, as a matter of public importance, with the relationship of vagrancy and destitution with serious juvenile crime became more

fully appreciated. It was recognised that the establishment of a type of school different from a reformatory would be desirable to deal with children who had not committed offences but who, through want, neglect, or lack of parental control might drift into crime. To meet this need the industrial schools were established. (Ireland, 1936: 4)

The objective was to resuscitate the spirit of reform which had originally given birth to the regime of compulsory training (see Carpenter, 1968), shifting the administrative focus from the punishment of crime to the administration of poverty (Ireland, 1936: 45). Explaining that the public cost of the schools should be understood as relief rather than punishment, the Commission was critical of the existing mode of training, which echoed the punitive rules of the Magdalen penitentiary examined in chapter 3, with the homogeneous inmate body subjected to a monotonous discipline, enforced silence and isolation from the outside world. In some schools the rule of silence extended to meal-times, while sleeping quarters were emptied of any adornment unnecessary to the functioning of the regime. Limitations on annual home leave – generally two weeks – were deemed to be too strict, while the tendency to use boys as 'juvenile labourers' was seen as inappropriate (Ireland, 1936: 22–3, 30–1).

Though expressing these reservations the Commission was none the less a conservative agent of reform, and it concluded by noting that 'the present system of reformatory and industrial schools affords the most suitable method of dealing with children suffering from the disabilities to which we have referred, and we recommend its continuance' (Ireland, 1936: 27–8). The Commission also thought it appropriate that the schools remain under the authority of the religious orders, and thus the system went largely unquestioned. And while it took up the cause of ending committal, this would again prove ineffective. What was novel, however, as noted in the last chapter, was the way the Commission aimed to disassemble the corporate inmate body, breaking it down into individual units to be inspected for signs of abnormality and infectious disease, and most importantly, susceptibility to training (Ireland, 1936: 26–7). Closer inspection would allow for the quarantine of those bearing infectious diseases and for the separation of those who could not be trained. The inmate body was to be reclassified and purified: to shed its contagious and defective parts so that its productive elements could be placed in the service of the National Society.

Redirecting the social model

In the context of the Great Depression, international organisations such as Save the Children International Union issued warnings about the possible long-term social consequences of unemployment. The Irish Free State set up a special interdepartmental committee under the authority of the minister of education to consider a practical counter-measure: raising the age of compulsory schooling to 16 years (*Irish Press*, 1934a; see also Finn, 1987).[2] Professional teachers also had a stake in this enterprise, with some demanding that the age of compulsory schooling be raised even higher, to 18 years of age. A letter to the *Irish Press* in 1937 explained that 'there is no sadder sight in Ireland today than that of the scores of youths . . . one meets on the streets of our Irish towns at all hours of the day and night, completely free from control, discipline, mental training and all cultural and civilising contacts'. Compulsory attendance at 'vocational schools or any other kind of post-primary school' would not only ensure that the nation's youth were exposed to 'educational and civilising influences', it would also 'provide work for every unemployed teacher in the Saorstat, and absorb the output of our training colleges and universities for some years to come' (O'Floinn, 1937). The General Secretary of the Irish National Teachers Organisation (INTO) also threw his weight behind the call for more state control over children by pressing the government to amend the School Attendance Act, arguing that 'people who employed children under 14 . . . during school hours should be rendered liable to prosecution and fine' (O'Connell, 1937). It seemed that young people were both dangerously idle *and* unacceptably employed. There was less confidence regarding what young people were actually doing than what they should be doing: sitting attentively in the classroom.

The bid to institute a regime of compulsory training was not confined solely to the school-going population, however. Germany's Labour Service had its supporters among those who thought a compulsory regime of physical education, hygiene and civics would both prevent juvenile delinquency and 'rehabilitate' unemployed youths (Beere, 1938). Cast in the mould of General Booth's cooperative common-wealth, the labour camp would be a regime of hyper-vitality, its governing principles a blend of labour, physical fitness, military drill, instruction in national politics and history, and community singing in the evenings, all of which would provide a 'training ground for the citizens of the State' (Beere, 1938: 41–7).

Perhaps the only practical manifestation of this scheme in Ireland was the Construction Corps. An experiment in organised employment relief, which more usually took the form of urban sewerage schemes and rural bog development works (Ireland, 1945b), the 1st Battalion of the Construction Corps was paraded past Government Buildings in December 1940, moving the editors of the *Irish Times* to note that 'discipline has a formidable name' (*Irish Times*, 1940b). The editors of the *Irish Press* agreed, writing that 'no onlooker could have failed to appraise these young men, their good colour, fitness and their smart military bearing' (*Irish Press*, 1940a, 1940b; McCourt, 1940). There was, however, a punitive side to this militaristic mode of employment relief. During 1942, 8,571 men were disqualified from unemployment assistance for refusing to accept work at the turf camps in County Kildare, and 6,000 under the age of 25 were 'disallowed' assistance for refusing to join the Construction Corps (*Irish Times*, 1943a). Eoin O'Duffy's Blueshirts were not the only hint of fascism in Ireland during the 'emergency'.

Between the labour camp and the school lay a variety of strategies to secure Society, each aiming to strike a balance between freedom and discipline. In 1943 Justice Mac Eachach denounced the NSPCC for its 'foolish and faddish attack on birching'. Fortunately, noted the judge, the whipping law remained in full force, and 'there was nothing to prevent it from being put into operation if and when it became necessary' (*Irish Press*, 1943c; see also Molony, 1927). In fact, in the midst of reports concerning a 'growing army of young criminals', it was less a question of if than when (*Irish Times*, 1940a). As 'a product of the age we live in', the 'ugly crop' of delinquent youths had to be taken in hand, for 'the whole future of any country depends on the proper training of its youth' (*Irish Times*, 1940a; also King, 1940). Cast in the mould of sovereign power, the punitive technique of the lash was limited to the offence – to what had already been done. Against this, and with its strategic objective that of governing future conduct, the potential of education was boundless.

The field of instruction known as civics was, for a while at least, posited as the solution to the problem of untrained youth, one that would be more carrot than stick. James Hickey, TD for Cork, argued in the Dáil that he wished:

> [T]o see civics compulsorily taught in the schools in order to develop that social sense and the idea that education is not merely preparation for a job, that it is a preparation for life and that the children when they grow up are expected to give service to the community and to display a sense of obligation to the community when they go into the world to earn their living.[3]

At the same time the assistant general of the Irish Christian Brothers called for civics to be taught in all post-primary schools. An *Irish Press* editorial at this time noted that 'civics is a word of comparatively recent coinage, but what it connotes is as old as Rome. It has to do with the behaviour of the individual citizen in relation to the interests of the community at large.' In particular the character-forming function of civics was directed at the urban poor, because the 'slums . . . are of their very nature inimical to the Civic Spirit [and] the children whose misfortune it is to live in them can hardly be expected to grow up with an appreciation of beauty or a respect for the dignity of the city in which they live, for all around them is an environment of dirt and squalor'. As General Booth had put it, for the residuum 'the world is all slum'. And even for those removed from the slums to the new suburban 'colonies':

> It would take time to instil in their minds a respect for order and property . . . We do not of course suggest that slum children are the only ones for whom the disciplines of civics should be taught . . . they are an essential part of the education of all children . . . because their effect on the moulding of character during the impressionable years is incalculable. (*Irish Press*, 1943a)

The editorial speaks not to the slum children themselves but to a readership already schooled in respect for 'order and property'. Given that this is the *Irish Press* – a bastion of Irish nationalism at this time – the representation is instructive, identifying as it does a segment of the population still to be incorporated into the project of Society.

Whether the answer to the problem was to be found in education or the labour camp, in military discipline or 'the disciplines of civics', discipline itself remained a question of *character*. But this was about to change. A little more than a decade later, during a Dáil debate on language revival, Dr Noel Browne denounced corporal punishment:

> In regard to the beating of children in schools, I do not mind how lightly they are beaten or for what reasons: I do not think an adult should ever use physical violence on a child . . . all of us who believe in the power of persuasion . . . must accept this . . . Beating a child teaches it that the final argument in any discussion . . . is violence . . . It teaches the child the power of violence . . . I have met many school teachers from English and American schools who have never laid a finger on children at all . . . It is about time that it should be accepted that the beating of children is not desirable or even effective.[4]

Browne conceded that the teacher faced difficulties, with which he sympathised, yet he maintained that the rule of fear was ineffective and corporal punishment was misdirected. It was pointless to punish the child for the overcrowding in classrooms, which both invited disorder and offered little opportunity to 'the backward, the maladjusted and the mentally defective child'. This was part of a drive to institute a more discerning mode of administration, with the programmes to mould character now giving way to new techniques which would connect up with the field of mental defect and derive their authority from the psychiatric sciences.

Youth unrest

During his speech on corporal punishment, Noel Browne also made reference to 'Teddy boys', his argument being that violence begets violence. Every generation no doubt produces its symbols of freedom and hope, but what seemed to characterise the era of rock 'n roll was a spirit of defiance and rebellion. As the 1950s became the 1960s the rebellious generation also spawned a new discourse: vandalism (see Kilcommins, O'Donnell, O'Sullivan and Vaughan, 2004: 210–11). Speaking on this topic in the Dáil in 1959, Captain Patrick Giles speculated that 'there must be some weakness in the character of the people. It is up to us here and the Department of Education to see that our youth are moulded to be the best type of citizens.'[5] A year later, as a new Criminal Justice Bill made its way through the Dáil, Giles was predicting a crime wave, the origins of which lay not in poverty but in the 'rotten' home life of a 'minority of people who are dangerous, low and dirty', and against which 'society must be defended'.[6] The notion of a dangerous residuum was again invoked.

The agent of vandalism was the 'hooligan', associated with irrational acts of 'rampaging' which belied the existence of an 'age of improving social conditions' (*Irish Press*, 1967a). Vandalism and hooliganism symbolised a youth out of control, with clerics warning against the dangers of intemperance among adolescents, especially females, and a declining morality which was evident in the prevalence of improper dress, dangerous literature and films, and unsupervised attendance at ballrooms (*Irish Press*, 1961a, 1967g, 1967j). As the 1960s drew to a close, vandalism was explained not as a question of character or weak moral fibre, but in Freudian terms: an untamed instinct which had somehow escaped the rule of reason.

When a number of new, unoccupied houses in Dublin were vandalised it became apparent that the hooligan did not even respect the sacred national emblems of home and sod. An *Irish Press* editorial on the incident suggested that there were 'no apparent reasons' other than the urge for destruction itself. The disposition to destroy without reason was defined as a 'lamentable instinct', the 'symptom of a malaise that seems to be affecting young people everywhere'. The 'urge to destroy' was 'a product of some sort of frustration, based in its turn on the lack of anything better to do'. Youthful energies had to be harnessed and channelled 'into some useful and productive purpose' so that 'there would be less temptation for them to go on the rampage' (*Irish Press*, 1967a; also 1967h).

Anthony Burgess published his controversial *A Clockwork Orange* (1962) at this time, a text which became even more notorious when Stanley Kubrick made it into a movie nine years later. Burgess described a world where youths engaged in violent crime not for reasons of material gain – 'the prospect of getting money easily without having to work for it honestly', as assumed by the Free State Prisons Board in 1925 – but for the sake of violence itself. *Clockwork Orange* described a world where the 'new and unsatisfied desires' of modern youth (again the words of the Prisons Board) had become an end in itself, where young males engaged in 'ultra-violence' (Burgess's phrase) purely for the pleasure of it. Kubrick exaggerated all this, using dance choreography, a Beethoven score and slow-motion camera work to aestheticise scenes of brutal violence and rape. Between the book and the movie was a critical commentary on the intimate relation between the prison and the clinic, which is to say punishment and treatment, and though Kubrick's movie was banned in Ireland, life would none the less mimic art as it mimicked life. Before looking at this moment of discursive formation I want to sketch the debate on youth at this time in more detail.

The Irish State published an influential report in 1965 called *Investment in Education* (Ireland, 1965b), and a plan was finally in place to increase the age of compulsory school attendance to 15 years (see also Kellaghan, 1989).[7] *Investment in Education* codified the problem of education as one of inequality, underlining the low participation rate among the lower classes. Two years later the minister for education, Donogh O'Malley, etched his name into the history books by announcing the introduction of free second-level education. This is often taken as *the* sign of growing equality in Irish society, evident for example in an *Irish Press* editorial which – against the backdrop of the fiftieth anniversary of the 1916 Rising – presented the new policy as the fulfilment of the 'egalitarian promise built into the fight for independence', one 'designed to honour the promise of 1916 to "cherish all the children of the nation"' (*Irish Press*, 1967k). There was more to this than simply fulfilling the wishes of the founding fathers, however.

The expansion of compulsory education by making it 'free' was also a way of governing freedom (see Finn, 1987). Education had long been in the service of the national interest; this at least was by no means specific to Ireland. In the Irish case it was clear that the meaning of the national interest was shifting away from the peasant idealism of the de

Valera days. In a way commensurate with the broader post-war doctrine of modernisation, those forms of life associated with 'tradition' were now discursively framed as dysfunctional. The Industrial and Economic Council of Ireland argued that purpose and will were required to achieve full employment and secure rising living standards. This had specific implications for the poor – those who removed their children from school at the first opportunity so that they could work 'on the farm or in the shop' – a tradition which had become a fetter on a new developmental vision with the rather idiosyncratic title of 'a programme' (not a 'plan') for 'economic expansion' (Ireland, 1958b, 1963b). Self-sacrifice, or 'self-denial' as it was phrased, on the part of the poor was in the long-term interests of the modernising 'nation' (*Irish Press*, 1967c, 1967d, 1967e).

Anticipating a rapid increase in the school-going population as a result of this policy, the Christian Brothers studied the international data and found that somewhere between 30 and 50 per cent of children would not take up free post-primary education. This was 'a social problem' which had to be solved if the project of 'educational development' was to succeed (*Irish Times*, 1967c). The Association of Secondary Teachers of Ireland (ASTI) concurred, and called for a study into low participation and high drop-out rates in post-primary education (*Irish Press*, 1967f). What might have been interpreted as a sign of resistance or refusal on the part of the poor in earlier times was now a question of combating inequality. The 'social problem' of low participation in education was not a problem of rising unemployment, or of growing juvenile crime, or even of the desire for economic growth; it was about cherishing the children equally and fulfilling the promise of the National Society. Addressing an Irish Congress of Trade Union conference in 1973, an International Labour Organisation representative paid tribute to James Connolly, who had described the linen mills of Dublin as 'slaughter houses for women and penitentiaries for children' (*Irish Press*, 1973b). No doubt the factories were brutal, but the fact that the school was itself modelled on the factory, with its timetable, working week and unaccountable mode of authority, was missed amid the resounding applause for the new equality.

An essay on the topic of 'Youth Unrest' won Marie Edgeworth a European Schools Day Award in 1970. Edgeworth was also the reigning Young Scientist of the Year, and her conception of Youth Unrest was the antithesis of vandalism and hooliganism:

[W]e have great and noble designs for ourselves and most of all we believe profoundly in Ireland's destiny – we know Ireland's 'finest hour' is imminent . . . for too long has this yet vulnerable nation of ours been buffeted by verbal blows, both from within and without. When years of honest effort did not realise the ideal Ireland we seem to have resorted to bearing under a load of pessimism and disappointment. But let us not forget than only a short fifty years ago this whole society had to make a tremendous break with an order centuries old, and make an overnight change to that of a domestic democracy . . . Not only have we developed and progressed, but by the inspiration of our liberators have led other peoples to gain the inalienable rights of nationhood . . . We in 1970 are gradually taking our place in a new world that has a new explanation . . . a world for which the panacea will not be separatism but rather brotherly association and a common good [based on] Christian standards and rec- ognition of the human rights and dignity of the individual in society . . . Irish society will . . . hardly be a leader in the world of politics and economics, but it will indeed be a leader – a leader in the realm of mind and spirit. (Edgeworth, 1970)

Ireland's historical role was to be Hegelian rather than Marxist; part of a 'new world' with a 'new explanation' (see also McLoone, 1984: 5). In a way that resonates with news reports on educational reform, Edge- worth traces a line of continuity and development between past and present, but there was a limit condition to this articulation of youth unrest: its darker underside of irrational rampage, hooliganism and vandalism. Or maybe the latter was more rational than its representa- tions allowed for: a rage born out of discontent. Could it be that the project of Society was both Hegelian Spirit and Nietzschean nihilism, or did the truth of 'Ireland's destiny' harbour a lie?

The occasional call for the reintroduction of the birch could still be heard; at the very least parents and teachers should be encouraged to give delinquents a 'good flogging' (*Irish Press*, 1967i, 1967c; Farrell, 1967). But this was now an outmoded approach to discipline, and only brutish 'animal trainers' continued to believe in the power of the lash (Byrne, 1967). The animal trainers had had their day, and the whipping laws had given way to a new mode of treatment, one set out in detail in the Kennedy Report on the reformatory and industrial schools. We have already looked at this from the perspective of disability and it can be dealt with here in brief.

The normal family and the normal child

The Kennedy inquiry correctly diagnosed the existing model of institu- tional care as an outcome rather than a design, in effect a historical accretion; and it was to be replaced by an integrated child-care system purpose-built for the job. As things stood child care was in the hands of a plethora of agents, engendering a situation whereby 'anomalies have arisen where children in similar circumstances have been dealt with by different Departments under different Acts' (Ireland, 1970a: 26). The Department of Education had responsibility for children committed through the courts to the industrial and reformatory schools, the Department of Health was responsible for children admitted to the schools under the Health Acts as well as those boarded out under the Children's Acts, while the Department of Justice was responsible for the Adoption Board and for minors committed to St Patrick's juvenile prison. Amalgamating existing functions, the proposed child-care system was to be administered by a single department: Health (Ireland, 1970a: 26; see also Lee, 1989: 548–53). Here we come full circle to the scheme put before the Poor Law Commission of 1927: the 'single mixed authority'. No longer equated with disorder, the model now signified efficiency and progress.

As we have seen, the envisioned mode of residential care (the 'home unit') was intended to simulate the 'normal' family home, with the housemother taking care of day-to-day matters, and the housefather going out to work during the day (see also Bowlby, 1965). This was a time when the idealised family was celebrated in sitcoms such as *The Partridge Family* (1970–4) and *The Brady Bunch* (1969–74). Minor upsets and problems provide moral lessons within the fictive space of these 'normal' families, with even the odd hint of misbehaviour functional to the preservation of harmony. Within its wider cultural context the normativity of the Kennedy Report mirrored these fictional representations of family life, but the factual was something else, with the domestic sphere shaken both by the women's movement and by a significant rise in alternative types of family (Flanagan and Richardson, 1992; CPA, 2003: 8). The family was fundamentally disturbed, and yet the discourse of securing order by saving children and preserving the family relation – a relation where the mother cherishes and the father provides – continued to exert a hegemonic grip on the social imaginary.

The medicalisation of youth unrest

Reading along the conjunctural axis, a range of actors converged on and helped to consolidate an apparatus which dovetails with the innovations we have encountered in the fields of Traveller and disability discourse: the administrative technologies of community care and the expert team. The ISPCC threw its support behind the central recommendation of the Kennedy inquiry: preventative measures to keep the 'normal' family intact (also Power, 1979). The Galway Godparents Association endorsed the idea of 'integrated child care', recognising it as commensurate with community care and thus promising to provide a means to gather information on children, inspect homes, and treat 'physically, mentally, and educationally retarded' children according to their specific needs (McDermott, 1970). Likewise the Men's Federation of Catholic School Unions (MFCSU) held a seminar on 'the important subject of student–teacher–parent communication'. Parents wanted to find out more about how their children were getting on in school, while teachers wanted to know more about the child's home life. Communication across the student–teacher–parent relation would enable teachers and parents to work together in addressing the 'special problems' of the 'difficult' child, the 'nervous' child, the 'sick' child and the 'precocious' child. This communicative mode of surveillance would bridge the hitherto distinct worlds of the child, folding school life and home life into each other so that the child could be fully monitored for any sign of abnormality (*Irish Press*, 1970f).

There is a memorable scene in Kubrick's rendering of *A Clockwork Orange* which describes the enfolding of authorities, and it does so at the exact historical moment when this takes place in Ireland. The plot is organised around a young character called Alex, who, in the jargon used by him and his 'droogs',[8] is the agent of ultra-violence. Alex is eventually caught, sentenced and inserted into the penal system, transformed from a subject into a bureaucratic object. Stripped of possessions and identity, the individual becomes a number and a uniform, absorbed into the monotonous routine of prison life. But this is not to be Alex's fate, and he is given a reprieve of sorts, being selected as the guinea pig in a scientific experiment to cure violence. The mode of treatment – aversion therapy – is designed to create an involuntary reflex in the mind–body complex, with violent thoughts, desires and intentions triggering a crippling nausea in their author. The scene I have in mind is the moment when Alex is marched into the Ludovico medical centre, military style, by a prison warden who snaps out a crisp command calling Alex to attention before signing him over to the doctors. Attired in their lab-coats, the doctors are casual and relaxed, reassuring young Alex that he is now to be cared for and cured of his illness. In its mode of treatment, however, the Ludovico clinic closes off the distance between the dangerous individual and a science that claims to be impartial and objective, serving only the cause of humanistic progress. Alex discovers to his horror that he is to be subjected to a mode of treatment which is as brutal as the prison and no less violent than the violence he is to be cured of. While a graphic (and of course exaggerated) representation, this blurring of authority and its object was taking place in Ireland at precisely this time. As the penitentiary model went into terminal decline, so the ordering techniques became one, the enfolded whole coded through a discourse of educational equality and therapeutic care.

Lelia Doolan wrote an article for the *Irish Press* in 1970 while observing Justice Eileen Kennedy presiding over the Children's Court in Dublin. Reflecting on her own socialisation, Doolan explained that 'by the age of 17 the regulations had somehow taken root inside me. Their life had, curiously, become transplanted into mine. I never knew how it happened. External commands simply became internal impulses' (Doolan, 1970). But this no longer applied, apparently, so that controls formerly internalised in an unreflective manner had somehow been externalised by the new generation of restless youth. Individuals could now apparently refuse social norms, inhabiting a new world, to cite Marie Edgeworth, in need of a new explanation. Yet nobody seemed qualified to provide this explanation. The explanations that *were* proposed had recourse to the old, tried and tested formula: poverty and pauperism. There was still little to suggest that the problem of untrained youth was *internal* to the project of Society, that is, intrinsic to the modern epoch. It could only be the uneven distribution of the modernising (civilising) process that was causing the problem: the pockets of privation amid plenty (see Murray, 1976b; *Irish Press*, 1976a, 1976b). Thus the causes of disorder were such things as 'overcrowding' and 'cramped housing', with the poverty of exhausted mothers, depressed fathers and neglected children resulting in an increase in crime. The discourse of pauperism had returned. But there was also a niggling doubt, a hint that this might not be something left over from colonial domination or a temporary glitch before Ireland finally caught up with the leaders in the race towards the end of history. Perhaps it was something else, something the project of Society had not anticipated.

Managing youth

Speaking at an International Seminar on Youth Unemployment run by the Organisation for Economic Cooperation and Development (OECD) in 1970, the minister for labour considered what he called the 'paradox of our age'. By this he meant the continuing problem of youth unemployment at a time when 'our young people everywhere are staying at school longer, and when the overall level of employment is higher than ever before' (*Irish Times*, 1970b). A few days later the minister for education announced the launch of 'an experiment which represents a comprehensive attack on the problem of educational failure'. This was a Special Education Project for pre-school children at Rutland Street School, in the midst of Dublin's impoverished north inner city, co-funded by the Irish State and the Bernard van Leer Foundation (Bernard van Leer Foundation, 1979; Kellaghan and Brugha, 1972). The minister noted that 'the reasons for educational failure are at best complex and at worst unknown', with the Special Project intended to function as a research laboratory. Children were to be given access to 'essential pre-school experience' from 3 years of age, while school management would busy itself compiling comprehensive data on the progress of each child. In the new age marked by the paradoxical, the complex and the unknown, *information* had become the crucial currency of government, and, in a way that resonated with the communicative mode of discipline proposed in the context of the Kennedy inquiry, the minister urged parents to 'regard yourselves as helpers in this important work' (*Irish Times*, 1970d). The age of paradox heralded a new, inclusive mode of government.

By the 1980s it was no longer possible to claim that the level of employment was on an upward trend; on the contrary, by 1985 Ireland was second in the OECD unemployment league (Lee, 1989: 519; Kennedy, Giblin and McHugh, 1988; McLoone, 1984). It was time to abandon the perfectionist project of Society and move to a strategy of management, and one way of doing this was to extend (further) the duration of 'youth' itself, this time not by raising the age of compulsory schooling, but by recasting the old regime of industrial training. In chapter 6 we saw an innovation within the field of disability discourse: the invention of the permanent trainee. During the 1980s the youth unemployment problem spawned a constellation of make-work schemes for the worker-as-trainee: work experience programmes, social employment schemes, environmental improvement schemes, community training programmes and workshops, and placements with voluntary organisations (Corcoran, O'Connor and Mullin, 1984; Brennan, 1984: 29–32; *Irish Times*, 1982a, 1982b). The disciplinary apparatus of vocational training moved out of the penitentiary and into the community, now coded by the pervasive logic of rehabilitation. This was not the rehabilitation we have seen in the case of the disabled and Travellers, however, for that was about being absorbed into *Society*. In the age of paradox, rehabilitation derived its meaning from the register of 'risk': dangerous dispositions, desires and relations could no longer be defined outside of their context, and the context was dynamic.

The theme of risk already had an international platform, an example being the Conference of Ministers Responsible for Family Affairs which met in 1973, under the auspices of the Council of Europe, to discuss

'Children and Young Persons at Risk' (UNICEF, 2005: x; Bernard, 1973). Here the causes of risk were framed in psychological terms as 'social maladjustment' and 'personality disorders', together defining the causes of delinquency. As recommended by the Kennedy Report, the child was to remain as far as possible within the 'natural family environment', and 'psychological and financial aid should be given to prevent difficulties'. And while the 'natural family' was the ideal source of crime prevention, the risk of maladjustment could be offset by placing the child with a 'substitute family', thus restoring the balance between the individual and the social order.

Back in Ireland a survey by the Association of Remedial Teachers in 1975 found that some 22 per cent of students entering post-primary schools had difficulty reading, while 20–25 per cent of primary and post-primary pupils were 'in the category of slow learner' (on primary schools see Fontes and Kellaghan, 1977). The survey prompted a letter to the *Irish Times* on the 'care of the school child', calling for all children to be 'screened from babyhood to school leaving age', with special attention to 'at risk' children (Cowhey, 1976). Again, it was the increasingly ubiquitous apparatus of the expert team and community care that was called upon to address the problem of 'underachievement', with pupils to be brought under the gaze of psychiatrists, psychologists, speech therapists, social workers, family doctors and 'other supportive services', together ensuring the 'full psychological assessment' of the child (Bernard, 1973; see also Swan, 1979; McCarthy and O'Boyle, 1988; Boehnlein, 1989).

Truancy – now 'no longer a trivial offence' (for those incarcerated in the industrial schools, it had never been a trivial offence) – was recoded as 'school phobia', while the problem of illiteracy among the adult population was said to be 'reaching an embarrassingly high percentage'. From the novel themes of risk, underachievement and educational failure was assembled a familiar object: a 'growing delinquency problem' (Cannon, 1976). Possible explanations abounded even as the field of investigation expanded: perhaps it was the child–parent relationship, or bullying by classmates, or an 'unethical teacher', or in the case of 'underprivileged children' it might be an alcoholic father or a wife-beating husband. The *Irish Press* recommended a truancy-scale based on 'degree of seriousness', from the 'soft offender' to the 'more serious offender', with the latter revealing a 'hidden ambivalence': she or he might come from a 'prosperous home' and might be of 'reasonable intelligence' (Cannon, 1976). Social class was still a key indicator, with poor 'scholastic performance' correlating positively with poverty (and delinquency), but the real surprise was that even wealthy and

intelligent youths might be at risk of educational failure, a revelation
which enlarged the field of discourse so that it began to envelop youth
as such.

By the end of the decade the 'reading nightmare' of illiteracy was
defined as both a 'defect' and a 'disability'. The chief psychiatrist at St
Joseph's Hospital in Limerick proposed two years' 'preventative detention' for school 'drop-outs', to be organised as a 'graded system of
training, education and work'. The rationale was a slippery-slope thesis:
drop-outs had 'all sorts of reasons . . . for not being qualified to take up
a job; and therefore are never fit for work . . . next they fall into gangs
[and] begin the downward trail of drugs, alcohol and promiscuous living
and later, robbing, petty thievery, vandalism and living rough' (*Irish
Times*, 1976b). Punishment and education had long worked together to
correct socially undesirable habits and conducts. The difference here
was that they were no longer operating as discrete fields; inadequate
education was placed on a continuum with the criminal act, and the
discourse of risk erased the distinction between the penitentiary and the
social disciplines. A survey conducted by the Educational Research
Centre of St Patrick's College in Drumcondra found that 12–13 per cent
of primary school-leavers in the Republic had reading and writing
disabilities. The 'serious questions' this raised concerned the socio-
economic profile of the problem population, with children in this class
found among poor and middle-class families alike (*Irish Times*, 1979;
Walshe, 1979; Swan, 1979). Again it was the 'hidden ambivalence' of
educational underachievement and underperformance that seemed to
cause alarm. On the one hand every child was at risk, but on the other
the specific problems associated with risk prevailed among the poor
(Edwards, 1974; McCarthy and O'Boyle, 1988; Boehnlein, 1989). That
truancy and 'dropping out' might be a form of resistance, a way of refusing the hegemony of an educational system which was no longer compulsory in the coercive sense but instead operated through the register
of equality, simply went unsaid.

The theme of risk bridged the poverty of 'ill-clad beggars at every
corner' and the invisible poverty 'behind the closed doors of comfort-
able looking homes': the loneliness, isolation and stress caused by financial pressure and 'mental block' (Kennedy, 1973). Just as the new
poverty broke the bounds of social class, so the problem of untrained
youth now traversed the social field in its entirety. As a symptom of all
social ills, 'school phobia' explained everything and so explained nothing,
yet it was the emptiness of this sign that gave it its value in the orders
of discourse: a prize to be won in the politics of truth-formation. Between
educational failure and 'the growing delinquency problem' would

emerge the notion of 'multiple' and 'cumulative risk factors' which, as we will see shortly, provides an epistemic support for the discourse of 'anti-social' behaviour (Squires and Stephen, 2005a).

Controlling the context

Corporal punishment was abolished in Ireland in 1982, provoking a search for alternative methods to maintain discipline in the classroom (Ireland, 1985a). The Catholic Primary School Managers Association discussed the effects of this at their annual conference in 1988, describing the deterioration in discipline as 'frightening'. The Association called on the minister for education to consult parents on the question of corporal punishment, but the minister ruled out any return to the old regime (Holmes, 1988). Instead an expert Committee was commissioned to control the context:

> [A]gainst a background of uncertainty and rapid change, it has become normal for people to question and indeed challenge the decisions of those in authority. Children are less inhibited nowadays and ask why it is necessary for them to adopt particular modes of behaviour . . . some parents . . . are so incapable of coping with the pressures of life that in exasperation, confusion and anger they ill-treat members of their families. Children from homes where violence occurs regularly or where the behaviour of a parent is in some way abnormal tend to be emotionally disturbed and to adopt disruptive behaviour in school . . . Some children with learning difficulties tend to compensate for their lack of educational progress by being aggressive towards their peers and insubordinate to those in authority . . . Some parents are so preoccupied with their business, professional or social pursuits that they fail to give enough attention to their children . . . Some people have a tolerant and permissive approach to rearing children. Others have a repressive and rigid view of how children should be controlled . . . *The absence of a clear consensus among parents as to what constitutes adequate discipline makes it more difficult for teachers to maintain discipline within the schools.* (Ireland, 1985a: 11–13, emphasis added)

The meaning of 'discipline' was conflicted and unstable, in part disturbed by a social force which is generally not counted among the new social movements: a restless youth disposed to question authority. Attempts to reinstate some kind of disciplinary apparatus – to orchestrate a hegemony – saw the experts looking out *from* the perspective of the fictional normal family and normal child to the less than ideal realities of actual families and actual children, with 'disruptive' behaviour bridging the distance between home and classroom (see also Garvey, 1989).

The new disciplinary code proposed by the Committee was based on three principles which would order the lived worlds of the child into a more tightly knit relation. First was the identification of 'special needs', together with the pastoral care of disruptive children; second, the continuous training of teachers combined with the continuous monitoring of the new disciplinary code; and third, the need for vigilance on the part of teachers, parents and school managers to identify potential and manifest behavioural problems. The 'code' required all schools to be equipped with remedial teachers and psychologists (also Swan, 1989). Day-care centres were to be established in urban areas to cater for the educational needs of pupils whose behaviour was 'so disruptive as to infringe on the constitutional right of others to education'. The code would combine remedial education with behavioural management, home–school liaison, career guidance, counselling, and consultation with parents and pupils. It would ensure a continuous flow of information between the school and the home, enabling teachers, clinicians and parents to hone their powers of observation for any signs of maladjustment. Schools should also have, with the agreement of parents/guardians, the capacity to refer a student directly to the child-guidance services under the authority of the health boards, and within the bounds of the Constitution it should be made easier for the state to take children into care when they were being seriously neglected or subjected to cruelty by their parents/guardians (Ireland, 1985a: 15–6, 23–31). The logic of the *Planning for the Future* document published the previous December (Ireland, 1989a) was clearly in evidence here: the new disciplinary code would take the form of a therapeutic regime, tracing out the life of the student as she or he moved within the enfolded spheres of home, clinic and school. While this could not cure the malaise of modernisation, it could make sure the players stayed in the game, preventing them from opting out by sniffing solvents, engaging in crime, or exiting altogether through the option of suicide.

In the 'age of paradox' neither the practices of the past nor the great promise of modernisation provided answers to the problem of order; there was nowhere to go other than to turn into the problem itself: it was now a management problem, with the worlds of the child brought together and governed as a single, inclusive relation.

The field of youth is now firmly encased in the register of risk, and in the remainder of this chapter I want to examine three dimensions of this discourse: sexual abuse, anti-social conduct, and educational performance.

Touching children

For a while it seemed as though the Kennedy process had written the concluding chapter to the history of the certified schools, but it was not to be so. The argument posed by the 1936 Commission on the reformatory and industrial schools – that there existed a 'misconception in the public mind' concerning the nature of the institutions – would prove to be prophetic, but not in the way intended. Context is important here, specifically the process of cultural transformation concerning matters of sexuality. After a protracted struggle spearheaded by the women's movement, contraceptives became available without prescription in 1985. Two years later the status of illegitimacy was abolished, marital rape was recognised in law in 1991, and homosexuality was decriminalised in 1993. The timing of these changes coincides with the emergence of child sex abuse as an intensely ethico-political issue, not only in Ireland but internationally (ICCL, 1985; LRC, 1989; Ireland, 2005b).

The Limerick Federation of Women's Organisations held a seminar on 'Child Sexual Abuse and Incest' in 1988. A senior psychologist with the Eastern Health Board spoke at the gathering and explained that in Ireland, by comparison to other countries, large numbers of brothers sexually abused their sisters. It was suggested that drug addiction, alcoholism, mental retardation and mental instability were not major factors contributing to the offence in Ireland. Instead it was the large size of Irish families which was causally significant, with the typical offender socially immature and unable to develop close relationships or communicate emotional needs (*Irish Times*, 1988a). Again, as with the debate on educational underachievement, it was 'tradition' that provided an explanation; more specifically the anomalous relation between the 'traditional' Irish family and the 'modern' nuclear family. It was not so much the closeness of the large Irish family that was the problem, but rather its *closed-ness*, meaning its insulation against surveillance. The profile of the typical offender was particularly troubling in this respect, with the vast majority of offenders known to the abused child, usually a family member (McKeown and Gilligan, 1990; ICCL, 1985; O'Morain, 1988). The recommendations of the Kennedy inquiry – that the family relation should be maintained at all costs – was inappropriate in the case of incestuous families, with research showing that if offenders are allowed back into the family, even after counselling and therapy, they must be kept under surveillance for life.

Between 1984 and 1987 the number of confirmed cases of sexual abuse in Ireland increased from 33 to 456, a trend which did not abate (LRC, 1989: 2). During the first few months of 1994 (the same year as the Catholic church in Ireland was implicated; see below) news reports of abuse included a male employee of the Madonna House Children's Home, a former Olympic swimming coach, a primary school principal, a man who had sexually assaulted a 5-year-old boy in the toilet of a public house, a 53-year-old man who had repeatedly raped his daughter, a 75-year-old man convicted of sexually assaulting two girls aged 10 and 12, and a 73-year-old man accused of sexually assaulting a boy.

By this time the sexual abuse of children was framed as a systemic rather than an episodic problem. Speaking at a conference on 'Healing Child Sex Abuse' in 1997 organised by Children at Risk in Ireland (CARI), Dr Alice Swann, from a Belfast-based child protection consultancy agency, explained that the impact of abuse on the child caused confusion, guilt, shame, low self-esteem, sadness, mistrust, anxiety and fear, and in terms of treatment it crossed the spheres of health, education, law and psychology. Eileen Prendeville, a therapist with CARI, explained that 'we now know that child abuse occurs in all areas, within all income groups, and that any child can be at risk' (Newman, 1997). In Belgium the Dutroux case[9] implicated the police and judicial system in an organised paedophile ring, with experts warning that the paedophile was 'Mr Everybody' (Downing, 1997; cf. ICCL, 1985). In Ireland, however, it was not Mr Everybody but the Catholic priest Brendan Smyth who became the symbolic centre of this discourse (Ireland, 2005b: 12).

Smyth was put on trial twice, first in 1994 and again during 1997.[10] The Smyth case made it increasingly clear that the Catholic hierarchy had concealed knowledge of clerical involvement in the sexual abuse of children. Although the psychologists warned that the paedophile was Mr Everybody, the Smyth case created a monster out of the man, transforming the individual into something the public could hate, consume and excrete; a creature so exceeding the desires and conduct of normal people that it was again possible to feel secure about Mr Everybody. Smyth was described in words and images as a vicious predator, the embodiment of evil, and the antithesis of civilised values. Photos depicted him snarling at the camera like an animal, with the images framed by words describing him as 'calculating', 'the most evil man in Ireland', the 'thief of innocence' and 'the predator'. It was as if it might be possible to represent Smyth in such a way that the truth of the horror would be fixed as an innate quality of the man himself. That Smyth might be the symptom of something else, something more routine, something that moved within the undergrowth of Irish culture was avoided like the plague. And this reluctance to confront the issue on any level other than that of seeing the church as the culprit, at most extending this to the state as co-conspirator, has persisted. The fact that complicity might include all those who placed women and children in the grip of the penitentiary complex – the philanthropic agents of rescue and child saving; those who allowed their daughters and sons, brothers and sisters, neighbours and acquaintances to be removed to the institutions, or even delivered them in person – has still to be broached.

As it reaches back into the archives of the penitentiary complex, so the investigation into abuse places the cherished resource of Irish history under intense suspicion, with those long coded as delinquent, defective, handicapped, illegitimate, backward and fallen now demanding justice and inclusion. At the 1997 CARI conference mentioned above, the minister for state at the Department of Health, Frank Fahey, could earnestly claim that 'until recently there was no widespread awareness of child sex abuse'. It might be more accurate to suggest that it has long been part of a regime of truth wherein knowledge takes the form of a shared secret. That it has been brought within the realm of the sayable is part of a larger transformation. The dislocations of the 1970s and 1980s no more brought the issue of sex abuse out into the open than the disclosure of sex abuse was the cause of dislocation; instead they are both constitutive dimensions of an event which has spawned an inclusive mode of governance.

Inclusive governance is predicated on the recognition that order cannot be perfected, and the discourse of child sex abuse just might remind us of this if we listened closely. But it seems that we are not (yet) willing to do so, with the figure of the abuser replacing that of the unmarried mother as the symbol of sexual excess and transgression (see chapter 8). Amid periodic calls for registers of known paedophiles to be made public are the cases of vigilante attacks on suspects, with 'communities' attempting to purify their living space and protect their children. And here the notion of 'community care' takes on a different – an urgent and at times violent – meaning. Even as more and more people are caught browsing child pornography on the internet, and as sex tourists satiate their desire for the novel, the unconventional and the prohibited beyond the prying eyes of family and friends, so there is an ever-greater effort to resuscitate the perfectionist logic of Society by seeking to know the 'kind of people who offend' (LRC, 1989). If the monster is known then it can be controlled and, if necessary, excluded for the safety of children and the social good. However, if we attend to the inclusion/exclusion problematic, that is, if we examine it as a governmentality (which is not to equate this with the single issue of paedophilia), then we find a growing recognition that the politics of order wraps an elusive object, with order at best a tenuous and provisional state of stability. The register of risk points to the fundamental undecidability of the social and presents us with a disturbing question: what if the monster is ineradicably with us and in us; what if the monster is us? Perhaps it is this which characterises the 'age of paradox'.

Anti-social behaviour

Introduced in Britain under the Crime and Disorder Act 1998, the Anti-Social Behaviour Order (ASBO) has its opponents on both sides of the Irish Sea and has been met with a number of criticisms. First among these is the problem of defining 'anti-social behaviour', with the legal definition both vague and varied. In the UK, the 1998 Act defines it as acting in a manner which has caused or is 'likely' to cause 'harassment, alarm or distress to one or more persons' (London, 2002; Ramsay, 2004). The more recent Anti-Social Behaviour Act 2003 incorporates this definition and adds behaviour 'capable of causing nuisance or annoyance to any person' (Padfield, 2004). For critics the problem is one of defining public nuisance or menace with a sufficient degree of precision. Behaviour associated with annoyance, for example, is likely to involve the contextual interplay of perspective and interpretation. Coupled to this is legislation which goes beyond acts which *have* caused harassment, alarm or distress to behaviour which is *likely* to cause these things. Designed in part to address the problem of witness intimidation, the Crime and Disorder Act empowers the professional witness and removes the need for an actual victim and a vulnerable witness (Jones and Sagar, 2001). However, critics point to the danger of a legally enforceable sanction that moves beyond things which have happened to the judgement of future misdeeds. When added to the legal vagueness of 'anti-social behaviour', the concern is over discretionary power which is exercised without being sufficiently constrained by due process, thus encroaching on individual rights and liberties.

A second concern is the hybrid nature of the ASBO, which blurs the distinction between civil and criminal law. An ASBO is made in a civil court, which admits hearsay evidence and prohibits the subject of an ASBO from doing anything described in the order. Breaching an ASBO, however, is a criminal offence, and may lead to a custodial sentence of up to five years (Jones and Sagar, 2001; IYJA, 2005). A third concern is the way the ASBO shifts the role of the state from social support to control and exclusion. An example is the practice of 'naming and shaming' whereby local authorities distribute flyers with photographs and details of young people who have been issued with an ASBO, the objective of which is to ensure compliance on the part of ASBO recipients by recruiting local residents into the work of surveillance and sanction (Squires and Stephen, 2005b; also Jones and Sagar, 2001).

Taken together, this bundle of criticisms sees in the ASBO a slippery slope to an authoritarian state. By prohibiting conduct which is otherwise lawful, the ASBO individualises the subject's relation to the rule of law, specifying duties and making civil rights conditional on present and future compliance with the ASBO (Ramsay, 2004). Yet the reach of the disciplinary complex assembled around the discourse of anti-social behaviour is much greater than the ASBO itself. Acceptable Behaviour Contracts (ABCs), for example, which supplement the ASBO, are voluntary agreements that organise 'people involved in anti-social behaviour' (including their parents or guardians) into partnerships with local police, housing authorities and school authorities. Augmenting this is the technique of the Crime Prevention Partnership which, under the Crime and Disorder Act 1998, imposes a duty on the local state to cooperate with a variety of local agencies – probation committees, health authorities, voluntary sector agencies (such as victim support and drug action teams), and the private for-profit sector – in developing a crime reduction strategy. Between the ASBO and the ABC is the means of inserting incompetent and recalcitrant subjects within a micro-social relation of community governance modelled on the expert team: on one side a voluntary contract and on the other a compulsory order. While it clearly has its punitive moment as it passes from civil injunction to crime, the ASBO/ABC nexus might be described as a technology of citizenship directed simultaneously at social conduct and individual character (see Cruikshank, 1994). It aims to create a civil subject and a mode of civility, linking social context (its intersubjective moment) to individual dispositions (the character of the anti-social individual) (Ramsay, 2004). While the old problem of liberal government – how to combine freedom with discipline – is being rethought here, it also remains largely intact.

In Ireland the current government is preparing legislation for the introduction of the ASBO,[11] but by no means does it have a monopoly on the issue. In fact all the major parties are striving to responsibilise individuals and 'communities'. While acknowledging the link between anti-social behaviour and disadvantage, the Labour Party's position, for example, which goes by the name of 'Taking Back the Neighbourhood', emphasises 'responsibility' and endorses the introduction of the ASBO (Labour Party, 2005). Fine Gael stands over a similar message, arguing that:

Anti-social behaviour is hurting our society. Every day, in every neighbourhood, it spoils our sense of community, degrades our environment, reduces our quality of life. It chips away at our sense of security, our civic pride, our peace of mind. Anti-social behaviour ranges from petty incivility to outright criminal damage to people and to property. (Fine Gael, 2005)

As part of its 'safe streets' campaign, Fine Gael published a website and hired billboards, populating both with images of 'real people in real incidents and settings . . . taken at night in a variety of locations around Ireland'. Contextualised by the caption 'Ireland: A Night in the Life', the images frame Fine Gael's depiction of anti-social behaviour as something which emanates from a 'culture of poverty' (figure 7.1). And while sympathetic to the plight of marginalised communities, the Party is emphatic in its stance on the necessary consequences of anti-social behaviour: 'it's the perpetrator, not the law-abiding citizen and community, who must pay the price'.

In the discourse of anti-social behaviour we can see how the theme of 'risk' articulates a struggle between competing interpretations as to the causes of disorder. In Ireland support for the ASBO marks a shift in policy focus and public perception to the notion of a moral underclass, or the discourse of disorder so apparent in the United States, targeting individual conducts and 'community' contexts marked by a lack of (self-)discipline. Child welfare agencies oppose this interpretation of risk and the way the ASBO threatens to contradict and undermine the Children Act of 2001. Replacing the Children's Charter of 1908 (and amending the Child Care Act 1991), the new child-care legislation promises to bring the juvenile justice system into alignment with the UN Convention on the Rights of the Child, ensuring that the detention of juveniles 'shall be used only as a measure of last resort and for the shortest appropriate period of time' (Dooley and Corbett, 2002). Here the theme of risk accords with notions of disadvantage and marginalisation. Against detention, whether in a residential home or a juvenile prison, the 2001 Act lays the groundwork for an apparatus of prevention, diversion, supervision and counselling within the community. While the legal terminology is different in Ireland and England, it must be noted that the same basic apparatus is in evidence. In Ireland, according to the 2001 Act, young people are to be admitted to diversion programmes if they accept responsibility for their criminal behaviour, while the management of young offenders within the community is to be effected through the technique of the conference. In accordance with the principles of restorative justice, a facilitator is charged with formulating an action plan with and for the offender, in partnership with his or her parents/guardians, in consultation with the victim, and with the assistance of police, health services, probation and welfare services and

Figure 7.1 Ireland: a night in the life

school authorities. Furthermore a court may make a parental supervision order, instructing the parents/guardians of an offender to undergo treatment for alcohol or substance misuse, and/or to attend a parenting course (Ireland, 2001).

Though widely perceived as the opportunity to break finally and decisively with the old penitentiary mode of treatment, in its emphasis on community-based non-custodial measures, family group conferences and diversion programmes, the 2001 Act is a cautious break with the past. While the penitentiary waits in the wings to punish those who breach the ASBO, more interesting is what lies between the competing interpretations of risk and between the disciplinary technologies of the penitentiary and the contract: a parochial mode of administration cast in the mould of community care and the expert team. More specifically, this is a governmental apparatus that brings a variety of authorities and subjects into a relation of partnership.

As an administrative apparatus and a technology of citizenship, the discourse of anti-social behaviour circumscribes a multi-dimensional strategy:

1 It positions conduct within the space of a problematic conjoining freedom and (self-)discipline. Going by the name of 'responsibility', this is both individual and social.
2 It places conduct and character under the authority of a discourse which has its central points in sovereign power (the police, the law, the prison) but is otherwise dispersed throughout the social field (crime reduction partnerships, diversion programmes, the conference).
3 It aims to secure order by creating a wholly negative representation of undesirable conducts, dispositions and relations. The 'anti-'social signifies pure negation, reaching beyond the concern with anti-social individuals to the government of social order and social relations.

In Britain the list of behaviours to be tackled by the ASBO and the ABC include writing graffiti, using abusive and intimidating language, creating excessive noise, littering, substance misuse, begging, prostitution and vandalism (London, 2002). In the Irish case the minister for justice has pledged a less draconian version of the ASBO, but either way it seems that the problem of the 'perishing and dangerous classes' has returned (Carpenter, 1861, 1968), precisely those forms of conduct that gave birth to the industrial and reformatory schools (Barnes, 1989; Raftery and O'Sullivan, 1999). By enlarging the role of the state in governing unruly bodies, the new disciplinary complex poses a challenge to the established authority of the 'psy' sciences, a mode of authority with its origins in the 'dangerous individual' of the nineteenth century (Foucault, 1975). On the one hand it replicates the discourses of dangerous 'types' such as the 'moral lunatic' (Rimke and Hunt, 2002), and thus continues to blur the boundary between socially undesirable behaviour and criminal acts, and thus between the authorities of state and science. However – and here we can see an explicit connection with the Citizen Traveller campaign examined in chapter 5 – the means of governing conduct is now coded by the logic of partnership and implemented through technologies of contract, with those who cannot or will not discipline themselves inserted into a disciplinary relation at the local 'community' level, and here again is another articulation of 'community care'. Individuals and communities are to be responsibilised through a parochial mode of control (Crawford, 2003), with the perpetrator, the victim and the technicians of conduct inhabiting the same discursive space. I will examine this in greater detail in chapter 9, for now noting that inclusive governance gathers together the actual and the potential act, the actual and the potential consequences of the act, and the well-founded or imagined fears and concerns that pass between the possible and the manifest. As these are ordered into discourse, so they become the objects of inclusive governance (see Squires and Stephen, 2005b: 522).

Inclusion?

In 1997 the junior minister for education announced that the government was considering a proposal to test the literacy of primary school pupils before allowing them to make the transition to second level, a move deemed necessary in countering the 'growing numeracy and literacy problems in Ireland'. The Irish National Teachers Organisation interpreted this as a move towards British-style league tables, a move it was prepared to resist. However, the proposal was defended as an 'early warning system', consistent with programmes to combat educational disadvantage. Whether through this measure or some other, what is being assembled is a strategy to prevent students from 'falling behind and being condemned to an adult life of sub-literacy' (Walshe, 1997). Rooted in practices of protection and rescue, the problem of 'sub-literacy' is new-speak for abnormality, and while the social disciplines have been greatly dispersed since the time of Bentham, the school remains the principal arena within which the struggle to define the mode of subjectivation takes place. Education, and remember we are now in the time of 'life-long education', is implicated in the recalibration of panopticism.

Attention Deficit and Hyperactivity Disorder (ADHD) provides a critical perspective on this. In January 2002 the Northwest ADHD Support Group organised a conference in Sligo called 'Living with

ADHD'. Speaking at the conference, Dr Philp Tyndall, consultant child and adolescent psychiatrist with the North Western Health Board, suggested that approximately 5 per cent of children suffer from ADHD, and even in the absence of clinical diagnosis children with the disorder could be identified in the classroom by their 'fidgeting, squirming, restless, and very easily distractable' behaviour (Judge, 2002; see also McCarthy and O'Boyle, 1988). Research has found that as many as 40–60 per cent of children with ADHD-type symptoms have at least one other disorder, including disruptive behaviour disorder (oppositional-defiant disorder and conduct disorder), mood disorders (mania/bipolar disorder), anxiety disorders (panic attacks and dizziness), tics and Tourette's Syndrome (sudden, rapid, recurrent, non-rhythmic movements or vocalisations; barking a word or sound, repetitive flinching and eye-blinking), and learning disabilities (see Munden and Arcelus, 1999: 58). The Irish National Council of ADHD Support Groups (INCADDS, working in cooperation with the Department of Health and Children) lists seventeen characteristics of ADHD and Hyperkinetic Disorder (HKD) under four subheadings – inattentiveness, impulsivity, hyperactivity and 'other frequent features' – explaining to the prospective client that 'if you answered yes to at least eight characteristics listed, for over a period of six months, the chances are that the person meets the criteria for further investigation and assessment by a trained professional' (INCADDS, 2001).[12] INCADDS also explains that the disorder is a neurobiological condition which may be genetically transmitted. In parenthesis is the more accessible version of this: it 'often runs in families' (also Munden and Arcelus, 1999: 9–10, 57–9; Green and Kit, 1995: 19–20). The old debate on the hereditary transmission of defective dispositions and conducts has returned, now a concern with the familial origins of learning difficulties, language problems, clumsiness, opposition to authority, disorderly conduct, mood swings and low self-esteem.

The critical literature on ADHD notes that the recent increase in diagnosis correlates with the increased demands of the educational system and is concurrent with a general decrease in funding for schools and psychiatric health programmes. It is also the case that self-diagnosis is on the increase, with the drugs used to treat the condition, such as methylphenidate, linked to the short-term enhancement of cognitive performance. So-called objective symptoms also tend to mirror prevailing conceptions of deviance and norm violation (Searight and McLaren, 1998; Castel, Castel and Lovell, 1982: 207–9; Schrag and Divoky, 1975). In a survey of the literature and clinical research, H. Russell Searight and A. Lesley McLaren note that 'teacher and parental pressure to diagnose ADHD and initiate methylphenidate treatment is an experience common to many paediatricians and family physicians' (1998: 481). Sociologically this is both intriguing and troubling, a phenomenon which might, under different circumstances and notwithstanding the level of voluntary diagnosis, be interpreted as a mode of resistance, perhaps even a healthy refusal of a normative order which is obsessed with optimising the performance of everything from individual bodies to zones, 'sectors' and systems. If it is a form of resistance then it seems ineffective, with parents and children requesting diagnosis and inscribing themselves into the new hegemonic logic of 'performative inclusion' (Levitas, 1998: 158)

The rise of ADHD correlates with a larger process of social transformation, of which the abolition of corporal punishment and the issue of child sex abuse are a part. Given the recent proscription of physical contact between adults and children, it is perhaps unsurprising that we are witnessing 'the medicalisation of misbehaviour' (Searight and McLaren, 1998). However, there are reasons why we should be cautious about leaning too heavily on the medical as the basis of explanation.

I began the last chapter by noting the great and enduring division within the realm of mind: between disordered and deficient minds. It was also noted that this has long been entangled in questions of deformed and defective bodies, and the point was made that these have never been wholly distinct from each other, despite the many attempts at precise classification. As we reach the end of this chapter it would seem that the condition of ADHD reproduces this ambivalence, except that its reach is far greater than the old categories of defectiveness and handicap. How would one class ADHD in terms of the disordered/deficient/deformed mind–body complex? Is it the sign of a disordered mind, a deficient mind or an (abnormally) restless body? Or is it a symptom of the social itself, something which passes through the family relation to the communicative mode of ordering, finding its outer limit in the juvenile prison? At the very least it is among a new horizon of 'emerging disabilities' which exceed the old categories, the established policies and practices, and the conventional form of critique, with the latter predicated on a distinction between the medical and the social (see Fox and Kim, 2004). ADHD encompasses a range of disorders embodied in individuals, transmitted within families, and governed by techniques which bring parents, teachers, doctors and children into a relation. To identify this as a process of medicalisation is to overlook how encompassing this enfolded structure is, particularly when supplemented by coercive technologies like the ASBO.

While it has its clinical meaning, ADHD is also a mark of disadvantage and the risk of failure, both of which converge on the life-chances of the individual. Diagnostically ADHD is a potential source of exclusion which is perceived to originate in the individual and/or the individual's genetic inheritance. However, the condition becomes *social* through its outward manifestation – the child's observable behaviour and cognitive performance – which is managed through a relation that brings a variety of authorities into a direct and indirect relation. I visited a friend in hospital during January of 2002, and when I got there a family was already gathered around the bed of our mutual friend, talking about their son's ADHD. They were explaining how grateful they were to have found a doctor in the UK to help their son with his condition, and they described the first encounter with the doctor in some detail, recalling how he had immediately put the boy (and his parents) at ease by explaining that 'it's all right, we're going to help you'. Like young Alex in *A Clockwork Orange* this young man was surrounded by care and concern, with responsibility for his condition forming a bond between himself and his significant others: the parent–teacher–doctor nexus. As he began his course of medication and counselling it was not only his own 'disorder' that was being repaired, it was also the world around him that was being ordered. The boy was present as his story was told. Fully included in the decisions affecting his life, everything was out in the open; everything, that is, except the disciplinary grip of the diagnosis and the normalising effects of the treatment.

8

Unmarried motherhood and lone parenting

We don't worry and starve the soil of a garden incessantly for fear of weeds. If we did, we should have no flowers. (Miss Menella Smedley, 1880)

With the recognition that illegitimacy is not only a question of individual sin but a problem which involves the whole range of inherent and environmental factors, the community will realise that it has a duty toward the unmarried mother and her child . . . It remains for the twentieth century to assist society to function properly by reducing illegitimacy to a minimum. (Percy Gamble Kammerer, 1918)

Introduction: the unmarried mother and public assistance

From the time of Bentham to Booth and beyond, the meanings articulated by the figure of the 'unmarried mother' exhibit a remarkable degree of stability, as do the associated practices.[1] Laws to punish 'lewd women' and recover the cost of maintaining 'bastards' from the putative father had existed since the beginning of the classical epoch, but the old poor laws also provided the unmarried mother with a number of options – some of which allowed her to keep her child and to remain at large in the community – that would vanish with the birth of liberal government (Higginbotham 1985: 7). Those who testified before the Royal Commission of 1834 railed against the 'illicit intercourse' and 'successful bastardy adventures' encouraged by public assistance, arguing that it rewarded the wrongdoing of the woman while compelling the putative father either to flee or to marry through fear of punishment. Poor relief was alleged to be the cause of vice and improvident marriages, while the affiliation laws were said to encourage women to accuse wealthy men falsely so as to secure their maintenance. The problem, then, was that the unmarried mother was guaranteed a standard of subsistence over and above that of hard-working families, and was free to use relief as a 'sort of pension to herself' (Checkland and Checkland, 1974: 261–4).

Malthus himself had commented on the problem of bastardy by proposing that illegitimate children be left entirely at the mercy of private charity with no claim on parish assistance. The Malthusian argument appeared in pristine fashion in the testimony before the Royal Commission by a Mr Walcott, who argued that the provision of relief to the mothers of bastards impinged on 'one of the punishments naturally consequential on the offence, the burthen of supporting a child'. He also argued that the measure of a woman's 'fall from grace', and thus the basis of her claim on public assistance, was whether or not it was her 'first offence' (Checkland and Checkland, 1974: 269–70). Accepting the weight of testimony, the Royal Commission recommended that a bastard be 'what providence appears to have ordained that it should be': a burden on its mother; and as the penalties inflicted by nature were sufficient there was no need for other legal punishments (Checkland and Checkland, 1974: 481–2). In fact the resulting law did not conform this closely to the recommendations of the Commission, with unmarried mothers simply excluded from out-relief and subjected to the workhouse test in the same way as able-bodied males. Walcott's reference to first offence, however, more widely known as 'first fall', did play a central role in this field of discourse, and would continue to do so right up to the present.

The new poor law was introduced to Ireland in 1838 following a series of inquiries that culminated in the reports of George Nicholls. Presenting a very different picture of bastardy by comparison to England, Nicholls described Irish women as 'generally correct in their conduct', exhibiting habits of modesty, industriousness and sobriety. He thus recommended that things be left as they were, with women in Ireland remaining the 'guardians of their own honour' (London, 1837a: 28). However, the logic of exclusion found its way into the Irish poor law code via the Benthamite distinction between poverty and indigence. Unmarried mothers were to be dealt with in the same manner as other destitute persons and subjected to the workhouse test of less eligibility. The suppression of mendicancy would allow no exception to the prohibition on outdoor relief, not to unmarried mothers and their bastard offspring, not to the sick, aged or infirm, or to harmless pauper idiots and lunatics. There was to be no possibility of confusing the distinction between '*poverty* and *destitution*' (London, 1837b: 19–22, original emphasis). Though founded on arguments derived from Malthusianism in the case of England and Benthamism in the Irish context, unmarried mothers would be excluded from the project of Society in both cases.

At the turn of the twentieth century, and as the theory of hereditary pauperism reached its zenith, the penal logic of first and repeat offence was reproduced intact, with the 1906 Viceregal Commission on Poor Law Reform in Ireland expressing its opposition to the workhouse as a refuge for unmarried mothers because it exposed 'first lapse' girls to dangerous associations.[2] To substantiate its position, the Commissioners cited the case of 'four illegitimate generations in the female line' in one workhouse; the illegitimate baby, her illegitimate mother, illegitimate grandmother, and illegitimate great-grandmother proof that the workhouse lessened the 'sense of shame' and caused such women to lapse into 'confirmed immorality':

> Workhouses in Ireland have been the means of keeping up the numbers of this most undesirable special class of women, and also of developing the tendency that exists for the continuation and multiplication of the class from hardened mothers to shameless daughter, owing to the unnatural and unhealthy environment in which they are placed . . . no child which has to be supported out of the rates, ought to be allowed to remain with a women who is the mother of two or more illegitimate children. (London, 1906: 42–4)

It was recommended that those guilty of a 'first lapse' be sent to a special institution prior to their confinement, after which the girl should be found a position while the child would be boarded out with a respectable family. As for the 'more degraded cases' of repeat offenders, they were to be interned in the 'excellent institutions' already in existence: the Magdalen penitentiaries. As we saw in chapter 3, the object of the Magdalen asylums, penitentiaries and refuges was originally the 'social evil' of prostitution. However, as the rescue enterprise became more organised and extensive its focus shifted to the sources of vice. Unmarried mothers were already being interned in the convent penitentiaries by the end of the nineteenth century, but in twentieth-century Ireland this would become the strategic objective of the institution (see MacInerny, 1922).[3]

As the Irish Free State was established the unmarried mother was governed through a three-way mode of authority: the workhouse under the authority of the state, the social disciplines under the authority of an embryonic social work profession born from social economy and scientific philanthropy (Skehill, 1999), and the large penitentiary under the authority of religious orders. In this three-way diagram we see the elements of an administrative apparatus which proved to be remarkably resilient. It is not that the unmarried mother was totally encased within this regime, and I am not suggesting that there is no scope for resistance. Among the unmarried mothers 'strategies for survival' (Higgenbotham 1985) were family support, if available, which may have allowed the mother to work while caring for her child within the family home. Many also fled the country, although the emergence of Catholic welfare agencies during the twentieth century established a practice of tracking down and repatriating at least some of those who managed to escape (Garrett, 2000; MacInerny, 1922: 253; 'Sagart', 1922: 146; Devane, 1928: 566). These moments of resistance are important, but they did not have a significant impact on the mode of government. Something else was responsible for that.

The Poor Law Commission on the fallen woman

On the question of unmarried mothers and illegitimate children the Poor Law Commission suggested that there were two distinct classes to be considered: those who were amenable to reform and those who were not (Ireland, 1927: 68; see also Devane, 1928; MacInerny, 1922; Glynn, 1921). The 'first offender' class was to be subjected to a blend of firmness, discipline, charity and sympathy, together providing the necessary 'moral upbuilding'. The health authorities would exercise discretion in dealing with this class through 'the agency of rescue societies and voluntary organisations'. It was also noted that a 'residue', immune to 'good influences', existed within this class. The logical thing to do, being mindful of the need for economy, was to incorporate this residual group into the second class of repeat offender (Ireland, 1927: 68; see also *Irish Times*, 1925b). Those first fall women who had merely lapsed would, though marked by their shame and probably minus their child, be given a second chance, while those incapable of reform would be subjected to harsh and punitive control, though there was less certainty regarding how exactly this was to be accomplished.

According to figures available to the Commission, as of 1926 there were 629 unmarried mothers in the county homes and the Dublin workhouse[4] who could be classed as first time offenders, and another 391 'who had fallen more than once' (Ireland, 1927: 68). As the law stood there was no power of compulsory detention available to prosecute the offence of unmarried motherhood, but the Commission argued that if a woman applying for assistance was willing to enter a home for a period not exceeding one year, then there should be power to retain her for that period, and this should be extended to two years for a second occurrence, and in the case of a third or subsequent child the period of detention should be determined by the local authority (Ireland, 1927: 69). The mode of regulation would ensure that treatment was dispensed 'according to individual requirements', while 'in the most degraded cases' it would allow for the segregation of those 'who have become sources of evil, danger, and expense to the community' (Ireland, 1927: 69). While the Commission did have something to say about the fathers of illegitimate children, their main concern in this respect was the cost of support. Under the Criminal Law Amendment Act of 1885[5] it was sufficient defence on the part of a man accused of unlawful carnal knowledge to have believed the girl to be over 16 years of age at the time of the act, while no prosecution could be brought against him if three months had lapsed since the commission of the offence (extended to six months by the Prevention of Cruelty to Children Act 1904). What the Commission wanted from the point of view of the putative father was the enforcement of affiliation orders, so that the cost of maintaining and educating the child could be recovered (Ireland, 1927: 71–2, 128).

In the absence of laws to apprehend and detain females guilty of extra-marital sex, the Commission could only hope to strengthen the existing laws and practices relating to sexual offences. Important here was the argument that 16 years of age was 'entirely too young for many girls to have full knowledge of and realise the consequences of an act that may be brought about by the thoughtlessness and the seductive pleadings of the male partner in guilt' (Ireland, 1927: 72). Here the unmarried mother was brought within the scope of mental deficiency discourse. In England, as codified by the Mental Deficiency Act of 1913, female sexuality was already coming under the complex authority of law, professional social work and the psychiatric sciences (Walmsley, 2000). In the Irish case there would be less of a role for positive law, and it would be some time before psychiatrists played more than a supplemental role in this field. Medical knowledge was none the less available to the agents of religious authority, and the Free State was also taking tentative steps towards a more comprehensive public health and assistance system. Drawing on established and emerging discourses of moral insanity, moral imbecility, feeble-mindedness and mental deficiency, clerics and representatives from the public health and assistance authorities were more than willing to diagnose any sign of sexual waywardness as a first step on the slippery slope to unmarried motherhood. 'Little more than children', girls under 16 years of age were considered to be 'mentally unstable' – incapable of understanding the morality or consequences of the sexual act – and so the question of consent was irrelevant. For Rev. R. Devane, purity campaigner and city missionary, those guilty of 'morally perverse conduct' – meaning the 'semi-imbecile' and the 'mentally deficient' – were to be given 'the protection of the law' (Devane, 1928: 569; 1924a; 1924b). A few years later at a meeting of the health and public assistance authorities, speakers made it clear that the discourse of mental defectiveness provided a means to prevent at least some women from becoming unmarried mothers, because, coded as *patients*, they could be controlled without the need for a criminal conviction (Ireland, 1930: 51, 88–93). We will return to this theme of protection shortly.

Importantly the Commission saw the problem of illegitimate births as something that would inevitably abate, and while there had been a slight upward trend during the previous decade this was explained by the upheavals of war and civil strife as the Free State came into existence. There was thus no apparent reason to believe that the 'evil' would continue to increase in the future; on the contrary, the Commission presumed that 'with returning stability of government and the gradual tightening of the reigns of discipline, both governmental and parental, we may look forward to a decrease in the number of these births' (Ireland, 1927: 73; also Devane, 1928).

In this way the Irish Free State reinstated the figure of the unmarried mother as a symbol of 'moral' excess and dangerousness. With the illegitimate children of first offenders coded as 'children in danger', and those of repeat offenders deemed to be 'dangerous children', the nineteenth-century fascination with the perishing and dangerous classes was also set to continue (Kilcommins, O'Donnell, O'Sullivan and Vaughan, 2004: 83). It was only as the twentieth century came to a close that the sin-crime-illness of unmarried motherhood would be (partially) unhinged, the process of reconstruction framed in humanistic terms as a sign of greater equality and inclusiveness.

Protecting women and securing order

By the end of the 1920s mother and baby homes had been established under the management of religious orders and were being funded by local assistance authorities in Dublin, Clare and Galway.[6] There was also one extern institution in County Cork (Bessborough), opened in 1922 and run by the Sisters of the Sacred Hearts of Jesus and Mary (see MacInerny, 1922). Unlike the Pelletstown home in Dublin, criticised for its failure to 'grade cases according to age, degree of guilt and social station' ('Sagart', 1922: 148), the Bessborough facility was:

> [I]ntended primarily for young mothers who have fallen for the first time and who are likely to be influenced towards a useful and respectable life. In the Home they are trained in domestic work, cookery, needlework, dairy work, poultry keeping and gardening and instructed in their religion. After a period of training each is provided with a suitable situation and put in the way of self support and the children are boarded out with reliable foster mothers. (DLGPHa, 1929: 113)

The technique of isolating first offenders moved in the groove of nineteenth-century reformatory punishment, with the logic of quarantine directed at 'protecting' those who had committed the error of first fall from the 'degrading influences' of the more hardened cases: the problem of moral contagion. As with General Booth's social lifeboat institution, the Bessborough model was to help first fall penitents to 'regain a footing in the world' (DLGPHa, 1929: 114). As things stood, however, some 70 per cent of unmarried mothers with first-born children in the care of the state still remained in the county homes, 'where they cannot be dealt with apart from other inmates' (DLGPHa, 1929: 113). There was a need for greater protection.

What was sought within the meaning of 'reform' was a regime of 'appropriate training and example' which would also attend to matters of economy. Unless 'active measures' were taken, there was a danger that unmarried mothers would become a 'permanent burden on the ratepayers' and/or 'drift into a life of degradation' (DLGPHa, 1931: 130). Reports published by the Department of Local Government and Public Health at this time claim that progress was being made, although a caveat was added in relation to Bessborough, where the matron warned that 'a number of the girls are very weak willed and have to be maintained in the Home for a long period to safeguard them against a second lapse' (DLGPHa, 1931: 130). Regarding these 'less hopeful cases', the report for 1932 noted that 'these women appear to be feeble-minded and need supervision and guardianship ... The Magdalen Asylum offers the only special provision at present for this class' (DLGPHa, 1932: 129). Efforts were also being made to track down and repatriate girls who had slipped through the net and made their way to England (DLGPHa, 1932: 130; 1935: 180; Garrett, 2000). While this regime of surveillance, detection, repatriation and incarceration had at best a tenuous basis in positive law, it was being assembled and instituted to protect women 'for their own good'. As was the case with itinerants, defectives and delinquents at this time, this class was subject to be dealt with by the technicians of conduct.

Speaking on the 'true Christian ideal of morality' in 1931, the Rev. H. B. Kennedy explained that legislation on sexual offences in the Free State lagged behind Britain and Northern Ireland. Local government reports described a pervasive 'sexual sin and debased moral standard', the proof of which was 'the disgraceful number of unmarried mothers in County Homes, where they are maintained at the public expense instead of being supported by their partners in sin' (*Irish Independent*, 1931a). An editorial in the *Irish Times* three years later endorsed this theme of moral decline, noting that 'the practice of certain vices and crimes had increased in the Free State during recent years', one sign being 'the growth of infanticide – that dreadful sequel of illegitimate births' (*Irish Times*, 1934a).[7] Between Rev. Kennedy's speech and the editorial was a 'suppressed report' compiled by the Carrigan Committee (after William Carrigan, who chaired the inquiry) on the Criminal Law Amendment Acts. Though never published, the report none the less created positive effects – very much a statement in the Foucaultian sense – which established a point of tension in the ongoing struggle between the penitentiary model and the social model. The Carrigan Committee wanted to address the problem of moral decline by cutting transgressors out of the social fabric altogether. The Free State's Department of Justice, however, was concerned with the more ambitious project of constituting and consolidating the National Society.

Anticipating resistance to its recommendations, the Carrigan inquiry concluded that 'if some of our proposals ... appear to be ... too drastic ... it is to be remembered that our function has been to provide remedies for an abnormal ailment and therefore the use of some new curative might be expected' (Ireland, 1931: 16). The abnormal ailment in question was the 'degeneration in the standard of social conduct', with the Committee agreeing with the diagnosis (but not the prognosis) of the 1927 Poor Law Commission in attributing this to the 'loss of parental control and responsibility during a period of general upheaval' (Ireland, 1931: 12). The Committee singled out 'the new popular amusements' as a principal cause in 'the ruin of hundreds of young girls', meaning dance halls, picture houses, and the 'opportunities afforded by the misuse of motor cars for luring girls'. Rev. John Flanagan of Dublin called for the names and addresses of all offenders to be published; Rev. Canon Lee from County Limerick described the dance halls as 'schools of scandal'; while Father Fitzpatrick of Limerick referred to the displays of public indecency as a sign of 'rampant ... defiance of priests and police' (Ireland, 1931: 12–3).

Armed with such incontrovertible evidence the Committee went on to rehearse the prevailing wisdom concerning the moral imbecility and mental instability of young women: 'the number of girls who begin to lead immoral lives at 16 is large' and 'we consider that this is due to the fact that the girl of 16 is often mentally and emotionally unstable; she is not finished growing and developing; and though she may be excited and her passions awakened, yet she cannot really appreciate the nature and result of the act to which she consents'. Again we see the science of emotional instability provide a support for normalising power. Exhibiting feeble-mindedness and weakness of will, young women were both incapable of mastering their sexual passion and vulnerable to the predatory instincts of males. The period from 16 to 19 years of age was the most dangerous because this was the time when girls were 'most susceptible emotionally and least capable of self-control'. Men would also be subject to the new moral code, and the Committee wanted 'male prowlers' punished for preying on 'weak-minded females' and bringing 'ignorant girls to ruin' (Ireland, 1931: 20). There was to be no room for ambiguity in governing this problem; the Committee recommended the straightforward criminalisation of sexual transgressions, with those found guilty sentenced to the lash followed by a two-year prison term with hard labour (Ireland, 1931: 15). Contraceptives too were denounced as 'a means of avoiding the consequences of sexual indulgence among the unmarried', and it was recommended that 'the articles in question should be banned by an enactment similar to the Dangerous Drugs Act 1920'.[8]

The Department of Justice responded with a fourteen-page memo denouncing the recommendations as partial, inappropriate and likely to undermine social order. From the perspective of the state the problem of illicit intercourse lay in its consequences, of which the illegitimate child was merely the visible tip of the proverbial iceberg. Less visible, as identified by the Poor Law Commission of 1834, were the problems of blackmail and improvident marriages, which now threatened the project of the National Society. The Department of Justice was of the opinion that the Committee was making an error in proposing punishment rather than prevention as the solution to the problem, which could only serve to create 'an enormous increase in the number of crimes committed in the country, of which only a small proportion will come to light':

> It is not unusual for a girl who has to confess to her parents as to her condition, to blame the most eligible man of her acquaintance, the reason not being the hope of financial gain, but the dread of admitting to her parents that she had been intimate with a man who by reason of his being already married, or because he is a man of a much lower social plane, she cannot have contemplated as a probable husband.[9]

The moral code proposed by the Carrigan Committee would undermine the institution of marriage and invite conspiracy: the motive of the girl might not be one of financial gain, but it might be precisely that, and the stakes for the accused would be raised if the recommendations of the Committee were enacted because he would face a prison term and a whipping. Given that the risk for the woman was minimal and the accusation difficult to disprove, women would also have an incentive to get pregnant for the purpose of blackmail. The memo concludes by noting that:

[T]he authors did not face their task in a judicial and impartial frame of mind. Their recommendations are invariably to increase penalties, create offences, and remove existing safeguards for persons charged. Their main concern seems to be to secure convictions: they do not consider the case of a man charged in the wrong . . . they did not avert to the fact that it is the essence of successful blackmail that it does not become public . . . These recommendations would undoubtedly . . . increase the opportunities for blackmail while removing practically every existing safeguard against it. Apart from the question as to whether the Report should be adopted, is the question whether it should be published. The view of the Department of Justice is that it should not be published.[10]

We have to examine this episode not by isolating it as a question of prostitution, unmarried motherhood and illegitimacy, but by positioning it within the wider context of overlapping discursive fields, including itinerancy, mental defectiveness and juvenile delinquency. The Carrigan Committee was intent on establishing a punitive mode of discipline which would focus on the offence and the offender, with those who transgressed stripped of their status as citizens and denied their liberty, while punishment inflicted on their bodies would compel free subjects to conform to social and legal norms: the logic of punishment as communicative code rather than reformative technique. The state, however, envisioned a mode of ordering which would close the gap between governors and governed, bringing each and all into a relation through the project of the National Society, and this returns us to the theme of 'protection'.

One of the key phrases used in the report, seized on by the Department of Justice and the public alike, which is interesting given that it was not published, was 'protection' (Devane, 1928; also Kammerer, 1918; Hooper, 1992). According to the priests, professionals, public officials and citizens who either served on the Criminal Law Amendment Committee, gave testimony before it, or found other ways to participate in the debate,[11] the problem was the 'protection of women'. Yet this was part of a more substantive code: Ireland's future was endangered by alien influences. Even as contraception was banished from the Free State a different type of prophylactic was sought to preserve the essential purity of the Irish. The inward-looking and insular period of modern Irish history is often attributed to the protectionist regime of the de Valera era, after which, or so the myth goes, the expansionist vision of Lemass and Whittaker turned the ship of state towards the future by sailing upon the 'rising tide' of modernisation. Such a history is written from the point of view of elites, as if they are the sole authors of social order and social change. Protection in the sense of cultural/ national/racial purity was an intrinsic part of the big idea which was the Irish Nation, and there was an extensive *societal* investment in this project which cannot be reduced to elites. Something had to bear the burden of giving symbolic form to the big idea, and the unmarried mother was positioned to play this role. That the thing to be protected was a myth created from within the project of sovereignty itself was overlooked, with the calls for 'protection' – the desire to wrap the symbolic Virgin Mother Ireland in the swaddling clothes of certainty – a yearning for that state of ordered perfection which is Society. Awarded a symbolic role in this drama, the bastard child and its fallen mother were the dark side of all that could be, all that should be, and all that was still to come.

The Great Silence

After the Poor Law Commission and the Carrigan inquiry something rather strange happened; it was as if the meanings invested in this particular subject were so stable that there was little need for debate, with the figure of the unmarried mother defined by a peculiar silence.[12] The problem for the researcher is how to read this silence, which is less a void than an extensive labour of displacement and evasion. The transcripts from parliamentary debates, for example, indicate that the question of unmarried mothers was raised quite frequently, in particular between 1926 and 1938. However, this related primarily to the Poor Law Commission's recommendations, with elected representatives concerned on the one hand with the removal of defectives and unmarried mothers from the workhouse, and on the other with implementing the Commission's proposal to separate first fall women. Even as recently as the 1960s, despite some discussion on the relation between unmarried mothers and welfare reform, there is little evidence of any significant change in this field of discourse, the exception being two questions posed by Dr Noel Browne during February of 1961. Browne inquired from the minister for health as to 'whether there was any compulsion permissible to cause unmarried mothers whose children are born in local authority institutions to remain in [those] institutions after the normal period of parturition'. The minister, Mr McEntee, simply replied in the negative.[13] In June of the same year Browne asked the minister for health whether there was any legislation 'which allows those in local authority institutions caring for unmarried mothers to carry out censorship of letters of those mothers maintained in those institutions'. Dr

Ryan, speaking for the minister, again replied in the negative.[14] Important questions, and evidence too of how the unmarried mother could be brought within the scope of political debate at this time. Yet the unmarried mother was of minor concern, at least in terms of what is *said* in the public domain.

What about the wider cultural context? It is of course possible to go into the records of the workhouses and penitentiaries, investigating the life of the penitents, how they were classified, how long they remained inside, the circumstances surrounding their discharge, whether they resisted the regime, and so forth (Finnegan, 2001; Raftery and O'Sullivan, 1999; Luddy, 1995; Higginbotham, 1985). While this is without doubt important research it none the less fails to explain the Great Silence as a societal phenomenon, which seems most pronounced during the period from the mid-1930s to the mid-1960s. Of course the silence is not absolute, for traces can be found in the archive regarding how things are *not* spoken about. Foucault noted this in his analysis of Victorian sexuality, finding within the 'repressive hypothesis' a strategy he theorised as the 'will to knowledge':

> Silence itself – the things one declines to say, or is forbidden to name, the discretion that is required between different speakers – is less the absolute limit of discourse, the other side from which it is separated by a strict boundary, than an element that functions alongside the things said, with them and in relation to them within all over strategies. There is no binary division to be made between what one says and what one does not say; we must try to determine the different ways of not saying such things . . . There is not one but many silences, and they are an integral part of the strategies that underlie and permeate discourses. (Foucault, 1998: 27)

The unmarried mother was the centre of such a silence, not forgotten in the orders of discourse so much as governed through a code which defies the analytical distinction between the tangible and the symbolic, the real and the ideal, or in Weber's historical scheme, the authority of convention and the authority of law (Weber, 1978b: 33–8, 215–54).

Slavoj Žižek calls such a code the superego, or the 'obscene "nightly" law that necessarily redoubles and accompanies, as its shadow, the public Law':

> Such a code must remain under the cover of night, unacknowledged, unutterable – in public, everybody pretends to know nothing about it, or even actively denies its existence. It represents the 'spirit of the community' at its purest, exerting the strongest pressure on the individual to comply with its mandate of group identification. Yet, simultaneously, it violates the explicit rules of community life. (Žižek, 1994: 54)

Žižek is describing a practice that bounds a collectivity and exerts its authority most forcefully when someone tries to get it out in the open: by speaking it, by making it part of 'language' or 'discourse' in the conventional sense of those terms. It is not that people are cultural dupes or in the grip of false consciousness. On the contrary, there is a kind of pleasure in embodying and enacting the language of the Great Silence. The obscene nightly law is the normative force of convention as it sediments in power/knowledge/practice, existing in the interstices of rational debate, positive law and codified rights: a secret shared by all but uttered by none.

In her research on the Magdalen asylums in Ireland, Frances Finnegan attempted to breach this code. Having moved to Ireland from the UK in the early 1980s, Finnegan described her surprise at discovering that 'former penitents' still lived in the Irish convents (the last Magdalen asylum closed in 1996):

> Over the course of my research, *the real nature of the system emerged.* Equally disconcerting was what appeared to be a general indifference to the experience of these women, and to the injustice done. As an English historian working on what soon became a controversial topic – exposing as it did, a discreditable episode in recent Irish history – I encountered various difficulties. *Criticism of the system was resented as misplaced or exaggerated; and it became evident that a treatment of the subject was acceptable, only if confined to the Victorian period, to which the notion of 'different standards' could be conveniently applied . . .* Campaigners for women's rights were apparently unmoved, both by the history of the subject and by the fact that as late as the nineteen-sixties women were still being consigned . . . to 'Magdalen' Homes. *This curious indifference* to a movement so oppressive, so outdated and so blatantly at odds with the notions of sexual equality and personal liberty, requires some explanation. (Finnegan, 2001: ix–x, 2, emphasis added)

Finnegan was describing a society which (in the 1980s) had been pursuing a determined programme of modernisation for over twenty years; a society which had been a member of the European Community and had been addressing gender inequalities for over a decade, yet also a society in deep and increasingly open conflict over questions of sexuality, in particular contraception, divorce, abortion, gay and lesbian rights and marital rape. In the figure of the unmarried mother, Finnegan not only discovered the endurance of practices excluded from the realm of the sayable; she also experienced the weight of Žižek's superego: the 'real nature of the system' was less the Magdalen penitentiary itself than a curious discourse which takes the form of a shared secret.[15]

This field of discourse is autistic in form. On the one hand the unmarried mother is guilty of having had sex done to her: too simple or weak-willed to govern her sexuality, she is locked away for her own safety and the good name of her family. At the same time she is the embodiment of evil: a siren who brings respectable men to ruin, and is locked away to punish her and secure the safety of Society. In both cases, as victim of temptation or evil temptress, the unmarried mother is removed from the public gaze and excluded from public debate, and yet there is an extensive labour involved in accomplishing this. At once a threat and an object of desire, the unmarried mother is subject to a discourse which simultaneously encloses and forecloses, which is how the realm of the (im)possible is circumscribed. The unmarried mother articulates the relation between fear and desire, shame and lust, compliance and transgression; a horizon of meaning along which the forbidden is cast as it defines the normative parameters of admissible conduct.

The silent sequestering of unwed mothers involved careful planning and subtle strategies; the 1930/1 report of the Department of Local Government and Public Health, for example, explains how girls and women were dispatched to the Pelletstown institution for unmarried mothers in Dublin. Having come to recognise 'that the method of admission is a matter of importance', the Board of Assistance had devised a 'system by which publicity is avoided'. Members of the Board, dispensary medical officers and public assistance officers were all empowered to issue admission tickets in such a way that 'no discussion takes place' (DLGPHa, 1931: 130). Provision was made, plans laid and practices designed to remove the unmarried mother to the penitentiary with a minimum of dialogue. Nobody need 'know' (although everyone would know) who was guilty of a crime which had at best a very tenuous basis in law.

In an old Irish joke a man goes into a chemist and asks for an aspirin while winking at the pharmacist, because 'aspirin' signifies 'condom'. Condoms could not exist openly, partly because they were illegal and partly because the premeditated sexual act – meaning sex for pleasure rather than for procreation – was prohibited. People knew how to use condoms, of course, and how to procure them by smuggling them into the country in brown packaging from England, suspicious-looking booty occasionally rifled and confiscated by the local post-master. But even then no accusation would be made, the matter existing only as a pocket of silence, and perhaps as a gossiping whisper, between those who knew and those who were known about. The acquisition of condoms, like the premeditated act of sex, must always *appear* to be an accident; nobody ever means it and so nobody is responsible, it just happens somehow.

Deniability is part of the code. But, as pointed out in the testimonies of the Royal Commission of 1834, someone must bear the consequences: those women who 'get themselves in trouble'. There were many ways of not talking about unmarried mothers.

The 1937 Constitution of Ireland, drafted in close cooperation with the church (Keogh, 1996: 117–30), is another important region of the Great Silence. Article 41 codifies the meaning of 'woman' in Irish society in relation to the family, which is defined as 'the necessary basis of social order' and 'indispensable to the welfare of the Nation and the State' (see also Ireland, 1930: 19–22). It also ascribes to women the role of wife and mother within the institution of marriage, which is defined as the source of the 'common good'. Article 41 never mentions the unmarried mother and yet it speaks about nothing else, as does Article 45 on Social Policy. Article 45 makes it incumbent on the state 'to promote the welfare of the whole people by securing and protecting as effectively as it may a social order in which justice and charity shall inform all the institutions of the national life'. To this end the state is charged with safeguarding 'the economic interests of the weaker sections of the community, and, where necessary, to contribute to the support of the infirm, the widow, the orphan, and the aged' (Ireland, 1937). Again the unmarried mother is simultaneously connoted and excluded, a class of woman deviating from the ascribed roles of wife and mother. And when it comes to 'justice and charity' and the entitlements of the 'weaker sections of the community', the unmarried mother is cast beyond the meaning of the National Society.

During their Easter meeting in 1944 the Catholic hierarchy discussed the moral implications of a new sanitary product for women called 'Tampax'. It was thought that the product posed the danger of harmfully stimulating girls at an impressionable age, which might lead to the use of contraceptives, and the archbishop of Dublin, Dr Charles McQuaid, contacted the Department of Local Government and Public Health to make known the hierarchy's misgivings (Barrington, 1987: 149). Important here is the fact that the moral hazard is *imagined*, and what is imagined is the piercing of a prohibited virginal-vaginal space: Irish Womanhood. That the repressed sexuality of Irish Womanhood might be awakened was *actively imagined* by these men as they met in private, with the new sanitary product providing a context for detailed discussion of what might happen as a girl inserts a tampon into her vagina. For the clerics this was certain to encourage the act of sex, and hence it had everything to do with the unmarried mother even though she may not have been mentioned in the discussion at all. Both the prohibited act and the new sanitary technology enabled these austere men to engage in detailed thought and debate regarding female genitalia and sexual pleasure. The humble tampon was, to cite Foucault again, an incitement to discourse (1998). How must this meeting have been conducted? This was a group of serious and learned men, celibate according to church doctrine, debating the triggering effect of something that vaguely resembled a penis – a dildo to be exact. The tampon was perceived by the patriarchs, exhibiting the ignorance and sexual immaturity of pre-pubescent boys, to be an instrument of pleasure. It would provoke masturbation, which was a practice innocent Irish women could apparently have no knowledge of by themselves but might acquire if Irish culture was penetrated by foreign and unnatural influences. For the Church hierarchy, tampons symbolised the possible impregnation of traditional Ireland by the corrupt seed of modernity. As noted by Foucault, there is no one locus or cause to the Great Silence. Instead there are many silences.

Reconstructing the unmarried mother

By the early 1960s the prognosis of the 1927 Poor Law Commission – that the problem of illegitimacy would be resolved as order was restored – was definitively overwritten by reports of a 'phenomenal' increase in illegitimate births in Ireland.[16] In 1970 the extraordinary degree of continuity in the governance of illegitimacy begin to unravel, and at a phenomenal pace. Conventional explanations for this sudden transformation tend to draw on the idea of a change in attitudes and the influence of the women's movement. At best this type of explanation provides a partial account, and the inference of a 'more enlightened' society is something I want to treat with caution. We need to know why this change happened at this time and why it took a particular discursive form. It is necessary to look for forces less coherent, less *unified* than the idea of movements and shifts in consciousness, both of which invoke images of autonomy and the onward march of reason. In the case of the unmarried mother it is possible to outline a field of force comprised of a number of relatively distinct elements.

Within this field of force are a number of important reference points, among them a Council of Europe Resolution on *The Social Protection of Unmarried Mothers and their Children*, published in 1970 and intended 'to make public opinion aware of the problems of unmarried mothers and their children . . . with a view to doing away with prejudice against them and to secure their acceptance on an equal footing with other families' (Kilkenny, 1972: 54–9; also *Irish Times*, 1970e).[17] Second was a Commission on the Status of Women, established in

1970 and publishing its report two years later. Mandated to consider 'the participation of women on equal terms and conditions with men in the political, social, cultural and economic life of the country', the Commission made only one reference to unmarried mothers, however, recommending that 'an unmarried mother who keeps her child should be entitled to a social welfare allowance at the same rate and on the same conditions that apply to a deserted wife, for a period of not less than one year after the birth of the child' (Ireland, 1972: 153). Finally, the 1972 Kennedy Report on the industrial and reformatory schools brought the unmarried mother within the compass of the fictional normal family:

> [To] develop a rational approach to the problem of the preservation of the family unit, the causation of family break-up must be identified . . . [all] families, *together with the special case of the unmarried mother and her child*, may be saved from break up by the provision of adequate financial benefits and a system of family support to enable them to overcome their difficulties. (Ireland, 1972: 61–4, emphasis added)

At both the national and the supranational levels a consensus was forming that the unmarried mother was to become a supplement to the 'normal family' and was to be encouraged and assisted to keep her child. This was the aspiration. However, a significant gap existed between the aspiration and prevailing practices. The lofty statements on rehabilitating the unmarried mother – now part of a newly emerging regime of truth – were positioned within a highly conflicted socio-political context, with the unmarried mother used as a resource in both challenging and defending the project of Society. I will discuss this under four headings: rehabilitation, the women's movement, the pro-life movement, and the illegitimate act.

Rehabilitation

The most comprehensive statement in reconstructing the unmarried mother was not a public inquiry, as was the case with the other case studies, but a conference on Community Services for the Unmarried Parent organised by the Kilkenny Social Services organisation in 1970. This brought together members of the clergy, professional social workers and social scientists, with the proceedings published two years later as *The Unmarried Mother in the Irish Community* (Kilkenny, 1972). Deriving its impetus from the Council of Europe Resolution, the Kilkenny framework tapped into policy innovations in the international arena to advance a programme of rehabilitation based on a mixture of medical care, vocational training, and integration into the community. Part of the background context was the pervasive problem of youth unemployment and vandalism, with the illegitimate child, or rather child of 'inadequate' parents, moved to the centre of international debate on the causes of escalating crime and social disorder.

The starting point in rehabilitating the unmarried mother was to make room for her within the constitutionally enshrined space of the family. Article 41 of the Irish Constitution was grafted onto the 1916 Proclamation so that the state was to 'honour its constitutional responsibility towards the illegitimate child by "cherishing it equally" with all of the rest of the State's children whether born in or out of wedlock' (Kilkenny, 1972: 6). However, even as the unmarried mother and her illegitimate child were inscribed into the space of the family, they were defined in 'factual terms' as a 'fatherless' or 'incomplete family'. It was proposed that the incomplete family receive the same social, financial and material support as a two-parent family, so that the child of the unmarried mother could be 'developed' under 'optimal conditions' (Kilkenny, 1972: 5). This would be accomplished through a regime of practices organised along two 'axes': a 'functional axis' and a 'structural axis' – essentially another version of community care and the expert team.[18]

Adopting a certain biblical style, the 'four commandments' of the functional axis were 'integration', 'coordination', 'continuity of care' and a 'multi-disciplinary approach' (Kilkenny, 1972: 7–8, 15–16, 32–4). This would facilitate 'easy interchange of information, rapid communication and good working relations' among the professionals engaged in this field. Social workers, medical experts, statutory bodies and sympathetic volunteers would form a continuous, multi-disciplinary and flexible ethos of care, and again we see the organisational logic of the 'team' or partnership invoked. It was also suggested that a single expert should be able to trace the progress of individual 'clients' through the entire system: from the diagnosis of pregnancy to the final placing for adoption or, alternatively, retention of the child. The system was mapped as a grid of human and material resources, from guidance to financial assistance, accommodation and training, fitting the mother for employment after the birth of her child.

The structural dimension mirrored the Kennedy inquiry in seeking to dispense with the penitentiary mode of treatment. While expressing 'enormous praise' for the services provided by the old mother and baby homes, it was suggested that the large institution was no longer relevant. The 'modern philosophy of delivery of care in many areas of human functional impairment demands that all people suffering from such conditions as mental illness should not be taken from the community and held together in one place', because when 'psychotically disturbed people [are] herded together' there is a tendency 'to exacerbate each other's condition' (Kilkenny, 1972: 36–7). As with psychotic patients so too did concentrations of pregnant women and young children create 'large resonating waves of disturbance and turbulence'. These resonating waves of 'emotional damage and trauma' would be relieved by placing unmarried mothers in 'small family group homes'.

One proposal tabled at the conference was the 'family placement scheme', a practice which had emerged through 'spontaneous voluntary effort' and was later organised by the Church of Ireland. The scheme worked by identifying suitable families willing to take the mother-to-be into their home 'on an *au pair* basis', so that she would help around the home to cover the cost of bed and board (Kilkenny, 1972: 42–5). While this was cast as part of the new community care model, it was clear that the unmarried mother was being brought within the scope of the established techniques of boarding out and rehabilitation. However, Rev. G. Colleran from the Catholic Protection and Rescue Society pointed out a minor glitch in the scheme: the practice could be 'dangerous to marriage' because of the temptation the girl would pose to the man of the house (*Irish Press*, 1970e). Here we see the symbolic role of the unmarried mother, with the 'danger to marriage' a hyper-sexualised phantasm: a narrative of sexual adventure entangled in menace and peril. The *femme fatale* is imaginatively freed from the normative constraints and conventions governing sexual relations; both desired and dangerous, she is a symbolic surface upon which is inscribed the detail of prohibited acts. Again, as with the bishops on the threat of tampons, this danger has to be *thought* before it is spoken, with the warning originating in the hypothetical mind of a hypothetical husband who is exposed to an imagined predatory female sexuality in a fictitious family home.

The contradictory representations of the fallen woman reappear intact here, as does the long-standing tension between the penitentiary and the social disciplines. A symbol of sexual transgression, the unmarried mother can be desired by all irrespective of sex or gender: for women she is the sexual freedom they deny in themselves and each other; for men she is the possibility of forbidden pleasures. But encountered as a real person, the unmarried mother is transformed into a normative excess that threatens to make public all the disavowed thoughts and illicit actions of ordinary people in their ordinary lives. The fantasy ends where reality begins, with the errant female desired only up to the point where she becomes a thing of responsibility and consequence, that is, when her desirability gives way to the burden born from her womb. The 'danger to marriage' was less the fallen women than the forces of social transformation, with those things long sequestered within the Great Silence – from the sexual abuse of children to recreational sex and unconventional sexual practices – now articulated within a new regime of truth.

The women's movement

In 1971 the Irish Women's Liberation Movement (IWLM) published a thirty-two-page manifesto called *Chains or Change? The Civil Wrongs of Irish Women*:

> The unmarried mother who keeps her child does not officially exist as a class as far as this State is concerned. It is time she was recognised. The unmarried mother does exist. We need a system for dealing with her problems which is less punishing and more aware of her and her child as a fatherless family. (cited in Farren and Dempsey, 1997: 15; also Smyth, 1993: 252)

It is interesting to note that the representation of the unmarried mother in the *Chains or Change* manifesto offers little evidence of deconstructing the 'normal' family, with the unmarried mother still marked out by a void in the form of the absent father.[19] In fact it was very difficult for the unmarried mother to form a nodal point in feminist discourse in Ireland because she was the symbolic centre of two divisive questions which threatened the unity of the movement: contraception and abortion (see Smyth, 1993: 253–65). The contraception issue became more complex as elements of the women's movement shifted from a reformist to a radical agenda, while the HIV-Aids issue both helped to explode the silence surrounding gay and lesbian relationships in Ireland and redefined the landscape on which the battle for and against contraception was waged. While disagreements over the contraception issue gradually subsided, the abortion question continued to fracture the unity of feminist discourse. From the point of view of the unmarried mother, statements such as the *Chains or Change* manifesto complemented rather than challenged the reformist debate concerned with enlarging the scope of the welfare code so that the unmarried mother could keep her child (see Ireland, 1970a: 61–4; 1972: 153).

Another organisation, Cherish, which derived its name from the 1916 Proclamation, was established by and for 'single unmarried mothers' in 1972, its ethos one of 'self-help and self-empowerment' (Farren and Dempsey, 1997). In retrospective terms the organisation is presented as radical, and in some respects it was, but it is also the case that its strategy was (and remains) one of including the unmarried mother for the sake of the child rather than challenging the order of things from the position of the woman. When Cherish published a booklet to celebrate its twenty-fifth birthday in 1997, titled *From Condemnation to Celebration*, it continued to justify itself in this way:

> An organisation which works with single parents may be accused of 'condoning wrongdoing', even encouraging promiscuity and irresponsibility. But Cherish is very clear about its attitude to single mothers ... children may be as loved and nourished in one parent families as in two ... nor is it necessary to have a union sanctified by marriage for children to be happy and secure. (Farren and Dempsey, 1997: 7)

The women's movement certainly had something to say about the unmarried mother, but outside of single-issue groups such as Cherish there was a profound difficulty in representing the unmarried mother beyond framing her as a supplement to the larger issues around which consensus could be built: equal rights and equal pay.

The pro-life movement and the 'child of chance'

In a sort of ironic twist, a number of conservative actors claimed the unmarried mother as an ally in their opposition to contraception, divorce and abortion, all of which posed a threat to Catholic Ireland. As the fight against contraception lost ground those who in the past might have condemned unwed mothers to the Magdalen penitentiaries began to speak on their behalf. The Society for the Protection of the Unborn Child (SPUC) in Liverpool, for example, attempted to stem the flow of Irish women travelling to England for an abortion by arguing that the pregnant mother should be protected and not punished by society, diagnosing 'the unplanned pregnancy' as the result of 'insecurity' and 'emotional deprivation' (*Irish Press*, 1973a). By 1979 one of the organisers of a pro-life march in Dublin extended a welcome to unmarried mothers, explaining that 'it was not enough to be anti-abortion ... We must [also] be pro-mother and pro-child' (Daly, 1979a, 1979b). This position was facilitated by the development of a psychoanalytical theory of illegitimacy (Bowlby, 1965; Young, 1954), enlarging the scope of the old discourses concerning moral imbecility and mental instability so that the 'sin' of unmarried motherhood was recast as a problem of unconscious 'instincts' – the procreative equivalent of a Freudian slip.

The strategy had been formulated twenty years earlier by Joseph Folliet in France. Folliet was director of the Social Institute of the Facultis Catholiques de Lyon, and had written the introductory chapter to Marie-Gabrielle Dervan's book *The Problem of the Unmarried Mother*, published in 1958, with the English translation published in Ireland three years later by Mercier Press. The influence of this book might well be disputed by asking questions such as who read it and how it influenced events in Ireland. This is not the kind of 'influence' I am interested in, however. What makes this book interesting is the way it resonates with the emerging regime of truth. Folliet himself may not have been on the lips of the pro-lifers in Ireland, but his text gives discursive form to what they were doing and saying. Folliet discussed the illegitimate 'child of chance' in relation to 'new types of unmarried mother', by which he meant the educated, professional and possibly lesbian woman 'who deliberately seeks a child of her own, outside of marriage' by having 'recourse to artificial insemination in order to avoid a masculine contact which repels [her]'. Folliet was attempting to control the new type of unmarried mother – the solo mother who is both solo and a mother by choice – by assimilating her to the instituted practices, arguing that she belonged 'to the study of social and mental diseases because they equally imply a subversion of values'. Tapping into the logic of child-saving and re-collecting the 19th-century discourse of moral insanity, Folliet explained that 'the child does not exist for the satisfaction of the mother, but the mother for the training and formation of the child':

> In accepting the consequences of her error, in devoting herself to this child of chance, the unmarried mother gives proof of her courage and of a comparative moral sanity. She could have procured an abortion, as did so many others; she did not do so. She could have abandoned her child to the care of the community or to the process of adoption, as did so many others; she refused to do so. Originally the victim of her instinct she consents at least, in spite of all the difficulties, to follow it properly to its conclusion. This attitude deserves respect and . . . effective encouragement . . . The unmarried mother has committed a grave offence. She can redeem it and make reparation for it . . . The child she bears starts life with a handicap for which he is not responsible. His mother, in giving him her love, can compensate for the inferiority which has its origin therein, and society, without casting any slight upon the respect due to the institution of the family, must not attempt to make the child expiate the weakness of the mother. (Folliet, 1961: 19–23)

Folliet reasoned that in the midst of the 'hyper-sexualised atmosphere' of contemporary society 'everyone is in duty bound to have compassion upon her and to help her', because 'we ourselves may perhaps be carrying some of the responsibility, indirect but all too real, for her offence' (Folliet, 1961: 20). The rehabilitation of the unmarried mother was part of a strategy to defend the old order, the significance of this social subject transformed, no longer a sin to be atoned or a crime warranting incarceration but an accidental slip to be corrected in defence of Society.

The illegitimate act

An unlikely alliance: the agents of welfare reform, feminists and Catholic conservatives together lay bare a horizon of contingency as each of them staked a claim in the child. That the meaning of the unmarried mother was subject to strategic manipulation had been made explicit, and a space was opened in the orders of discourse for innovation. An event in 1976 prised open this space and further dislodged the fixity of the unmarried mother. The curious thing about this particular episode was that it could, potentially, have happened many years earlier. The event, which I shall call an 'illegitimate act' because of the response to it, goes back to the inquiry on the poor law commissioned by the Irish Free State (Ireland, 1927). During the proceedings Rev. R. Devane (cited above)[20] railed against the 'terrible evils of baby farming' and solicitation, recommending that the state should recognise, as the church already did, that an illegitimate child could be legitimised if the natural parents married subsequent to the birth (Devane, 1924a, 1924b, 1928; *Irish Independent*, 1925e). Devane wanted 'the law of the land' brought into alignment with canon law, and the Legitimacy Act of 1931 gave legal effect to this. An illegitimate child could now *become* legitimate, yet this attempt to align the authority of church and state, or the validity of convention and law in Weber's terminology, etched a concrete possibility for innovation into the orders of discourse, and it would be enacted forty-five years later.

It was the practice of adoption – part law, part convention – which provided the precise location for the enactment of the illegitimate act. Adoption in Ireland was a practice assembled from the disciplines of the workhouse, the convent asylum and social economy. Babies were routinely taken from unmarried mothers interned in the Magdalen asylums and either raised in industrial schools or boarded out. With the establishment of a statutory Adoption Board (An Bord Uchtala) in 1952 the practice was given a legal basis,[21] so that legal adoption continued to apply only to children classed as illegitimate or orphaned (Ireland, 1984c). The legally reformed system thus retained the normative force of convention. In 1976 this started to come undone.

The event in question involved an unmarried mother who had placed her son in foster care in 1970, subsequently agreeing to have him adopted. She later married the father, thus legitimising the child in accordance with the Act of 1931, after which the couple initiated proceedings to recover their child. After failing in the High Court in 1974, the couple filed an appeal with the Supreme Court (Murray, 1976a; *Irish Times*, 1976c). So here was an unmarried mother who was no longer unmarried, and an illegitimate child who was no longer illegitimate, both of which added up to an anomaly within the established regime of practices. And this made it possible, or at least it was no longer *impossible*, for the unmarried mother to inscribe herself in the constitutionally protected space of 'the family'. The event – repeatedly referred to as 'exceptional' – caused a moral panic.

There were in fact two possible ways of interpreting the event. One concerned the relation between the natural parents and the adopted child: the domain of constitutional law. The other concerned the failure of the Adoption Board to follow procedure. Section 14 of the Adoption Act stated that an adoption order could not be made without the consent of the mother, and consent could be withdrawn at any time prior to the order being made. The Adoption Board had apparently failed in its duty to make this known to the woman. The judgement of the Supreme Court was that:

> Where the relief which a plaintiff seeks rests on two such distinct grounds, as a general rule the court should consider first whether the relief sought can be granted on the ground which does not raise a question of constitutional validity . . . there may be circumstances of an exceptional nature where the requirements of justice and the protection of constitutional rights make the larger enquiry necessary. Such, in my view, do not exist in this case.[22]

The ruling (by a majority of four to one) was made on the basis of the Adoption Board's oversight, and confrontation with the Constitution was avoided. But the innovation caused a major disturbance. Importantly, it also illustrated the degree of societal complicity in the exclusion of this composite social subject. The child was immediately moved to the political centre by a variety of agencies, among them the Irish Federation of Women's Clubs, the Campaign for the Care of Deprived Children, Children First, the Joint Committee of Women's Societies, the Irish Association of Social Workers, lawyers, child psychiatrists, academics, everyone it seemed who had a stake in the child. The effect was to channel the meaning of the episode so that it was framed almost without exception from the perspective of adopted children and adoptive parents.[23] The concerns of the child's natural parents and the long history of unmarried motherhood forming the backdrop to the event were all but excluded from the field of representation.[24]

Strictly speaking the force of the act was that of problematising the status of illegitimacy rather than the status of unmarried motherhood. It was after all the fact of having married subsequent to an illegitimate birth which provided the means to act at all, and the debate which grew out of this episode continued to focus on the child. The response to the act indicates the extent to which the unmarried mother remained excluded from the socio-political imaginary of 'Ireland'. It is for this reason that I think the act can be classed as illegitimate: an innovative act which lacked the validity or social recognition associated with the notion of legitimacy. As the various individuals and agencies rushed to protect the 'child of chance' it became apparent that, while willing to act on *behalf* of the unmarried mother, they were not willing to permit a breach in the limited autonomy which had been granted to her. Now ordered into the space of the family the unmarried mother was acknowledged as a legitimate type of parent, but as she moved to act on her own behalf – to become a political subject – the force of response was that of fixing meaning back in its conventional place. The innovation was possible not because other social actors were willing to confirm its validity (see Haugaard 2003, 1997) but because law was called upon to govern a disturbance in the fields and orders of discourse. It was law that conferred legitimacy on the illegitimate act, but it did so reluctantly by deliberately constraining the scope of the innovation. A certain threshold had been crossed, however. The act continued to resonate in the field as the ghosts of countless unmarried mothers suddenly took on new significance. An army of women stretching into the past reappeared along the horizon of the future, now – at least potentially – armed with constitutional rights. At the very least 26,000 adoption orders going back to 1952 suddenly became contingent, creating further disturbances and necessitating additional legislative reforms (Ireland, 1984c: 4; Glennon, 1979).

It was becoming increasingly apparent that the project of Society was an impossible project, because order tends to deconstruct *itself*, with social dislocation not only resulting from external shocks and the failure of internal engineering projects, but also originating in the margins of order. Deconstructive forces are born from within the social field through the surplus of meaning which contaminates the fields and orders of discourse. In terms of anticipating this phenomenon, and in terms of building it into governmental practices, the reconstruction of the unmarried mother provides an important lesson which has gradually been incorporated into the new ordering modality of inclusive governance. Yet even as this came into being, and as the unmarried mother was transformed into the lone parent, there were also signs that under certain conditions the old meanings could be reinstated. We will look at two examples of this before examining how the lone parent is positioned within the new regime of practices.

The return of the unmarried mother

That the reconstruction of the unmarried mother was partial and incomplete was demonstrated by two episodes which I will examine very briefly: one within the realm of the Great Silence, which became known as the 'Kerry Babies' affair, and more recently an attempt to introduce the figure of the 'welfare mother' to Ireland.

The Kerry Babies and the limits of rehabilitation

The Kerry Babies controversy is one of those episodes that pose the question of 'why': why did the issue emerge at this time and why was it so politically charged? Why was a young unmarried mother, Joanne Hayes, put on trial and subjected to public humiliation, not for the murder of a baby, for which she had been acquitted, but for something else entirely?

The bare facts of the case are as follows. In 1984 a newborn baby was discovered off the coast of Cahirciveen in County Kerry, and it transpired that the child had been murdered. While certain suspect types were brought within the scope of the ensuing investigation – strangers and those who seemed somehow *different* – the gaze of suspicion came to rest on a particular type of woman: Joanne Hayes was a single woman in an open relationship with a married man. The couple already had one illegitimate child,[25] and it was known that Hayes had become pregnant a second time. Crucially, it was also known that she had recently had a miscarriage or delivery of some sort, but not in hospital (McCafferty, 1985). When questioned by police Joanne Hayes admitted killing the Cahirciveen baby, but the story became more complex when a second baby was found dead on the Hayes family farm, wrapped in a bag and submerged in a shallow pool. Forensic anomalies, in particular the fact that the Cahirciveen baby had a different blood group to Hayes and her partner, saw a number of theories produced to explain the puzzle, the most spectacular being the super-fecundity thesis. Here Hayes was alleged to have given birth to twins conceived from separate fathers, meaning she had sex with two men within a short space of time.

Further complexities arose following allegations that the Hayes family had been bullied by police into admitting the crime.[26] Finally there was the storm surrounding the 'trial', with Joanne Hayes, who had come to symbolise the crime of unmarried motherhood, very publicly put on trial at a tribunal convened to investigate allegations against the Gardai (see Inglis, 2002). The tribunal established a context both to decriminalise *and* to recriminalise the twice-fallen woman, with Hayes forming a political frontier between elements of the women's movement and a number of conservative actors defending Catholic Ireland against contraception and abortion.

While politicising the issue of unmarried motherhood and further disturbing this field of discourse, the episode also demonstrated just how deeply the Great Silence ran in Irish culture. The silence surrounded Hayes during her pregnancy, it continued after her lonely miscarriage in a field in the middle of the night, and it enveloped her the next morning when her family carried on as if nothing had happened. It can be extremely difficult to keep secrets in rural Ireland, but there are certain forms of knowledge which play an integrative role: the publicly disavowed 'spirit of the community' that Žižek writes about (1994: 54).

The welfare mother

The other example exhibits more by way of ideological strategy in representing the lone parent as a 'welfare mother'; a derivative of the underclass thesis. We have already looked at this in chapter 1 and here I simply want to sketch the brief appearance of this debate in Ireland in 1997, the year after the community and voluntary (C&V) sector was fully incorporated into social partnership.

It was the neo-liberal Progressive Democrats (PDs) who made the intervention, attempting to score a political point by defending the booming 'tiger' economy against those who acted as a drag on growth. In its election manifesto the leader of the Party, Mary Harney, called attention to the spectre of the welfare mother, arguing that young single mothers should be given incentives to stay at home with their parents. The PDs took their cue from the Clinton reforms in the US, where Federal Aid to Families with Dependent Children was being dismantled. Harney attempted to trigger a moral panic by arguing that 'it is time to wake up to the social time-bomb that is ticking around us and come up with real solutions to our problems'. To this end she proposed a 'pro-family, pro-work, pro-self-reliance society', and a new 'parenting allowance' intended to provide financial incentives to young single parents to remain at home with their parents. The proposal reproduced the long-standing theme of public assistance as the cause of single motherhood, and while Harney used the genderless term 'single parent' what she really meant was single *mother*. Behind the idea of a 'pro-family society' lay the normative assumption that young single mothers with a poor education and/or from a poor background were using welfare entitlements as, to cite the 1834 Royal Commission again, 'a sort of pension to [themselves]'.

Lone-parent groups quickly denounced the proposal, as did Fianna Fáil – the PDs' most likely coalition partner. The PDs responded by saying that Harney was simply voicing what everyone else was thinking. At the time over 50,000 adults were in receipt of the Lone Parent's Allowance,[27] but this included widowed, separated and deserted spouses, and research also indicated that the issue was more complex than the PDs allowed for, with most solo mothers drawing on welfare for three to five years before taking up employment or (re)marrying.[28] It was not that Harney's attempt to responsibilise single mothers was completely off the mark, more that she was slightly out of step with the emerging hegemony of self-help, mutual assistance and participatory forms of 'community' governance. Lone parenting groups were already pursuing all of these things themselves, having established a national network to coordinate individual efforts along these lines in 1994.[29] By 1996 the One Parent Exchange Network (OPEN), along with other C&V-sector groups, were incorporated into national-level partnership negotiations under the Partnership 2000 framework. If Harney was voicing what everyone else was thinking, then she had phrased it in the wrong way. The way into the new regime of truth was not to denounce the delinquency of welfare recipients but to responsibilise them by targeting their poverty, to speak of empowering them, and to augment their employability.

Inclusion?

The problem of unplanned pregnancy is now cast in the registers of 'crisis' and 'risk'. In 2001 the Crisis Pregnancy Agency (CPA) was established under the auspices of the Department of Health and Children, defining its object as 'a pregnancy which is neither planned nor desired by the woman concerned, and which represents a personal crisis for her' (CPA, 2003: 6). Charged with formulating and implementing a strategy to address the issue of crisis pregnancy, the Agency published its three objectives in 2003:

1 reduce the number of crisis pregnancies through the provision of education, advice and contraceptive services;
2 reduce the number of women with crisis pregnancies who opt for abortion, offering services and supports which make other options more attractive;
3 provide counselling and medical services after a crisis pregnancy. (CPA, 2003: 6; chapters 3–5)

The Agency positions its subject within a specific type of governmental relation, on the one hand 'empowering men and women' to acquire 'skills and knowledge to prevent unwanted conception', and on the other 'fostering a culture which supports decisions in favour of safe sexual health and motivates and stimulates individuals to make safe choices' (CPA, 2003: 12, 22). Mandated by an all-party Oireachtas (legislative) committee on the Constitution,[30] the CPA is essentially charged with securing consensus on the contentious issue of abortion through a framework of consultation, research, information and advice. To this end the Agency brings the state into partnership with voluntary bodies with a stake in sexually transmitted infections and crisis pregnancies, together with other 'key communicators' such as parents, teachers, youth leaders, GPs, health service professionals and employers (CPA, 2003: 8–10; cf. London, 1999). Communication is a crucial part of the strategy, and the CPA uses text messaging, online resources, television, cinema, press, radio and washroom advertising, even providing 'consumer tips' in its Golden Pages listings. To keep tabs on the effectiveness of its product, the Agency commissioned Lansdowne Market Research to assess the level of awareness and recall among its target audience. Employing the techniques of business, articulating the new, inclusive mode of governance and implementing a strategy of empowerment, this is about the conduct of conduct: the 'concept of safe sexual health' is to 'become synonymous with normal behaviour' (CPA, 2003: 22).

In 2004 the CPA launched a public information campaign to deliver the message: 'Think Contraception'. Part of the campaign involved distributing 400,000 information packs on the theme of 'Baby?' to 18–30-year-olds at key events and in third-level educational settings (CPA, 2004: 12). Images designed for the campaign play on the word 'Baby' by juxtaposing it with 'babes': desirable bodies placed in front of a Christmas tree (in the case of the female babe) and surf (the male babe) (figure 8.1). As a paradigmatically biopolitical strategy, the 'Baby' campaign targets two periods in the year when unplanned pregnancies peak: Christmas and summer holidays. Whether at home or abroad, winter or summer, the annual holidays are times when too much alcohol is consumed, normal inhibitions and self-controls abate, and young people find themselves in a crisis situation.

For those facing such a crisis, the CPA is ready to provide information through its Positive Options Programme, which houses the 'Baby' campaign and delivers the message: 'No Judge No Jury Just Information'.[31] Information is normatively neutral, with the 'non-confrontational' ethos

Figure 8.1 Think contraception

of the Agency anchored in facts which are disseminated in 'public space in a non-judgemental way':

> The Crisis Pregnancy Agency neither questions the moral basis for teaching sexual abstinence or [*sic*] the deeply felt ethos of those who believe in it. What we know is that young people, even those so young that we consider them now to be children, will make their own decisions. (CPA, 2003: 4)

Pregnancy out of wedlock is no longer a social problem so much as an individual crisis which necessitates an informed decision, and the Crisis Pregnancy Agency is charged with providing impartial advice. Not only is contraception now legal in Ireland, it is also actively encouraged – but to what end?

'Crisis' pregnancies are by no means limited to teenagers or young adults, and CPA research has found that the number of births to teenagers has remained relatively stable over the last three decades in Ireland, yet the message of the 'Baby' campaign moves in the groove of the now familiar theme of 'babies having babies' (see London, 1999; Albert, Brown and Flanigan, 2003). The message: parties and holidays are a dangerous mix of booze and liberty, with the rule of reason giving way to sexual desire which is fuelled, for young men at least, by a diet of sexually explicit imagery provided by the media industries (see Hyde and Howlett, 2004). The 'Baby' campaign recasts the unmarried mother, no longer a fallen penitent, a weak-willed slave of passions or the victim of unconscious drives and inaugurates a new strategy to govern sexuality by acting upon the autonomous individual's capacity for action (cf. Tapia, 2005). The three-pronged strategy of the CPA is positioned within the degrees of freedom available to the (hetero-)sexually active subject: contraception, pregnancy, adoption and abortion. Adoption remains an option, although having fallen from 37.6 per cent of non-marital births in 1978 to 0.4 per cent in 2001, it is unlikely to play a significant role in managing crisis pregnancies (CPA, 2003: 13; cf. London, 1999: 57). Abortion *is* among the Positive Options on offer, although, because it is prohibited by law and discouraged by the Agency, it means travelling to another country.[32] Prevention is the primary objective of the CPA, and whether this is accomplished through abstinence or contraception is left to the informed individual. The discourse of crisis pregnancy positions its subject within an apparatus designed to prevent undesirable choices and manage the consequences of unplanned actions. Once again this apparatus bears the hegemonic stamp of inclusive governance: a mode of ordering that governs through the regulation of self-regulation.

Another dimension of unplanned, which is to say unmanaged, pregnancy, is the risk of poverty and exclusion:

> Teenage mothers are less likely to finish their education, less likely to find a good job, and more likely to end up both as single parents and bringing up their children in poverty. The children themselves run a much greater risk of poor health, and have a much higher chance of becoming teenage mothers themselves. Our failure to tackle this problem has cost the teenagers, their children and the country dear. (Blair, 1999)

Unlike Britain, which has the highest rate of teen pregnancy in (Western) Europe and where the link between teen pregnancy and social exclusion was the subject of a lengthy report in 1999 (London, 1999), the rate of pregnancy among teenagers in Ireland is considered to be on a par with the European average (CPA, 2003: 13). That said, in Ireland the risk of poverty and exclusion is a feature of lone parenting regardless of age.

Organisations such as the Irish Congress of Trade Unions (ICTU) and the Conference of Major Religious Superiors began to highlight the poverty of lone parents in the 1980s (*Irish Times*, 1985a, 1985d; CORI, 1993, 1995). As the 1980s became the 1990s, the Report of the Second Commission on the Status of Women made the case that 'single mothers' were trapped in the 'cycle of poverty', explaining that 'the effect of public policy towards lone mothers has been to discourage their participation in the labour market rather than provide them with training and other supports which might help them to hold a job' (Ireland, 1993: 166).[33] Drawing explicitly on the discourse of exclusion, the Commission noted that 'young single mothers' were in 'situations of particular disadvantage', as were older women, women with disabilities, lesbian women, Traveller women, female prisoners and women involved in prostitution (1993: 163). A more recent study by the Vincentian Partnership for Social Justice provided further evidence, the case study of a 33-year-old lone mother, living in a large flat complex on the outskirts of Dublin with her two children, apparently typical. Though they are in receipt of a basic Lone Parent's Allowance, a Child Dependent Allowance, and a monthly Child Benefit payment, one of the most pressing problems for this family is debt, and while this woman was willing to work there was no affordable child care in the area. Contrary to the myth of the welfare mother, the study concluded that the poverty experienced by this family was not due to dependency or the mismanagement of financial resources. Instead it was a reflection of inadequate support services and an insufficient income (MacMahon, Delaney and Lynch, 2001: 6–8; see also Bookle, 2001).

The crime of sexual transgression which long posed such a threat to the safety of Society has given way to the problem of equipping individuals to manage themselves. While there may be disagreement on questions such as the funding of crèches, there is general agreement that single motherhood increases the risk of individuals becoming socially excluded. The principal strategy is to prevent unplanned pregnancy, and if this fails, then those experiencing the crisis of pregnancy and confronting the risk of poverty are steered into programmes to enhance their employability. Both techniques are built into the new Teenage Pregnancy Strategy in the UK (Kidger, 2004: 291–2; London, 1999), and while Ireland does not have a Teenage Pregnancy Strategy it does have a range of programmes directed at the management of sexual conduct and the employability of lone parents.

For the moment at least the single mother in Ireland would seem to pose no great threat to order, although she may face definite constraints as an individual and as a parent, particularly if her family is dependent on an inadequate income, whether from welfare or a low-paid job. And while they are no longer subjected to the old disciplinary techniques of penitence and punishment, this is not to say that solo mothers are no longer subjected. Like the old techniques of normalisation, *social inclusion is a mode of subjection*, and this necessitates a closer look at the new, inclusive mode of governance.

9

Inclusive governance: encircling and encircled by exclusion

We cannot doubt the existence of a great power ready to hand and capable of being directed with vast benefit as soon as we shall have learnt to understand and to apply it. (Francis Galton, 1901)

I try to chase Trouble but it's chasing me . . . Trouble with a capital T. (Horslips, 2000)

Introduction

For nearly two hundred years the politics of order has been shaped by the problem of how to govern the relation between the spheres of state, market and society. At the centre of this problem is the subject, defined in various contexts as the individual bearer of freedoms and responsibilities or as a collective entity: a shared will, identity and purpose. Either way the subject is positioned within grids of power/knowledge/ practice that name, visualise, sort and segregate, the effect of which is the creation of both order and waste. This waste – this immanent domain of exclusion – has long been the source of instability, with the relation between order and exclusion articulated by specific forms of authority that were deeply problematised in the closing decades of the twentieth century. This final chapter considers the aftermath of this process of problematisation. It begins with a brief analysis of inclusive governance in the Irish case, focusing on how this is conceptualised and codified. Following this I attempt to look out from the specificities of the Irish case to the more general problem of managing postmodernity.

Inclusive governance: the enfolding

Key statements in the newly emerging regime of truth include 'the Third Way' (Giddens, 1998, 2000), 'triangulation' (Clinton), 'the middle way' (Blair and Schroeder, 1999), the 'third sector' (Borzaga and Defourny, 2001; Spear, Defourny, Favreau and Laville, 2001) and, if we extend the idiom to social theory, 'third space' (Soja, 1996). Eschewing the old oppositions between left and right, liberalism and socialism, business and labour, society and state, inclusive governance effaces boundaries and orders the political, the economic and the social into an enveloping whole: a fluid field of bodies, technologies, sectors, zones and networks to be programmed, audited and managed. In Ireland this is called 'social partnership'.

Social partnership was instituted in 1987 through the *Programme for National Recovery*, which was intended to 'overcome the serious obstacles which at present . . . impede economic and social development' (Ireland, 1987: 5). Nine years later the hand of partnership was extended to the community and voluntary sector (third sector), with some seventeen organisations participating in a National Agreement called *Partnership 2000 for Inclusion, Employment and Competitiveness* (Ireland, 1996c).

Now an institutionalised feature of the political landscape, social partnership was recently defined by the National Economic and Social Council (NESC) as a three-dimensional process: (1) functional interdependence through bargaining and deal-making; (2) solidarity through inclusiveness and participation; and (3) deliberation geared to 'shaping and reshaping the understanding, identity and preferences' of participants (NESC, 2002: 55–6).[1] Established in 1973, the NESC derives its legitimacy both from its dual mandate of economic development and social justice, and from the composition of the Council, which brings together representatives from the state, business, labour unions, farming organisations and the third sector,[2] the last represented on the NESC since 1998.[3] The NESC produces comprehensive policy programmes called Strategies, and a series of these have been produced in tandem with the National Agreements. The NESC has published three Strategies since the third sector was incorporated into partnership: *Opportunities, Challenges and Capacities for Choice* (1999), *An Investment in Quality: Services, Inclusion and Enterprise* (2002), and *The Developmental Welfare State* (2005). In the first part of this chapter I want to use these texts to unpack some of the key features of inclusive governance in Ireland.

The Strategy coupled to the 'Sustaining Progress' Agreement (2003–5) tells us that 'the successful society must be visible' to its subjects, with partnership creating the discursive lens through which all will perceive the same world in the same way. It is through such a lens that each and all will perceive the 'shared pressures' and 'new possibilities' which define the parameters of the possible (NESC, 2002: 35, vi–vii). This is the narrative form of inclusive governance in the Irish context, and I will examine each dimension in turn.

Shared pressures: folding conflict into consensus

As a technology of government, social partnership strategically breaks with the past and orients the social field towards the future. This is not the distant future, however, for partnership dispenses with the perfectionist impulse that characterised the project of Society. Instead the present is projected into the near future by constructing a set of targets that – precisely because they are provisional and contingent on a dynamic context – will soon be revisited and, if necessary, revised. Partnership governs the present by setting it against the bad old days of social conflict, and thus aims to consign the 'vicious circle' of 'adversity' to the past so as to make way for the 'virtuous circle' of 'managing success' (NESC, 1999: 8; 2002: 63). If the past signifies the failure of big government and the polarisation of social classes, 'partnership' is the sign of what can be accomplished through negotiated agreements and strategies.

Though built on democratic principles of participation and negotiated agreement, the partnership process is ultimately subject to sovereign power – or what in the literature is called 'meta-governance' – so that inclusive governance always operates in the 'shadow of hierarchy' (Torfing, 2005: 203). The capacity to override devolved decision-making is built into the process itself, so that while local participants are given the freedom to set goals and determine the means to achieve them, they are also obliged to comply with the organisational logic of innovation and performance. It is here that we can see how inclusive governance articulates a performative norm which is also a mode of *authority*; an ordering technology that, according to the NESC, enables a multiplicity of agents to 'pool' and 'rank' information while ensuring that 'the centre' retains the 'right to sanction those who continually fail' (NESC, 2002: 45–7). However, this sovereign 'centre' is not exactly the state, at least not in the sense that we tend to refer to *the* state as a unified entity. In so far as it is meaningful to speak of 'the' state (and I will return to this shortly), the state merely articulates a mode of authority which is essentially decentred.

For example, in the context of what was (at the time) perceived to be a global economic downturn, a public-sector strike during July of 2003 portended growing dissent over the implementation of the 'Sustaining Progress' Agreement.[4] This little altercation – one of many frictions which characterise the 'consensual' nature of inclusive governance – also revealed a struggle over the meaning of the sign of necessity: 'reality'. With representatives from business and labour both claiming to be acting in the interest of 'jobs', the minister for finance argued that 'we must adjust our expectations to the new reality', i.e. protect competitiveness in the uncertain environment of the global market. Sean Healy of the Conference of Religious of Ireland countered this by arguing that 'the principle beneficiaries of the economic growth of the Celtic Tiger have not been Ireland's poorest and most excluded, and this reality needs to be addressed in policy'. With the unifying emblem of 'jobs' defining the context, it was *the* reality of a changed global economy which determined the realm of the possible, with domestic policy cast as a necessary (hence politically neutral) response to the contingency of external conditions. From the standpoint of the third sector the economic gains made through social partnership were of little benefit to vulnerable individuals and groups, and it was *this* reality that should determine policy. Despite the attempt to represent economic development and social justice as compatible aims (NESC, 2002, 2005), in this case they clearly meet in a conflicted relation. The global economy (*the* reality) occupies the position of the universal and articulates the particular (*this* reality), so that the latter is necessarily subject to the authority of the former. Whether defined in economic, social or cultural terms, globalisation is without doubt a fundamentally contested concept, a discursive stage upon which manifold struggle are currently waged, and yet a reality it is, apparently, and one that we must adapt ourselves to. In other words the reality of the global economy must be managed, for it cannot be mastered.

Social partnership places the problem of order on a horizontal plane, distributing it among the various partners or stakeholders. Yet in the context of disagreements like the one above it is clear that the relation is one of hierarchy, with the possibility of social justice deferring to 'jobs', which in turn defers to the primacy of economic competitiveness and performance. It seems to be difficult if not impossible, however, to represent inclusive governance in this way. Some agencies from the third sector have stepped outside (or have been cast out, depending on the interpretation) of the current National Agreement, objecting to a lack of commitment concerning poverty reduction and social inclusion (CWC, 2003a: 1). From the perspective of dissenting third-sector agencies, social partnership has discarded the façade of facilitating equality and democracy and revealed its underlying logic as a 'problem solving mechanism' (CWC, 2003a: 5; 2003b: 6; Fahy, 2003).[5] And yet these dissenting groups remain committed to the ideal of 'true social partnership' and continue to contribute from 'outside' of the Agreement (CWC, 2003c: 2). Partnership exhibits a certain precious quality which is protected by participants, and when threatened with dissolution it tends to generate rapid repair work. On the one hand this is the nature of the practice itself, with National Agreements negotiated every three years or so, thus establishing the possibility for a fresh start. On the other hand when partnership is threatened then we see demands from participants to return to the moment of 'true' social partnership (CWC), which is to say the original moment when alternatives have yet to be foreclosed. The sign of 'reality' articulates the democratic imaginary, and its meaning is a prize to be won through political struggle.

The logic of enfolding becomes explicit when the NESC asks 'how the developmental and welfare aspects of public policy can be related to one another'. The answer lies in the symmetry of the 'flexible developmental state' and the 'developmental welfare state', two halves of the most recent Strategy which are merged in the idea of the 'flexible developmental welfare state' (NESC, 2002, 2005). Constructing vague yet impressively technical concepts such as 'network management' and 'associational activism', governance is defined as a matter of 'activating, orchestrating and modulating the activities of networks' and 'webs' of 'interdependent actors' and 'autonomous service providers' (NESC, 2005: ix–xii, 159). I will examine this conception of governing in more detail in the next section. Here I want to look at how the NESC Strategy recasts welfare as an integral part of economic performance, with state, economy and society brought together as an enfolded structure which is visualised in the NESC documents as a series of triangular Venn diagrams. Severing the link with outdated 'traditions', inclusive governance instantiates its own singularity by abandoning the notion of modernisation as a 'linear, deterministic, or predictable' path of development (NESC, 2002: 45–6). Partnership builds a (porous) seal around the problem of order by constructing a self-contained and interconnected figure of government that takes the discursive form of a triangle (figure 9.1).

Folding the spheres of state, market and society into an autotelic whole, the triadic structure stabilises the potential and manifest conflicts articulated by the inclusion/exclusion problematic. The state is neither wholly internal nor wholly external to this relation, nor can it be said to be aligned to any one region of it (see NESC, 2002: 55–6). Instead,

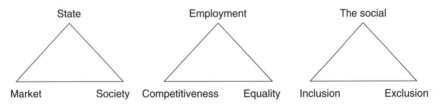

Figure 9.1 The structure of inclusive governance

depending on the context, and notwithstanding the power to enact disciplinary sanctions (a point to which I will return), the state is both mediator and marketing agent, investing the process with legitimacy by sponsoring, steering and endorsing (branding) the Agreements and Strategies produced through the partnership process.

In a way similar to that in which structural linguistics breaks the sign down into the elementary phoneme, partnership can be broken down analytically into its constituent elements. But as with the phoneme, the elements of inclusive governance are meaningless unless reassembled into a relational whole. Meaning slides around within a structure which is held together by this very slippage, so that from the standpoint of any one agent it is possible to view all dimensions as necessarily articulated by the agent's own particular position. For example, some third-sector agencies are concerned with social justice, or more specifically with reducing poverty and empowering the excluded. Empowerment requires educative, counselling, mentoring and training programmes funded through public and private investment. Poverty reduction is dependent on forms of income maintenance secured through the redistribution of wealth and/or remuneration through paid employment in the market economy and employment schemes in the social economy. Thus if we take the 'employment–competitiveness–equality' diagram (figure 9.1) as a core statement in the discourse of social partnership, then it can be noted that the programmes to combat poverty and exclusion require a combination of employment opportunities and wealth creation. In other words those who struggle in the name of 'equality' can only hope to hegemonise the field by defining the meaning of 'employment' and 'competitiveness' in such a way that these are harnessed to the goal of social justice. In this way, the subject of inclusive governance is dispersed throughout the state–market–society relation. Decentring the subject, inclusive governance enables a variety of actors to contest and articulate meaning from a variety of positions without disturbing the ordering apparatus itself.

New possibilities: domesticating the constitutive outside
Interestingly, the primacy of competitiveness defers to something else: a realm of possibilities which is fundamental to innovation but cannot be brought into conscious thought or planned action in any positive sense. This horizon exceeds the reach of human knowledge, and while in the past this ungovernable realm applied primarily to economy it now fully envelops the social:

> More important than the substance of the new view, is the way in which actual developments differ from our best strategies, and how this forces

us to alter how we think strategies, models and plans . . . an effective
public system is one which learns from experience and experimentation
to continuously improve policy and implementation . . . Rather than see
public policy as guided by timeless high-level goals, it understands it as a
problem-solving process which is guided by action-oriented co-ordination
and information. This reflects the fact that the life of the society – like
that of individuals, the public system and the economy – is realised in
history . . . new possibilities . . . are more often disclosed through action
and experimentation, than through analysis or ideological debate.
(NESC, 2002: 36–8, 46)

Even the best-laid plans are vulnerable to that which is excluded. This
is clearly stated in the section on 'delivering a fair and inclusive society'
in the current Agreement. The text notes the importance of identifying
'*emerging* causes of exclusion or inequality' so that it becomes necessary
to 'review and revise social inclusion programmes and initiatives as
appropriate, and in consultation with the relevant actors' (Ireland, 2003:
56, emphasis added; also NESC, 2002: 129). To the mechanisms for
anticipating possible problems can be added the deliberative dimension
of partnership, or 'the idea that identity can be shaped in interaction',
together with knowledge derived from 'rights discourse': the 'modern
consensus that it is not possible to establish rights on universally valid
foundations' (NESC, 2002: 108). Social partnership governs through the
insight that order, membership, identity and rights are all contingent on
an unstable context. In other words it aims to manage the surplus of
meaning which penetrates and encircles the social as both danger and
opportunity. Though this cannot be brought within the realm of knowledge we can learn how to harness and direct it. The perfectionist project
of Society was one in which the growth of knowledge would be harnessed
to rational techniques of economic planning and social engineering, but
this is now thought to have engendered stagnation, which is the greatest
threat of all. To offset this risk we must govern ourselves and each other
through innovating and adapting to emergent conditions of possibility,
and this means that our very identities and subjectivities must be rendered contingent and subjected to programmes of re-formation. Inclusive governance seeks to harness, direct and manage rather than master
aleatory forces. The 'radical negativity' of postmodern theorising – the
insight that a 'constitutive outside' is the possibility and impossibility of
order – becomes the target and the means of inclusive governance.

Inclusive governance is an autotelic mode of ordering which displaces
the great modern promise of progress. If politics is about power and
antagonism, then partnership is an open and variable structure that
secures order by anticipating and managing antagonism. It transforms

the political into an aesthetic symmetry which cuts itself away from the teleological and perfectionist discourse of Society, securing order through an inclusive process of exclusion.

Meta-governance and discipline: performance, auditing and contract

In stating that governance aims to activate, orchestrate and modulate the activities of autonomous actors and agencies, the latest NESC Strategy captures and codifies the transformations I have tracked in the case studies above: from itinerancy to citizenship, from defectiveness to rights, from delinquency to risk, from the punishment of unmarried mothers to the management of crisis pregnancies, or in a more general sense, from exclusion to inclusion. The project of Society has given way to a mode of ordering that governs through the autonomous decisions and choices of individuals and other entities such as 'sectors' and various type of 'community'. Autonomy is exercised and decisions are calculated in multiple contexts – markets, workplace, school, family, voluntary organisation – yet choices do not go unnoticed, with autonomy acted upon by recording, monitoring and measuring the performance of decision-making actors and entities, the strategic objective of which is to promote a type of autonomy which is both disciplined and responsible. Importantly given the focus of this particular study, the new governmentality reconfigures the relation between disciplinary control and biopolitical regulation.

Marking a shift from bureaucracy to business, from planning to competition, and from the logic of systems to one of markets (Rose, 1999: 150), inclusive governance is denoted in a variety of ways: network governance, self-regulating inter-organisational networks, and new public management. Whichever label we settle on, the strategic aim is to find a middle ground between markets and hierarchies by importing business practices into public-sector contexts, in particular cost control, financial transparency, decentralised authority, the creation of markets and quasi-markets, and the introduction of mechanisms to make service providers accountable to customers (Verheijen and Coomes, 1998; Rhodes, 1996; Eliassen and Kooiman, 1993). In normative terms this is framed as a response to consumer demand for cheaper, more efficient and more effective services, empowering the tax-paying citizen by prising open the organisation and the domains of expertise so that managers and professionals are subject to scrutiny and made accountable (Power, 1997: 44; Rose, 1999: 147).

The dominant way of creating this type of accountability – evident not just in Ireland but internationally – is through the technique of audit

(Power, 1997). As an idea and as a technology it is not always entirely clear what auditing is, yet this essential fuzziness is precisely what facilitates its dissemination across a variety of organisational contexts. As Michael Power puts it, 'the word is not used simply *descriptively* to refer to particular practices, but *normatively* in the context of demands and aspirations for accountability and control' (1997: 6). Audit combines knowledge with practice in shaping our understanding of the problem for which it is the solution (Power, 1997: 7).

Audit has thoroughly penetrated what Nikolas Rose calls the old 'enclaves of power' – the 'fiefdoms of local government' and 'enclosures of professional expertise' – making these domains both autonomous and responsive to the expectations of users. At the same time this also 'reinstates the state' by instituting new methods of control and by reinforcing the centres of calculation that manage budgetary regimes, set targets and monitor performance (Rose, 1999: 146–7). Audit and accounting become the means and the measure of legitimacy, with auditable standards of performance a ruler against which the organisation, agency or individual is measured and disciplined, an example being the audit commissioned by the Irish minister for justice prior to terminating funding for the Citizen Traveller campaign. Notwithstanding this example of how audit can reinstate the sovereign power of the state, it is also allows the state to shift to enabling strategies by promoting various types of partnership, devolving responsibilities to actors and agencies embedded in 'webs of knowledge and circuits of communication' (Rose, 1999: 147).

As government shifts to the regulation of discrete governable entities, so the space of governing is reconfigured as zones and networks, or in the case of Ireland, 'sectors'. Rose notes that the experts and authorities populating these zones are subjectified in two related ways: first as *objects* of calculations, monitored in accordance with standards of performance; and secondly as *relays* of calculations, induced or commanded to evaluate their own performance and the performance of those around them (1999: 152). In this way the power of decision-making is devolved and made visible at the same time. In other words, the same action or operation can be measured, costed and compared, whether the provision of hospital beds in London and Copenhagen, a programme to reduce road deaths in neighbouring regions of Italy, or the performance of two schools in a disadvantaged area of Dublin.

Notwithstanding the alleged openness and efficiency of these techniques, Power notes that the audit process itself requires trust in those charged with conducting the audit, and the documents they produce may in fact establish a 'dead end in the chain of accountability' (1997:

127–8). More interesting from the point of view of examining the relation between order and exclusion, however, is not the integrity of the practice – the degree of fit between the claims and the actuality of auditing – but the way this recalibrates the disciplinary technology of the penitentiary and the regulatory technologies of social government by keeping observational practices under observation (Power, 1997: 129). It is here that we can see how the problem of governing social exclusion articulates a disciplinary apparatus relating to questions of employability, dependency and educational disadvantage.

As noted in the introduction, as the social state came into existence T. H. Marshall defined welfare as a social right which filled out the status of citizenship and offset the inequalities created by a market economy. This is no longer the case. As we have seen in the chapters on disability and youth – in the notion of 'activation' and the invention of the permanent trainee – welfare now imitates training, and there are to be no exceptions to the rule of managing one's employability, with individuals encouraged and induced to take responsibility for their employability by anticipating and offsetting the obsolescence of marketable skills and credentials (Rose, 1999: 162–4). In other words, the individual must continually update existing skills or acquire new ones in accordance with the shifting requirements of the economy (CEC, 1993).

The danger of unemployability has seen public assistance and earned benefits recoded in the language of 'active' welfare. Recast as a 'job-seeker', the unemployed person is steered into education and training programmes and, depending on the context, may be subjected to workfare programmes as a condition of eligibility for public assistance. The experience of unemployment must at least resemble the experience of work, with the unemployed individual tutored in the arts of disciplined and responsible freedom (Rose, 1999: 164). In Ireland the current minister for social and family affairs is redesigning the One Parent Family Payments, the aim of which is to insert claimants into a one-to-one relation with a personal mentor, who will provide advice and guidance on how to acquire marketable skills and credentials. Unemployment itself is technologised so that it becomes a form of pedagogy which connects up with discourses of educational disadvantage and 'life-long learning'. As we have seen in some detail in chapter 7, it is only very recently that education was coded in the language of equality, and since then it has become the guarantor of inclusion, the dominant meaning of which is the autonomy made possible through paid employment (Levitas, 1996). As with the programmes of Bentham and Booth, a set of rationalities, programmes and technologies is brought to bear on the problem of creating the subject of rule. Responsible, independent and prudent, the subject of the inclusive society must be capable of governing his or her 'self' as an enterprise, offsetting the risks of lived life by keeping skills and credentials up to date with the shifting demands of the market and taking out insurance against risk: health insurance, mortgage protection, life assurance, income protection – the list is potentially extensive (Rose, 1996; O'Malley, 1992). This is one indication of how the new governmentality recalibrates the subject. We might call this the core of inclusion. But what about those individuals and groups who are unable or unwilling to enterprise their 'self' in this way: those beyond the inner core who, through their marginality, bound order from within?

This requires another look at strategies such as Citizen Traveller, Anti-Social Behaviour Orders (ASBOs) and the new child-care legislation, and in particular the focus of the last of these on restorative justice. All of these bear the stamp of a new actuarial penology known as 'situational crime prevention'. It is apparently no longer useful to know the mind or the disposition of the criminal. Instead prevention strategies target the situational contexts within which crimes (may) occur (O'Malley, 1992; Feeley and Simon, 1992, 1994). The aim is to avoid trouble rather than understand it, and so it no longer really matters whether the offender is 'bad or mad' (Young, 1999: 66–7). The strategy assumes all people to be capable of criminal acts, and it assumes all people to be rational choosers in the light of a given set of opportunities, and so the objective shifts from knowledge of the criminal or the criminal mind to the task of adjusting the crime rate in a given context. This might involve the removal of coin-operated phone boxes, or placing security cameras over cash-dispensing machines, or establishing local crime reduction partnerships. The last of these techniques, which is codified in England and Wales by the Crime and Disorder Act of 1998, closes off the distance between public and private and disperses responsibility for securing order (Crawford, 2003: 480). It discards the concerns of penal welfarism – justice and rehabilitation – and dispenses with the separation between law-abiding citizen and agents of the penal system, so that citizens are now enlisted into a corporate strategy of crime prevention and management (Crawford, 2003: 484–6).

Adam Crawford (2003) identifies an important trend in this type of contractual governance: 'modes of control that mimic and deploy contracts and agreements in the regulation of deviant conduct and disorderly behaviour'. Contractual governance often operates in the shadow of the law in the sense that the contractual form is not always legally codified. Instead it is a flexible technology to regulate self-regulation: structuring the distribution of responsibilities and obligations, establishing a relation of reciprocity through exchange, and operating through the freedom to choose. The last point is crucial to understanding how the contractual form reorganises disciplinary power. To enter into a contract is a voluntary decision, or at least it may be experienced as such, even in cases where there is little choice to be made. In this way contract is the voluntary acceptance of imposed obligations: a way of entering into a set of constraints which narrows the scope of future choices and actions (Crawford, 2003: 489–90). Discipline thus takes the form of a transaction, the strategic aim of which is to secure compliance by conferring the power of choice upon those who are to be tutored in the arts of self-government.

Contractual governance looms large in the battle against anti-social behaviour. As noted in chapter 7, the ASBO is a sanction designed to fit the precise circumstances of a given 'anti-social' individual, limiting the scope of his or her choice by prohibiting behaviours specified in the order. Connecting civil and criminal law, the ASBO is a switching mechanism or transmission point: it attempts to regulate conduct without removing the individual from the space of liberties, yet at the same time it constrains the exercise of freedom, and it does this with a mixture of the carrot and the stick. It is a type of licensed freedom which is surrounded by coercion: a technology that can quickly remove the 'anti-social' individual from the zones of inclusion and pass her or him over to the coercive apparatus of the state. In other words the ASBO is an explicitly punitive example of the contractual form, and one that marks the edge between inclusion and exclusion.

Other types of contractual devices are more subtle. Examples from the UK are the Acceptable Behaviour Contract (ABC) discussed in chapter 7, or the Referral Orders provided for under the Youth Justice and Criminal Evidence Act 1999, covering all 10–17-year-old offenders who plead guilty on a first offence (Crawford, 2003). With the Referral Order, which is similar to the objectives of the 2001 Children Act in Ireland, the young offender is referred to a panel governed by principles of restorative justice. The panel draws up a contract which, when signed, both activates the court order and provides a forum wherein the offender, victim, family and members of the wider community can discuss the crime and its consequences. The panel also monitors the contract, keeping a record of the offender's compliance or non-compliance.

Experiments to regulate fly-posting in the UK are also modelled on the contract, with designated 'street sites' and bollards offering free advertising. With city leaders focusing on the problem of how to brand and market their city, behaviour which may be construed as a nuisance is not prohibited but 'placed': drawn into designated zones which are designed to anticipate and manage undesirable conduct (Crawford,

2003: 487). Less benign examples are the 'zones of tolerance' in Scotland to contain prostitution, or the city-subsidised premises in Germany, Switzerland and Holland where heroin is administered to addicts (Young, 1999: 65–6). Regulated in this way, deviance is managed as a technical rather than a moral problem; not a question of 'why' someone transgresses norms or violates laws, but a question of 'what' is to be done with undesirable choices and actions (Crawford, 2003: 487).

Membership is fragmenting into zones and circuits, each with tentative and revocable 'rules of inclusion', with contractual governance displacing the fiction of the social contract as the basis of citizenship (Crawford, 2003: 499–500). The subject of the ASBO, the subject of the ABC, and the subject of the youth Referral Order are all positioned within what Crawford calls a parochial mode of control, which has direct and indirect connections to the sovereign powers of the state. Each of these technologies trims and shapes the bundle of rights and responsibilities associated with citizenship so that the right to exercise freedom is made conditional on compliance with the terms of the contract. The Citizen Traveller strategy is an example of how the contractual form has been used in the Irish context. Individuals move within and between various zones, networks and circuits of inclusion: shopping malls, lines of credit, ethnic identities, offshore tax havens, online communities, faith-based charities; the list is easily extended.

Public management technologies modelled on contracts, on principles of restorative justice, and on the placement of otherwise prohibited conduct both empower and discipline, simultaneously conferring power on individuals and enveloping the space of autonomy with a blend of responsibilities and (potential) sanctions. In structuring the zones within which choice is exercised, and in making decisions and actions both visible and accountable, contractual governance connects the logic of performance and the technology of auditing to the subject of inclusive governance. The disciplinary technology of contract brings those who are unable or unwilling to practise responsible autonomy under a specific mode of tutelage which instructs them in the arts of self-government. Acting upon these technologies of control is the actuarial logic of performance and the technologies of auditing and accounting. Performance, audit and contract together secure order. In the wings, now as in the past, is the penal sanction, or the power to exclude.

Managing postmodernity

As we have seen in the preceding chapters, the discourse of in/exclusion is plural rather than singular. To paraphrase Robert Goodin (1996), this

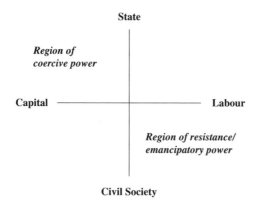

Figure 9.2 Power and resistance in modernity

plurality can be organised as three statements: the excluded have been 'left out' (sociological thesis); they have 'opted out' (moral underclass thesis); they have been 'kept out' (power thesis). From the perspective of the political left, which has arguably had the most to say on modern forms of domination, it is the power thesis which characterises conflict in modernity, as shown in figure 9.2.

In this figure we see how power, or rather powers, have a definite place (see Newman, 2004). Coercive power is concentrated between the capitalist economy and the state and is exercised over those subject to forms of exploitation and domination. Opposite and opposed to this repressive power is an emancipatory power, which takes the form of individual autonomy and/or organised resistance. In the classic Marxist narrative this is articulated by the labour movement as it contests the power of a capitalist class supported by a duplicitous state. The Marxist narrative of emancipation is one in which structural relations of domination are erased as labour seizes control of the means of production. In turn this leads to a withering of the state as class divisions are effaced, leaving a community of people no longer in the grip of false consciousness and no longer alienated from the material world they produce through their individual and collective labour. Another well-known (liberal) version sees the region of resistance articulated by civil society organisations as they limit government and/or powerful private interests, thus protecting private and public autonomy. There are of course many variations on this theme, such as feminist critiques of patriarchal power. Irrespective of the presumed, alleged or actual sources of domination and resistance, the structure itself exhibits the longevity of an epoch.

In fact what seems to have transpired in recent decades is not entirely dissimilar to the Marxist narrative, minus the utopian end-state. The boundaries defining the spheres of state, market and society have blurred, and the old distinctions – distinctions at times experienced, at other times normatively advocated – have blended into each other: the public folds into the private, work mixes with leisure, the separation between culture and nature is increasingly difficult to define, and 'government' can no longer be thought as something external to its subject. Inclusive governance dissolves the axes and lines of opposition shown in figure 9.2, folding the spheres of state, market and society into each other as each and all are recruited into the task of securing a manageable order.

Despite the frustration on the part of some actors among the third sector in Ireland – the apparent inability to locate an 'outside' space of dissent – there is such a space and a corresponding mode of action: violence. The riots that began in the *banlieue* of Paris during October of 2005 are an example of this. Inclusive governance does not *re*place so much as *dis*place the old oppositions, but these can be re-invoked, as was the case in France, with the words of one youth a stark reminder of what is at stake: 'we burn because it's the only way to make ourselves heard, because it's solidarity with the rest of the non-citizens in this country, with this whole underclass. Because it feels good to do something with your rage' (Henley, 2005). Note, however, that this is neither the revolutionary subject of socialism nor the liberal subject of rights and responsibilities. This is the voice of *les exclus*, and it articulates the difference and the distance between order and its others.

Thus far the Republic of Ireland has not produced this kind of conflict, at least not on any significant scale, with the many frictions relating to inequality contained by the apparatus of social partnership. So how do we explain this stability? Important is the way social partnership resonates with what David Osborne and Ted Gaebler call, from the North American perspective, the 'reinvention of government' (1992). The Weberian subtitle of their book underlines the perceived agent of reinvention: 'how the entrepreneurial spirit is transforming the public sector'. Their hope is 'to unleash new ways of thinking and acting', with the lean and flexible firm providing a template for public-sector reform. The watchwords are innovation, competition and enterprise. In Europe Tony Blair's Third Way, Gerhard Schroeder's *Neue Mitte* and the local partnership initiatives sponsored by the European Union are among the most widely cited attempts to translate the new thinking into practice, but the practice is more than the sum of these programmatic statements.

As the preceding chapters have shown, governmentalities are assembled over time as an accretion of programmes, apparatuses and technologies born from the intersection of alliances, frictions and, yes, competition and innovation. Order is never the product of design or intention, and the new governmentality recognises this.

In contrast to the modern narratives of progress, the problem is now one of defining and staying *a* course. In Ireland, as noted above, this is accomplished through social partnership, an inclusive apparatus of governance which operates by constructing envelopes of agreement, the scope of which varies depending on the specific context. While this mode of ordering is institutionalised at local and national levels, it would be a mistake to equate it with well-defined places of negotiation; indeed there are signs that the existing model of National Agreements is under strain. While social partnership has its specific places (such as negotiations at the national level, or within the Strategic Policy Committees of local government) and its specific objectives (wage agreements, promoting sustainable development), inclusive governance is more than the singularity of place or the specificity of objectives. It is at once a modality – of enunciation, of representation, of reporting, of organisation – and a context in which 'consultation' and 'dialogue' are mobilised to secure agreement on a course of action. Inclusive governance organises a variety of stakeholders – agents that might otherwise meet in relations of conflict – into forums and spaces of negotiation through which a programme of action can be agreed upon. This is a mode of governing that moves cautiously, step by step, pitching objectives into a future no more than a few years away, with the decision never more than provisional and hence (potentially) open to revision.

The problem of order is now explicitly a *management* problem, with government seeking to activate and augment individual, 'sectoral' and 'community' capacities for self-help and mutual assistance. Far from being subjected to this shift in the mode of administration, Travellers, lone parenting groups, disability organisations and youth agencies are pursuing these things themselves. Indeed all of these groups now participate in governance, as do representatives for the aged, homeless, poor, unemployed, gays and lesbians, refugees, drug users and prisoners. Inclusive governance dispenses with the old practices of exclusion, making it incumbent on each and all to secure the governability of democracy: *together* we enclose a range of possibilities within an agreed set of objectives, and by default we foreclose on alternatives. Crucial to this is the process of securing agreement through consultation and negotiation, because this confers legitimacy on the decision, and indeed inclusive governance can be conceptualised as a mode of legitimate authority for the postmodern world.

The concept of legitimacy clearly occupies a privileged place in modern political thought. Rooted in debates on the source and scope of political authority, it is arguably *the* normative yardstick against which the relation between sovereign power and social order is assessed. In what became a classic study of authority and domination, Max Weber delineated two broad types of legitimate order. The first, concerning the validity of convention, was based on a combination of tradition and faith, while the second, based on the validity of law, he associated with the growth and consolidation of the rational bureaucratic state (1978b: 33–8, 215–54). The Weberian scheme continues to influence political thought today, notable for example in the work of Jürgen Habermas (1996: 30–3). For Habermas the continued viability of democracy depends on the extent to which law can secure legitimacy in a context marked by a proliferation of demands for recognition, inclusion and rights. At stake is the potential for a democratic order which is both inclusive and open to difference.

Habermas's understanding of positive law is quite specific – related but not equivalent to legal positivism. William Rehg provides a succinct definition: 'a system of coercible rules and impersonal procedures that also involve an appeal to reasons that all citizens should, at least ideally, find acceptable' (1996: xi). Crucial to Habermas's theory is the generalisability of validity claims ('reasons') and the way these are reflected in positive law, so that the rule of law becomes a 'consciously enacted framework of norms' which seeks, in fact needs, universal recognition (Habermas 1996: 38). For without recognition on the part of *all* who are subject to it, the rule of law would be experienced, at least by some, as the force of law – a mechanism of coercion which lacks the legitimacy to secure social integration. Again it is worth recalling the example from France of the rioter who finds solidarity in violence and rage.

In the context of inclusive governance we might ask whether the relation between negotiation and decision corresponds to Habermas's discourse ethics. The new governmentality certainly resembles Habermas's normative ideal, but the resemblance is no more than superficial. Inclusive governance moves the problem of exclusion to the centre, making it an explicit target and thus securing social recognition (legitimacy) for the policies and programmes which are the output of governance. Inclusive governance is also a setting where certain things are convention-*alised*: principles of competitiveness, flexibility, employability and consumption. While obviously derived from the sphere of economy these are now stretched over the social in its entirety, becoming the means and ends of public programmes and private projects. Inclusive governance belongs to a context where things long thought of as analytically distinct or dialectically related are folded into each other: state, market and society, citizens and consumers, capital and labour, the public and the private, work and leisure; or in more general terms, the inside and outside of organisation (Clegg, 1990; Dean, 1996; Lash, 2002; Wittel, 2001). Crucially important, this is not a question of deceit: the consciousness-distorting power of ideology; but neither does it reflect Habermas's discourse ethics: normative agreement uncontaminated by manipulative strategies. Instead it is the power of social knowledge when it is reified as truth. The truth we now individually and collectively enact in the course of routine social life concerns the necessarily partial and provisional nature of order, and this is neither ideologically hidden from view nor something we have learnt from listening to each other's claims to validity.

If the nineteenth century was the era of progress and the twentieth century the time of the plan, then the twenty-first century seems set to become the age of strategy. The language of strategy has become ubiquitous, and it connects up with the truth of our present: *performance.* While this can be interpreted in a variety of ways, as the mark of efficiency or effectiveness for example, its deeper significance concerns immanence. Closely aligned to the technology of audit, performance is both the measure of legitimacy and the means of legitimation, for we have abandoned the project of mastering uncertainty and eradicating ambivalence. And while it must be managed for the purpose of ordering, the margin which is squeezed out from regimes of power/knowledge/practice – the surplus which for so long threatened order but also made order possible – is at once the source of risk and our most precious resource: the possibility for innovation. In a word, the problem of government is that of managing the relation between inclusion and exclusion, enclosure and foreclosure, with the *telos* of social and human perfection born in the wake of the Enlightenment displaced by an autotelic mode of social organisation. Poststructuralism tells us that the immanent surplus of meaning is both the possibility and impossibility of order. This is now embraced as we strive for the innovative edge, and inclusive governance appropriates the core insight of poststructuralist critique.

For Habermas law is a *consciously enacted* system of norms, reflecting the duality of his notion of consensus: communicatively accomplished understanding and normative agreement. This is both the strength and weakness of his theory; its strength: to give form and substance to a yearning for something better, something missing from lived life; its weakness: an inability or unwillingness to confront the specificity and multiplicity of 'empirical realities' (Clegg, 1990). Against the Habermasian ideal, we have seen examples of how the social is disturbed and reordered through strategic forces and alliances which by no means accord with the ideal of communicatively accomplished agreement. Referring back to the classic Weberian scheme, and drawing again on the notion of the illegitimate act discussed in chapter 8, it can be argued that convention and law are not separate or related orders but are of the same order of social knowledge. To speak of convention is to denote social knowledge which is deeply sedimented in practices, and when this is problematised the rule of law restores order. In other words law brings convention and the modification of convention into alignment. Law stands between order and those meanings which have been prised apart from convention through political struggle, and it articulates the relation between order and those meanings which are fighting their way into the space of possibilities. Legitimacy, then – and this is the Nietzschean twist – is the sign of victory amid perpetual struggle. What I am suggesting is that inclusive governance turns this paradigmatically modern mechanism into an ordering technology which anticipates disturbances.

Inclusive governance is a comprehensive articulation of the social mode of ordering that was born with the modern epoch. Unlike the project of Society, the logic of which was to create a bounded order by controlling the abnormal and banishing the anomalous, inclusive governance works by managing a fluid social field which is open at its boundary. The register of 'inclusion' floats in the fields and orders of discourse: mobile, anticipating, ready to domesticate the immanent and ineliminable horizon of antagonism which necessarily inhabits the social. Morphologically the sign of 'inclusion' is both porous and absorbent: open at the level of the signifier and amorphous and fluid at the level of the signified. Discursively it is a mobile and empty space for the inscription of meaning. In contrast to the perfectionist discourse of Society, the problem of order is now cast in the negative sign of 'exclusion' and its mirror-image 'inclusion'. It is not simply that social inclusion is worth fighting for; it is that the *meaning* of inclusion is worth fighting for, and the struggle for meaning is a struggle for truth, for hegemony, for order. As an empty space and an open invitation, inclusion is a 'dotted line' ('...........') in the fields and orders of discourse: anticipating and ready for the inscription of as yet unforeseen demands and challenges: to receive, envelop and *direct* conflict and contestation.

Inclusive governance wraps a finite spectrum of possibilities, at once open to everything while deferring those alternatives that pose a challenge to its truth. Whereas the strength and the weakness of Society were its perfectionist impulse, those of inclusive governance are its fundamental contingency. Travellers have not (yet) acquired the kind of justice they demand, the disabled have not (yet) secured the rights they have been fighting for, and lone parents have not (yet) achieved the kind of equality they seek, and nevertheless the organisations and bodies representing these groups continue to fight for inclusion and to participate in inclusive governance. As for the question of youth, whether a young person at risk is defined as an offender or an under-performer, she or he is subjected to programmes that govern through inclusion. The categories endure even as their content changes – from itinerant to Traveller, defective to disabled, unmarried mother to lone parent, delinquency to risk – and though winning the right to recognition, the more difficult questions of redistribution and social justice are endlessly deferred. But maybe to look for happy endings is to risk missing the larger significance of governmental transformation. Between the Citizen Traveller campaign, the Crisis Pregnancy strategy, the rights-based approach to disability, and the various strategies articulated by the discourses of attention deficiency and anti-social behaviour, we can begin to see an outline of the subject of inclusive governance: a constellation of norms at once ill-defined and yet circumscribing a definite field of possibilities and limitations. As the historically excluded are included, so they are gently coerced into embodying norms of responsibility and employability.

Inclusive governance secures order by folding means and ends into an all-enveloping logic of performance, a regime of truth that defers only to itself as origin, cause and purpose. But its narcissistic structure may also be its Achilles heel. Unlike the project of Society the new regime of truth can only effect closure by remaining open: by bounding itself through the logic of a dotted line which waits to recognise and give the name of 'inclusion' to any and all 'excluded' subjects, identities and forces that pose a threat to order. The modern space of resistance and the postmodern space of refusal (the constitutive outside) are either dissolved or absorbed, and there is a cost attached to the moment of inscription: as the excluded turn on the hinge of the social and move into the realm of inclusion, so they reinforce the regime of truth. But this can also be refused, and so nothing is certain.

The goal of 'inclusion' is enunciated repeatedly in the various forums of governance; hence it takes the discursive form of reiteration. But because it derives its significance from something which is permanently in question – the social – so the meaning of inclusion is never quite defined, and the struggles waged in its name defer the present to a future which need never arrive. Social inclusion is the modern promise of equality/emancipation made into a postmodern technology of government: it provides direction and secures legitimacy in a context where both are routinely contested.

Notes

Introduction

1 Marshall citing Patrick Colquhoun (1806) *A Treatise on Indigence*, London: Hatchard.

Chapter 1

1 This is placed in scare quotes because the register of crisis frames a situation of imminent change as normatively undesirable, which might not be the case if all perspectives are considered (see Raboy and Dagenais, 1992; Hay, 1999).
2 See also CEC (1991) for discussion on these themes.
3 On the debate surrounding Lewis and Wilson see Maxwell (1993).
4 In fact Gunner Myrdal coined the term as early as 1963 (Gans, 1996), yet the work of Wilson has become the 'origin' of this debate.
5 At the time of writing the Bush administration is pressing for a constitutional amendment to prohibit same-sex couples from marrying.
6 Now widely referred to as policy transfer (Dolowitz and Marsh, 2000). For a relevant theoretical framework see Clegg (1989).
7 The vision of social Europe was predicated on the idea of 'industrial citizen-ship', a pragmatic framework aimed at securing agreement at the inter-governmental level of the European Community, but silent on those excluded from this economic conception of citizenship (Room, 1990).
8 Ian Hacking calls this the 'looping effect' (Hacking, 2004), or in a slightly different formulation, actor network theorists propose that the social sci-ences 'enact' the world (Law and Urry, 2004).

Chapter 2

1 Karl Popper could also be included here. See his *Open Society and its Enemies* (1962) and *Poverty of Historicism* (2002b).
2 For a more detailed account of this argument see Foucault (1977: 195–228).

3 While this phrase is used by Foucault and Foucaultian scholars, Roseberry takes it from the work of E. P. Thompson.
4 Laclau proposes an equivalent to the episteme in his concept of 'imaginary'. However, if the categories 'episteme' and 'imaginary' are conceptually equivalent then there is nothing to be gained by adding unnecessary complexity to the theoretical vocabulary used here.
5 Poststructuralist thinkers such as Chantal Mouffe and Ernesto Laclau also identify with the organic intellectual, although they would not subscribe to the idea of a closed cultural unity or emancipation in any final sense. Instead they write of counter-hegemony and emancipation in a radically plural and provisional sense.

Chapter 3

1 This public theatre of signs is what Foucault called 'the gentle way in punishment' (1977: 104–31).
2 Both Karl Polanyi in 1944 and J. R. Poynter in 1969 made the connection between Bentham and the amended Poor Law of 1834. Recent Bentham scholarship seems to accept this (see Bentham, 2001).
3 Chadwick had access to at least some of Bentham's unpublished work on the topic (see Bentham, 2001: xxxv; xlvii).
4 Extended to Ireland in 1860 as the Dublin-based Mission to Friendless Females.
5 Guidelines were also published at this time by the Reformatory and Refuge Union as a *Handbook for Lay Missionaries and Refuge Workers* (Finnegan, 2001). In fact there was a proliferation of such rules at this time, the Sisters of Mercy, for example, also publishing *The Rules and Constitution of the Religious Sisters of Mercy* in 1863.
6 Some commentators argued that indulging the comfort of sinners would reward vice rather than ensure repentance, and here we can trace the discourse of penitence to the Benthamite principle of less eligibility (see Finnegan, 2001: 227). The context is important here. When the rescue movement was at its height during the second half of the nineteenth century poverty was at its worst, and the refuges had to contend with the possibility that rendering life within the homes more eligible than the comforts afforded by paid labour would cause rather than cure vice.
7 There is a strong imprint of Bentham's plan for pauper management in these principles, which is examined in chapter 4.
8 A relatively recent MA thesis (1961) on the Good Shepherd homes demonstrates the extent to which the Rules endured. As of that time the dormitory Mistress continued to lock herself into her cell at night, training herself to wake several times so that she could detect transgressions, using 'mechanical listening devices' to 'magnify even the slightest noise' (Finnegan, 2001: 234). The central inspection principle is well known from Foucault's work on Bentham's panopticon (1977), but Bentham also envisioned an ingenious

'trumpet' through which the inspector could listen to and speak to her or his charges from within the inspection tower (see Bentham, 1995: 36, 111).

Chapter 4

1 The phrase used in this subheading is borrowed from Poynter (1969: 130).
2 Civil parishes in England had been allowed to combine as Unions since the introduction of the Workhouse Test Act of 1743 (Slack, 1990: 45).
3 'Panopticism' is borrowed from chapter 3 in part 3 of Foucault's *Discipline and Punish* (1977).
4 The problem of unemployment is also the central concern of Charles Booth's *Life and Labour of the People of London*, although he frames it as a problem of underemployment (Booth, 1969: 309).
5 On the history of the casual ward see Rose (1988: 77–86).
6 Eugenics discourse saw the phrase 'submerged tenth' used in Ireland during 1906–7, an example being David Barry, canon of Doneraile, who published several articles on the topic in the Catholic *Irish Theological Quarterly* (Jones, 1992: 91).
7 Framed in authoritarian terms by Booth, this also maps onto various forms of twentieth-century social democracy.
8 Booth's little commonwealth traced the paternal-patriarchal conception of authority right down to the family unit, with his 'fundamental law of the family' derived from the 'fundamental laws of nature'. If 'woman's rights' were an issue, then for Booth the first of those rights should be to train a woman in her trade as 'queen of her household, and mother of her children' (Booth, 1890: 235).
9 I am indebted to Mark Haugaard for drawing my attention to the significance of Booth's lithograph.
10 Constructed in the 1860s, the London Embankment become a place for the homeless to gather and sleep within easy reach of the theatres and restaurants of the West End, offering opportunities to beg, to receive scraps of food occasionally distributed by chefs, and to secure casual work such as cab-touting (Rose, 1988: 92).
11 The Cab Horse Charter is now part of the Salvation Army's heritage <www.salvationarmy.org/heritage.nsf?Open>, accessed 1 April 2004.
12 This resonates strongly with Bauman's notion of the gardening state (1989, 1991).
13 A similar rationale was used in Ireland in 1920 by the Rev. Michael J. O'Donnell, professor of dogmatic and moral theology at Maynooth and co-editor of the *Irish Theological Quarterly*. In defence of eugenic policies, O'Donnell argued 'If public authority may segregate a lunatic, criminal or leper, may it not also, by adopting the same moral and reasonable method, prevent acts leading to the birth of children who, in all human probability, will have to be supported at the public expense or become centres of moral and physical contagion' (cited in Jones, 1992: 92).

Chapter 5

1 See Pavee Point <www.paveepoint.ie> and the Irish Traveller Movement <www.itmtrav.com>; also McDonagh (2000).

2 During the second half of the nineteenth century there were so many Irish immigrants in North American asylums that the Irish were also associated with insanity (Robins, 1986: 121).

3 See also *Irish Times* (1955); *Irish Press* (1958a).

4 The Bill was enacted in 1947 in a much diluted form, in part due to opposition by the church to state interference in matters of welfare (Barrington, 1987). The punitive powers proposed by this piece of legislation are similar to the infamous Contagious Disease Acts at the end of the nineteenth century (see Luddy, 1995; Finnegan, 2001).

5 Dáil debates, vol. 105, 1 May 1947, 'Committee on Finance: Health Bill 1947: Second Stage'.

6 It is interesting to note that this page of *The Times* carried several reports on anti-racist actions taking place in the UK at this time, but the problem of racism is perceived only in terms of colour.

7 The practice of child removal was intended to 'absorb' indigenous Australians by 'breeding out the colour' (Bird, 1998: 1). A public inquiry from 1995 to 1997 by the Human Rights and Equal Opportunities Commission concluded with the prime minister, John Howard, refusing to issue a public apology (Reynolds, 1998; Paisley, 1997).

8 Transcripts from parliamentary debate on tinkers and itinerants at this time are published under the heading 'Vagrancy'.

9 Dáil debates, vol. 126, 18 July, 'Questions, Oral Answers: Protection from Itinerants'.

10 In 1971 Sharon and George Gmelch identified 102 local settlement committees registered with the Irish Council, although 30 were found to be inactive (Gmelch and Gmelch, 1974: 15).

11 An MA thesis, titled 'Itinerancy and Poverty: A Case Study in the Subculture of Poverty' (1971, UCD), was a key reference point in this shift (Gmelch, 1987: 306; Helleiner, 2000: 92).

12 See also *Irish Times* (1976a, 1976f); *Irish Press* (1976c).

13 Also *Irish Times* (1976d); *Irish Independent* (1976).

14 Victor Bewley also served on the Travelling People Review Body from 1981 to 1983 (see Gmelch, 1987: 306).

15 There was a marked increase in the number of arrests under Section 30 the Act at this time, few of which, however, resulted in prosecution (see Gmelch, 1987: 311; Kilcommins, O'Donnell, O'Sullivan and Vaughan, 2004: 154–5).

16 The text itself was written by Des Curley, a school teacher in County Roscommon whose wife was a national coordinator for Traveller social work services. The document itself was developed under the auspices of the Irish Centre for the Study of Human Rights (Gmelch, 1987: 315).

17 The 1996 National Agreement called *Partnership 2000 for Inclusion, Employment and Competitiveness* (Ireland, 1996c) saw two Traveller organisations represented in the Community Platform: the Irish Traveller Movement and Pavee Point. The subsequent *Programme for Prosperity and Fairness* (Ireland, 2000) saw a third organisation incorporated: the National Traveller Women's Forum.

18 RTE is the state radio and television broadcasting company.

Chapter 6

1 The first industrial day school was established in Aberdeen in 1844. Tired of sentencing children to prison terms for beggary and petty theft, the city sheriff decided to undertake an enterprise in 'reclaiming' children by 'putting them on their feet on the first steps to usefulness'. As a residential institution (as opposed to a day school), the industrial school was an outgrowth of the reformatory school, a technology of prevention which was formally introduced to Ireland by statute in 1868. With local authorities reluctant to implement the legislation, the role of the state in the Irish context was limited to licensing and funding the schools, with management taken over by the religious orders. (For a history of the schools in Ireland see Raftery and O'Sullivan, 1999; Barnes, 1989. Carpenter, 1968, is perhaps the definitive primary source, a text written explicitly to promote public support for the introduction of special schools to govern the children of the 'perishing and dangerous classes'.)

2 See also the proceedings from a conference on public health and public assistance in 1930 (Ireland, 1930: 51–9, 89). One delegate from the public health and assistance authorities spoke of the 'drivelling idiotic children' who were a 'daily butt for the other school children and a source of annoyance and trouble to the teacher' (Ireland, 1930: 51). Others advocated the 'removal', 'isolation' and 'control' of mental defectives, the objective one of preventing the 'ordinary school' from placing 'a most undesirable citizen' among the 'normal community'.

3 Most likely to refer to St Teresa's institute, opened in Stamullen, County Meath, in 1942, for the reception and training of adult male mental defectives in 'agricultural pursuits'. The colony was an auxiliary to St Augustine's colony in Blackrock, County Dublin, for 'high-grade educable boys over six years of age' (DH, 1943–6).

4 Comprising the National Council for the Blind, the Infantile Paralysis Fellowship, the National Association for Cerebral Palsy, and the Rehabilitation Institute.

5 A Commission on Mental Illness was conducted simultaneously but I have focused on the Report of the Commission on Mental Handicap for purposes of brevity. While distinguished by their object, they are broadly similar in analytical approach, style of reasoning, and practical recommendations. In Foucaultian terms they can be treated as a single statement.

6 On mental illness in rural Ireland see Nancy Scheper-Hughes (1982).
7 An editorial in the *Irish Times* saw this as an 'honest admission' on the part of the Commission. The spectre of 'inbreeding' in 'small rural communities' was also floated as a possible cause of mental illness (*Irish Times*, 1967b).
8 Since at least 1961 the problem of overcrowding in the mental hospitals had seen the inspector of mental hospitals urging the hospital authorities to take care that 'unsuitable' elderly patients were not admitted.
9 For examples see *Irish Press* (1970b, 1979a); O'Byrnes (1973).
10 A discretionary and revocable form of public assistance going back to the poor law.
11 The Irish Psychiatric Association published a study in March 2003 titled *The Stark Facts*, which assessed the implementation of the community care model. Since *Planning for the Future* the main components of the plan have been instituted, including 'sectors', 'catchment areas', 'community mental health teams' and 'community residences'. The report also identifies significant inequalities with respect to accessing psychiatric services, a combination of 'idiosyncratic administrative structure' and local political machinations (O'Keane, Jeffers, Moloney and Barry, 2003).
12 These have since become performance verification groups (Ireland, 2003: 118–21).
13 'Sectors' in this context include clothing and textiles, mechanical engineering, electronics, plastics, chemicals and pharmaceuticals, sea-fishing and aqua-culture, dairy, beef, building and construction, marketing, and industrial technology (Ireland, 1984b: 157–72).
14 The NDA was established by the National Disability Authority Act (1999) as an independent statutory body operating under the aegis of the Department of Justice, Equality and Law Reform.
15 My copy of this report was retrieved over the internet and I am citing paragraph numbers.
16 A recent survey by Rehabilitation International reports that on the question of rights for the disabled 'no reply was received from the Government of Ireland' (see Institute on Independent Living, <www.independentliving. org/standardrules/RI_Answers/RI.pdf>, accessed 21 November 2005).

Chapter 7

1 The phrase 'baby farming' denoted a type of provision for orphaned, foundling and illegitimate children, which was motivated by monetary gain, i.e. private nurses who received payment from the state.
2 Dáil Èireann, vol. 54, 18 December 1934: 1521, 'Questions, Oral Answers: School-leaving Age'. For debates on public works at this time see Dáil Èireann, vol. 54, 28 November 1934: 431–78, 'Private Deputies Business: Unemployment Problem'.
3 Dáil Èireann, vol. 90, 13 May 1943: 188, 'Committee on Finance, Vote 45: Office of the Minister for Education (Resumed)'.

4 Dáil Èireann, vol. 168, 3 June 1958: 1089–92, 'Committee on Finance, Vote 37'; also *Irish Press* (1958b).
5 Dáil Èireann, vol. 174, 8 April 1959: 114–15, 'Committee on Finance, Vote 36'.
6 Dáil Èireann, vol. 183, 29 June 1960: 614–15, 'Criminal Justice Bill 1960, Second State (Resumed)'.
7 Put into effect in 1972 through an amendment to the 1926 School Attendance Act.
8 Burgess created a special vocabulary for the characters in his book, derived primarily from Russian. The term 'droog' denotes friend and fellow gang-member.
9 Marc Dutroux was convicted of kidnapping, torturing and sexually abusing six girls, aged between 8 and 19, during 1995 and 1996. The handling of the subsequent investigation led to a serious loss of trust in the Belgian criminal justice system and to allegations that Dutroux and his accomplices were part of a larger European network of paedophiles that reached to the upper echelons of the Belgian state.
10 See the *Irish Times*, *Irish Independent* and *Irish Press* June–October 1994, and March–July 1997.
11 For a defence of the proposed reforms see DJELR (2005).
12 This is similar to, though not quite consistent with, both the definition of HKD provided under the World Health Organisation's International Classification of Diseases (ICD10) (Cooper and O'Regan, 2001: 106–8) and the Diagnostic Criteria for Attention Deficit/Hyperactivity Disorder published by the American Psychiatric Association (DSM-IV, 1994) (Munden and Arcelus, 1999: 17; Green and Kit, 1995: 171–3).

Chapter 8

1 Anticipating a point made later in this chapter (see note 5 below), it is worth mentioning the Salvation Army's stake in this field. In 1884 Bramwell Booth, son of William, elicited the help of a journalist with the *Pall Mall Gazette*, W. T. Stead. Together they concocted a scheme to prove to the public that girls could be bought and imprisoned in brothels. With the help of Rebecca Jarrett, a reformed procuress who had spent time in the care of the legendary Josephine Butler, Stead fronted the scheme and acquired an illegitimate girl called Eliza Armstrong for the purpose of prostitution. The action openly violated criminal law and the perpetrators were charged with abduction. Stead received a prison sentence, Booth was acquitted, and the trial proved to be a very public embarrassment for the Salvation Army, although it did go on to establish one of the most significant rescue missions in London (Begbie, 1920: I, 336–38; II, 40–4; Booth, 1912; Higginbotham, 1985: 106).
2 The programmes of both Bentham and Booth, as discussed in chapter 4, spiral through the Viceregal Commission. The Commission recommend

that the existing 'system of *aggregation* should cease, and that workhouse inmates should be *segregated* according to their condition – that is, in place of the 159 workhouses for all classes [in Ireland], the sick should be treated in hospitals; the infirm and the aged in almshouses; the lunatics in asylums; the infants and their mothers in "nurseries"; the vagrants, casuals, and adults of bad character in labour houses' (Eason, 1907: 131, original emphasis).

3 From the perspective of Catholic Rescue agencies the unmarried mother was a prime candidate for Protestant 'soupers' or proselytisers, alleged to prey on 'girls in trouble' by offering them 'shelter, hospitality and secrecy' in return for their soul (see MacInerny, 1921).

4 The Dublin Poor Law Union was the last administrative area to be incorporated into the new County system of the Irish Free State, and thus the Dublin workhouse was still called a workhouse at this time, as opposed to the old workhouses elsewhere in the country, which had been recoded as County Homes.

5 Also known as Stead's Act, in recognition of W. T. Stead's efforts to stem 'White Slavery' (see note 1 above; also Devane, 1924a, 1924b).

6 The facility at Pelletstown (Dublin) was run by the Sisters of Charity of St Vincent de Paul, while the Sisters of Mercy ran the Auxiliary Home for the local authority at Kilrush (Clare) and the Bons Secours Nuns ran the Children's Home in Tuam (Galway).

7 On the long-standing mythology surrounding the child murdress and the dead child in Irish folklore see O'Connor (1991).

8 The Criminal Law Amendment Act 1935, which followed in the wake of this report, rendered contraception illegal in Ireland (see McAvoy, 1999).

9 Department of Justice, National Archives, File S5998: 3.

10 Department of Justice, National Archives, File S5998: 13.

11 See Mellone and Macnaghten (1934); Kirwin (1934).

12 Michael Viney wrote a series of articles for the *Irish Times* in 1964 titled 'No Birthright'. In part 3 of the series Viney described the mother and baby homes run by the religious orders as the 'secret service' (Viney, 1964).

13 Dáil Debates, vol. 186, 15 February 1961: 363.

14 Dáil Debates, vol. 190, 21 June 1961: 627.

15 Despite evidence that some of the more rebellious Magdalens were ordered out of the institutions for 'unsatisfactory' behaviour, that some were determined enough to escape, that many were incarcerated because they had been raped, were the victims of incest or sexual abuse, or had been shut away because the 'neighbours might find out', there is no evidence of former inmates issuing formal complaints about their unlawful detention (Finnegan, 2001: 4).

16 It was also the case that some 10 per cent of illegitimate births recorded in London were attributed to unmarried mothers from the 'twenty-six counties', and this did not account for the numbers travelling to the UK for abortions (Flanagan and Richardson, 1992: 61–7; CPA, 2003: 12–14).

17 This supported the European Social Charter, which laid down the rights of mothers and children, irrespective of marital status and family relations, to appropriate social and economic protection.

18 The Kilkenny framework is similar to the 1984 Report on the Psychiatric Services (*Planning for the Future*; London, 1984a) in posing the model of community care as presupposed. While the later retroactively discovered community care in the 1945 Mental Treatment Act, the Kilkenny Conference found it in a circular issued by the Local Government Board of Ireland in 1916. This was said to have 'encouraged local authorities to provide nursery centres and crèches, home help, and above all to make provision for the unmarried mother to *keep her child* and to spell out the methods by which this might be done' (Kilkenny, 1972: 31, original emphasis).

19 While contesting the issue of justice for unmarried mothers, the women's movement had little to say on the penitents then residing in the Magdalen asylums (Finnegan, 2001).

20 Devane also gave evidence before the Carrigan Committee on the Criminal Law Amendment Acts and Juvenile Prostitution (Devane, 1924a, 1924b; Ireland, 1931; McAvoy, 1999).

21 Following a campaign by the Legal Adoption Society (Ireland, 1984c).

22 Judgement by O'Higgins, CJ: M and M, plaintiffs, versus An Bord Uchtala and The Attorney General, Defendants (1974 No. 1689p), Supreme Court [1977] IR 287; Hearing Dates: 15–16 March 1976, 12–14 May 1976, 2 June 1976.

23 See the *Irish Times*, *Irish Press* and *Irish Independent* (3–30 June 1976).

24 The only alternative (but not quite dissenting) agency was Cherish (*Irish Times*, 1976e; Farren and Dempsey, 1997).

25 The status of illegitimacy was abolished two years later through the Status of Children Act.

26 Joanne was told that her daughter Yvonne would be put into an orphanage while her mother would be jailed and the family farm sold if she did not confess. Other family members reported physical harassment (McCafferty, 1985: 74).

27 Before the new Lone Parent's Allowance was introduced there were specific payments for Widows and Orphans (Benefit and Assistance, introduced in 1935), Deserted Wife's Allowance (1970); Deserted Wife's Benefit (1973); Unmarried Mothers Allowance (1973); Single Women's Allowance (1974); Prisoner's Wife's Allowance (1974); and the generic Supplementary Welfare Allowance (1977), the last of these replacing Home Assistance as a legacy of the Poor Law (Curry, 1993: 19).

28 See Farren and Dempsey (1997: 8).

29 One Parent Exchange Network (OPEN), <www.oneparent.ie>.

30 All Party Oireachtas Committee on the Constitution, Fifth Progress Report, Abortion, November 2000 (see CPA, 2003: 6).

31 See Crisis Pregnancy Agency, <www.positiveoptions.ie>, accessed 16 September 2005.

32 Prior to the fourteenth amendment to the Constitution (1992) it was illegal to provide information on abortion. Following the amendment, Article 40.3.3° (the right to life of the unborn) no longer limits freedom to obtain or make available information relating to services lawfully available in another state.

33 Under the guidance of the European Community, the Unmarried Mothers Allowance was transformed into the gender-neutral Lone Parent's Allowance in 1989. In 1997 this became the One Parent Family Payment (OPFP). Under the rules governing the OPFP, a claimant is required to make 'efforts' to seek maintenance from the other parent of the child/children. While 'taking due account of any sensitive issues involved, such as a risk of violence towards the one-parent family involved', non-compliance may lead to disqualification. On this last point, and contrary to the alleged gender-neutrality of the welfare code, it is interesting to note that a 'she' is presumed on the part of the state (see Department of Social and Family Affairs, <www.welfare.ie/foi/onepfp.html#part7>, accessed 28 November 2005).

Chapter 9

1 From the perspective of the third sector the Community Workers Cooperative defines social partnership as 'an approach to government where interest groups outside of elected representatives play an active role in decision taking and policy making. This form of participative democracy enables the social partners to enter discussions with government on a range of social and economic issues and to reach a consensus on policy' (<www.cwc.ie/work/sp.html>, accessed 17 January 2006).

2 Some organisations within the third sector have recently been removed from the NESC in response to their dissenting views on the 'Sustaining Progress' Agreement.

3 The third sector is also engaged with the partnership process through the National Economic and Social Forum (NESF), established in 1993 for the purpose of achieving consensus on policy. Since 1998 the Forum's work has focused on evaluating the implementation of policies dealing with equality and social inclusion. At the time of willing a Bill has just been finalised which will incorporate the NESC, NESF and National Centre for Partnership and Performance (NCPP) within a new National Economic and Social Development Office (NESDO).

4 The information used here is taken from a televised news report on the strike, which included commentary from state, business, labour and the third sector (RTE1 6/1 News, 18 July 2003).

5 See O'Morain (2003); Holland (2003); CWC (2003d).

References

Official publications

CEC (1988) 'The Social Dimension of the Internal Market', *Social Europe*, Special Edition, Commission of the European Communities, CB-PP-88-005-EN-C, Brussels.

CEC (1991) *Final Report on the Second European Poverty Programme 1985–1989*, Commission of the European Communities, COM (91) 29 Final, Brussels.

CEC (1993) *Growth, Competitiveness, Employment*, Commission of the European Communities, White Paper, Supplement 6/93, Brussels.

CEC (1995) *Final Report on the Implementation of the Community Programme Concerning the Economic and Social Integration of the Economically and Socially Less Privileged Groups in Society 'Poverty 3' (1989–94)*, Commission of the European Communities, COM (95) 94 Final, Brussels.

DH (1943–6) *Annual Reports of the Inspector of Mental Hospitals*, Department of Health, Dublin.

DJELR (2005) 'Address by Minister to Forum on ASBOs', 18 July, Department of Justice Equality and Law Reform, <www.justice.ie/80256E01003A02CF/vWeb/pcJUSQ6EPLDX-ga>, accessed 15 September 2005.

DLGPHa (1928–45) *Annual Reports*, Department of Local Government and Public Health, Dublin.

DLGPHb (1926–31) *Annual Reports of the Inspector of Mental Hospitals*, Department of Local Government and Public Health, Dublin.

Ireland (1927) *Report of the Commission on the Relief of the Sick and Destitute Poor, Including the Insane Poor*, Dublin.

Ireland (1930) *Report of the Conference between the Department of Local Government and Public Health and Representatives of Local Public Health and Public Assistance Authorities held at the Mansion House, Dublin on the 8th and 9th July, 1930*, Dublin.

Ireland (1931) *Report of the Committee on the Criminal Law Amendment Acts (1880–85), and Juvenile Prostitution*, Dublin.

Ireland (1936) *Commission of Inquiry into the Reformatory and Industrial School System 1934–1936*, Dublin.

Ireland (1937) *Bunreacht na hÉireann (Constitution of Ireland)*, Dublin.

Ireland (1945a) *Mental Treatment Act: An Act to Provide for the Prevention and Treatment of Mental Disorders and the Care of Persons Suffering Therefrom and to Provide for Other Matters Connected with the Matters Aforesaid*, Number 19 of 1945, Dublin.

Ireland (1945b) *Guide to the Social Services: A Summary Designed for the Information of Individuals and Groups*, Dublin.

Ireland (1958a) *Economic Development*, Dublin.

Ireland (1958b) *Programme for Economic Expansion*, Dublin.

Ireland (1963a) *Report of the Commission on Itinerancy*, Dublin.

Ireland (1963b) *Second Programme for Economic Expansion*, Dublin.

Ireland (1965a) *Commission of Inquiry on Mental Handicap*, Dublin.

Ireland (1965b) *Investment in Education: Report of a Survey Team Appointed by the Minister for Education in Conjunction with the OECD*, Dublin.

Ireland (1966) *Commission of Inquiry on Mental Illness*, Dublin.

Ireland (1970a) *Reformatory and Industrial Schools Systems Report*, Dublin.

Ireland (1970b) *Towards Better Health Care: Management in the Health Boards*, Department of Health and McKinsey, Dublin.

Ireland (1972) *Commission on the Status of Women: Report to Minister for Finance*, Dublin.

Ireland (1975) *Training and Employing the Handicapped: Report of a Working Party Established by the Minister for Health*, Dublin.

Ireland (1983a) *Report of the Travelling People Review Body*, Dublin.

Ireland (1983b) *The Education and Training of Severely and Profoundly Mentally Handicapped Children in Ireland: Report of a Working Party to the Minister for Education and the Minister for Health and Social Welfare*, Dublin.

Ireland (1984a) *The Psychiatric Services – Planning for the Future: Report of a Study Group on the Development of the Psychiatric Services*, Dublin.

Ireland (1984b) *Building on Reality 1985–1987*, Dublin.

Ireland (1984c) *Adoption: Report of the Review Committee on Adoption Services*, Dublin.

Ireland (1985a) *Report of the Committee on Discipline in Schools*, Dublin.

Ireland (1985b) *Serving the Country Better: A White Paper on the Public Service*, Dublin.

Ireland (1987) *Programme for National Recovery*, Dublin.

Ireland (1993) *Report of the Second Commission on the Status of Women*, Dublin.

Ireland (1994) *Programme for Competitiveness and Work*, Dublin.

Ireland (1995) *Report of the Task Force on the Travelling Community*, Dublin.

Ireland (1996a) *Towards an Independent Future: Report of the Review Group on Health and Personal Social Services for People with Physical and Sensory Disabilities*, Dublin.

Ireland (1996b) *Commission on the Status of People with Disabilities: A Strategy for Equality*, Dublin.

Ireland (1996c) *Partnership 2000 for Inclusion, Employment and Competitiveness*, Dublin.

Ireland (1999) *National Disability Authority Act*, Number 14 of 1999, Dublin.

Ireland (2000) *Programme for Prosperity and Fairness*, Dublin.

Ireland (2001) *Children Act*, Number 24 of 2001, Dublin.

Ireland (2002) *Value for Money and Management Audit of the Citizen Traveller Campaign and the Preparation of a Report on Financial Position: Final Report*, Department of Justice, Equality and Law Reform, Dublin.

Ireland (2003) *Sustaining Progress: Social Partnership Agreement 2003–2005*, Dublin.

Ireland (2004) *United Nations International Convention on the Elimination of All Forms of Racial Discrimination: First National Report by Ireland*, Dublin.

Ireland (2005a) *Disability Act*, Number 14 of 2005, Dublin.

Ireland (2005b) *The Ferns Report: Presented to the Minister for Health and Children*, Dublin.

Ireland (2005c) *Planning For Diversity: The National Action Plan Against Racism 2005–2008*, Dublin.

London (1826) *Third Report of the Commissioners of Irish Education Inquiry*, House of Commons Parliamentary Papers 1826–7 (13) viii.

London (1837a) *Report of George Nicholls to Her Majesty's Principal Secretary of State for the Home Department on Poor Laws Ireland*.

London (1837b) *Second Report of George Nicholls to Her Majesty's Principal Secretary of State for the Home Department on Poor Laws Ireland*.

London (1906) *Report of the Vice Regal Commission on Poor Law Reform in Ireland. Volume 1*.

London (1999) *Teenage Pregnancy: Report presented to Parliament by the Prime Minister by Command of Her Majesty, June 1999*, Social Exclusion Unit.

London (2002) *A Guide to Anti-Social Behaviour Orders and Acceptable Behaviour Contracts*, Home Office.

NBCGC (1953–8) *Annual Reports of the National BCG Committee*, St Ultan's Hospital, Dublin.

Primary and secondary sources

Acton, Thomas (1994) 'Categorising Irish Travellers', in May McCann, Seamus O Siochain and Joseph Ruane (eds), *Irish Travellers: Culture and Ethnicity*, Belfast: Institute of Irish Studies, Queen's University.

Albert, Bill, Sarah Brown and Christine Flanigan (eds) (2003) *14 and Younger: The Sexual Behavior of Young Adolescents (Summary)*, Washington DC: National Campaign to Prevent Teen Pregnancy.

Ashenden, Samantha (1996) 'Reflexive Governance and Child Sex Abuse: Liberal Welfare Rationality and the Cleveland Inquiry', *Economy and Society*, 25: 1 (February): 64–88.

Barnes, Jane (1989) *Irish Industrial Schools, 1868–1908: Origins and Development*, Dublin: Irish Academic Press.

Barrington, Ruth (1987) *Health, Medicine, and Politics in Ireland 1900–1970*, Dublin: Institute of Public Administration.

Barry, Andrew, Thomas Osborne and Nikolas Rose (1996) 'Introduction', in Andrew Barry, Thomas Osborne and Nikolas Rose (eds), *Foucault and Political Reason: Liberalism, Neo-Liberalism and Rationalities of Government*, Chicago: University of Chicago Press.

Barthes, Roland (1985) *The Grain of the Voice: Interviews 1962–1980*, trans. L. Coverdale, London: Jonathan Cape.

Barthes, Roland (1993) [1957] *Mythologies*, London: Verso.

Bauman, Zygmunt (1989) *Modernity and the Holocaust*, New York: Cornell University Press.

Bauman, Zygmunt (1991) *Modernity and Ambivalence*, New York: Cornell University Press.

Bauman, Zygmunt (1998a) *Globalisation the Human Consequences*, Cambridge: Polity.

Bauman, Zygmunt (1998b) *Work, Consumerism and the New Poor*, Buckingham: Open University Press.

Bauman, Zygmunt (2001) *Community: Seeking Safety in an Insecure World*, Cambridge: Polity.

Bauman, Zygmunt (2002a) *Society Under Siege*, Cambridge: Polity.

Bauman, Zygmunt (2002b) *Liquid Modernity*, Cambridge: Polity.

Beck, Ulrich (1992) *Risk Society: Towards a New Modernity*, trans. Mark Ritter, London: Sage.

Beere, T. J. (1938) 'Schemes for the Rehabilitation of Youth in Certain Countries, with Special Reference to Labour Service', *Journal of the Statistical and Social Inquiry Society of Ireland*, 16 (December): 33–52.

Begbie, Harold (1920) *Life of William Booth*, 2 volumes, London: Macmillan.

Bentham, Jeremy (1843a) *Works. Volume 1*, ed. J. Bowring, Edinburgh: William Tait.

Bentham, Jeremy (1843b) *Works. Volume 8*, ed. J. Bowring, Edinburgh: William Tait.

Bentham, Jeremy (1995) [1787] *Jeremy Bentham: The Panopticon Writings*, Miran Božovič (ed), London and New York: Verso.

Bentham, Jeremy (2001) *Writings on the Poor Laws: The Collected Works of Jeremy Bentham. Volume I*, ed. Michael Quinn, Oxford: Clarendon.

Bernard, François (1973) 'European Children at Risk', *Irish Times*, 13 November, page 14.

Bernard van Leer Foundation (1979) *Project Information Handbook: Special Education Project, Rutland Street*, Dublin: Bernard van Leer Foundation and Department of Education.

Bewick, Tom (1997) 'The Poverty of US Welfare Reform: Lessons from California', *Working Brief*, August/September: 21–6.

Bewley, Victor E. H. (1976a) 'Travelling People', *Irish Independent*, letter, hon. secretary Dublin Committee for Travelling People, 21 December, page 6.

Bewley, Victor E. H. (1976b) 'Aid to Itinerants', letter, *Irish Press*, hon. secretary Dublin Itinerant Settlement Committee, 1 April, page 8.

Bierer, Joshua and Richard I. Evans (1969) *Innovations in Social Psychiatry: A Social Psychological Perspective through Dialogue*, London: Avenue Publishing.

Billig, Michael, Susan Condor, Derek Edwards, Mike Gane, David Middleton and Alan Radley (1988) *Ideological Dilemmas*, London: Sage.

Bird, Carmel (1998) *The Stolen Children – Their Stories*, Australia: Random House.

Blair, Tony (1999) 'Foreword', in *Teenage Pregnancy: Report presented to Parliament by the Prime Minister by Command of Her Majesty, June 1999*, London: Social Exclusion Unit.

Blair, Tony and Gerhard Schroeder (1999) 'Europe: The Third Way/Die Neue Mitte', speech delivered to the Labour Party in London, 8 June, Frontier Centre for Public Policy, <http://fcpp.org/publication_detail.php?PubID=349>, accessed 17 March 2004.

Blakely, Edward J. and Mary Gail Snyder (1997) 'Divided We Fall: Gated and Walled Communities in the United States', in Nan Ellin (ed.), *Architecture of Fear*, New York: Princeton Architectural Press.

Boehnlein, Mary Maher (1989) 'Reading Recovery: Helping At-Risk readers Learn to Read and Succeed', *Learn*, II (Summer): 23–8.

Bookle, Susan (2001) 'Piloting a Support Programme for Lone Parents: "New Opportunities"', anti-poverty work in action supplement in *Poverty Today*, 50 (March/April), Combat Poverty Agency, Dublin.

Booth, Bramwell (1912) 'W. T. Stead – The Loss of a True Friend', *Salvation Army International Heritage Centre*, <www2.salvationarmy.org.uk/uki/www_uki_ihc.nsf/vwdynamicindex/1E2D6EB051C2288580257059003AE0F6?OpenDocument>, accessed 5 January 2006.

Booth, Charles (1969) *Charles Booth's London: A Portrait of the Poor at the Turn of the Century Drawn from his 'Life and Labour of the People of London'*, eds Albert Fried and Richard M. Elman, London: Hutchinson.

Booth, General William (1890) *In Darkest England and the Way Out*, London: William Burgess Carlyle Press.

Borzaga, Carlo and Jacques Defourny (eds) (2001) *The Emergence of Social Enterprise*, London and New York: Routledge.

Bottomore, Tom (1992) 'Citizenship and Social Class, Forty Years On', in T. H. Marshall and Tom Bottomore, *Citizenship and Social Class*, London: Pluto.

Bourdieu, Pierre (1989) 'Social Space and Symbolic Power', *Sociological Theory*, 7: 1 (Spring): 14–25.

Bowlby, John (1965) [1953] *Child Care and the Growth of Love*, 2nd edition, London and New York: Penguin.

Brennan, Séamus (1984) 'A Political Response to Unemployment', in James McLoone (ed.), *Young Ireland: Realism and Vision*, Galway: Social Study Conference.

Broberg, Gunnar and Nils Roll-Hansen (eds) (1996) *Eugenics and the Welfare State: Sterilisation Policy in Denmark, Sweden, Norway, and Finland*, Michigan: Michigan University Press.

Broberg, Gunnar and Mathias Tydén (1996) 'Eugenics in Sweden: Efficient Care', in Gunnar Broberg and Nils Roll-Hansen (eds), *Eugenics and the Welfare State: Sterilisation Policy in Denmark, Sweden, Norway, and Finland*, Michigan: Michigan University Press.

Browne, Noel C. (1986) *Against the Tide*, Dublin: Gill and Macmillan.

Burgess, Anthony (1972) [1962] *A Clockwork Orange*, London: Penguin.

Burke, Helen (1987) *The People and the Poor Law in 19th Century Ireland*, Littlehampton: Women's Education Bureau.

Burt, Cyril L. (1917) 'The Unstable Child', *Child Study: The Journal of the Child Study Association*, 10: 3: 61–79.

Burt, Cyril (1923a) 'The Causal Factors of Juvenile Crime', *British Journal of Medical Psychology*, 3: 1–33.

Burt, Cyril (1923b) 'Delinquency and Mental Defect (II)', *British Journal of Medical Psychology*, 3: 168–78.

Burt, Cyril L. (1931) [1925] *The Young Delinquent*, London: University of London Press.

Byrne, Anne (1982) 'Female Poverty and the Irish Welfare System', unpublished MA thesis, Department of Political Science and Sociology, National University of Ireland Galway.

Byrne, D. (1967) 'Corporal Punishment', letter, *Irish Press*, 30 September, page 8.

Byrne, David (1999) *Social Exclusion*, Buckingham: Open University Press.

Cannon, Michael (1976) 'Truancy: Has the Time Come to Take More Serious Note of this Problem?', *Irish Press*, 18 February, page 7.

Carpenter, Mary (1861) 'On Educational Help from Government for the Destitute and Neglected Children of Great Britain', *Journal of the Statistical Society of London*, 24: 1 (March): 22–9.

Carpenter, Mary (1968) [1851] *Reformatory Schools for the Children of the Perishing and Dangerous Classes and for Young Offenders*, London: Woburn.

Castel, Robert, Françoise Castel and Anne Lovell (1982) [1979] *The Psychiatric Society*, New York: Columbia University Press.

Checkland, S. G. and E. O. Checkland (eds) (1974) *The Poor Law Report of 1834*, Harmondsworth: Penguin.

Clarke, Dermot C. (1967) 'Itinerants', letter, *Irish Press*, 6 March, page 9.

Clarke, Dermot C. (1970a) 'Itinerants', letter, *Irish Times*, 8 April, page 9.

Clarke, Dermot C. (1970b) 'Itinerants', letter, *Irish Press*, 8 April, page 11.

Clarke, John (2005) 'New Labour's Citizens: Activated, Empowered, Responsibilised, Abandoned?', *Critical Social Policy*, 25: 4: 447–63.

Clarke, Simon (2006) *From Enlightenment to Risk: Social Theory and Contemporary Society*, Basingstoke and New York: Palgrave Macmillan.

Clarke, Vivienne (1991) 'Unemployed Suffer More from Mental Illness', *Irish Press*, 30 January, page 13.

Clegg, Stewart, R. (1989) *Frameworks of Power*, London: Sage.

Clegg, Stewart, R. (1990) *Modern Organisations: Organisation Studies in the Postmodern World*, London: Sage.

Clifford, Dr Louis S. (1939) 'Investigation into the Incidence of Mental Deficiency amongst Dublin School Children', *Journal of the Statistical and Social Inquiry Society of Ireland*, 16: 29–48.

Connacht Tribune (1964) 'People who Need Rescue from a Life of Depredation', 11 April, page 3.

Connacht Tribune (1973) 'Itinerant Settlement: Good Progress Reported', 16 February, page 7.

Cooper, Paul and Fintan J. O'Regan (2001) *Education Children with AD/HD*, London: Routledge Falmer.

Corcoran, Terry, David O'Connor and Sile Mullin (1984) *The Transition from School to Work: Situation of 1981/82 School-Leavers in Late 1984*, Dublin: Youth Employment Agency.

CORI (1993) *Growing Exclusion: A Review of Aspects of the Current Socio-Economic Situation with Recommendations for the 1993 Budget*, Dublin: Conference of Religious of Ireland Justice Commission.

CORI (1995) *Ireland For All: Recommendations for the 1996 Budget*, Dublin: Conference of Religious of Ireland Justice Commission.

Cousins, Christine (1996) *Social Exclusion in Europe: Paradigms of Social Disadvantage in Germany, Spain, Sweden and the UK*, University of Hertfordshire Business School Working Paper Series 1, 19.

Cowan, Rory (1964) 'Itinerants', letter, *Irish Times*, 25–8 December, page 11.

Cowhey, Ellen (1976) 'Child Health', letter, *Irish Times*, 24 April, page 9.

CPA (2003) *Strategy to Address the Issue of Crisis Pregnancy*, Dublin: Crisis Pregnancy Agency.

CPA (2004) *Annual Report*, Dublin: Crisis Pregnancy Agency.

Crawford, Adam (2003) ' "Contractual Governance" of Deviant Behaviour', *Journal of Law and Society*, 30: 4 (December): 479–505.

Cruikshank, Barbara (1994) 'The Will to Empower: Technologies of Citizenship and the War on Poverty', *Socialist Review*, 23: 4: 29–55.

Cruikshank, Barbara (1999) *The Will to Empower: Democratic Citizens and Other Subjects*, Ithaca, NY and London: Cornell University Press.

Cummins, Mary (1991) 'Travellers Urged to Vote Tactically in Elections', *Irish Times*, 20 May, page 4.

Curry, John (1993) *Irish Social Services*, 2nd edition, Dublin: Institute of Public Administration.

CWC (2002a) 'More Info on Protest on May 2nd', news bulletin, 30 April, Galway: Community Workers Cooperative.

CWC (2002b) 'Minister Martin Cullen Reneges on his Commitment to Traveller Groups', news bulletin, 2 July, Galway: Community Workers Cooperative.

CWC (2003a) 'Nothing in New National Agreement to Address Poverty or Inequality', *News and Views*, 8 (March): 5, Galway: Community Workers Cooperative.

CWC (2003b) 'National Social Partnership: Where to from Here?', *News and Views*, 10 (September): 6, Galway: Community Workers Cooperative.

CWC (2003c) *Draft Strategic Plan 2004–2007*, Galway: Community Workers Cooperative.

CWC (2003d) 'Community Platform National Conference on Sustaining Progress', news bulletin, 3 March, Galway: Community Workers Cooperative.

Daly, E. D. (1891) 'Our Industrial and Reformatory Systems in Relation to the Poor', *Journal of the Statistical and Social Inquiry Society of Ireland*, 9: 71: 523–42.

Daly, Paul (1979a) 'March Against Abortion', *Irish Independent*, letter, 12 May, page 6.

Daly, Paul (1979b) 'Pro-Mother and Pro-Child', *Irish Independent*, letter, 18 May, page 8.

Darwin, Charles (1998) [1859] *The Origin of Species*, Ware: Wordsworth.

Dean, Mitchell (1991) *The Constitution of Poverty: Toward a Genealogy of Liberal Governance*, London and New York: Routledge.

Dean, Mitchell (1992) 'A Genealogy of the Government of Poverty', *Economy and Society*, 21: 3 (August): 215–51.

Dean, Mitchell (1996) 'Foucault, Government and the Enfolding of Authority', in Andrew Barry, Thomas Osborne and Nikolas Rose (eds), *Foucault and Political Reason: Liberalism, Neo-Liberalism and Rationalities of Government*, Chicago: University of Chicago Press.

Dean, Mitchell (1999) *Governmentality: Power and Rule in Modern Society*, London: Sage.

Delaney, Paul (2001) 'Representations of the Travellers in the 1880s and 1900s', *Irish Studies Review*, 9: 1: 53–68.

Delaney, Paul (2003) 'A Sense of Place: Travellers, Representation, and Irish Culture', *Republic*, 3 (July): 79–89.

Dervan, Marie-Gabrielle (1961) [1958] *The Problem of the Unmarried Mother*, Cork: Mercier Press.

Devane, Rev. R. S. (1924a) 'The Unmarried Mother: Some Legal Aspects of the Problem', *Irish Ecclesiastical Record*, 23: 55–68.

Devane, Rev. R. S. (1924b) 'The Unmarried Mother: Some Legal Aspects of the Problem', *Irish Ecclesiastical Record*, 23: 172–88.

Devane, Rev. R. S. (1928) 'The Unmarried Mother and the Poor Law Commission', *Irish Ecclesiastical Record*, 31: 561–82.

Devenney, Mark (2002) 'Critical Theory and Democracy', in Alan Finlayson and Jeremy Valentine (eds), *Politics and Post-Structuralism: An Introduction*, Edinburgh: Edinburgh University Press.

Devenney, Mark (2004) *Ethics and Politics in Contemporary Theory*, London and New York: Routledge.

Dickens, Charles (1994) [1838] *Oliver Twist*, Oxford: Oxford University Press.

Dolowitz, David and David Marsh (2000) 'Learning from Abroad: The Role of Policy Transfer in Contemporary Policy-Making', *International Journal of Policy and Administration*, 13: 1 (January): 5–24.

Donzelot, Jacques (1979) [1977] *The Policing of Families*, Baltimore and London: Johns Hopkins University Press.

Doolan, Lelia (1970) 'My Well-Trained Sense of Guilt', *Irish Press*, 15 April, page 8.

Dooley, Raymond and Maria Corbett (2002) 'Child Care, Juvenile Justice and the Children Act, 2001', *Irish Youthwork Scene: A Journal for Youth Workers*, 36 (June), <www.childrensrights.ie/pubs/ChildCareJuvenileJustice.doc>, accessed 13 November 2005.

Downing, John (1997) 'Protecting Children Everywhere', *Irish Independent*, 28 July, page 14.

Dreyfus, Hubert L. and Paul Rabinow (1983) *Michel Foucault: Beyond Structuralism and Hermeneutics*, 2nd edition, Chicago: University of Chicago Press.

Eason, Charles (1907) 'The Report of the Viceregal Commission on the Irish Poor Law', *Economic Journal*, 17: 65 (March): 131–8.

Edwards, J. R. (1974) 'Characteristics of Disadvantaged Children', *Irish Journal of Education*, VIII: 1: 49–61.

Edgeworth, Marie (1970) 'A Nation of True Freedom and Justice', *Irish Press*, 7 December, page 9.

Eliassen, Kjell A. and Jan Kooiman (eds) (1993) *Managing Public Organisations*, London, Sage.

Englander, David (1998) *Poverty and Poor Law Reform in Britain: From Chadwick to Booth, 1834–1914*, London and New York: Longman.

Fahy, K. (2003) 'Notes on the Community Platform National Conference on Sustaining Progress 2003–2005', Ashling Hotel, 3 March 2002, Dublin.

Farragher, M. A. (2001) 'Degradation of the Dodder', *Irish Times*, letter, 14 November, page 14.

Farrell, Y. (1967) 'Corporal Punishment', letter, *Irish Press*, 27 September, page 9.

Farren, Grainne and Anne Dempsey (1997) *From Condemnation to Celebration: The Story of Cherish 1972–1997*, Dublin: Cherish.

Feeley, Malcolm and Jonathan Simon (1992) 'The New Penology: Notes on the Emerging Strategy of Corrections and its Implications', *Criminology*, 30: 4: 449–74.

Feeley, Malcolm and Jonathan Simon (1994) 'Actuarial Justice: The Emerging New Criminal Law', in David Nelken (ed.), *The Future of Criminology*, London: Sage.

Fine Gael (2005) *Safe Streets*, <www.safestreets.ie>, accessed 30 November 2005.

Finn, Dan (1987) *Training without Jobs: New Deals and Broken Promises*, Basingstoke and London: Macmillan Education.

Finnegan, Frances (2001) *Do Penance or Perish: A Study of Magdalen Asylums in Ireland*, Piltown: Congrave Press.

Flanagan, Niamh and Valerie Richardson (1992) *Unmarried Mothers: A Social Profile*, Dublin: University College Dublin, Department of Social Policy and Social Work/Social Science Research Centre.

Folliet, Joseph (1961) [1958] 'Preliminary Study', in Marie-Gabrielle Dervan, *The Problem of the Unmarried Mother*, Cork: Mercier Press.

Fontes, Patricia J. and Thomas Kellaghan (1977) 'Incidence and Correlates of Illiteracy in Irish Primary Schools', *Irish Journal of Education*, XI: 1: 5–20.

Foucault, Michel (1972) [1969] *The Archaeology of Knowledge and the Discourse on Language*, trans. A. M. Sheridan Smith, London: Tavistock.

Foucault, Michel (ed.) (1975) [1973] *I, Pierre Rivière, Having Slaughtered my Mother, my Sister and my Brother . . . A Case of Parricide in the 19th Century*, Lincoln, NE and London: University of Nebraska Press.

Foucault, Michel (1977) [1975] *Discipline and Punish*, trans. Alan Sheridan, London: Penguin.

Foucault, Michel (1980) *Power/Knowledge: Selected Interviews and Other Writings 1972–1977*, ed. Colin Gordon, New York: Pantheon.

Foucault, Michel (1983) 'The Subject and Power', in Hubert L. Dreyfus and Paul Rabinow, *Michel Foucault: Beyond Structuralism and Hermeneutics*, 2nd edition, Chicago: University of Chicago Press.

Foucault, Michel (1984a) 'Nietzsche, Genealogy, History', in Paul Rabinow (ed.), *The Foucault Reader*, New York: Pantheon.

Foucault, Michel (1984b) 'What is Enlightenment?', in Paul Rabinow (ed.), *The Foucault Reader*, New York: Pantheon.

Foucault, Michel (1988) [1961] *Madness and Civilisation: A History of Insanity in the Age of Reason*, New York: Vintage.

Foucault, Michel (1991a) 'Questions of Method', in Graham Burchell, Colin Gordon and Peter Miller (eds), *The Foucault Effect: Studies in Governmentality*, Hemel Hempstead: Harvester Wheatsheaf.

Foucault, Michel (1991b) [1978] 'Governmentality', in Graham Burchell, Colin Gordon and Peter Miller (eds), *The Foucault Effect: Studies in Governmentality*, Hemel Hempstead: Harvester Wheatsheaf.

Foucault, Michel (1994) [1966] *The Order of Things*, New York: Vintage Books.

Foucault, Michel (1997) [1994] *Ethics, Subjectivity and Truth: The Essential Works of Foucault 1954–1984. Volume 1*, ed. Paul Rabinow, New York: New Press.

Foucault, Michel (1998) [1976] *The History of Sexuality. Volume One: The Will to Knowledge*, London: Penguin.

Foucault, Michel (2000) [1994] *Power: The Essential Works of Foucault 1954–1984. Volume III*, ed. James D. Faubion, New York: New Press.

Foucault, Michel (2003) [1999] *Abnormal: Lectures at the Collège de France 1974–1975*, trans. Graham Burchell, eds Valerio Marhetti and Antonella Salomoni, New York: Picador.

Fox, Michael H. and KyungMee Kim (2004) 'Understanding Emerging Disabilities', *Disability & Society*, 19: 4 (June): 323–37.

Fraser, Nancy and Linda Gordon (1997) 'A Genealogy of Dependency', in Nancy Fraser, *Justice Interruptus: Critical Reflections on the Post-Socialist Condition*, London and New York: Routledge.

Fukuyama, Francis (1995) *Trust: The Social Virtues and the Creation of Prosperity*, New York and London: Free Press.

Gaffikin, Frank and Mike Morrissey (1992) *The New Unemployed*, London: Zed.

Gallagher, Jackie (1994) 'Union Told Women with Disabilities Suffer an Irish Form of Apartheid', *Irish Times*, 18 April, page 6.

Galton, Frances (1901) 'The Possible Improvement of the Human Breed Under the Existing Conditions of Law and Sentiment: The Second Huxley Lecture of the Anthropological Institute', *Nature*, 64: 1670: 659–65.

Gannon, Brenda and Brian Nolan (2005) *Disability and Social Inclusion in Ireland*, Dublin: National Disability Authority and the Equality Authority in association with the Economic and Social Research Institute.

Gans, Herbert J. (1996) 'From "Underclass" to "Undercaste": Some Observations about the Future of the Post-Industrial Economy and its Major Victims', in Enzo Mingione (ed.), *Urban Poverty and the Underclass*, Oxford: Blackwell.

Garrett, Paul Michael (2000) 'The Abnormal Flight: The Migration and Repatriation of Irish Unmarried Mothers', *Social History*, 25: 3: 330–43.

Garvey, Criona (1989) 'The Disturbed and Disturbing Child', *Learn*, II (Summer): 69–78.

Garwood, John (1853) *The Million-Peopled City, or One Half of the People of London Made Known to the Other Half*, London: Wertheim and MacIntosh.

Geddes, Mike and John Bennington (eds) (2001) *Local Partnerships and Social Exclusion in the European Union*, London and New York: Routledge.

Giddens, Anthony (1984) *The Constitution of Society*, Cambridge: Polity.

Giddens, Anthony (1994) 'Living in a Post-Traditional Society', in Ulrich Beck, Anthony Giddens and Scott Lash, *Reflexive Modernisation: Politics, Tradition and Aesthetics in the Modern Social Order*, Cambridge: Polity.

Giddens, Anthony (1998) *The Third Way: The Renewal of Social Democracy*, Cambridge: Polity.

Giddens, Anthony (2000) *The Third Way and its Critics*, Cambridge: Polity.

Gill, Micheal (2005) 'The Myth of Transition: Contractualising Disability in the Sheltered Workshop', *Disability & Society*, 20: 6 (October): 613–23.

Glennon, Christ (1979) 'Referenda Issues to be Explained to 2.3m Voters', *Irish Independent*, 18 May, page 9.

Glynn, Joseph (1921) 'The Unmarried Mother', *Irish Ecclesiastical Record*, 18: 461–7.

Gmelch, Sharon B. (1987) 'From Poverty Subculture to Political Lobby: The Traveller Rights Movement in Ireland', in Chris Curtin and Thomas M. Wilson (eds), *Ireland from Below: Social Change and Local Community*, Galway: Galway University Press.

Gmelch, Sharon B. and George Gmelch (1974) 'The Itinerant Settlement Movement: Its Policies and Effects on Irish Travellers', *Studies: An Irish Quarterly Review*, 63: 1–16.

Goffman, Erving (1961) *Asylums: Essays on the Social Situation of Mental Patients and Other Inmates*, Harmondsworth: Penguin.

Goodin, Robert E. (1996) 'Inclusion and Exclusion', *Archives Européennes de Sociologie*, 37: 2: 343–71.

Gordon, Colin (1986) 'Question, Ethos, Event: Foucault on Kant and Enlightenment', *Economy and Society*, 15: 1 (February): 71–87.

Gordon, Colin (1991) 'Governmental Rationality: An Introduction', in Graham Burchell, Colin Gordon and Peter Miller (eds), *The Foucault Effect: Studies in Governmentality*, Hemel Hempstead: Harvester Wheatsheaf.

Gramsci, Antonio (1971) *Selections from the Prison Notebooks*, eds and trans. Quinton Hoare and Geoffrey Nowell Smith, London: Lawrence and Wishart.

Green, Christopher and Kit Chee (1995) *Understanding Attention Deficit Disorder: A Parent's Guide to A.D.D. in Children*, London: Vermilion.

GTSG (1999) *Annual Report*, Galway: Galway Travellers Support Group.

Habermas, Jürgen (1984) [1981] *The Theory of Communicative Action. Volume I: Reason and the Rationalisation of Society*, trans. Thomas McCarthy, Cambridge: Polity.

Habermas, Jürgen (1987) [1981] *The Theory of Communicative Action. Volume II: Lifeworld and System*, trans. Thomas McCarthy, Cambridge: Polity.

Habermas, Jürgen (1996) *Between Facts and Norms: Contributions to a Discourse Theory of Law and Democracy*, trans. William Rehg, Cambridge, MA: MIT Press.

Habermas, Jürgen (1999a) *The Inclusion of the Other: Studies in Political Theory*, eds Ciaran Cronin and Pablo De Greiff, Cambridge: Polity.

Habermas, Jürgen (1999b) 'The European Nation State and the Pressures of Globalisation', *New Left Review*, 235 (May/June): 46–59.

Hacking, Ian (2004) 'Between Michel Foucault and Erving Goffman: Between Discourse in the Abstract and Face-to-Face Interaction', *Economy and Society*, 33: 3 (August): 277–302.

Hajer, Martin (1995) *The Politics of Environmental Discourse*, Oxford: Clarendon.

Hancock, W. N (1855) 'The Workhouse as a Mode of Relief for Widows and Children', *Journal of the Dublin Statistical Society*, 1 (April): 84–91.

Harvey, David (1990) *The Condition of Postmodernity*, Oxford: Blackwell.

Haugaard, Mark (1997) *The Constitution of Power*, Manchester and New York: Manchester University Press.

Haugaard, Mark (2003) 'Reflections on Seven Ways of Creating Power', *European Journal of Social Theory*, 6: 87–113.

Haughey, Nuala (2002) 'Travellers Launch Court Challenge as Trespass Bill Becomes Law', *Irish Times*, 4 November, page 3.

Hay, Colin (1999) 'Crisis and the Structural Transformation of the State: Interrogating the Process of Change', *British Journal of Politics and International Relations*, 1: 3 (October): 317–44.

Hayek, Friedrich A. (1991) [1944] *The Road to Serfdom*, London: Routledge.

Healy, Mairin (1964) 'Itinerant Camps', letter, *Irish Times*, 21 December, page 13.

Healy, Séan and Brigid Reynolds (1998) 'Progress, Paradigms and Policy', in Séan Healy and Brigid Reynolds (eds), *Social Policy in Ireland*, Dublin: Oak Tree Press.

Helleiner, Jane (2000) *Irish Travellers: Racism and the Politics of Culture*, Toronto, Buffalo and London: University of Toronto Press.

Henley, Jon (2005) 'We Hate France and France Hates Us', *Guardian*, 9 November, page 17.

Hennessy, Mark (2001) 'FG Plan to Move Travellers Camping Illegally', *Irish Times*, 6 November, page 3.

Herrnstein, Richard J. and Charles Murray (1994) *The Bell Curve: Intelligence and Class Structure in American Life*, New York and London: Free Press.

Higginbotham, Ann Rowell (1985) 'The Unmarried Mother and Her Child in Victorian London, 1834–1914', unpublished PhD thesis, Indiana University.

Hoare, Quinton and Geoffrey Nowell Smith (1971) 'Introduction', in Antonio Gramsci, *Selections from the Prison Notebooks*, eds and trans. Quinton Hoare and Geoffrey Nowell Smith, London: Lawrence and Wishart.

Hochschild, Adam (1999) *King Leopold's Ghost*, Boston and New York: Mariner.

Holden, Winifrede (1934) 'Criminal Law Amendment Acts', letter, assistant hon. secretary, Women's Social Studies Guild, *Irish Times*, 11 June, page 6.

Holland, Kitty (2003) 'Voluntary Groups "Excluded" from Key Decisions, Organisations "Left on the Outside" After Opposing Partnership Deal', *Irish Times*, 23 June, page 4.

Holland, Stuart (1993) *The European Imperative: Economic and Social Cohesion in the 1990's*, Report to the Commission of the European Communities, Nottingham: Spokesman.

Holmes, Pat (1988) 'Minister Rejects Cane Call', *Irish Press*, 27 June, page 7.

Hooper, Carol-Ann (1992) 'Child Sexual Abuse and the Regulation of Women: Variations on a Theme', in Carol Smart (ed.), *Regulating Womanhood: Historical Essays on Marriage, Motherhood and Sexuality*, New York: Routledge.

Howarth, David (2000) *Discourse*, Buckingham: Open University Press.

Howarth, David and Jacob Torfing (2005) *Discourse Theory in European Politics: Identity, Policy and Governance*, Basingstoke and New York: Palgrave Macmillan.

Hughes, Robert (1986) *The Fatal Shore: The Epic of Australia's Founding*, New York: Alfred A. Knopf.

Humphreys, Joe (2002) 'Calls to Withdraw the Disability Bill Rejected', *Irish Times*, 11 February, page 7.

Huxley, Thomas, H. (1898) *Evolution and Ethics and Other Essays*, New York: Macmillan.

Hyde, Abbey and Etaoine Howlett (2004) *Understanding Teenage Sexuality in Ireland*, Dublin: Crisis Pregnancy Agency.

ICCL (1985) *Information on Child Sexual Abuse*, Dublin: Irish Council of Civil Liberties.

Ignatieff, Michael (1978) *A Just Measure of Pain: The Penitentiary in the Industrial Revolution 1750–1850*, New York: Columbia University Press.

INCADDS (2001) *Attention Deficit Hyperactivity Disorder (ADHD)/ Hyperkinetic Disorder (HKD)*, Dublin: Irish National Council of ADHD Support Groups.

Inglis, Tom (2002) 'Sexual Transgression and Scapegoats: A Case Study from Modern Ireland', *Sexualities*, 5: 1: 5–24.

Irish Independent (1925a) 'Helping the Children', editorial, 22 January, page 4.

Irish Independent (1925b) 'Family Starving without Fire and Beds', 22 January, page 9.

Irish Independent (1925c) 'Scientist's Views: The Unstable Child', 2 September, page 5.

Irish Independent (1925d) 'Lunacy in Ireland – No Increase, Dublin's Position', 4 November, page 9.

Irish Independent (1925e) 'The Protection of Girls: A Jesuit's View', 6 November, page 8.

Irish Independent (1928) 'The Industrial Schools', editorial, 14 June, page 6.

Irish Independent (1931a) 'Law and Sexual Crimes: Dean Kennedy's Opinion', 2 March, page 10.

Irish Independent (1931b) 'Dublin Father and His Children: Custody Issue', 20 May, page 14.

Irish Independent (1976) 'Itinerants Plead for New Deal in Fresh "Rahoonery"', 25 October, page 5.

Irish Independent (1997a) 'Disabled Demand Extra Funding', 26 May, page 3.

Irish Independent (1997b) 'Authority New Dawn for Disabled', 19 November, page 9.

Irish Press (1934a) 'A Problem', editorial, 25 April, page 6.

Irish Press (1934b) 'Industrial Schools: Madame MacBride Criticises Existing System', 11 June, page 14.

Irish Press (1940a) 'The Nation's Work', editorial, 9 December, page 6.

Irish Press (1940b) 'Taoiseach Takes Salute from New Corps', 9 December, page 7.

Irish Press (1943a) 'Citizenship', editorial, 1 March, page 2.

Irish Press (1943b) 'Where Men Live Dreamy Life of Children', 14 September, page 3.

Irish Press (1943c) 'Boys May Still Be Birched, DJ warns', 10 November, page 4.

Irish Press (1949) 'Combating T.B.', editorial, 26 September, page 4.

Irish Press (1958a) 'TB Still a Major Public Health Problem', 7 January, page 5.

Irish Press (1958b) 'Dr. Browne on "Illiteracy"', 4 June, page 7.

Irish Press (1958c) 'Jobs Got for 600 Former TB Patients', 10 June, page 4.

Irish Press (1961a) 'Synod Warns of Youthful Drinkers', 6 July, page 5.

Irish Press (1961b) 'Unable to Cope with Demands', 20 July, page 11.

Irish Press (1961c) 'Irish Delegates to see Holland's Itinerant Class', 8 September, page 5.

Irish Press (1961d) 'Give Work to the Handicapped: Doctors Call to Employers', 27 September, page 11.

Irish Press (1964a) 'Itinerants Evicted', 28 April, page 3.

Irish Press (1964b) 'Minister Praises New Attitude to Mental Disorders', 28 April, page 4.

Irish Press (1967a) 'Vandalism', editorial, 26 January, page 8.

Irish Press (1967b) '15 Bodies Join New Youth Council', 26 January, page 4.

Irish Press (1967c) 'Full Employment', editorial, 18 March, page 8.

Irish Press (1967d) 'Full Employment Possible – But', 18 March, page 7.

Irish Press (1967e) 'The Extra Year or So', editorial, 30 March, page 8.

Irish Press (1967f) 'Problem of Dropouts', 30 March, page 4.

Irish Press (1967g) 'Conduct at Fleadh Deplored', 30 March, page 5.

Irish Press (1967h) 'Not Using Vandalism as Excuse', 19 May, page 4.

Irish Press (1967i) 'Corporal Punishment', unsigned letter, 18 September, page 9.

Irish Press (1967j) 'Priest on Threat to Morals of Youth', 18 September, page 3.

Irish Press (1967k) 'Ard-Fheis', editorial, 22 November, page 10.

Irish Press (1970a) 'Hospital "Dumping"', editorial, 24 February, page 10.

Irish Press (1970b) 'False Hopes for the Retarded', 30 March, page 3.

Irish Press (1970c) 'Vandalism Condemned', 3 June, page 10.

Irish Press (1970d) 'Shantalla's Example', editorial, 12 October, page 8.

Irish Press (1970e) 'The Illegitimate Child', editorial, 1 December, page 8.

Irish Press (1970f) 'Background of Child is Vital', 7 December, page 7.

Irish Press (1973a) 'Problems of Abortion Now Very Real', 2 April, page 4.

Irish Press (1973b) 'Move against Child Labour by the ILO', 4 July, page 5.

Irish Press (1976a) 'Deprived Children', editorial, 2 February, page 6.

Irish Press (1976b) 'CARE Film on Deprived Children', 2 February, page 5.

Irish Press (1976c) 'Itinerant Village Go-Ahead', 13 October, page 3.

Irish Press (1979a) 'Parents Allege Ill-Treatment at Mental Unit', 12 July, page 3.

Irish Press (1979b) 'Haughey on the Right to Work', 25 September, page 4.

Irish Times (1925a) 'Mental Healing', editorial, 4 November, page 6.

Irish Times (1925b) 'The Relief of the Poor', 5 November, page 8.

Irish Times (1928) 'Problem of Boarded Out Children', 1 November, page 8.

Irish Times (1934a) 'A Suppressed Report', editorial, 29 January, page 6.

Irish Times (1934b) 'Industrial Schools: Committal and After Care', 3 July, page 8.

Irish Times (1934c) 'Industrial Schools', editorial, 3 July, page 6.

Irish Times (1940a) 'The Young Idea', editorial, 4 April, page 4.

Irish Times (1940b) 'Work', editorial, 9 December, page 4.

Irish Times (1943a) 'Emigration Solved a Problem', 3 September, page 1.

Irish Times (1943b) 'The Treatment of Mental Defectives', 3 September, page 1.

Irish Times (1955) 'TB Theory on Emigrants Refuted', 26 November, page 8.

Irish Times (1961a) 'Census of Itinerants Completed', 4 January, page 6.

Irish Times (1961b) 'Employers Criticised', 16 January, page 9.

Irish Times (1961c) 'Commission Studies Dutch Care for Itinerants', 28 September, page 11.

Irish Times (1961d) 'The Travelling Folk', editorial, 28 September, page 7.

Irish Times (1961e) 'Care of the Aged a Growing Problem', 28 September, page 5.

Irish Times (1964a) 'Coming Here to Study Problem of Itinerants', 15 October, page 10.

Irish Times (1964b) editorial, 21 December, page 7.

Irish Times (1967a) 'New Council to Study Needs of Youth', 26 January, page 8.

Irish Times (1967b) 'All in the Mind', editorial, 30 March, page 9.

Irish Times (1967c) 'More than 30% of Children Neglect Scheme', 19 May, page 7.

Irish Times (1967d) 'New Camp Site for Itinerants', 29 May, page 11.

Irish Times (1967e) 'Psychiatrist Calls for New Approach: No Mental Hospitals', 26 June, page 7.

Irish Times (1970a) 'Hospitals Overcrowded by 400 Unnecessary Patients', 24 February, page 4.

Irish Times (1970b) 'Brennan on Youth Unemployment', 15 April, page 8.

Irish Times (1970c) 'New Centre to Help Handicapped', 23 April, page 11.

Irish Times (1970d) 'Pre-School Centre is opened in Dublin', 23 April, page 11.

Irish Times (1970e) 'Protecting the Unmarried Mother', 2 June, page 6.

Irish Times (1970f) 'Garda Watch Furey Home in Galway', 12 October, page 1.

Irish Times (1973) 'Many More Seeking Psychiatric Help', 27 March, page 16.

Irish Times (1976a) 'Itinerant's Village Plan Meets Strong Opposition', 2 February, page 11.

Irish Times (1976b) 'Lock up and Educate "Drop-Outs" says Limerick Psychologist', 2 February, page 11.

Irish Times (1976c) 'Supreme Court Orders Return of Adopted Boy to Natural Parents', 3 June, page 13.

Irish Times (1976d) 'Council Called on to Quit over Itinerants', 4 June, page 11.

Irish Times (1976e) 'Senator Robinson Calls for New Approach to Family Law', 15 June, page 5.

Irish Times (1976f) 'Tully Backs Galway Plan to House Itinerants', 13 October, page 4.

Irish Times (1979) '12%–13% School-Leavers have Literacy Defects – Survey', 8 March, page 11.

Irish Times (1982a) 'FG put Youth Jobs Plan', 3 February, page 6.

Irish Times (1982b) 'New Job Training Scheme', 9 June, page 13.

Irish Times (1985a) 'ICTU Seeks 8½% Welfare Increase', 24 January, page 7.

Irish Times (1985b) ' "Irish Apartheid" Protest', 8 July, page 10.

Irish Times (1985c) 'Jobless More Likely to be Sick, 12th World Conference on Health Education in Dublin', 3 September, page 7.

Irish Times (1985d) 'System Increasing Social Inequality Says Book by Religious', 13 September, page 9.

Irish Times (1988a) 'Incest due Mainly to Large Families', 29 February, page 9.

Irish Times (1988b) 'A Law on Rahoonery', editorial, 17 December, page 11.

Irish Times (1991a) 'Travellers in Protest', 22 March, page 2.

Irish Times (1991b) 'Disabled not Objects of Pity', 10 July, page 4.

Irish Times (1991c) 'Care of Mentally Ill Criticised', 25 July, page 4.

Irish Times (1997a) '£12m Funding for Disabled Urged', 15 January, page 4.

Irish Times (1997b) 'Funding Protests for Disability Body', 27 May, page 9.

IYJA (2005) *Anti Social Behaviour Orders (ASBOs): A Briefing Paper prepared by the Irish Youth Justice Alliance*, Irish Youth Justice Alliance, 23 February, <www.iprt.ie/>, accessed 20 November 2005.

Jacques, Carlos T. (1997) 'From Savages and Barbarians to Primitives: Africa, Social Typologies, and History in Eighteenth-Century French Philosophy', *History and Theory*, 36: 2 (May): 190–215.

Jones, Greta (1992) 'Eugenics in Ireland: The Belfast Eugenics Society, 1911–15', *Irish Historical Studies*, 28: 109 (May): 81–95.

Jones, Helen and Tracy Sagar (2001) 'Crime and Disorder Act 1998: Prostitution and the Anti-Social Behaviour Order', *Criminal Law Review*, November: 873–85.

Judge, Theresa (2002) 'Large Differences in Care for Attention Disorder', *Irish Times*, 28 January, page 4.

Kahn, Joel (2001) *Modernity and Exclusion*, London: Sage.

Kammerer, Percy Gamble (1918) *The Unmarried Mother: A Study of Five-Hundred Cases*, Criminal Science Monographs No. 3, Boston: Little, Brown.

Kearns, Kevin (1997) *Dublin Tenement Life: An Oral History*, Dublin: Gill and Macmillan.

Kellaghan, Thomas (1989) 'Performance in Second-Level Education in Ireland', *Irish Journal of Education*, 23: 2: 65–84.

Kellaghan, Thomas and Deirdre Brugha (1972) 'The Scholastic Performance of Children in a Disadvantaged Area', *Irish Journal of Education*, 6: 2: 133–43.

Kennedy, Geraldine (1973) 'A Caring Society', *Irish Times*, 12 September, page 6.

Kennedy, Kieran, Thomas Giblin and Deirdre McHugh (1988) *The Economic Development of Ireland in the Twentieth Century*, London: Routledge.

Keogh, Dermot (1996) 'The Role of the Catholic Church in the Republic of Ireland 1922–1995', in *Building Trust in Ireland*, Studies Commissioned by the Forum for Peace and Reconciliation, Dublin: Blackstaff.

Kidger, Judi (2004) 'Including Young Mothers: Limitations to New Labour's Strategy for Supporting Teenage Parents', *Critical Social Policy*, 24: 3: 291–311.

Kilcommins, Shane, Ian O'Donnell, Eoin O'Sullivan and Barry Vaughan (2004) *Crime, Punishment and the Search for Order in Ireland*, Dublin: Institute of Public Administration.

Kilfeather, Frank (1982) 'Consult Us Too, Say Travellers', *Irish Times*, 9 June, page 5.

Kilkenny (1972) *The Unmarried Mother in the Irish Community: A Report on the National Conference on Community Services for the Unmarried Parent*, Kilkenny: Kilkenny Social Services and Kilkenny People.

King, Harold (1940) 'Juvenile Delinquency', letter, hon. secretary of the Standing Conference of Youth Organisations of Northern Ireland, *Irish Times*, 19 April, page 2.

Kirwin, K. (1934) 'Criminal Law Amendment', letter, Women's Social Guild, *Irish Press*, 6 July, page 6.

Kitching, John (1857) 'Lecture on Moral Insanity', *British Medical Journal*, 25 April: 334–6.

Labour Party (2005) *Taking Back the Neighbourhood: A Strategy For Tackling Anti-Social Behaviour*, Labour Party Discussion Paper, April, <www.labour.ie/download/pdf/take_back_neighbour.pdf>, accessed 14 December 2005.

Laclau, Ernesto and Chantal Mouffe (1987) 'Post-Marxism Without Apologies', *New Left Review*, 166: 79–106.

Laclau, Ernesto and Chantal Mouffe (2001) [1985] *Hegemony and Socialist Strategy: Towards a Radical Democratic Politics*, London: Verso.

Laing, R. D. (1990) [1960] *The Divided Self: An Existential Study in Sanity and Madness*, London: Penguin.

Lash, Scott (2002) *Critique of Information*, London: Sage.

Law, John and John Urry (2004) 'Enacting the Social', *Economy and Society*, 33: 3 (August): 390–410.

Lawson, J. A. (1847) 'On the Connexion between Statistics and Political Economy', *Dublin Statistical Society*, 1 (December): 3–9.

Lee, Joseph (1989) *Ireland 1912–1985: Politics and Society*, Cambridge: Cambridge University Press.

Levitas, Ruth (1996) 'The Concept of Social Exclusion and the New Durkheimian Hegemony', *Critical Social Policy*, 46: 16: 5–20.

Levitas, Ruth (1998) *The Inclusive Society? Social Exclusion and New Labour*, Basingstoke and New York: Palgrave.

Lewis, Oscar (1961) *The Children of Sánchez*, Harmondsworth: Penguin.

Long, Siobhan (2002) 'State Fails to See that Disability Law Should Focus on Rights, not Duties', *Irish Times*, 22 February, page 14.

Love, Sean (2002) 'Travellers Being Pushed Further to the Edge of Society', letter, director Amnesty International (Irish Section), Dublin, *Irish Examiner*, 15 April, page 14.

LRC (1989) *Consultation Paper on Child Sex Abuse*, Dublin: Law Reform Commission.

Luddy, Maria (1995) *Women and Philanthropy in Nineteenth-Century Ireland*, Cambridge: Cambridge University Press.

Mac Gréil, Micheál (1996) *Prejudice in Ireland Revisited*, Maynooth: Survey and Research Unit, St Patrick's College.

McAvoy, Sandra L. (1999) 'The Regulation of Sexuality in the Irish Free State, 1929–35', in Elizabeth Malcolm and Greta Jones (eds), *Medicine, Disease and the State in Ireland, 1650–1940*, Cork: Cork University Press.

McCafferty, Nell (1985) *A Woman to Blame: The Kerry Babies Case*, Dublin: Attic Press.

McCarthy, Paul W. and Ciaran A. O'Boyle (1988) 'Prevalence of Behavioural Maladjustment in a Social Cross-Section of Irish Urban School Children', *Learn*, Summer: 66–75.

McCourt, James E. (1940) 'Training Our Youth', letter, *Irish Press*, 11 October, page 6.

McDermott, Lily (1970) 'Some of Our Children', letter, hon. secretary Galway Godparents Association, *Irish Press*, 7 December, page 8.

McDonagh, Michael (2000) 'Nomadism', in Frank Murphy and Cathleen McDonagh, *Travellers: Citizens of Ireland*, ed. Erica Sheehan, Dublin: Parish of the Travelling People.

McDonagh, Michelle (2001) 'Travellers Move from Boycott School Area', *Irish Times*, 8 September, page 20.

McDonnell, R. (1863) 'Observations on the Case of Burton, and So-Called Moral Insanity in Criminal Cases', *Journal of the Dublin Statistical Society*, 3 (December): 447–55.

McGrath, Finian, John Mitchell, Phillip Flynn *et al.* (1985) 'Support for Travellers', letter, Finian McGrath (INTO), John Mitchell (IDATU), Phillip Flynn (LGPSU), Joe O'Toole (DCTU), Anne Speed (ITGWU), Pat Gibbons (ITGWU), Paddy Healy (TUI), Eamonn McCann (NUJ), Maire Ni Breithiunaigh (ASTI), Tom Dowling (INTO), Patricia McCarthy (LGPSU), Molly O'Duffy (INTO), Joe Duffy, Tome Kellegher, Joe Lally, Liam Morrissey, Elizabeth Murphy, Kieran Allen, Angela Lombard, Nora Hamill and Bernard Maguire (INTO), *Irish Times*, 15 July, page 11.

McHale, John (1976) 'Handicapped are Being Exploited by the State', *Irish Independent*, 29 March, page 7.

MacInerny, Rev. M. H. (1921) 'The Souper Problem in Ireland', *Irish Ecclesiastical Record*, 18: 140–56.

MacInerny, Rev. M. H. (1922) 'A Post-Script to the Souper Problem', *Irish Ecclesiastical Record*, 19: 246–61.

McKeown, Kieran and Robbie Gilligan (1990) 'Child Sexual Abuse in the Eastern Health Board Area of Ireland: An Analysis of all Confirmed Cases in 1988', paper presented to the Sociological Association of Ireland, Health Research Board, 3 March.

MacLaughlin, Jim (1995) *Travellers and Ireland: Whose Country, Whose History?*, Cork: Cork University Press.

McLoone, James (ed.) (1984) *Young Ireland: Realism and Vision*, Galway: Social Study Conference.

MacMahon, Bernadette, Margo Delaney and Gemma Lynch (2001) 'Struggling to Live on a Low Income – Anne Burke's Story', *Poverty Today*, 51 (June/July): 6–8, Combat Poverty Agency, Dublin.

Malešević, Siniša (2002) *Ideology, Legitimacy and the New State: Yugoslavia, Serbia and Croatia*, London: Frank Cass.

Malešević, Siniša (forthcoming) *Identity as Ideology: Understanding Ethnicity and Nationalism*, Basingstoke and New York: Palgrave Macmillan.

Malthus, Thomas (1872) *An Essay on the Principle of Population or View of its Past and Present Effects on Human Happiness*, 7th edition, Fairfield: Augustus M. Kelly.

Malthus, Thomas (1992) [1803] *An Essay on the Principle of Population or View of its Past and Present Effects on Human Happiness*, ed. Donald Winch, Cambridge: Cambridge University Press.

Marshall, J. D. (1985) *Poor Law Origins and Development: The Old Poor Law 1795–1834*, 2nd edition, Economic History Society, Basingstoke and London: Macmillan.

Marshall, T. H. (1972) 'Value Problems of Welfare Capitalism', *Journal of Social Policy*, 1: 1: 15–32.

Marshall, T. H. (1992) [1950] *Citizenship and Social Class*, London: Pluto.

Martin, James (1998) *Gramsci's Political Analysis: A Critical Introduction*, Basingstoke and London: Macmillan.

Maxwell, Andrew, H. (1993) 'The Underclass, "Social Isolation" and "Concentration Effects"', *Critique of Anthropology*, 13: 3: 231–45.

Mead, L. M. (1993) 'The Logic of Workfare: The Underclass and Work Policy', in W. J. Wilson (ed.), *The Ghetto Underclass*, London: Sage.

Mellone, Dora and Ethel Macnaghten (1934) 'Criminal Law Amendment', letter, *Irish Times*, 15 June, page 4.

Mingione, Enzo (ed.) (1996) *Urban Poverty and the Underclass*, Oxford: Blackwell.

Molony, Thomas (1925) 'The Probation of Offenders', *Journal of the Statistical and Social Inquiry Society of Ireland*, 14 (October): 181–96.

Molony, Thomas (1927) 'The Treatment of Young Offenders', *Journal of the Statistical and Social Inquiry Society of Ireland*, 14 (June): 437–53.

Morgen, Sandra (2002) 'The Politics of Welfare and Poverty Research', *Anthropological Quarterly*, 75: 4 (Fall): 745–57.

Mouffe, Chantal (2000) *The Democratic Paradox*, London: Verso.

Munden, Alison and Jon Arcelus (1999) *The AD/HD Handbook: A Guide for Parents and Professionals on Attention Deficit/Hyperactivity Disorder*, London and Philadelphia: Jessica Kingsley.

Murphy, Frank and Cathleen McDonagh (2000) *Travellers: Citizens of Ireland*, ed. Erica Sheehan, Dublin: Parish of the Travelling People.

Murray, Charles (1994) *Underclass: The Crisis Deepens*, London: Institute of Economic Affairs Health and Welfare Unit in association with the Sunday Times.

Murray, Paul (1976a) 'Court Ruling Dismays Adoption Workers', *Irish Times*, 3 June, page 1.

Murray, Paul (1976b) 'Child-Care Report will be Test', *Irish Times*, 2 February, page 13.

NDA (2003) *Review of Access to Mental Health Services for People with Intellectual Disabilities*, Dublin: National Disability Authority.

NESC (1994) *New Approaches to Rural Development*, Dublin: National and Economic Social Council.

NESC (1999) *Opportunities, Challenges and Capacities for Choice*, Dublin: National and Economic Social Council.

NESC (2002) *An Investment in Quality: Services, Inclusion and Enterprise*, Dublin: National and Economic Social Council.

NESC (2005) *The Developmental Welfare State*, Dublin: National and Economic Social Council.

Newman, Christine (1997) 'Conference on Child Sex Abuse', *Irish Times*, 19 November, page 9.

Newman, Saul (2004) 'The Place of Power in Political Discourse', *International Political Science Review*, 25 (April): 139–57.

Nicholls, George (1967) [1856] *A History of the Irish Poor Law*, New York: Augustus M. Kelly.

O'Brien, Eileen (1967) 'This Hostel is Like Home', *Irish Times*, 2 January, page 8.

O'Byrne, D. (1987) 'Health Education for Youth', *Health for All – Meeting the Challenge*, 12th World Conference on health Education, 1–6 September 1985, Dublin: Health Education Bureau.

O'Byrnes, Stephen (1973) 'The Domain-Delecato Method', *Irish Press*, 2 April, page 12.

O'Connell, M. J. (1880) 'Poor Law Administration as it Affects Women and Children in Workhouses', *Journal of the Statistical and Social Inquiry Society of Ireland*, 8 (April): 20–31.

O'Connell, T. J. (1937) 'School Attendance', letter, general secretary INTO, *Irish Press*, 25 February, page 11.

O'Connor, Anne (1991) 'Women in Irish Folklore: The Testimony Regarding Illegitimacy, Abortion and Infanticide', in Margaret MacCurtain and Mary O'Dowd (eds), *Women in Early Modern Ireland*, Edinburgh: Edinburgh University Press.

O'Cuanaigh, Liam (1982) 'When Psychological Help is Needed', *Irish Press*, 16 August, page 9.

O'Donoghue, Martin (1970) 'Wheelchairs at Croke Park', letter, president Disabled Drivers Association of Ireland, *Irish Press*, 24 February, page 11.

O'Floinn, Sean (1937) 'School Attendance Act', letter, *Irish Press*, 27 February, page 11.

O'Keane, V., A. Jeffers, E. Moloney and S. Barry (2003) *The Stark Facts: A Survey of Irish Psychiatric Services in Ireland*, Dublin: Irish Psychiatric Association.

O'Malley, Pat (1992) 'Risk, Power and Crime Prevention', *Economy and Society*, 21: 3 (August): 252–75.

O'Morain, Padraig (1988) 'Child Abuse Sentences too Low', *Irish Times*, 4 April, page 9.

O'Morain, Padraig (2003) 'Dirt Poor Pay Deal', *Financial Times Information*, 13 March, page 16.

Osborne, David and Ted Gaebler (1992) *Reinventing Government: How the Entrepreneurial Spirit is Transforming the Public Sector*, Reading MA: Addison-Wesley.

O'Shaughnessy, Mark S. (1862a) 'Remarks on the Necessity of a State Provision for the Education of the Deaf and Dumb of Ireland, by C. Stoker', *Journal of the Dublin Statistical Society*, 3 (December): 459–60.

O'Shaughnessy, Mark S. (1862b) 'Some Remarks upon Mrs Hannah Archer's Scheme for Befriending Pauper Girls', *Journal of the Dublin Statistical Society*, 3 (April): 143–55.

Padfield, Nicola (2004) 'The Anti-Social Behaviour Act 2003: The Ultimate Nanny-State Act?', *Criminal Law Review*, September: 712–27.

Paisley, Fiona (1997) *Race and Remembrance: Contesting Aboriginal Child Removal in the Inter-War Years*, <www.lib.latrobe.edu.au/AHR/archive/Issue-November-1997/paisley.html>, accessed May 2002.

Pasquino, Pasquale (1991) 'Theatrum Politicum: The Genealogy of Capital – Police and the State of Prosperity', in Graham Burchell, Colin Gordon and Peter Miller (eds), *The Foucault Effect: Studies in Governmentality*, Hemel Hempstead: Harvester Wheatsheaf.

Peterson, Paul, E. (1991) 'The Underclass and the Poverty Paradox', in Christopher Jencks and Paul E. Peterson (eds), *The Urban Underclass*, Washington, DC: Brookings Institution.

Piven, Francis Fox and Richard A. Cloward (1971) *Regulating the Poor: The Function of Public Welfare*, Pantheon, New York.

Polanyi, Karl (2001) [1944] *The Great Transformation*, Boston: Beacon Press.

Pollack, Andy (1997) 'New Disability Authority to Oversee Policy and Services', *Irish Times*, 19 November, page 4.

Popper, Karl R. (1962) [1945] *The Open Society and its Enemies*, 2 volumes, 4th edition, London: Routledge & Kegan Paul.

Popper, Karl R. (2002a) [1935] *The Logic of Scientific Discovery*, London and New York: Routledge.

Popper, Karl R. (2002b) [1957] *The Poverty of Historicism*, London and New York: Routledge.

Powell, Frederick W. (1992) *The Politics of Irish Social Policy 1600–1990*, New York, Lampeter and Ontario: Edwin Mellen.

Power, Catherine (1979) 'Loughan House', letter, Southern Area secretary Connolly Youth Movement, *Irish Press*, 25 September, page 8.

Power, Michael (1997) *The Audit Society: Rituals of Verification*, Oxford: Oxford University Press.

Poynter, J. R. (1969) *Society and Pauperism: English Ideas on Poor Relief, 1795–1834*, London: Routledge & Kegan Paul.

Pro Bono Publico (1931) 'Tinkers' Children', *Irish Times*, letter, 16 May, page 5.

Procacci, Giovanna (1991) 'Social Economy and the Government of Poverty', in Graham Burchell, Colin Gordon and Peter Miller (eds), *The Foucault Effect: Studies in Governmentality*, Hemel Hempstead: Harvester Wheatsheaf.

Prunty, Jucinta (1998) *Dublin Slums 1800–1925*, Dublin: Irish Academic Press.

Putnam, Robert (2000) *Bowling Alone: The Collapse and Revival of American Community*, New York and London: Simon and Schuster.

Raboy, Marc and Bernard Dagenais (eds) (1992) *Media, Crisis and Democracy: Mass Communication and the Social Order*, London: Sage.

Raftery, Mary and Eoin O'Sullivan (1999) *Suffer the Little Children: The Inside Story of Ireland's Industrial Schools*, New York: Continuum.

Ramsay, Peter (2004) 'What is Anti-Social Behaviour?', *Criminal Law Review*, November: 908–25.

Rehg, William (1996) 'Translator's Introduction', in Jürgen Habermas, *Between Facts and Norms: Contributions to a Discourse Theory of Law and Democracy*, trans. William Rehg, Cambridge, MA: MIT Press.

Reynolds, Henry (1998) 'The Stolen Children – Their Stories: An Afterword', <www.lib.latrobe.edu.au/AHR/archive/Issue-February-1997/reynolds2.html>, accessed May 2002.

Rhodes, R. A. W. (1996) 'The New Governance: Governing without Government', *Political Studies*, 44: 4: 652–67.

Rimke, Heidi and Alan Hunt (2002) 'From Sinners to Degenerates: The Medicalisation of Morality in the 19th Century', *History of the Human Sciences*, 15: 1: 59–88.

Robins, Joseph (1980) *The Lost Children: A Study of Charity Children in Ireland 1700–1900*, Dublin: Institute of Public Administration.

Robins, Joseph (1986) *Fools and Mad: A History of the Insane in Ireland*, Dublin: Institute of Public Administration.

Roche, John D. (1984) *Poverty and Income Maintenance Policies in Ireland 1973–80*, Dublin: Institute of Public Administration.

Rodgers, Gerry (1995) 'What is Special about a Social Exclusion Approach?', in Gerry Rodgers, Charles Gore and José Figueiredo (eds), *Social Exclusion: Rhetoric, Reality, Responses*, Geneva: International Institute for Labour Studies.

Rodgers, Gerry, Charles Gore and José Figueiredo (eds) (1995) *Social Exclusion: Rhetoric, Reality, Responses*, Geneva: International Institute for Labour Studies.

Room, Graham (1990) *New Poverty in the European Community*, Basingstoke and London: Macmillan.

Room, Graham (1995) 'Poverty in Europe: Competing Paradigms of Analysis', *Policy and Politics*, 23: 2: 103–13.

Rose, Lionel (1988) *'Rogues and Vagabonds': The Vagrant Underworld in Britain 1815–1985*, London and New York: Routledge.

Rose, Nikolas (1985) *The Psychological Complex: Psychology, Politics and Society in England, 1869–1939*, London: Routledge & Kegan Paul.

Rose, Nikolas (1996a) 'Governing "Advanced" Liberal Democracies', in Andrew Barry, Thomas Osborne and Nikolas Rose (eds), *Foucault and Political Reason: Liberalism, Neo-Liberalism and Rationalities of Government*, Chicago: University of Chicago Press.

Rose, Nikolas (1996b) 'The Death of the Social? Re-Figuring the Territory of Government', *Economy and Society*, 25: 3: 327–56.

Rose, Nikolas (1999) *Powers of Freedom*, Cambridge: Cambridge University Press.

Roseberry, William (1994) 'Hegemony and the Language of Contention', in Gilbert M. Joseph and Daniel Nugent (eds), *Everyday Forms of State Formation: Revolution and the Negotiation of Rule in Modern Mexico*, Durham, NC and London: Duke University Press.

'Sagart' (1922) 'How to Deal with the Unmarried Mother', *Irish Ecclesiastical Record*, 20: 145–53.

Said, Edward (1991) [1978] *Orientalism*, London: Penguin.

Saussure, Ferdinand de (1983) [1916] *Course in General Linguistics*, trans. Roy London: Harris Duckworth.

Scheper-Hughes, Nancy (1982) *Saints, Scholars and Schizophrenics: Mental Illness in Rural Ireland*, Berkeley and London: University of California Press.

Schrag, Peter and Diane Divoky (1975) *The Myth of the Hyperactive Child and other Means of Child Control*, New York: Pantheon Books.

Scott, Joanne (1995) *Development Dilemmas in the European Community*, Buckingham and Philadelphia: Open University Press.

Searight, H. Russell and A. Lesley McLaren (1998) 'Attention-Deficit Hyperactivity Disorder: The Medicalisation of Misbehaviour', *Journal of Clinical Psychology in Medical Settings*, 5: 4: 467–95.

Sigerson, G. (1886) 'The Law and the Lunatic', *Journal of the Statistical and Social Inquiry Society of Ireland*, 9 (July): 7–30.

Silver, Hilary (1994) 'Social Exclusion and Social Solidarity: Three Paradigms', *International Labour Review*, 133: 5–6: 551–78.

Silver, Hilary (1995) 'Reconceptualising Social Disadvantage: Three Paradigms of Social Exclusion', in Gerry Rodgers, Charles Gore and José Figueiredo (eds), *Social Exclusion: Rhetoric, Reality, Responses*, Geneva: International Institute for Labour Studies.

Silver, Hilary (1996) 'Culture, Politics and National Discourses of the New Urban Poverty', in Enzo Mingione (ed.), *Urban Poverty and the Underclass*, Oxford: Blackwell.

Skehill, Caroline (1999) *The Nature of Social Work in Ireland*, Lewiston, Queenstown and Lampeter: Edwin Mellen.

Slack, Paul (1990) *The English Poor Law 1531–1782*, Basingstoke: Macmillan.

Small, Albion (1909) *The Cameralists: The Pioneers of Social Polity*, Chicago: University of Chicago Press.

Smart, Barry (1986) 'The Politics of Truth and the Problem of Hegemony', in David Couzens Hoy (ed.), *Foucault: A Critical Reader*, Oxford: Blackwell.

Smedley, M. (1880) 'Comparison between Boarding-Out and Pauper Schools', *Journal of the Statistical and Social Inquiry Society of Ireland*, 8 (April): 31–41.

Smith, Adam (1976a) [1776] *An Inquiry into the Nature and Causes of the Wealth of Nations*, 2 volumes, eds R. H. Campbell and A. S. Skinner, Oxford: Clarendon.

Smith, Adam (1976b) [1754] *The Theory of Moral Sentiments*, eds D. D. Raphael and A. L. Macfie, Oxford: Clarendon.

Smith, Anne-Marie (1994) *New Right Discourse on Race and Sexuality: Britain 1968–90*, Cambridge: Cambridge University Press.

Smyth, Ailbhe (1993) 'The Women's Movement in the Republic of Ireland 1970–1990', in Ailbhe Smyth (ed.), *Irish Women's Studies Reader*, Dublin: Attic Press.

Soja, Edward (1996) *Third Space*, Oxford: Blackwell.

Spear, Roger, Jacques Defourny, Louis Favreau and Jean-Louis Laville (eds) (2001) *Tackling Social Exclusion in Europe: The Contribution of the Social Economy*, Burlington: Ashgate.

Spensky, Martine (1992) 'Producers of Legitimacy: Homes for Unmarried Mothers in the 1950s', in Carol Smart (ed.), *Regulating Womanhood: Historical Essays on Marriage, Motherhood and Sexuality*, London and New York: Routledge.

Squires, Peter and Dawn E. Stephen (2005a) *Rougher Justice: Anti-Social Behaviour and Young People*, Cullompton: Willan.

Squires, Peter and Dawn E. Stephen (2005b) 'Rethinking ASBOs', *Critical Social Policy*, 25: 4: 517–28.

Staten, Henry (1985) *Wittgenstein and Derrida*, Oxford: Blackwell.

Sunday World (2001) 'Travellers Make a Racist Division', 2 December, page 26.

Swan, Desmond (1979) 'Illiteracy in Ireland', letter, head of the Dept of Education UCD, *Irish Times,* 12 July, page 9.

Swan, Desmond (1989) 'Cherished Equally? Educational and Behavioural Adjustment of Children: A study of Primary Schools in the Mid-West Region', review article, *Learn*, II (Summer): 79–81.

Szasz, Thomas (1960) 'The Myth of Mental Illness', *American Psychologist*, 15: 113–18.

Tapia, Ruby C. (2005) 'Impregnating Images: Visions of Race, Sex and Citizenship in California's Teen Pregnancy Prevention Campaigns', *Feminist Media Studies*, 5: 1: 7–22.

Thomas, L. (1964) 'Itinerants', letter, *Irish Times*, 6 August, page 11.

Times, The (1961) 'Irish Immigrants who Enter UK without Jobs or Prospects', 13 November, page 7.

Times, The (1963) 'Action against Irish Tinkers', 7 October, page 6.

Tod, Isabella (1878) 'Boarding out Pauper Children', *Journal of the Statistical and Social Inquiry Society of Ireland*, 7 (August): 293–9.

Torfing, Jacob (1999) *New Theories of Discourse: Laclau, Mouffe and Žižek*, Oxford: Blackwell.

Torfing, Jacob (2005) 'The Democratic Anchorage of Governance Networks', *Scandinavian Political Studies*, 28: 3: 195–218.

UNICEF (2005) *Council of Europe Actions to Promote Children's Rights to Protection from All Forms of Violence*, United Nations International Children's Emergency Fund Innocenti Research Centre, <www.unicef-icdc.org/publications/pdf/european_standards.pdf>, accessed 12 August 2005.

Varley, Tony (1988) *Rural Development and Combating Poverty: The Rural Projects of the Second European Combat Poverty Programme (1985–9) in Historical and Comparative Context*, Galway: Centre for Community Development Studies/Social Science Research Centre.

Varley, Tony and Mary Ruddy (1996) 'Partners Worthy of the Name? The State and Community Groups in the Forum Project', in *Partnership in Action*, Galway: Community Workers Cooperative.

Verheijen, Tony and David Coomes (eds) (1998) *Innovation in Public Management: Perspectives from East and West Europe*, Cheltenham: Edward Elgar.

Vincent, Joan (1993) 'Framing the Underclass', *Critique of Anthropology*, 13: 3: 215–30.

Viney, Michael (1964) 'Secret Service', *Irish Times*, 15 September, page 8.

Walby, Sylvia (1994) 'Is Citizenship Gendered?', *Sociology*, 2: 28: 379–95.

Walmsley, Jan (2000) 'Woman and the Mental Deficiency Act of 1913: Citizenship, Sexuality and Regulation', *British Journal of Learning Disabilities*, 28: 65–70.

Walshe, John (1979) 'Reading Nightmare for 8,000 of Our Children', *Irish Independent*, 8 March, page 11.

Walshe, John (1997) 'Students May Face New Test to Measure Literacy Skills', *Irish Independent*, 17 November, page 8.

Weber, Max (1978a) *The Protestant Ethic and the Spirit of Capitalism*, London: Allen and Unwin.

Weber, Max (1978b) *Economy and Society. Volume 1*, eds G. Roth and C. Wittich, Berkeley, Los Angeles and London: University of California Press.

Whelan, Christopher T., Damian Hannan and Sean Creighton (1991) *Unemployment, Poverty and Psychological Distress*, Dublin: Economic and Social Research Institute.

Williams, R. H. (1996) *European Union: Spatial Policy and Planning*, London: Paul Chapman.

Wilson, James J. (1967) 'New Approach to Psychiatry', letter, *Irish Times*, 4 July, page 14.

Wilson, William Julius (1987) *The Truly Disadvantaged: The Inner City, the Underclass, and Public Policy*, Chicago and London: University of Chicago Press.

Winterson, Jeanette (1996) *Art Objects: Essays on Ecstasy and Effrontery*, London: Vintage.

Wittel, Andreas (2001) 'Toward a Network Sociality', *Theory, Culture & Society*, 18: 6: 51–76.

Yeates, Padraig (1988) 'Racism at the Root of Problem Facing Travellers', *Irish Times*, 26–8 December, page 17.

Yeates, Padraig (1994) 'Travellers Challenge Ethnic Claims', *Irish Times*, 21 February, page 2.

Young, Jock (1999) *The Exclusive Society: Social Exclusion, Crime and Difference in Late Modernity*, London: Sage.

Young, Leontine (1954) *Out of Wedlock*, Westport, CT: Greenwood.

Žižek, Slavoj (1989) *The Sublime Object of Ideology*, London: Verso.

Žižek, Slavoj (1994) *The Metastasis of Enjoyment*, London: Verso.

Audio

Horslips (2000) [1976] *The Book of Invasions: A Celtic Symphony*, Demon Records.

Index